HMRC Investigations and Enquiries

HMRC Investigations and Enquiries

General Editor: John T. Newth

Tottel publishing

Tottel Publishing Ltd, Maxwelton House, 41–43 Boltro Road, Haywards Heath, West Sussex, RH16 1BJ

A CIP Catalogue record for this book is available from the British Library.

ISBN 978 1 84766 169 2

Typeset by Kerrypress Ltd, Luton, Bedfordshire, UK.

Printed and bound in Great Britain by CPI Antony Rowe, Chippenham, Wiltshire

Preface

The main functions of the combined Her Majesty's Revenue and Customs are clearly compliance and investigation. This is demonstrated by the HMRC Enquiry Manual, other HMRC Manuals and the pronouncements and statistics published by the Department.

Some, but not all, of the actions of HMRC investigators are governed by statutory legislation. However, many of the procedures used by Revenue investigators in enquiries and investigations are practices devised by the Department, some of them longstanding, others more recent, but all constantly under review and subject to change.

It is the task of the tax adviser, whether he or she is a lawyer, accountant or tax consultant, to represent the client under investigation to the very best effect, within current law and ethical practice. This is no easy task as the issues involved are complex and specialised.

It is for this reason that *HMRC Investigations and Enquiries* is being published. The various chapters are written by different experts who have day-to-day experience of investigations and enquiries and the text outlines and explains many of the issues that have to be faced. Practical solutions of complex problems are explored.

The book will be invaluable to the tax investigation specialist and also general practice accountants, lawyers and tax consultants who are faced with the occasional investigation or enquiry. Taxpayer businesses and individuals under enquiry will also find the book informative and helpful.

John T. Newth

Contents

Table of Statutes

Table of Statutory Instruments

Table of Cases

Chapter 1

Enquiries under self-assessment

Robert Maas FCA FTII FIIT, Partner Blackstone Franks

INTRODUCTION

1.1 An enquiry power is an essential element of a self-assessment system. Enquiries have two objectives. The first, and most obvious one, is to seek to detect fraud, errors and areas in which the applicable legal principles may be open to different interpretations so that HMRC may wish to challenge that adopted by the taxpayer. The second, less obvious one, is to test the system. If different taxpayers make the same error this may be due to poor design of the forms and guidance notes, or may suggest that an HMRC interpretation of the legislation is out of line with that adopted by others.

1.2 Direct tax enquiries are often categorised into full, aspect and random enquiries. These are not statutory divisions, but convenient descriptions. A full enquiry is one in which HMRC enquire into every aspect of the return – and in many cases seek to enquire into matters outside the return (albeit that it is questionable whether in most cases they have power to do so) to obtain an overall view of the taxpayer's financial affairs against which they can test what is shown in the return. An aspect enquiry is one that relates to only one, or selected, entries in the return. It is important to realise that an aspect enquiry can develop into a full enquiry, particularly if it is not handled well.

1.3 For example, in one case HMRC raised a number of questions in relation to estimates used in arriving at the figures of the taxpayer's Standard Accounts Information page. Conscious of costs, that estimates are to some extent a matter of opinion, and that the figures involved were all fairly trivial, the accountant made little effort to justify his figures but accepted without much protest the figures suggested by HMRC. The Inspector, not surprisingly, finding that every figure he had challenged was conceded, concluded that the rest of the figures shown in the return might well be unreliable and the enquiry, which had started in relation to fairly trivial issues, turned into a full enquiry.

1.4 The vast majority of enquiries begin because an Inspector or other HMRC Officer suspects that there is something wrong with the return. In other words there is either something on the face of the return that gives cause for concern or HMRC have information from other sources that conflict with what is shown on the return. A small number of returns are selected randomly for enquiry by the HMRC computer before the start of the tax year. These random enquiries are designed to test the tax system. They are not selected on the basis of risk (they are selected in advance of the return being submitted) and could well be cases where the HMRC risk assessment would not identify that anything might be wrong with the return. Random enquiries are full enquiries – although the Inspector working the case may be able to verify some of the entries on the return from internal sources, so would not necessarily raise questions on every aspect.

1.5 Where an enquiry is opened into a return, some accountants seem to assume that the enquiry is a random enquiry because they have absolute faith in both their client's honesty and their own ability to avoid errors. This is a dangerous stance to take. Roughly one in a thousand enquiries are random enquiries. If there is no obvious reason why HMRC have opened an enquiry it is accordingly most probable that it has been opened 'for cause' and that the factor or factors that caused the enquiry are simply not apparent to the accountant.

DISCLOSURE

1.6 Whilst it is not possible to avoid the risk of HMRC opening an enquiry into a tax return, the risk of an aspect enquiry at least can be reduced by anticipating which items in a return are likely to raise questions and forestalling such questions by providing the answer with the return. HMRC do not then need to open an enquiry in order to elicit that information. It needs to be realised that even if, when challenged, a convincing explanation can easily be given in relation to an item that looks odd, HMRC have only one bite of the cherry in relation to enquiries. Once they close an enquiry they cannot raise enquiries on any other issues in relation to the return (unless they can make a discovery). Accordingly if something in a return looks odd and HMRC have to open an enquiry to elicit why it does so, they are likely to review the remainder of the return much more thoroughly than they otherwise would have done, as once they close the enquiry they will close off their ability to raise any other issues. Accordingly, heading off an enquiry by forestalling questions about the oddity is also likely to head off the review of the return that would have been prompted by an enquiry into that item.

1.7 Accordingly, the pre-self-assessment strategy that many adopted of not volunteering information, but leaving it to the Inspector to inspect the return is a dangerous strategy in the era of self-assessment. Returns are selected for enquiry on the basis of an HMRC assessment of the risk that the return may not be wholly correct. Anything that can be done to reduce HMRC's perception of such risk therefore ought to be done. Explaining in advance items that are likely to call for an explanation might well eliminate the perception of risk in relation to such items, thus reducing the overall risk that HMRC place on the return.

1.8 Volunteering information can also have a second benefit of making it more difficult for HMRC to make a discovery in relation to the return at a later date. Unless they can establish negligence HMRC cannot make a discovery assessment unless at the time when the 'enquiry window' closed they could not have been reasonably expected, on the basis of the information made available to them before that time, to be aware of errors or omissions that they subsequently discover (Taxes Management Act 1970 (TMA), s 29(5)). Information which is contained in the tax return, or in any accounts, statements or documents accompanying the return (or in the return for either of the two previous years) is deemed to have been made available for this purpose, even if the Officer who reviewed the return at that time chose not to look at it. Accordingly, it makes sense to volunteer accounts, dividend schedules, capital gains tax computations and other information created or used in arriving at the figures to be included in the return in order to enhance protection from discovery (TMA 1970, s 25(6)). HMRC sometimes seek to discourage the submission of such information, but they have no power to prohibit a taxpayer from providing it. In the early days of self-assessment they sometimes returned such information. If they do so it is sensible to send it back again and point out that they have no statutory power to refuse to accept it and that s 29(6) clearly envisages a taxpayer being entitled to submit accompanying documents. Indeed the legislation requires no more than that the document accompanies the return. What HMRC then do with it cannot thwart the statutory protection given to the taxpayer; that is already in place before HMRC send it back, although it is probably easier to convince the appeal Commissioners of this if it can be shown that efforts were made to seek to persuade HMRC to accept the information. HMRC consider that 'reasonably expected' requires a taxpayer to point out that information sent to them is relevant to the return, but it is hard to imagine any body of Commissioners holding that an Inspector could not have expected something sent with the return to be relevant to it. Of course, an Inspector might well not be expected to read through a long document only part of which is clearly relevant, so if the taxpayer wants protection for something else in it he may well be expected to point it out. For example, if shares in a private company are sold and the sale agreement is sent with the return it should be obvious that the name of the vendor, the date, and the existence or otherwise of warranties and indemnities that might give rise to contingent liabilities, is relevant to the return. However, if the Inspector later discovers that the gain was declared in the wrong year because the contract was a conditional one, the Commissioners could uphold his right to make a discovery on the basis that the taxpayer could be expected to have pointed out the relevant clause.

HANDLING AN ENQUIRY

1.9 The enquiry process is laid down in the statute. However, HMRC have overlaid the statutory rules with their own, non-statutory, procedural rules. It is important to distinguish the two. A taxpayer is required to comply with a statutory request; if he wishes to comply with a non-statutory request or procedure he is free to do so, but is equally free not to do so. That is not to say that he ought not to, but rather to make the point that a taxpayer should volunteer something in the full knowledge that he is volunteering and having made a positive decision to do so, rather than volunteer it under the mistaken impression that he is required to provide it.

1.10 It is accordingly unwise to seek to deal with an enquiry without first familiarising oneself with the statutory rules. For income tax these can be found in TMA 1970, ss 8 to 28B and for corporation tax in FA 1998, Sch 18, paras 3 to 35. These provisions do not relate solely to enquiries. They also cover the rules on tax returns. It is important to be aware of these as the requirements for what is to be included in a return set the parameters for what HMRC might need in order to check that return.

1.11 There are no similar statutory rules for VAT enquiries. These are dealt with elsewhere in this work and not considered further here.

1.12 It is also important to know who you are dealing with. Whilst the enquiry legislation applies to all tax enquiries, the Special Civil Investigations Office (SCI) adopt a different approach to Inspectors in Local Tax Districts and need to be approached in a different manner. SCI (and its predecessor the Special Compliance Office (SCO) which merged the old Special Offices and Enquiry Branch) have traditionally dealt with two distinct areas, tax avoidance and serious civil tax fraud. Whilst they still do both, they currently seem to be concentrating on the former and are taking on new fraud cases only if they believe that the tax underpaid is at least £500,000. Smaller cases of suspected serious fraud, which used to be dealt with by SCI are being dealt with by local CIF (Civil Investigations of Fraud) Offices. These are headed by former SCI investigators, their staff are trained by SCI, and their cases need to be handled in the same way as SCI cases. Whilst in the past it was easy to recognise if a case was being handled by SCI, it is often more difficult to identify where a CIF Office is involved as this is not always apparent from the letterhead. For example, it is understood that Complex Personal Returns Offices have become CIF Offices. CIF Offices do not only deal with serious suspected fraud though. Where SCI or a CIF Office are dealing with such a case they will say that they are dealing with the case under COP (Code of Practice) 9. This is a procedure that replaces the old 'Hansard' procedure. Where COP 9 is issued, HMRC will not prosecute the taxpayer for the fraud; they are looking for a cash settlement. They may prosecute if false documents are given to them, or false statements made to them, in the course of the enquiry.

1.13 Smaller cases of serious suspected fraud, normally where the tax at risk is initially thought to be under around £75,000 are dealt with in the local tax office network. Local tax offices are not empowered to issue COP 9. Only SCI and CIF Offices can do so. This is not necessarily a good thing as COP 9 affords protection against prosecution. In practice though, a network enquiry is unlikely to result in prosecution, if only because unless the case is identified as warranting prosecution at a very early stage the network enquiries are likely to seriously prejudice the taxpayer's rights under the Police and Criminal Evidence Act (as network officers are not trained in PACE), which would make a prosecution very difficult.

1.14 There are also a couple of HMRC publications that are very helpful in handling an enquiry. The first is the HMRC Enquiry Manual which is available on the HMRC website. This is HMRC's internal staff guidance. It not only gives an invaluable insight into how HMRC expect an enquiry to be conducted but also highlights areas where there may be doubt on the legal position and points out the limitations on an Inspector's powers. The second is the relevant Code of Practice which is normally given to the taxpayer with the opening letter, at least where a full enquiry is involved. COP 11 deals with enquiries by local tax offices. SCI and CIF Offices use COP 9 (2005) in cases of serious suspected tax fraud and COP 8 for other cases.

THE START OF AN ENQUIRY

1.15 HMRC must start an enquiry by giving notice to the taxpayer of their intention to do so (TMA 1970, s 9A(1); FA 1998, Sch 18, para 24). The notice must normally be given by the first anniversary of the filing date, which is 31 January following the end of the tax year.

1.16 There is no right of appeal against such a notice. If there is something wrong with it, such as being given out of time, it is not a valid notice. However, the only way to establish whether or not it is valid is in the course of an appeal later in the enquiry process, such as an appeal against a section 19A notice, or an appeal against an HMRC amendment to the return – because if the original enquiry notice is not valid it will invalidate the entire enquiry process.

1.17 The formal enquiry notice is normally accompanied by a letter asking for the information that the Officer requires for the purpose of the enquiry. Officers are encouraged to ask up-front for everything they are likely to require, although they can, and often do, of course, ask for further information at any time during the course of the enquiry. The letter will normally give a time limit within which the Officer expects the information to be supplied. This is normally a minimum of 30 days.

1.18 This opening letter is not part of the statutory enquiry process. Accordingly, the time limit is not a statutory one; it is a figure plucked out of the air by the Officer. No penalty or other statutory sanctions arise if this time limit is not met. The Officer's only recourse is either to chase for a reply or to issue a formal notice under s 19A or para 27 for the information. It is obviously courteous to tell the Officer as early as possible if his target date cannot be met. However, there is no need to panic if the time limit is overlooked or, although the taxpayer or his agent aims to comply with it, he does not manage to do so.

1.19 Similarly, the Officer is not entitled to insist on the provision of information in response to the opening letter. He has two specific information powers, TMA 1970, s 19A (or FA 1998, Sch 18, para 27 in the case of a company) and TMA 1970, s 20. Section 20 is a general information power, but s 19A and para 27 are enquiry powers that are specific to self-assessment. However, each of these powers requires the use of a formal procedure (albeit a different one for each of the powers) that has built-in protections for taxpayers. Accordingly, in reality in his opening letter the Officer is requesting the taxpayer to volunteer information.

1.20 That is not to say that the taxpayer should not volunteer to do, so but instead insist on the use of the formal information powers. It is pointless to waste time on a statutory procedure when it is clear that at the end of that procedure the information is statutorily required to be provided. It will also clearly irritate the Officer, which may well influence his approach to doubtful issues that arise during the enquiry.

1.21 However, it is sensible to consider each item of information requested by the Officer in the context of s 19A or para 27. If it is clear that the item can be required under that provision it should be provided. If it is not clear, the taxpayer or his agent ought to consider whether he believes it to be in his best interest to provide it. For example, an extended trial balance prepared by the taxpayer's agent is unlikely to be within s 19A or para 27, as in most cases it is likely to belong to the agent and therefore will not be within the taxpayer's power to provide. Nevertheless, it is difficult to conceive of a reason not to volunteer it. Without it the Officer will be forced to ask far more questions than he otherwise would have done and may make incorrect assumptions that needlessly prolong the enquiry and thus increase its cost. Where it is decided to volunteer information, it is sensible to make the point to HMRC that the taxpayer or agent does not believe that it falls within s 19A (or para 27), but that the taxpayer is happy to nevertheless provide it. This indicates cooperation and helpfulness.

1.22 If the taxpayer or agent does not believe that the information requested falls within s 19A (or para 27) and he chooses not to volunteer it there is nothing to prevent his declining to provide it. It is sensible to do so politely, such as telling the Officer that its relevance to the tax return is not readily apparent and asking why he believes it to be relevant.

1.23 Each enquiry obviously depends on its individual facts. It is accordingly not possible to list what may or may not fall within s 19A or para 27.

Information that belongs to third parties, such as the taxpayer's spouse or children, or to his agent, clearly does not fall within these provisions. The author would normally challenge requests for the following:

1 An analysis of drawings or of a proprietor's capital account or a director's loan account. There are things that do not impact on the quantification of profit. They relate to how the profit is spent and how funds to finance the business are raised. Normally, neither of these things has any relevance to the enquiry into the tax return, which is a return of income. HMRC argue that if drawings are minimal that may be an indication that income has been diverted from the business. However, that is far too wide a generalisation. The proprietor's or director's spouse may be generating the income to meet living expenses; parents may be helping to support an adult child whose business acumen is such that he cannot generate adequate income; a person may be living off borrowings such as a bank overdraft or may be realising past savings or using an inheritance to supplement his living expenses. It is hard to see a justification for HMRC to pry into a taxpayer's private life on the off chance that he may be diverting income from his business. Many taxpayers strongly resent such an intrusion and it does not seem right to ask them to submit to it merely to seek to prove the negative that income has not been diverted. Where a business does not handle cash at all but receives all of its income by cheque, diversion is clearly improbable as banks do not allow a cheque made out to one person to be banked in the account of another, but that fact does not seem to deter HMRC requests for analyses of drawings or loan account. Furthermore, the author's experience is that in many cases where such information is volunteered this does not satisfy HMRC, but they often go on to raise further questions on the information provided because the Officer is searching for the possibility, no matter how remote, of some other theoretical source of undisclosed income.

2 Personal bank statements of a sole trader or partnership where he keeps his personal finances separate from those of his business, or personal bank statements of a director of a company. Again these have nothing to do with the tax return under enquiry and have been requested in the off chance that something in them may suggest diverted takings. In this connection it needs to be appreciated that if such bank statements are volunteered the Officer will often take the stance that, as it is for the taxpayer to disprove an assessment, he intends to assess every single receipt in the personal bank account as diverted business income and leave it to the taxpayer to prove that it is not. Very few people can identify – and evidence – the source of small payments into their bank accounts two years earlier. In most cases these are things like refunds from utilities or from mail order or online retailers for goods that are no longer available, receipts from friends for their share of a restaurant bill, premium bond or football pool winnings, insurance claims, cheques as

birthday presents and similar day-to-day personal receipts. It is of course highly improbable that if a person were to divert money from his business he would divert £8.46 or some other tiny sum, so the likelihood of such an item in a person's personal bank account representing diverted income is inherently improbable. However, such an improbability does not seem to deter most HMRC Officers.

Sometimes an Officer will put forward a non-business reason for needing to see personal bank statements. The author has seen for example claims that they are needed to check the receipt of dividends from quoted companies, and to check the amount of bank interest earned. In such cases it is worth considering whether there is an alternative means to do what the Officer says that he is trying to do. For example, in the dividends case we sent him the dividend counterfoils and pointed out that they provide far better evidence of the dividends than the bank statements do, particularly as the receipt of a dividend warrant is a receipt of income even if the warrant is not banked or is banked in a later year. In the case of interest most banks give a figure of interest for the year as a note on the first bank statement after 5 April. Accordingly, that one statement, rather than all of the statements for the tax year, will evidence that figure. A letter from the bank might be an alternative source of evidence. Providing such alternative evidence does not prevent HMRC from claiming that in the particular circumstances of the case the personal bank statements come within s 19A, but it is likely to make it difficult for them to convince the Appeal Commissioners that the information is 'reasonably required' for that purpose when they already hold better evidence of the item that they have said that they wish to check.

3 Appointment diaries. Most people do not keep their business and personal life separate. Accordingly appointment diaries invariably contain personal data for which the taxpayer is entitled to privacy. Furthermore, this author does not regard his diary as an historical record. It is merely a reminder of future engagements. If a client does not turn up for an appointment it does not get crossed out of the diary. If a client phones for an urgent appointment in a couple of hours time it will probably not get put in the diary. Some of the appointments are of meetings that the author will attend if he has time, but not if he is too busy at the time, and those that are missed may well not be crossed out. Accordingly, the diary is a wholly inappropriate tool as a basis for HMRC to assume that every item in it should have generated a fee and, if it does not, to assume that income has been diverted. Electronic diaries tend to delete past entries on a monthly basis. Clearly, whether a diary is kept manually or electronically can have no bearing on the accuracy of a business's accounts. If accounts can be assumed to be reliable if the diary is electronic and does not retain past data, they ought to be assumed to be equally reliable if the diary is kept in a different manner.

4 An accountant's working papers. These are the property of the accountant and therefore not in the power of the client to obtain.

5 A statement of a director's or proprietor's personal assets and liabilities. Such a statement has no bearing to the tax return of a company or to the profits of an unincorporated business. Even where the individual has non-business income it is hard to sec how a statement of assets can say anything about his income.

6 Joint bank account. The joint account holder is entitled to privacy. Also, it is unclear whether or not the bank statements of such an account are in the possession or power of the taxpayer as he is probably not entitled to disclose them to third parties, such as HMRC, without the consent of the joint holder.

7 Income of spouses or children. These are not normally in the possession or power of the taxpayer. They may be if the child is a minor and the taxpayer is the child's guardian, but this is unclear.

8 Assets such as premium bonds or National Savings certificates which do not produce taxable income or capital gains.

9 Assets held by the taxpayer as a trustee. It is not clear whether these are in his possession or power in relation to his personal affairs, so if necessary this probably ought to be tested before the appeal Commissioners.

10 Overseas assets and income of a non-UK domiciled taxpayer where there have been no remittances of income generated by such assets. It is hard to see how these can have any relevance to his UK tax return.

1.24 It does however need to be borne in mind that whether or not something is relevant depends on the circumstances. Although the above items are rarely relevant when an Officer opens an enquiry, if during the course of the enquiry it were to become apparent that the business accounts are unreliable and the only satisfactory way to arrive at the taxable profits is to reconstruct what probably happened from some other source, then it clearly becomes relevant to look at whether one of the above sources provides an appropriate means to do this. However, this becomes the case only when the accounts are unreliable – what HMRC used to call when they 'break the accounts'. A handful of small errors or a few small unexplained items does not necessarily suggest that the accounts are unreliable as a basis for measuring the profits for the year.

MEETINGS

1.25 HMRC tell their staff that 'meetings play a vital part in full enquiries under SA and will often be appropriate in aspect enquiries of substance' (Enquiry Manual, para 1821). However, Parliament does not appear to have regarded meetings as vital when it introduced self-assessment. Had it done so it would surely have given HMRC power to require a taxpayer to attend meetings and answer questions, which it did not do. Furthermore, some agents refuse to countenance meetings, either at all or except where there is a good reason for a meeting, and such agents seem to settle enquiries as much as anyone else without recourse to the appeal Commissioners. Accordingly 'vital' seems a wholly inappropriate adjective for HMRC to use.

1.26 HMRC tell their staff that meetings are vital because they enable you to:

'– obtain facts from the taxpayer about the business, how it is run and the records that are kept;
– obtain the facts in non-business enquiries;
– explain the purpose of your enquiry. Taxpayers may not always be fully aware of the extent of Revenue enquiries;
– establish whether the taxpayer wishes to disclose omissions;
– agree what action is required and by whom to move the enquiry towards conclusion;
– ensure that, where omissions have been found, the taxpayer is aware what offence has been committed and the likelihood of penalties and of the benefits of co-operating in bringing about an appropriate settlement at the earliest possible date, but you should make it clear that it is entirely a matter for them to decide. You should also at this stage give them the public funding leaflet.
– quantify and agree omissions;
– settle the enquiry.'

(Enquiry Manual, para 1822).

1.27 Curiously, they also tell them that when they encounter resistance to a meeting from an agent they might reduce this by:

'– explaining that meetings can actually reduce the costs and length of an enquiry, because so much more can be covered at a meeting than in protracted correspondence.
– saying why you want to meet the taxpayer. You should make it clear that you are entitled to enquire into the taxpayer's return, the information you need can only be given by the taxpayer in person, and in the absence of co-operation, you will not give up.

– asking if the agent has passed on your views about the desirability of a meeting to the taxpayer.

– confirming to the agent that he or she will be provided with a copy of your notes following the meeting. The agent and taxpayer will be able to correct any misunderstanding of what was said and will be able to revise any explanations or information given at the time if, on reflection, these are felt to be inaccurate.'

(Enquiry Manual, para 1861).

1.28 It seems curious that the reasons that they are told to give agents for wanting a meeting seem to bear little relationship to their actual purpose in wanting it.

1.29 HMRC also tell their staff that, 'asking for meetings at business premises should be the norm rather than the exception' (Enquiry Manual, para 1830). Again, it is odd that when self-assessment was introduced they did not seek to convince Parliament that they should be given power to hold meetings at business premises (although it should perhaps be mentioned that they are now seeking such a power).

1.30 In fact the tax legislation contains no references at all to meetings. These are purely voluntary. It follows that the terms on which they are held are equally voluntary. Sadly, most accountants can relate many horror stories of what has happened at meetings. The author's include the Inspector who, when the Jewish refugee client started to give an explanation, jumped in and said 'Don't try to explain; just answer yes or no to my questions', the Inspector who asked the Asian client how often his wife changed her underwear, and a number of Inspectors who sought to put words into the client's mouth or harangued a client because the Inspector seemed to think it incredible that a client could not remember details of a small transaction two or three years earlier. Clearly, an agent's reaction to a request for a meeting is likely to be coloured by his past experiences.

1.31 This author's own approach based on his personal experience is to welcome meetings between himself and HMRC, but to agree to meetings with the client present only where he can see a good reason for doing so.

1.32 The Enquiry Manual tells HMRC staff, 'On some occasions an early meeting with the business's book-keeper or accountant will be valuable in understanding how the business records were built up and link together. Such meetings should lead to a better understanding of how the accounts have been prepared and may enable some issues to be resolved without troubling the taxpayer' (Enquiry Manual, para 1821). Such meetings seem sensible. Unfortunately, the author's experience is that they are rarely offered and where the agent himself suggests such a meeting that suggestion is invariably rebuffed. In many cases such a meeting could actually achieve virtually all of the purposes set out above for which HMRC believe meetings vital.

1.33 What about taking clients to meetings with HMRC? The circumstances in which this author will consider such meetings are where:

- HMRC have issued in advance a detailed agenda of what they wish to cover at the meeting. It is unrealistic to expect a list of questions as these ought, to a large extent, to be dependent on the answers to earlier questions. On the other hand, 'I wish to discuss how the business operates and the taxpayer's lifestyle' (or 'the gross profit percentage and living expenses') is not a detailed agenda. Indeed it is so vague that it probably does not justify a meeting at all. A detailed agenda is important because it indicates that the Officer has identified what issues require help that only the taxpayer can give, and enables the accountant to satisfy himself that that is indeed the case and that some of the issues cannot be better resolved in advance of the meeting.
- All of the accounting issues and other issues that can be dealt with by the accountant have been resolved. HMRC tell their staff, 'You should bear in mind, however, that meetings can be expensive and inconvenient to taxpayers' (Enquiry Manual, para 1821). Sadly Officers rarely seem to take much notice of this. The reality is that many clients have no knowledge of how the detailed figures in their accounts have been put together. Nor indeed is there any rational reason why they should. It is not information that they need to manage the business. It is information that has been generated partly by their book-keeper and partly by their accountant and it is reasonable for them to rely on the expertise of such people. It is unreasonable for an Officer to expect a taxpayer to put aside running his business and attend a three-hour meeting, much of which is taken up by accounting issues that are outside the taxpayer's own knowledge and competence and which his accountant can deal with without the taxpayer's intervention.
- The taxpayer is the most appropriate person to deal with the remaining issues. Many HMRC Officers seem to take the view that as the taxpayer has ultimate responsibility for his tax affairs they need to interview him because he ought to know precisely how the business operates. Such Officers often become extremely suspicious when the client is unable to provide detailed explanations for things that his book-keeper or another staff member could well have been able to answer readily. If the taxpayer or company director is not the most appropriate person to provide the information that the Officer says that he is seeking from the meeting consider offering a meeting with the appropriate staff member instead. If such an offer is rebuffed then the reasons the Officer has given for wanting a meeting are probably not his real reasons. It is clearly inappropriate to

subject a client to a meeting where the agent has any suspicion that the reasons the Officer has given for wanting a meeting are either spurious or incomplete.

- If the agenda includes detailed questions on entries in the records that the accountant has been given an opportunity to deal with but has been unable to answer fully because the books and records were sent to HMRC at the start of the enquiry but have not been returned prior to the meeting. It is unreasonable to expect anyone to answer questions on individual transactions that occurred two or three years earlier without his having been able to review the records to refresh his memory in advance of the meeting.
- The issues that the Officer wishes to discuss need to be of sufficient importance in the context of the accounts to justify taking the taxpayer or director away from his business. A meeting for the sake of having had a meeting is never justifiable.

1.34 If it has been decided that a meeting is appropriate, where should this be held? The answer is normally at either an HMRC office or the accountant's office depending on which is more convenient. HMRC increasingly deal with a taxpayer's affairs a long distance away. In such a case a meeting at the accountant's office is usually sensible, although the Officer can usually arrange to hold a meeting at a local HMRC office if this is desired.

1.35 What about the HMRC desire to meet at the client's premises? If the records are voluminous, or it is clear that a number of staff members are likely to be called on to deal with specific issues this may be sensible. In most cases though a taxpayer does not want someone arriving at his office and announcing to the receptionist that he is from HMRC. Even less do clients want to risk people wandering round the building, perhaps looking for the toilets, and telling other staff that they are from HMRC. Staff are likely to wonder why the tax authorities are visiting the business and could well draw incorrect conclusions from the presence of such people, which can be damaging to the operation of the business. There is also the risk an Officer might add to his list of questions things that he notices while at the business premises but actually have no bearing on the enquiry – other, of course, than to needlessly prolong the meeting.

1.36 HMRC usually make detailed notes of meetings. They are prepared to provide a taxpayer or his agent with a copy of such notes, but do not always volunteer to do so. If they do not send a copy of their notes after the meeting, it is sensible to request a copy. Where HMRC send notes they tend to sign them and ask the taxpayer and his agent to read them, sign them if they agree with them and send back a signed copy. It is unwise to sign such notes. Many firms of accountants, including my own, decline to do so as a matter of policy and explain to HMRC that it is their policy never to ask clients to sign such notes. Curiously, SCI and its predecessors have always accepted this as reasonable, whereas some local offices get upset when notes are not signed. There are two good reasons not to do so. First, the notes tend to be slanted towards what the Officer wanted to know. That is probably not deliberate. Meeting notes do not purport to be a transcript of what was said. They are a summary. Any summariser is likely to include in his summary the things that he regards as important and to omit things that he considers trivial. When people take notes of a meeting they do the same thing; their notes tend to cover only the points they consider significant. The result is that the notes often downplay or omit entirely things that may have been said, the relevance of which may not assume any importance until a later date. If the taxpayer has signed the notes as a complete and correct record of the meeting it becomes difficult, if not impossible, subsequently to convince the appeal Commissioners that he said something at the meeting that is not covered in the notes. The language adopted can itself slant the emphasis of what was said. The obvious example is that taxpayers seem never to 'say' anything at HMRC meetings; they 'allege' things. To many people 'allege' carries a connotation that what was said is not readily believable.

1.37 Secondly, the reason that HMRC want the notes signed is that in the event of a later dispute they can point to the signature as evidence that what the taxpayer is then claiming that he said at the meeting was not said. There is no advantage to the taxpayer in signing HMRC's notes. Accordingly, why risk them being regarded at a later date of evidence of precisely what was said at the meeting?

1.38 The HMRC notes should, of course, be read and any significant errors or omissions pointed out to the Officer. Where the notes do not properly explain a point which the taxpayer was seeking to make it is sensible to re-explain that point. If the notes correctly reflect what was said but it has subsequently been found that the taxpayer's recollection was at fault, the information given at the meeting should of course be corrected. It is sensible to send HMRC any documentary evidence that shows that the corrected position reflects the facts. Often, if a taxpayer or his agent challenges what was said in an Officer's notes the Officer will seek to argue over what was said. Try not to get drawn into such a debate over the notes. At the end of the day, enquiries are resolved on the basis of the facts. If the appeal Commissioners are presented with a set of notes and a contemporary letter challenging aspects of those notes, they are likely to recognise that the issue is disputed and not regard the notes as evidence of what was said but look for alternative evidence to resolve the matter. If the purpose of a meeting is to ascertain the facts, it is also curious that the Officer should seem more concerned about what was and was not said than what the facts actually are.

BOOKS AND RECORDS

1.39 A person must keep all such records as may be requisite for the purpose of enabling him to make and deliver a correct and complete return

(TMA 1970, s 12B(1); FA 1998, Sch 18, para 21)(1)). In the case of a person carrying on a business such records must include records of:

(i) all amounts received and expended in the course of the trade, profession or business and the matters in respect of which the receipts and expenditure take place, and

(ii) in the case of a trade involving dealing in goods all sales and purchases of goods made in the course of the trade

(TMA 1970, s 12B(3), FA 1998, Sch 18, para 21(5)).

1.40 The records must be retained until the fifth anniversary of 31 January following the end of the tax year (the first anniversary for non-business records) or, if later, the completion of any HMRC enquiry. In the case of a company they must be kept for six years after the end of the accounting period (or if later the close of any HMRC enquiry). The duty to preserve the records listed at (i) and (ii) above is specifically stated to include a duty to preserve 'all supporting documents relating to such items': (TMA 1970, s 12B(1)(b) and 3(b); FA 1998, Sch 18, para 21(2), (3) and (6)). Supporting documents is defined to include 'accounts, books, deeds, contracts, vouchers and receipts' (TMA 1970, s 12B(6), FA 1998, Sch 18, para 21(6)). It should be noted that there is no specific requirement to keep (in the sense of bring into existence) such records. It is only if the business in fact keeps them that it becomes under an obligation to retain them for the requisite period.

1.41 It is a question of fact what records 'may be requisite' for the purpose of delivering a correct and complete return. Unless and until it is demonstrated that the return is not correct and complete there is a strong inference that the records that were in fact kept satisfy the statutory obligation as they have enabled the statutory objective to be achieved.

1.42 Comments in the course of an enquiry that the Officer considers the business records to be inadequate should be approached in the context of this statutory requirement. The records a taxpayer needs to keep are those that he considers appropriate, not those which the HMRC Officer considers appropriate. The HMRC Officer has no real knowledge of either the needs of the business or the abilities of its staff. Records that a person finds easy to keep are likely to be more accurate than more complex records that he finds it difficult to complete. This author's experience is that HMRC frequently expect records to be kept that are inappropriate to the circumstances of a business. For example, if cheques received are entered into a cash book and copied from there to a paying-in book, and the bankings agree with the cash book, it is hard to see any justification for keeping the paying-in book as that is not the prime record but is something prepared simply for the bank. Even if the paying-in-book is completed first, it is difficult to see why it should form part of the records under s 12B once it is ascertained that the bankings agree with the cash book (although in that case it may be a supporting document). Similarly, cheque book stubs are unlikely to come within s 12B if they are not the prime document.

1.43 HMRC Officers sometimes contend that the use of estimates breaches the requirement of s 12B. As the starting point for taxable profits is accounts prepared in accordance with UK GAAP (Generally Accepted Accounting Principles) and UK GAAP permits estimates, that cannot be right provided that the estimate can be justified under GAAP. Accounts that satisfy UK GAAP also satisfy the test of being correct and complete (subject to any adjustments required by law). Of course, if HMRC amend a taxpayer's return it is then up to him to justify any estimate used, but that is a different obligation from the record-keeping requirement.

1.44 The other issue in relation to books and records is that the s 19A obligation is to 'produce' documents to HMRC. It is up to the taxpayer where he produces them. He cannot be required to send them to HMRC. Nor can he be required to allow HMRC to come to his office to inspect them. In many, if not most, cases for a small business the most appropriate place to produce the records is its external accountant's office. The clients' staff are not then aware of the enquiry and the accountant will be able to volunteer to the HMRC Officer information in his working papers that assist an understanding of the accounts and may be prepared to make available to the Officer the staff member who prepared the accounts.

SECTION 19A AND PARA 27 NOTICES

1.45 Section 19A is a limited information power. It seems likely that the limitations reflect the amount of work that Parliament envisaged HMRC doing in relation to an enquiry. In particular, HMRC Officers frequently say that they have a duty to satisfy themselves that the accounts are correct and complete. That is not the case. Section 9A (or para 24) gives him a right 'to enquire into a return', but does not specify the objective of such an enquiry. Section 19A (or para 27 enables him to obtain documents and information 'for the purpose of determining whether and, if so, the extent to which the return is incorrect or incomplete', but s 28A (and para 32) which deals with the completion of an enquiry merely requires the Officer to 'state his conclusions and if necessary to amend the return to give effect to his conclusions'. It seems clear that if the Officer believes that the return is not complete and correct all that statutorily he is seeking to do is to reach a conclusion and to form an opinion as to what the amendment to the return ought to be; not to satisfy himself about anything.

1.46 Section 19A imposes three limitations on the information that the Officer can require (plus, of course, a valid enquiry notice must have been issued within the appropriate time limit).

1.47

- If he requires documents, these must be in the taxpayer's 'possession or power' (TMA 1970, s 19A(2)(a)).
- The documents or information sought must be required for the purpose of determining whether and to what extent the return is incorrect or incomplete.
- The documents or information must be 'reasonably required' for that purpose. (TMA 1970, s 19A(2); FA 1998, Sch 18, para 27).
- In the case of a company they can also require information (but not documents) to be produced in such form as they may reasonably require for the purpose of the enquiry (FA 1998, Sch 18, para 27(1)(b)).

1.48 As these provisions are central to the enquiry process, their limitations need to be looked at in more detail. Before doing so it may be worth noting that the draftsman has used the negative expression 'incorrect or incomplete' rather than the positive 'correct and complete'. The may well imply a lower test. In particular accounts require judgments to be applied in many areas. Using a judgment means that there cannot be one 'correct' figure of profit. There will be a range of figures permissible within the judgment and every one of those figures is potentially 'correct', or at least none of them are 'incorrect' (it is doubtful whether any of them can actually be described as correct when a different figure is equally correct). And what about estimates? By definition any estimate is unlikely to be correct because it is placing a value on something for which the actual value is unknown. Nevertheless, a reasonable estimate must surely make the return 'not incorrect' even though it may be uncertain whether it is 'correct'.

The expression 'possession or power' is a common legal expression. Nevertheless, its meaning is uncertain. In *Meditor Capital Management Ltd v Feighan* (2004 STC(SCD) 273) the Special Commissioner was asked to order disclosure of documents of another company with a common directorship. Reviewing the relevant law, he noted that:

> 'There is no case law on the phrase "possession or power" in the particular context of para 27, Sch 18 Finance Act 1998. Nor is there any case law on the same phrase in ss 20 and 20A of the 1970 Act. However, there is case law on the phrase in relation to the old disclosure rules, which confirms that the question is one of fact. RSC Ord 24, r 7(1) provided that the court had the power to order disclosure in certain circumstances if documents were in the "possession, power or custody" of a party. In *B v B* [1978] 3 WLR 624 a husband was ordered to disclose certain documents in divorce proceedings, although the documents belonged to a company which he controlled and of which he was a director. It was held by Dunn J

that the documents were within his power. The question of whether this was the case was a question of fact, depending on the individual's shareholding, whether the minority shareholders were adverse to him, the constitution of the board of directors and whether they objected to disclosure of the documents. Documents would not be within his power merely because he had a right under s 12 of the Companies Act 1976 to inspect them; but where a company was a director's alter ego, so that he had unfettered control of its affairs, company documents would be within his power. In *B v B* the individual was the chairman and individual director of the company, which is not the case with Mr Shakerchi at present. He is no longer a director of the company, nor is he a shareholder. It is difficult to say that MCM(B) is the "alter ego" of Mr Shakerchi in the manner that the company was the alter ego of the director in *B v B* (at 807). The fact that Mr Shakerchi is not a director of the company means that this rule cannot be invoked ... In *Lonrho Ltd v Shell Petroleum Co Ltd* [1980] 1 WLR 627 it was said that "in the context of the phrase 'possession, custody or power' the expression 'power' must, in my view, mean a presently enforceable legal right to obtain from whoever actually holds the document inspection of it without the need to obtain the consent of anyone else" (per Lord Diplock, [1980] 1 WLR 627 at 635). In that case, the question arose of whether holding companies had the power over documents in indirectly controlled subsidiaries. The following observations were made: "The articles of association of all the subsidiaries vest the management of the company in its board of directors. It is the board that has control of the company's documents on its behalf; the shareholders as such have no right to inspect or to take copies of them. If requested to allow inspection of the company's documents, whether by a shareholder or by a third party, it is the duty of the board to consider whether to accede to this request would be in the best interests of the company" (at 634). The rule was limited however thus: "I say nothing about one-man companies in which a natural person and/or his nominees are the sole shareholders and directors. It may be that, depending upon their own particular facts, different considerations apply to these." ' (at 636–37).

1.49 The upshot of the above cases is that in cases in which a company is not simply a one-man company, the refusal of a company to allow inspection of its documents must be respected (Lonrho). In the case of one-man companies, if the company is the alter ego of the individual the company's refusal will have no effect on the individual's 'power' over a document (*B v B*).

1.50 Where it is unclear whether something is in the taxpayer's possession or power it is up to the appeal Commissioner to decide the issue as a question of fact.

1.51 Whether or not something is required for the purpose of the enquiry requires an examination both of what the enquiry is and what its purpose is. The enquiry is 'into a return' (TMA 1970, s 9A(1); FA 1998, Sch 18, para 24(1)). This itself imposes a number of limitations. It is not a general enquiry in relation to the taxpayer's tax affairs. It relates only to one particular return; it does not extend to the return of any other year. It relates only to the return by the taxpayer; it does not extend to a return by the taxpayer's spouse or civil partner, to a return by a director of the taxpayer company or to a return by a subsidiary of the taxpayer company. It relates only to the income tax or company tax return under enquiry; it does not extend to a different return by the taxpayer such as a PAYE return or a return under one of the specific provisions requiring special returns (but a company return includes a return of tax due under ICTA 1988, s 419 (loans to directors)).

1.52 As indicated earlier, the purpose of the enquiry seems to be to enable the Officer to state conclusions and to amend the return to give effect to such conclusions. As HMRC are adept at raising estimated assessments, the information that is reasonably required to enable the Officers to amend a return to give effect to his conclusions may well not go beyond that which will enable him to make a rough-and-ready estimate of what amendment to make.

1.53 It needs to be realised though that this is a two-edged sword. If a taxpayer challenges a s 19A notice on the basis that the Officer's wish to enquire into details is not necessary for him to be able to state his conclusions, he will put an onus on himself to displace the estimate which he forces the Officer to make – and such an estimate is far more likely to be an overestimate than an underestimate.

1.54 Whether something is 'reasonably' required is a question of fact that must depend on the circumstances of an individual enquiry. It is not what a reasonable Officer requires, ie it is not a test of whether or not the Officer is being unreasonable. It is an objective test. What would 'the man on the Clapham omnibus' or the 'officious bystander with some knowledge of tax' think reasonable in the circumstances of the case.

1.55 This probably needs to be looked at in the context of what information the Officer already has. If he already has the dividend vouchers can the bank statements be reasonably required to check the dividends? Probably not. It also needs to be looked at in the context that the Officer is enquiring only into a single return, so what may be reasonably required to establish a course of conduct over several years may well not be reasonably required for the purpose only of enquiring into that single return.

1.56 An interesting issue arises in connection with electronic records. For income tax purposes the provision of a print-out seems to satisfy s 19A. In the case of a company the reason that the legislation enables HMRC to specify the form in which information is provided is to enable them to require the information on computer disk. The layout in the Queens Printer's version of the legislation and the version on the HMRC and Statute Law Database websites all tie 'in such form' only to information, not to documents. However, FA 1998, s 127(1) (which is headed 'Production of computer records') states that 'any provision made by or under the Taxes Acts which requires a person (a) to produce … any documents … shall have effect as if any reference in that provision to a document were a reference to anything in which information of any description is recorded'.

1.57 As para 27 deals separately with documents and information it may well be that the two are intended to be mutually exclusive and that something that constitutes a document cannot also constitute information. It is accordingly questionable whether HMRC are entitled to require the provision of a computer disk. The reason that they ask for such a disk is that they have an audit program that they wish to apply to it. The best advice is to provide a print-out of the information on the disk and to argue before the appeal Commissioners that HMRC have already been provided with a document containing all of the accounts information held by the computer so it is not reasonable for them to require the same information again in a different form, particularly bearing in mind that Parliament has not given them the right to require the form which a document should take.

1.58 Because whether not an item falls within s 19A or para 27 is wholly a question of fact, the cases that have come before the Special Commissioners give little or no help in determining what does and does not fall within the section. The fact that in a particular case something was held to be reasonably required does not mean that it will also be reasonably required in another case where the circumstances may be different. Most people would prefer to take such a question before the General Commissioners, so not that many cases have come before the Special Commissioners and those that have generally involve a point of principal.

1.59 *Meditor Capital Management Ltd v Feighan* (2004 STC (SCD) 273) related to evidence to support a transfer pricing issue and one of the issues was what was in the company's possession or power. *Accountant v Inspector of Taxes* (2000 STC (SCD) 522) and *Parto v Bratherton* (2004 STC (SCD) 339) both raised the question, which the Commissioners answered in the affirmative, whether a person could be required under information to produce a document that did not exist. *Mother v Inspector of Taxes* (1999 STC (SCD) 279) was concerned with reasonableness, but as the challenge was more to whether HMRC was being reasonable rather than what was reasonably required it was not surprisingly dismissed. It was also held that records of the taxpayer's business which may reveal information concerning other taxpayers must nevertheless be supplied, but providing as little information concerning other taxpayers as is compatible with the requirement to produce documents relating to the taxpayer's business. *Guyer v Walton* (2001 STC (SCD) 750) involved a solicitor who unsuccessfully tried to claim legal professional privilege in relation to his own affairs. In *Guest House Proprietor v Kendall* (2005 STC (SCD) 280) some of the items requested did not exist and others formed part of the accountant's working papers, but the Inspector told the Commissioners that he was not asking for documents to be produced that did not exist so it would be sufficient for the company to tell him that fact and which items were in the accountant's working papers and thus not within the taxpayer's possession or power. In *Murphy v Gowers* (2005 STC (SCD) 44) it was held that it was irrelevant that the information requested had been supplied to another part of HMRC by Mr Murphy's employer, but as Mr Murphy did not appear and was not represented it was a very one-sided case. *Spring Salmon & Seafood Ltd v RCC* (2005 STC (SCD) 830) involved a tax scheme and the Commissioners felt that the information requested was reasonably required to enable HMRC to assess the motivation and commerciality of the transactions. The challenge in *Asfar v RCC* (2006 STC (SCD) 625) was that the information requested went too wide and that it infringed the taxpayer's human right to privacy, but the information was held to be reasonably required. *Commane v RCC* (2006 STC (SCD) 81) was an appeal by a taxpayer in person who did not appear before the Commissioners, but his main objection seems to have been that he thought the enquiry as such was unreasonable so the appeal was dismissed. *Low v RCC* (2006 STC (SCD) 21) was another case of a taxpayer in person who did not appear before the Commissioners. He complained that he had already provided the information in response to a Tax Credits enquiry, but the Commissioner held that as that was different legislation HMRC were entitled to ask for it again. It was held in *Eder v RCC* (2007 STC (SCD) 334) that information shown on a tax return that related to the tax liability of a different year (in that case an election to carry back a gift aid payment) was 'something contained in the return for the later year and accordingly within the scope of the enquiry for the later year'. In *Jacques v RCC* (No 2) (2007 STC (SCD) 166) the Special Commissioner expressed a view that 'produce' in the context of s 19A means 'allowing sufficient unrestricted use of all the documents in question to HMRC for HMRC to do such work, tests and other things (such as photocopying) in relation to the documents as is reasonable for HMRC to do in order to progress that stage of the enquiry. It includes allowing HMRC sufficient time to do what is necessary'.

1.60 In *Sokaya v RCC* (2008 STC (SCD) 51) the Special Commissioner commented, in relation to a demand for personal bank statements, 'Clearly the enquiry need not be limited to the entries in the return because the officer can require information to determine whether the return is incomplete … The appellant says he has ordered his affairs so as not to pay any tax but has not said how. … Since his income cannot support his expenditure it seems entirely reasonable to me that the Revenue should check his taxable income'. This ought to be a salutary lesson. If HMRC can point to a clear inconsistency it is likely that the Commissioners will be sympathetic to allowing them access to whatever they claim that they need in order to resolve that inconsistency. It is accordingly advisable to identify in advance of the hearing that there is an obvious inconsistency and to seek to resolve it, if necessary by volunteering enough information that you believe falls outside s 19A for the Commissioners to realise that the information sought by HMRC is not needed to explain the inconsistency because it can be explained by something else. For example, although an apparent deficiency of income may point to the possibility of other income, it could equally well be explained by an increase in bank overdraft facilities, a loan or gift from a third party or the taxpayer's spouse having sufficient income or assets to make good the shortfall. If no explanation is offered for the shortfall it is not surprising for the Commissioners to feel it is reasonable for HMRC to assume that it suggests undisclosed income. If information to support the actual explanation has been proffered to HMRC the Commissioners will have to consider the reasonableness of the information that HMRC are seeking in the context that an alternative explanation for the shortfall has already been evidenced.

1.61 Do not be disheartened by the fact that most of the published Commissioners decisions have gone against the taxpayer. What is reasonably required is a pure question of fact. As such most taxpayers take s 19A appeals (and requests for closure notices (see below) which are similarly pure questions of fact) to the General Commissioners as they feel that a layman with commercial experience is more likely to appreciate the practical questions involved in what might reasonable satisfy someone than do the Special Commissioners with their legal training. It is probable that the cases that come before the Special Commissioners (which are the only cases publicly reported) are those where the taxpayer or his adviser is either seeking to establish some legal principle or mistakenly believes either that listing the case before the Special Commissioners is some sort of deterrent to HMRC or that the Special Commissioners are more likely to be sympathetic to his arguments.

THE S 19A PROCEDURE

1.62 A notice under s 19A (or para 27) must specify the time within which it must be complied with, which must not be less than 30 days (TMA 1970, s 19A(2), FA 1998, Sch 18, para 27(2)). The taxpayer has a right of appeal against such a notice. Such an appeal must be in writing and made within 30 days after the notice is given to the taxpayer (TMA 1970, s 19A(6) and (7); FA 1998, Sch 18, para 28(1) and (2)). A ground for appeal needs to be stated in the same way as for an appeal against an assessment (TMA 1970, s 19A(8)). This will normally be that some or all of the documents or information required by the notice does not fall within s 19A (or para 27). It could also be that the enquiry notice itself is invalid or that the s 19A (or para 27) notice is invalid. There have been several Special Commissioners' decisions dealing with the validity of both s 9A and s 19A notices.

1.63 The s 19A notice in *Wing Hung Lai v Bale* (1999 STC (SCD) 238) was held to be invalid as it was posted too late to have been received in the normal course of post by 31 January. HMRC sought, unsuccessfully, to overturn that principle in *Holly v Inspector of Taxes* (2000 STC (SCD) 50). In *Self-Assessed v Inspector of Taxes* (1999 STC (SCD) 253) a s 19A notice was held invalid as it required the information to be produced 'within 30 days of this notice', whereas the taxpayer was entitled under the statute to a minimum of 30 days from receipt of the notice. In *Hallamshire Estates Ltd v Walford* (2004 STC (SCD) 330), the taxpayer unsuccessfully sought to contend as a matter of construction that the time limit for enquiring into an amended return ran from the date of the return, not that of the amendment.

1.64 In *Murat v Ornach* (2004 STC (SCD) 115), the taxpayer sought to challenge the validity of the s 9A notice in an appeal against a penalty for not complying with the resultant s 19A notice. It was held that as the decision on the s 19A appeal is final it was too late to seek to challenge the s 9A notice. Mr Murat appealed to the High Court (77 TC 122), but his appeal was dismissed as hopeless. *Siwek v CIR* (2002 STC (SCD) 247) was a taxpayer in person taking a forlorn point. In *Bensoor v Devine* (2005 STC (SCD) 297), the taxpayer challenged whether a s 9A notice could be issued by an Officer who was not an Inspector and also challenged HMRC's right to broaden an aspect enquiry. Unsurprisingly, he lost on both points. In *O'Sullivan v Philip* (2005 STC (SCD) 51) the taxpayer amended his return and after some correspondence HMRC accepted the amendment. In response to a subsequent enquiry notice the taxpayer contended, unsuccessfully, that such HMRC acceptance amounted to the completion of an enquiry into the return so they were debarred from opening a further enquiry. *Moffat v CIR* (2006 STC (SCD) 380) concerned a technical challenge based on the wording of the closure notice, but it failed.

1.65 The appeal freezes HMRC's ability to obtain the information sought until it has been determined either on appeal or by agreement. An appeal lies either to the General or Special Commissioners. The Commissioners can (and probably must) confirm the notice if it appears to them that the production of the documents or information is reasonably required for the purpose of the enquiry, and set it aside if it does not so appear to them (TMA 1970, s 19A(9): FA 1998, Sch, para 28(4)). There is no onus of proof on the taxpayer. Nor is there any right of appeal by either the taxpayer or HMRC against the decision of the Commissioners. This is obviously because whether or not something is reasonably required for the purpose of the enquiry is a question of fact and the normal right of appeal against a Commissioner's decision applies only to questions of law (TMA 1970, s 19A(11), FA 1998, Sch 18, para 28(6)).

1.66 In practice it is generally accepted that the Commissioners are entitled to look at each document or item of information individually as if it were contained in a separate notice and therefore uphold part of the notice and set aside part. The appeal on the other hand seems to be an appeal against the notice in its entirety. If the Commissioners uphold the notice, the taxpayer has a period of 30 days from the determination of the appeal in which to provide the information (TMA 1970, s 19A(10), FA 1998, Sch 18, para 28(5)).

1.67 HMRC can issue as many s 19A (or para 27) notices as they wish during the course of an enquiry. Indeed there is nothing to stop them issuing a second notice for information that the Commissioners hold not to be reasonably required under an earlier notice. This is not unreasonable as information may not be reasonably required at an early stage of an enquiry, but something might come to light later in the enquiry which affects its relevance. It might be worth drawing this to the attention of the Commissioners. A decision that is adverse to the taxpayer is final whereas one that is adverse to HMRC is not necessarily so as they could issue a fresh notice for it at a later stage. Accordingly, if the decision is fairly evenly balanced justice might well require the notice to be set aside so that HMRC could revisit the need for the information at a later stage.

1.68 In practice HMRC rarely seem to list s 19A (and para 27) appeals for hearing. They generally make do without the disputed information provided that items that come clearly within the ambit of the provision are complied with.

1.69 Section 20 is considered in Chapter 10. There is nothing to prevent HMRC issuing a s 20 notice in relation to a self-assessment enquiry. However the following Ministerial statement of 19 April 1999 should be quoted if HMRC threaten a s 20 notice to obtain information that has been held not to be reasonably required under s 19A.

> 'Dawn Primarolo: The powers in TMA 1970 ss 19A, 20 are not mutually exclusive. However, the Inland Revenue would not normally issue a notice under s 20 in order to obtain information that they had failed to obtain under s 19A. Very rarely, it might become clear, after the taxpayer had appealed against an s 19A notice, that s 20 was in fact the more appropriate section to use. A notice under s 20 cannot be issued by an inspector unless the taxpayer has failed to take an opportunity to provide the information voluntarily, and may be issued only with the consent of an independent Appeal Commissioner.'

(Hansard, HC Written Answer, Vol 329, cols 425, 426, 19 April 1999)

1.70 The main instances in which HMRC seem to use s 20 notices in relation to self-assessment is to obtain information about the affairs of a company director when they are enquiring into the company's return. They cannot use s 19A in such circumstances, as the information is not in the possession or power of the company and the enquiry is not into the return of the director. Third party notices under s 20(3) might also be used where the taxpayer is not prepared to cooperate with the enquiry. It might be easier for HMRC to obtain the information by another route than to have to enforce a succession of s 19A notices.

OTHER WAYS TO OBTAIN INFORMATION

1.71 Sometimes HMRC ask for a mandate from the taxpayer authorising his bank or another third party to provide direct to HMRC such information as they may request. This is not a statutory procedure. It is wholly voluntary. A taxpayer should think carefully before agreeing to provide such a mandate. It is normally better for the taxpayer to volunteer to obtain information from the bank himself. If HMRC obtain information direct from the bank the taxpayer may well not know what information they have been given, which places him at a disadvantage in negotiating with HMRC. Furthermore, in practice banks made available information to HMRC under the authority of a mandate which they would not make available to the taxpayer himself. The obvious example is the bank's own file notes of telephone conversations with the taxpayer.

1.72 HMRC also tell their staff that there will be occasions in which they may want to invite the Commissioners to exercise their power to issue a precept under reg 10 of the General Commissioners (Jurisdiction and Procedure) Regulations 1994 or the Special Commissioners (Jurisdiction and Procedure) Regulations 1994, although in a normal self-assessment enquiry there is normally no opportunity to do so (Enquiry Manual, para 2270). On the face of it, to accede to such a request would be an abuse of the Commissioners' powers. Regulation 10 gives the Commissioners power to require the taxpayer to deliver to them such information as they may require for the purpose of determining any issue in the proceedings and to make available for inspection by the Commissioners or HMRC such documents as in the opinion of the Commissioners may contain information relevant to the subject matter of the proceedings. In other words, it is a power to enable the Commissioners to ensure that information that they think that they themselves need to determine the appeal is made available to them. It is not a power to assist HMRC in carrying out an enquiry. Indeed, as the onus on an appeal against an assessment is normally on the taxpayer to disprove the assessment, and it is for the taxpayer to present his case as he wishes, it is difficult to conceive circumstances where it would be proper for the Commissioners to use their Regulation 10 power in circumstances where the taxpayer has professional representation and is accordingly capable of himself identifying what information or documents he ought to put before the tribunal to prove his case.

COMPLETION OF ENQUIRY

1.73 An enquiry is completed when the Officer issues a closure notice to the taxpayer (TMA 1970, s 28(1), FA 1998, Sch 18, para 32(1)). The closure notice takes effect when it is issued (TMA 1970, s 28(3), FA 1998, Sch 18, para 32(2)). An income tax closure notice must inform the taxpayer that the Officer has completed his enquiries and state his conclusions. It must also state that in his opinion no amendment to the return is required, or must make the amendments to the return that are required to give effect to his conclusions (TMA 1970, s 28A(1) and (3)). This clearly implies that the conclusions must incorporate the amount of any adjustment that the Officer concludes is required, as otherwise he would not be able to amend the return. A corporation tax closure notice merely has to inform the company that HMRC have completed their enquiry and state their conclusions (FA 1998, Sch 18, para 32(1)). The company then has 30 days in which to amend its return to accord with the conclusions stated in the closure notice (FA 1998, Sch 18, para 34(1)). This seem to imply an obligation on HMRC to state their conclusions in a manner which are capable of being given effect to, ie to either state what amendment is needed or how the amendment is to be arrived at. If the company does not amend its return within the 30-day period HMRC are entitled, by notice to the company, to do so itself (FA 1998, Sch 18, para 34(2)).

1.74 At any time during the course of an enquiry the taxpayer can apply to the Commissioners for a direction requiring HMRC to issue a closure notice within a specified period. Such an application is heard and determined in the same way as an appeal. The Commissioners must give the direction applied for unless they are satisfied that there are reasonable grounds for not issuing a closure notice within a specified period (TMA 1970, s 28A(4)–(6); FA 1998, Sch 18, para 33). This places the onus on the Officer to convince the Commissioners that they ought not to direct a closure. The purpose of this provision is to prevent HMRC leaving an enquiry open indefinitely and thus defeating the taxpayer's right to finality in his tax affairs within a reasonable time. A taxpayer might make such an application where he considers that HMRC delays are unreasonable or where he feels that HMRC is raising new questions in relation to areas that have already been fully dealt with.

1.75 Such an application should not be made lightly, however. If successful, it does not force the Officer to abandon his enquiry; it forces him to reach a conclusion on the basis of the information that is available to him by the specified date. If this is incomplete information he is likely to conclude that a greater adjustment to the self-assessment ought to be made than he would have concluded had he been able to obtain the missing information. Accordingly, a successful application is likely to force the taxpayer to appeal against the Officer's amendment and on the appeal to disprove a larger assessment than he would have faced had he let the Officer continue with his investigation.

1.76 There is, of course, a right of appeal against the amendment to the self-assessment as a result of the closure notice or against HMRC's amendment of the assessment (TMA 1970, s 31, FA 1998, Sch 18, para 34(3)). Notice of such an appeal must be made in writing within 30 days in the normal way.

However, the issue of the closure notice brings to an end the self-assessment process and, in particular, the Officer's ability to seek information under s 19A (or para 27). It does not, of course, prevent the taxpayer volunteering further information or the Officer asking for further information informally.

1.77 The major case dealing with closure notices is *Jade Palace Ltd v RCC* (2006 STC (SCD) 419 which held that the legislation did not require the Officer to be satisfied – she might never be so that would undermine the purpose of the provision – but merely to form a conclusion. It also held that the Commissioner does not have to require the closure by the date requested by the taxpayer, but can reach his own decision as to the appropriate date. In *Vodafone* (*No* 2) (2006 STC 1530), which is concerned with the validity of the UK's CFC rules, the company asked for a closure notice so that the case could be brought before the ECJ. The Commissioners decided that the substantive issue was one that ought to be referred and ordered the closure. HMRC appealed on the basis that the Commissioners had no power to decide the substantive point so ought not to have ordered the closure. The Court of Appeal held that para 33 gives the Commissioners power to do anything they consider reasonably necessary to decide whether or not to require a closure and that included deciding incidental points of law.

DISCOVERY

1.78 Self-assessment is designed to give finality to the taxpayer. Once an enquiry has been closed or the enquiry window has passed without HMRC having opened an enquiry, they can no longer challenge the return.

1.79 The discovery power provides an exception to this general principle. It enables HMRC to assess tax in relation to closed years if they discover that tax has been under assessed and the under-assessment is attributable either to:

- fraud or negligent conduct of the taxpayer or a person acting on his behalf, or
- something of which the Officer could not have been reasonably expected to be aware at the time the enquiry window closed on the basis of the information made available to him before that time.

1.80 A discovery assessment can be made at any time up to the fifth anniversary of 31 January following the tax year to which it relates (or up to six years after the end of the accounting period in relation to a company) (TMA 1970, s 34; FA 1998, Sch 18, para 46). In the case of fraud or negligence, a discovery assessment can be made up to 20 years after 31 January following the tax year to which it relates or, in the case of a company up to 21 years after the end of the accounting period (TMA 1970, s 36; FA 1998, Sch 18, para 46(2)).

1.81 As discovery is not part of self-assessment, the self-assessment enquiry procedures do not apply. In particular, HMRC have no power to issue a s 19A or para 27 information notice. Indeed, apart from TMA 1970, s 20, they have no power at all to require the taxpayer to supply information in relation to an investigation leading up to a discovery. They have to rely on the taxpayer volunteering information – but where a discovery involves negligence their power to determine the level of penalty can act as a powerful inducement to volunteer information.

1.82 The reason for mentioning discovery in the context of enquiries is that HMRC take the view that in the absence of evidence to the contrary 'a presumption of continuity' can be made where an enquiry suggests that there is an understatement of income in the enquiry year and the reasons for that understatement provide a pointer to under-declarations in earlier years (Enquiry Manual, para 3309).

1.83 In practice, HMRC invariably seek to adjust the previous six years in addition to the enquiry year where they believe that a presumption of continuity can reasonably be made. In general they do not seek to investigate the omissions for such earlier years, but quantify the supposed omissions by assuming that the figure quantified for the enquiry year is representative of the level of under declaration in earlier years and reducing it on some rough and ready basis to allow for inflation.

1.84 There are two points that need to be borne in mind. The first is that before agreeing to an adjustment on an enquiry for the sake of an easy life when the taxpayer does not believe any adjustment to be legally due, it needs to be appreciated that the adjustment may result in a tax bill seven times the size of that which was anticipated when agreeing it. The second is that if the taxpayer does not believe that adjusting the current year's amendment to reflect the effect of inflation is likely to give a reasonable approximation of any underpayment for earlier years, he ought to seek to establish the size of any appropriate adjustment on a more realistic basis using whatever information he has available in relation to the years in question and seek to persuade the Officer to agree his calculation.

1.85 Where, in the course of a self-assessment enquiry, HMRC make a discovery in relation to earlier years they normally seek 'a contract settlement' rather than raise formal discovery and penalty assessments. A contract settlement is a contract between HMRC and the taxpayer under which the taxpayer offers to pay HMRC an agreed sum in respect of tax, interest and penalties in consideration of HMRC agreeing not to institute proceedings against him. The contract settlement will normally cover the enquiry year as well as the discovery years.

1.86 Where a contract settlement has been entered into the amount due is not tax; it is a civil debt. HMRC will accordingly enforce it as such a debt. They cannot use their power of distraint or other statutory powers that they have to enable them to recover tax.

1.87 Where a contract settlement is entered into, HMRC do not in practice issue a closure notice. The reason is that their computer system would then seek to recover the tax due under the amendment to the self-assessment, as well as the Collector collecting the debt under the contract settlement. In theory this leaves the enquiry window open indefinitely. The taxpayer could apply to the Commissioners for the issue of a closure notice, but as the issue of such a notice will trigger the computer problem and cause a lot of work and anguish for both the taxpayer and HMRC this is probably not a sensible thing to do. HMRC tell their staff, 'Once a contract offer has been accepted, it has the same effect as the issue of a closure notice. The year(s) included in the contract become final and you will not be able to make any further enquiries into those years, unless you consider that the conditions for making a discovery assessment are satisfied' (Enquiry Manual, para 6001). Whilst the legal basis for this statement may be dubious, the taxpayer can probably safely rely on it.

Chapter 2

Special Civil Investigations

Gary Ashford, Director National Tax Investigations, Grant Thornton

THE ROLE OF SPECIAL CIVIL INVESTIGATIONS OFFICE (SCI)

2.1 SCI is the successor office to SCO. It was previously the case that all investigations of suspected serious fraud, in terms of direct taxes, were handled by Special Compliance Office (SCO). Cases of Suspected Serious Fraud were and still are handled under Code of Practice 9.

2.2 SCO also handled large and complex avoidance-type cases, regularly involving offshore structures where significant liabilities were at risk. SCO would also conduct large-scale projects looking at such groups as high-profile entertainers or sportsmen, sectors where significant amounts of PAYE and NIC or other taxes were at risk; for example in relation to city traders, the pharmaceutical industry etc. This sort of work was and is still undertaken under a separate Code of Practice, Code of Practice 8 (Cases other than Suspected Serious Fraud).

2.3 Historically in the old SCO, staff were split into clearly defined roles within SCO dealing with the work arising under one or other of the Codes of Practice. SCO also was the home of the then Board's Investigation Office and Prosecution Groups. SCO also previously had responsibility for departments such as the Foreign Entertainers Unit (FEU); however, FEU became part of Centre for Non-Residents (previously FICO) and is now part of Charities Assets and Residence (CAR).

2.4 On 1 April 2005, the prosecution functions of the former Inland Revenue and former Customs and Excise were placed within a new independent prosecuting authority, the Revenue and Customs Prosecution Office (RCPO). This led the way for the criminal prosecution teams being removed to a new HMRC department, the Criminal Investigation Directorate Special Civil Investigations (SCI) was created to deal with all other special civil investigation work. There are SCI offices strategically located throughout the UK; in London, Bristol, Manchester, Solihull, Edinburgh, Nottingham and Leeds. Recently, various subsidiary SCI offices have been created to handle the large increase in workload on tax avoidance scheme arrangements, but the offices above remain the key SCI offices.

2.5 On 1 September 2005 the Civil Investigation of Fraud (CIF) procedures were introduced and specially trained CIF teams were set up within strategically located local Tax Districts throughout the UK to deal with the majority of cases which were suitable to be worked under the these new procedures.

2.6 SCI remains responsible for the largest Code of Practice 9 investigations and investigations under Code of Practice 8. (See Section 8 below for the thresholds applicable to the SCI and CIF teams for COP9 cases.)

STRUCTURE OF SPECIAL CIVIL INVESTIGATIONS OFFICE

2.7 SCI is headed by a Director who is responsible directly to the Board of HMRC. Each individual SCI office is headed by an Assistant Director. Various team leaders and investigators work directly to the Assistant Director.

Types of SCI investigation

2.8 SCI Investigations can arise in a range of ways and circumstances.

Suspected Serious Fraud (Civil Investigation of Fraud (CIF) Procedures (Code of Practice 9)

2.9 CIF investigations can arise in the following circumstances:

- from an investigation being conducted in the local area office where the local investigator identifies significant additions to profit as a result of an identified fraud, or activities which suggest that serious fraud may have taken place,
- from an investigation opened directly by SCI or CIF team as a result of their own intelligence and research work,
- alternatively, where a taxpayer or their adviser identifies an issue or issues where additional liabilities are likely resulting from suspected fraudulent activity, subject to the limits (see SCI thresholds), they might wish to approach the relevant CIF/SCI team direct to seek the protection of CIF procedures for their client or clients.

Cases other than Suspected Serious Fraud (Code of Practice 8)

2.10 SCI also investigates non-fraud cases as follows:

- where significant tax is at risk, perhaps as a result of the use of offshore structures or trusts,
- where SCI conduct projects for example to identify high-profile individuals, entertainers and sportsmen whose tax affairs may be complex or not up to date, or who have failed to register for tax altogether (an example of this is the well publicised football and rugby project of the late 1980s and 1990s),
- where SCI have been tasked to support local offices or for example the Anti Avoidance Group (AAG) by raising investigations into marketed avoidance schemes.

CRIMINAL INVESTIGATIONS

2.11 When considering cases of suspected serious fraud, with a view to CIF procedures, it is important to understand HMRC's approach to criminal investigation, as to some extent the two approaches overlap. There can be an overlap between a criminal investigation and a criminal prosecution.

2.12 The overlap results from the fact that when HMRC consider whether a case is suitable for CIF procedures they will first look at the suspected offences committed and whether they are sufficiently heinous to warrant a criminal investigation.

2.13 HMRC's published criminal prosecution policy states the following:

> 'HMRC's aim is to secure the highest level of compliance with the law and regulations governing direct and indirect taxes and other regimes for which they are responsible. Criminal investigation, with a view to prosecution by the Revenue and Customs Prosecutions Office (RCPO) in England and Wales – or the appropriate prosecuting authority in Scotland and Northern Ireland – is an important part of HMRC's overall enforcement strategy.
>
> It is HMRC's policy to deal with fraud by use of the cost-effective Civil Investigation of Fraud (CIF) procedures, wherever appropriate. Criminal Investigation will be reserved for cases where HMRC needs to send a strong deterrent message or where the conduct involved is such that only a criminal sanction is appropriate.
>
> However, HMRC reserves complete discretion to conduct a criminal investigation in any case and to carry out these investigations across a range of offences and in all the areas for which the Commissioners of HMRC have responsibility.'

2.14 Examples of the kind of circumstances in which HMRC will generally consider commencing a criminal, rather than civil investigations are:

- in cases of organised criminal gangs attacking the tax system or systematic frauds where losses represent a serious threat to the tax base, including conspiracy;
- where an individual holds a position of trust or responsibility;
- where materially false statements are made or materially false documents are provided in the course of a civil investigation;
- where, pursuing an avoidance scheme, reliance is placed on a false or altered document or such reliance or material facts are misrepresented to enhance the credibility of a scheme;
- where deliberate concealment, deception, conspiracy or corruption is suspected;
- in cases involving the use of false or forged documents;
- in cases involving importation or exportation breaching prohibitions and restrictions;
- in cases involving money laundering with particular focus on advisors, accountants, solicitors and others acting in a 'professional' capacity who provide the means to put tainted money out of reach of law enforcement;
- where the perpetrator has committed previous offences or there is a repeated course of unlawful conduct or previous civil action;
- in cases involving theft, or the misuse or un lawful destruction of HMRC documents;
- where there is evidence of assault on, threats to, or the impersonation of HMRC officials;
- where there is a link to suspected wider criminality, whether domestic or international, involving offences not under the administration of HMRC.

2.15 When considering whether a case should be investigated under the Civil Investigation of Fraud procedures or is to be the subject of a criminal investigation, one important factor will be whether the taxpayer has made a complete and unprompted disclosure of the offences committed.

2.16 However, there are certain fiscal offences where HMRC will not usually adopt the Civil Investigation of Fraud approach. Examples of these are:

- VAT Missing Trader Intra-Community (MTIC) Fraud;
- VAT 'Bogus' registration repayment fraud;
- organised Tax Credit fraud.

DEFINITION OF FRAUD

2.17 As well as understanding the HMRC Board's policy to criminal prosecution when considering cases of suspected serious fraud some understanding of what constitutes fraud is also clearly helpful. There is an abundance of common law (both tax and non-tax related) on this subject.

2.18 The HMRC Enquiry Manual, reference EM5106, publishes the following extract from Halsbury's Laws of England, published by Messrs Butterworth & Co, under the heading 'Misrepresentation and Fraud'.

> '**Section 757 What Constitutes Fraud?** Not only is a misrepresentation fraudulent if it was known or believed by the representor to be false when made, but mere non-belief in the truth is also indicative of fraud. Thus, whenever a person makes a false statement which he does not actually and honestly believe to be true, for purposes of civil liability, that statement is as fraudulent as if he had stated that which he did not know to be true, or knew or believed to be false*. Proof of absence of actual and honest belief is all that is necessary to satisfy the requirements of the law, whether the representation has been made recklessly or deliberately; indifference or recklessness on the part of the representor as to the truth or falsity of the representation affords merely an instance of absence of such a belief.
> A representor will not, however, be fraudulent if he believed the statement to be true in the sense in which he understood it, provided that was a meaning which might reasonably be attached to it, even though the court later holds that the statement objectively bears another meaning, which the representor did not believe.
> [* see *Derry v Peek* 14 App Cas 337, p374, per Lord Herschell: fraud is proved when it is shown that a false representation has been made (1) knowingly, or (2) without belief in its truth, or (3) recklessly, careless whether it be true or false; the third case being but an instance of the second.]
>
> **Section 759 Irrelevancy of Representor's Motive** It follows from the meaning of fraudulent misrepresentation that, given absence of actual and honest belief by the representor in the truth of the misrepresentation, his motive in making the misrepresentation is wholly irrelevant. It may be that he intended to injure the representee without benefiting himself, or to benefit himself without injuring the representee; it may be that he did not intend to do either, but solely to benefit a third person, or even the representee himself, or otherwise to do right. Lastly, he may have acted with no intelligible or rational notice whatsoever and told a lie from mere caprice, mischievousness or stupidity. In all these cases, provided that there was an absence of

actual and honest belief in the truth of his assertion, the misrepresentation is accounted fraudulent and no proof of any wicked or other intention (other than an intention to induce) on the part of the representor is required by the law; or if it is necessary to establish an intention to deceive or injure, that intention is immediately and irrebuttably presumed in law from the mere act of making the misrepresentation without such belief.

Section 760 Representation Subsequently Discovered by Representor to be False Where a representation is a continuing one and where, between the time when it was made and the time when the representee altered his position on the faith of it, either (1) the representor discovers that his original statement which, when he made it, he honestly believed to be true, was false, or (2) supervening events render, to the knowledge of the representor, his statement no longer true, a duty to disclose the changed situation to the representee may arise. In such cases the mere fact that the statement may have been innocently made, though false, or true when made, will not, it seems, prevent the representee from establishing fraud where he can show that the representor dishonestly failed to discharge the duty of disclosing the change in the situation.'

2.19 The above demonstrates that, particularly in terms of civil liability, the term fraud is widely drawn. For example it extends to the deliberate submission of understated accounts and incorrect tax returns.

2.20 Further guidance can also be drawn from the Fraud Act 2006.

THE FRAUD ACT 2006

2.21 In terms of the criminal law, the Fraud Act 2006 defines fraud in three categories:

(i) fraud by false representation;

(ii) fraud by failing to disclose information;

(iii) fraud by abuse of position.

2.22 The Act states that in all three categories the person committing the offence must have an intention to make a gain or loss, temporary or permanent, and defines loss or gain as extending only to money or other property (real or personal) but including things in action or other intangible property.

2.23 In terms of gain, this includes keeping what one has as well as what one does not have; and in terms of loss, this includes getting what one might get as well as parting with what one has.

CODE OF PRACTICE 9

2.24 In terms of direct taxes, Code of Practice 9 and its forerunner, the so-called 'Hansard procedure' has been around for a long time (its name derived from parliamentary statements made by the Chancellor of the Exchequer in relation to tax fraud) and dates from 1923.

2.25 Early versions of the Hansard procedures stated that where a person made a full disclosure of all tax irregularities as part of the formal Hansard process, the Board of the ex-Inland Revenue would take this into account when considering whether to accept a money settlement or institute criminal proceedings.

2.26 Whilst this provided no guarantee that criminal proceedings would not result from what amounted to full disclosure of tax fraud, in practice, the Inland Revenue approach was not to prosecute in such cases despite the legal facility to do so. (The approach of the ex-Customs and Excise was more clean cut, ie more like the current CIF procedures, in that once a case had been categorised as civil only in very defined circumstances could a criminal investigation occur.)

2.27 This position came to a head in the case of the case of *Regina v W & Another* [1998] STC 550. In this case the Crown did institute criminal proceedings, despite the custom and practice of HMRC for many years of non-prosecution where full disclosure was made, and the case of *R v Allen* STC 1537 HL in 2001, where the courts referred to the inducement of the wording of the COP 9 leaflet effectively preventing prosecution where a full disclosure was made. (The matter of the inducement was incidental to the outcome of that case as the taxpayer was found to have not made a full disclosure under the terms offered.)

2.28 In order to clarify the position, a new statement was made by the Chancellor of Exchequer in November 2002 which resulted in the issue of a revised version of COP 9. This statement explicitly guaranteed for the first time for direct tax purposes that no prosecution would result where a full disclosure was made.

2.29 Further changes took place following the case of *R v Gill & Gill* STC 1229 in 2003. In this case, the courts criticised the ex-Inland Revenue for not having formally cautioned the defendants before offering them an inducement to make a disclosure. (However, the courts did not free the defendants from their prison sentence, notwithstanding the criticism of the ex-Revenue procedures, as they found that the defendants had deceived despite the absence of the caution.)

2.30 As a result of this case, all the new Hansard investigations under the COP 9 procedures were suspended in the autumn of 2003, and new Hansard procedures were formulated to take account of the issues raised in the *Gill &*

Gill case. It is worth recognising that in terms of investigating the extent of any irregularities and preparing disclosure reports, there was little difference in all of these variations of the Hansard and COP 9 procedures. The differences largely affected the procedures adopted in the formal opening of a case by SCI, and, although the potential impact was significant, in practical terms the position only changed for those who did not make a full and complete disclosure when offered the protection of COP 9.

2.31 A new procedure was introduced by the ex-Inland Revenue to include a formal caution under The Police and Criminal Evidence Act 1984 (PACE) as well as the reading of the revised 2002 version of COP 9 which offered the inducement of non-prosecution in exchange for a full disclosure. The procedures for opening of Hansard cases under COP 9 was then amended to include a formal taped interview, at which the taxpayer would be formally advised of their rights under PACE. As a result of this, it became common for taxpayers and their advisers to attend the opening meetings with a criminal lawyer who could advise as to whether any self-incriminatory discussions could take place following the reading of the caution under PACE and the COP 9 questions. Consequently some opening meetings were very short, and were limited merely to the five formal questions (see para **2.56** The Five Direct Tax Questions) with no other discussion of the issues in the case.

2.32 Following the merger of the Inland Revenue and HM Customs and Excise in April 2005, it was inevitable that further changes would be needed to the Code of Practice 9 procedures, given the different approaches to civil investigation of fraud by the two departments. The Customs and Excise approach (730 procedures) made very clear that once the decision had been made to go down either the civil or criminal route there was no ambiguity about the protection, or otherwise, available to the taxpayer when making a disclosure of irregularities. There was also the cumbersome procedures of applying both COP 9 and the 730 procedures to the same case where both direct and indirect taxes arose from the same irregularity.

CIVIL INVESTIGATION OF FRAUD PROCEDURE

2.33 On 1 September 2005 a new Code of Practice 9 was published introducing the new Civil Investigation of Fraud (CIF) procedures to cover all taxes. The CIF procedures replaced all previous former Inland Revenue or former Customs and Excise procedures for the handling of serious fraud on a civil basis.

2.34 The most significant feature in the new CIF procedures from 1 September 2005 is an up-front guarantee, and HMRC will not conduct a criminal investigation in relation to the initial tax offence. The need for taped interviews under PACE has been disputed as there is no jeopardy of prosecution provided full disclosure is made. It is important to recognise that a criminal investigation might still be commenced if the taxpayer tries to deceive HMRC or provides false documents as part of the COP9 investigation.

2.35 At para **2.14** above reference is made to the various events that might result in a CIF investigation. Regardless of the origins of the investigation, the client will receive formal notification in writing from HMRC that their affairs are to be investigated in line with the CIF procedures under Code of Practice 9. A copy of the Code of Practice 9 booklet will be enclosed with that letter. The leaflet suggests that the taxpayer should consider seeking specialist advice. This is the recommended advice of the writer of this chapter.

2.36 The client who is the subject of the investigation under the CIF procedures will be invited to attend a meeting with a specialist investigator from a CIF team or from SCI. This is a formal meeting. The purpose of the meeting is for the HMRC investigator to set out in very prescribed terms the Board's approach to suspected serious fraud. Investigators are advised not to deviate from the Board's published statement.

2.37 The latest statement in relation to HMRC's approach to the civil investigation of fraud states the following:

> 'The Commissioners reserve complete discretion to pursue a criminal investigation with a view to prosecution where they consider it necessary and appropriate
>
> Where a criminal investigation is not considered necessary or appropriate, the Commissioners may decide to investigate using the CIF procedure
>
> Where the Commissioners decide to investigate using the CIF procedure they will not seek a prosecution for the tax fraud which is the subject of that investigation
>
> The taxpayer will be given an opportunity to make a full and complete disclosure of all irregularities in their tax affairs
>
> However, where materially false statements are made or materially false documents are provided with intent to deceive in the course of a civil investigation, the Commissioners may conduct a criminal investigation with a view to a prosecution of that conduct
>
> If the Commissioners decide to investigate using the CIF procedure the taxpayer will be given a copy of this statement by an authorised officer'

2.38 Having set out the formal policy, the investigator will hand out a printed copy of that policy to the client who is the subject of the CIF procedures.

2.39 The meeting then moves on to the point where the investigator asks a series of questions in relation to the taxpayer's affairs which are designed to result in either 'yes' or 'no' replies.

2.40 For investigations commenced before 1 September 2005 there were essentially five questions, which extended to all direct taxes and were without time limit (although HMRC was effectively time barred from action beyond HMRC's 20-year assessing time limit, clients could still be invited to pay out of date liabilities through voluntary restitution).

2.41 From 1 September 2005, the CIF procedures now include indirect taxes and there are also a series of four additional questions covering indirect taxes. (See para **2.55** for the nine questions.)

2.42 Depending on whether the CIF investigation resulted from a voluntary disclosure or from HMRC's own investigation work, the meeting will then move to discussions of the irregularities, and the CIF or SCI investigator will seek to understand more of the background to the disclosure. If the investigation has been opened by HMRC as a result of their own work they will ask the taxpayer whether they have anything to disclose or perhaps ask various questions around the issues already identified by the investigator or ask the taxpayer to respond to specific allegations.

2.43 Prior to any meeting where COP 9 is to be offered under the CIF procedures, it is clearly good practice to assist the taxpayer in preparing for the meeting. Such meetings can be very stressful for clients, and without any preparation they might inadvertently answer some or all of the questions incorrectly or provide misleading information to the investigator.

2.44 It is also good practice for the adviser to try and understand more about the client's affairs and identify any potential tax liabilities which might have arisen and which may have been overlooked by the taxpayer in compiling the disclosure. This should include a full review of areas where a liability might have resulted, including from technical points, as well as any liabilities that have arisen from any potential fraudulent activities.

2.45 The purpose of this is to assist the taxpayer in making an early disclosure of any such items, thus securing the maximum mitigation for penalties; but more importantly to demonstrate full cooperation and minimise any risk of losing the guarantee of no criminal proceedings and the withdrawal of Code of Practice 9, if the HMRC investigator believes the taxpayer is misleading them as part of the investigation.

2.46 A denial of any wrongdoing at the CIF meeting will result in the investigator conducting their own investigation, usually still within the protection of Code of Practice 9. If HMRC subsequently demonstrates that there are additional liabilities which were not disclosed, there is a risk of the withdrawal of COP 9. Mitigation for tax-geared penalties will be greatly reduced even if the case remains on a civil basis with COP 9.

2.47 The HMRC investigator will use the meeting to seek to understand the following information about the taxpayer's business. They will want to understand:

- detailed explanations around any disclosure being made;
- the taxpayers response to any specific allegations being put before them;
- the nature and structure of the taxpayer's business (if appropriate);
- the business records maintained and controls applied;
- accounting areas or practices where income/purchases may have been understated/overstated etc;
- any other areas where there might be a risk of a tax liability.

2.48 They will also use the meeting to understand fully the personal tax affairs of the taxpayer, including:

- personal history and background, including family relationships etc;
- details of sources of personal income and expenditure;
- details of personal assets and liabilities;
- any links to perceived tax-sheltering vehicles such as offshore trusts.

2.49 After the fact finding part of the meeting, the investigator will ask whether the taxpayer formally wishes to instruct their adviser to prepare a disclosure report. If the taxpayer confirms that he or she does wish for this to happen, the investigator will make it very clear that HMRC will expect the disclosure report within six months of the date of the opening Hansard meeting.

2.50 Following the formal meeting there will generally be separate meeting with the adviser who has been commissioned to prepare the disclosure report in order for both parties to agree on what should be covered and what work should be undertaken. This is an opportunity for the adviser to set out to SCI or the CIF team any practical difficulties that they may anticipate. This might include discussions on whether the six months expectation for the report should be extended because of special circumstances ie the case involves exceptional circumstances or is particularly large or complex.

2.51 Throughout the period of preparing the disclosure report there will be update meetings or telephone calls with the SCI or CIF team investigator and again this is also an opportunity to set out any difficulties that the adviser is experiencing.

2.52 HMRC will generally expect the final disclosure report to include the following completed certificates:

- a certificate of bank and credit card accounts operated;
- statement of personal assets and liabilities;
- certificate of full disclosure.

2.53 The disclosure report will also be required to be adopted by the taxpayer as their own full and complete disclosure.

2.54 Where HMRC decides to investigate using the Civil Investigation of Fraud procedures, SCI offices have remained responsible for the largest CIF cases and the remaining cases are dealt with by the CIF teams.

The nine questions of COP9

2.55 There are five direct tax and four indirect tax questions:

The five direct tax questions

2.56

> ‘1) Have any transactions been omitted from or incorrectly recorded in the books of any business with which you are or have been concerned whether as a director, partner or sole proprietor to the best of your knowledge or belief?
>
> 2) Are the accounts sent to the HMRC for each and every business with which you are or have been concerned whether as a director, partner or sole proprietor, correct and complete to the best of your knowledge and belief?
>
> 3) Are all the tax returns of each and every business with which you are or have been concerned whether as a director, partner or sole proprietor correct and complete to the best of your knowledge and belief?
>
> 4) Are all your personal tax returns correct and complete to the best of your knowledge and belief?

5) Will you allow an examination of all business books, and private statements and any other business and private records in order that HMRC may be satisfied that your answers to the first four questions are correct?'

The four indirect tax questions

2.57

'1) Have any transactions been omitted from, or incorrectly recorded, in the books and records of (name of legal entity) for which you are (responsible status)?

2) Are the books and records you are required to keep by HMRC for (name of legal entity) for which you are (responsible status), correct and complete to the best of your knowledge and belief?

3) Are all the VAT returns of the (name of legal entity) for which you are (responsible status) correct and complete to the best of your knowledge and belief?

4) Were you aware that any of the VAT returns were incorrect or incomplete at the time they were submitted?'

In cases where the main offence is Failure to Notify Chargeability, HMRC may also include an extra direct tax question.

CIVIL INVESTIGATION OF FRAUD THRESHOLDS

2.58 HMRC apply their own internal financial limits to cases of suspected serious fraud. Historically the main threshold for Hansard (Code of Practice 9) investigations was whether the tax liability previously exceeded £100,000. With the setting up of the CIF teams, two thresholds effectively apply:

– £75,000 to £500,000, including interest and penalties, being dealt with by the CIF teams;

– and over £500,000 being dealt with by SCI.

CODE OF PRACTICE 8 – CASES OTHER THAN SUSPECTED SERIOUS FRAUD

2.59 As well as cases of suspected serious fraud, SCI also carry out other types of investigation.

2.60 Code of Practice 8 has historically been the Code used by SCI to investigate complex tax planning structures, and high profile taxpayers with complex tax affairs, particularly involving offshore aspects, where HMRC believes there is a significant risk of substantial unpaid liabilities.

2.61 It is important to recognise that Code of Practice 8 does not bring with it any of the protections or guarantees of Code of Practice 9 (ie the guarantee of no prosecution where full compliance with the terms of the guidance on disclosure and cooperation are met). It must therefore be borne in mind that if SCI identify fraud during any Code of Practice 8 investigation, it cannot be assumed that a civil settlement will result, and the enquiry could instead be handed over to the Criminal Investigation Directorate to commence a criminal investigation.

2.62 With HMRC's recent drive against marketed avoidance schemes, Code of Practice 8 has been used to conduct investigations in this field.

2.63 Code of Practice 8 investigators have historically demonstrated a strong leaning towards technical challenges on complex issues. However in recent times it is the case that SCI investigators maintain a portfolio of both Code of Practice 9 and 8 work.

2.64 Code of Practice 8 investigations should be treated seriously and with care and the advice again would be that this should be handled by a specialist.

HANDLING SCI/CIF INVESTIGATIONS

2.65 SCI and CIF investigations involve highly specialised work and should only be handled in consultation with or by tax advisers with the appropriate specialist skills. Most professional indemnity insurers will state that they will not cover this work unless it is handled by specialists.

2.66 It is very important to recognise that all Inspectors operating within SCI or the CIF teams have been selected for their specific flair and interest in investigation work. These Investigators are also recognised as possessing excellent negotiating skills.

2.67 New staff joining SCI shadow colleagues and will work closely with experienced Investigators and team leaders to ensure that they meet the standards required. One should therefore never view Inspectors who have recently joined SCI, or of youthful appearance as an easy touch or less experienced. There is a huge support network there to protect them.

2.68 SCI Investigators will not be easily deflected where they believe there is a need for an explanation. They are the recognised experts on the use of formal information powers in terms of information notices within the UK and overseas.

2.69 It is also important to recognise that any case which is taken on by SCI will have been reviewed and identified as one where there is a clear risk of a significant loss of tax either as a result of fraud or otherwise.

2.70 SCI do not take on cases lightly. Prior to April 2006 cases transferred to SCI (and its predecessor named departments) resulted in an automatic credit in the yield records of the local tax office from where the case arose. From April 2006, the local area office will be given credit appropriate to the value of liabilities identified at the time of the transfer to SCI or to the CIF teams. SCI or CIF will only be able to claim the credit for the value they have added. It would therefore seem logical that they only take over cases where they are confident of additions substantially in excess of those already identified by the local area office.

2.71 Any case therefore registered by one of these specialist offices must be viewed as one which has passed all these tests and where the Investigator believes that there are substantial further liabilities. It is good practice to ensure clients are aware of this and emphasise that SCI and the CIF teams do not take on cases lightly. They believe there is a case to answer and will have strong evidence to support that view. Therefore as soon as an enquiry notice under either COP 8 or COP 9 is received, it is always worthwhile spending time with the client to explore if there is any reason they can think of why they are the subject of an SCI or CIF investigation.

2.72 That said, SCI or the CIF teams, like any other government agency, can occasionally get things wrong and so it is always worthwhile exploring with them their reasons for taking a case on. They may, of course, be reluctant to advise you of this, but a mature conversation can always help both parties explore the reasons for why the case has been selected.

2.73 Good practice is to treat SCI and CIF team staff professionally and courteously at all times whilst remaining firm and positive in your representation of your client. As experienced investigators they will not be put off track by an overly aggressive approach; SCI inspectors are well–trained, well-supported and more than capable of holding their own in difficult and uncomfortable situations. Conversely, because of their clear professionalism and experience, SCI personnel will generally respond very well where they are treated with respect, and will be more likely to share with you the reasons for the enquiry and the extent of the information which they already hold.

2.74 That said, there will be cases where it is necessary to stand your ground in representing your client and SCI recognise this. But the skills lie in selecting the battles and most certainly not winning pyrrhic victories and ultimately losing the SCI war. No client will thank you for starting (and generally) losing the long-term relationship with SCI.

Specialists within SCI

2.75 SCI is staffed not only by direct and indirect tax investigators. In each office, there is also a team of qualified accountants whose role it is to assist the Investigators in understanding accountancy issues.

2.76 SCI is also the home of a number of the liaison points for HMRC with other UK Government agencies or overseas fiscal authorities. For example, SCI London is the HMRC home for all UK exchange of information requests with other foreign fiscal authorities with whom the UK has reciprocal arrangements via such things as the OECD tax convention, double taxation treaties etc.

2.77 SCI is also home to HMRC's liaison with the Serious Organised Crime Agency (SOCA), specifically in terms of Money Laundering.

2.78 Where SOCA receives a Suspicious Activity Report (SAR) and tax offences are the predominant offence, the relevant SAR will be passed to SCI for consideration of a tax investigation. Where SCI decide they will not mount their own investigation, the SAR may then be handed over to the local office.

2.79 Whilst the criminal work of HMRC is no longer housed within SCI, again SCI is the liaison point for the Criminal Investigation Directorate.

Chapter 3

VAT and Revenue & Customs visits

Dennis Knowles, Partner, Deloitte & Touche

OVERALL CONCEPT

3.1 In April 2005 HM Customs and Excise ('HMCE') merged with the Inland Revenue ('IR') to create a new department 'HM Revenue and Customs' ('HMRC'). Historically, HMCE had developed a personal and tangible contact with their 'clients'. The Commissioners' experience with, *inter alia*, importers, exporters, breweries, distilleries and the control of purchase tax necessarily led the department to propose a system for controlling the administration of VAT based on hands-on inspections. Although steps will undoubtedly be taken to harmonise the practices of both departments, it is unlikely that the way VAT is currently controlled will change substantially. This is because, unlike corporation tax and other forms of direct taxation, VAT is an immediate tax. Every transaction made by a business impacts on the VAT affairs of that business, whether it be the liability of the supply made by the business or the amount of recoverable VAT that can be claimed by that particular business. The tax is, therefore, controlled at grass roots level and will involve, to some degree, Officers reviewing individual invoices on a sample basis.

3.2 Every business registering for VAT immediately enters the realm of the computer and the VAT Central Unit (VCU). This starts with VAT registration. Every business registered for VAT is allocated a VAT number. This is often initially notified to the business in a letter followed shortly after by a form VAT4 'Certificate of VAT Registration'. The VAT numbers are always in the same format 123 4567 89 and are based on what is referred to as a modulus 97 formulae. That is to say that, at a basic level, the validity of any VAT number can be checked. The calculation being:

VAT No:	5	2	4	9	3	4	0	4	7		
	x	x	x	x	x	x	x	x	x		
	8	7	6	5	4	3	2			=	40+14+24+45+12+12+0+ 47 divided by 97 = to a whole number (1,2,3 etc)

3.3 Since the merger a new organisational structure has been put in place to provide a unified approach to all taxpayers. The new structure is based upon four Business Streams: Operations, Product and Process Groups, Customer Units and Corporate Functions. Thirty-six Business Units sit within these Business Streams, each headed individually by a Director. These new Business Units will deal with all taxes for example, the Large Business Service will not only service VAT large businesses, but former IR large businesses.

3.4

1 Operations will be responsible for the delivery of services, including delivering 'customer' contact, processing and operational compliance, as well as enforcement capabilities and debt management and banking.

2 Product and Process Groups will focus on taxes, duties, credits and benefits and the process by which they are delivered.

3 Customer Units will focus on identifying and understanding the requirements and behaviour of 'customers' and associated risks.

4 Corporate Functions will include functions such as Human Resources and Finance.

3.5 The merger created the 'Commissioners for Revenue and Customs' who have in turn put in place a new high-level governance structure which comprises an Executive Committee, the supreme decision-making body in HMRC and the Board, whose role is to oversee the Commissioners in the discharge of their statutory duties.

1 The Executive Committee is split into three sub-committees which provide a strategic overview of security and business continuity, detailed oversight of the business and approval of top-level appointments.

2 The Board, which is split into two sub-committees, provides independent assurance on risk and control as well as advice on succession planning and talent management.

3.6 When VAT was introduced in 1973, the first visit to a business was a registration or educational visit. This enabled HMCE to ensure that a new business was aware of its obligations, that the accounts maintained by the business were adequate for VAT purposes and the liabilities of the supplies made by the business were correct. Previously, a newly registered business could expect to receive its first visit from the Local VAT Office (LVO) within about 18 months of being registered. These 'assurance visits', formed the basis of HMCE's control of the tax.

3.7 Now, the majority of assurance visits are assigned by a computer-based model on a series of factors that assess the risk of negligent or fraudulent returns. Occasional sector-based campaigns can also prompt a flurry of visits either nationwide or locally. For those businesses who remain under the compliance 'radar', more efficient ways of contact such as telephone advice to both correct and improve compliance are being trialled. As a result of this revised risk assurance methodology, some 'low-risk' types of businesses may not receive an assurance visit for ten years.

3.8 Most initial contact with HMRC is now routed through the National Advice Service ('NAS') (0845 010 9000). This centralised service takes all telephone enquiries and replaces the localised services which were provided by Business Advice Centres. The NAS also provides a centralised written enquiries service which can provide advice and rulings via email or letter.

ASSURANCE VISITS

3.9 It is likely that, in time, HMRC may choose to carry out joint visits consisting of Officers checking more than one tax. Initially this may take the form of two or more Officers conducting a joint visit although eventually visits may be undertaken by one Officer trained in all taxes. Different ways of working will no doubt be piloted to find the most cost-effective system. In normal circumstances however, HMRC should make it clear before the visit which taxes they will be inspecting.

3.10 VAT visit selection is now generally dictated by risk assessment teams. These teams have computer systems that draw data from a variety of sources such as a computer network terminal known as VISION (VAT Interrogation System Inter Office Network). This system allows the risk team to interrogate the trader database. Information contained on file includes core data such as name, address of the business, trade classification, date of last visit and VAT return data. The system will allocate points on the basis of the amounts of VAT declared on a return and on the time elapsed since the last visit. After each VAT assurance visit, Officers write a report allocating points based upon their findings and this is also fed into the visit selection process. The total level of points allocated to a business will dictate when the business is selected for subsequent visits.

3.11 When selected for an assurance visit, the Officer will have the following information available:

1 original VAT 1 application form;

2 copies of any correspondence between the business and HMRC including that with former HMCE;

3 printouts containing, typically, up to the last 18 months of VAT return details and credibility analysis automatically performed by the VCU computer system (D1600 series);

4 any earlier visit reports and internal departmental notes/memos; and

5 details of any written enquiries or telephone calls to the National Advice Service.

3.12 Additionally, if the business acquires goods from the EU, the Officer will be able to obtain information relating to the aggregate value of acquisitions by that business for each quarterly period. Each VAT authority in every member state submits the data from the individual European Sales Listings (ESLs) into the VAT Information Exchange System (VIES). The data contained on ESLs enables VIES to identify, by VAT number, the value of sales from each supplier/member state. The Officer can use this information to gain a knowledge of where a business purchases its goods, raw materials, etc and the level of such purchases prior to his visit. Clearly, if the value ascribed to a particular UK business by VIES is greater than the acquisition value shown on the VAT returns, some difficult questions can be expected. (With effect from 1 January 2010, suppliers of services which are subject to VAT where received will, when supplied to a business customer established in another member state, also be required to submit ESLs).

3.13 The Officer will also be able to access information about the business from the Internet. The Internet facility is now available to most VAT Officers, allowing them to 'surf' the net using various search engines to look for business information and websites.

3.14 Typically, the visit will be arranged by a centralised visit booking team, who usually telephone to make an appointment. This may then be followed up with a letter confirming the arrangements. When the VAT Officer arrives for the visit he will have an identity card bearing his photograph. This should always be inspected before allowing the Officer into the working area since bogus VAT visits have been known and are an effective way of finding out a lot about a business.

3.15 An assurance visit typically splits into three parts. First, general questions about the business and the way it operates, secondly a detailed review of at least one VAT period, and lastly an overview of the business.

General questions

3.16 For the first visit, the Officer will be required to complete a form VAT465A (Summary Trading Activities and Records). This contains the basic information concerning that particular business and forms a permanent record on the trader's VAT file. On subsequent visits to the business the form VAT465A will be reviewed and amended as necessary to reflect changes in the business. Since the introduction of a paperless electronic folder system this form will be held on the business's 'electronic folder', as will all other information regarding the business. However, the points covered on the form include:

1 name, status and contact details for the person responsible for VAT at the traders;
2 name, address and contact details for the auditors;
3 financial year end;
4 address of the principal place of business and registered office if different;
5 confirmation that the details on the VAT4 are still correct;
6 main and, if applicable, subsidiary business activities;
7 whether the business has contact with other parts of HMRC, eg whether the business has a bonded warehouse or operates under any HMRC duty regime;
8 whether the business imports or exports;
9 whether the business imports services;
10 principal sales (outputs) and purchases (inputs);
11 which retail schemes are operated (if applicable);
12 a list of the main, subsidiary and other non-accounting records maintained by the business;
13 structure of the business;
14 details of bank and building society accounts;
15 tax point information (eg optional/standard for retailers and whether the business uses the 14-day rule for invoices);
16 rulings given to the business; and
17 risk areas and special and unusual features.

3.17 The above information is generally obtained whilst conducting a general discussion about the business. The information obtained allows the Officer to establish an understanding of the business and how it is organised. It is often followed by a request to see the premises. This general walk around adds to the Officer's general understanding and allows him to see whether there is anything going on which was not disclosed in the general discussion. The Officer will also be noting specific items of stock or machinery so that he can check these out later when inspecting the accounting system.

Review of VAT returns submitted

3.18 The Officer will, as explained earlier, invariably check at least one VAT return in detail. This involves checking from source documents, eg purchase and sales invoices, through the various accounting records to the VAT account and the completed VAT return.

3.19 The Officer will also make other checks in order to verify the credibility of the VAT returns. For example, he will check that the sales figures indicated on VAT returns for a 12-month period correspond with the figures disclosed in the annual accounts for the same period. Similarly, Officers will check the annual accounts for any disposal of assets to ensure that output tax has been charged and declared or that the level of expenses declared in the accounts agrees with the input figures declared on the VAT returns. The credibility check used will often vary according to the specific activities of the business and the records available to the Officer. Other credibility checks commonly used include cash reconciliations (more commonly used in smaller cash businesses such as restaurants and pubs), bank reconciliations and mark-up exercises.

3.20 Officers increasingly cross-refer invoices inspected at one business with the information disclosed at another business. For example, sales of confectionery items sold by a wholesaler will be checked against purchases declared by the wholesaler's customers. Although, this might seem on the surface to suggest that eligible input VAT has not been claimed by a business, it is often a good indication, particularly in a cash business, that the business is not recovering input VAT in order to suppress sales. To continue to claim all input VAT whilst suppressing sales will eventually show that the business is being run on uneconomical margins. This will either mean that the business is in financial trouble or raise suspicions with HMRC that the business is failing to account for all of its sales.

3.21 The Officer is required to prepare a report (form VAT465 S (simplified) or B (normal)) of his visit noting specifically:

1 checks made and annual accounts examined (not on VAT465 S);

2 irregularities found, including particulars of misdeclarations and assessments made;

3 rulings given during the visit and general comment;

4 conclusions and comments on credibility; and

5 matters for consideration on the next visit.

3.22 Depending on the size and complexity of the business and its accounting system, more than one Officer may attend. It is unusual, however, for three or more Officers to attend on the same day. This is regarded by HMRC as over-burdensome on the business.

3.23 If the business uses a sophisticated computerised accounting system, it is possible that the visit will be made by a Computer Accounts Officer (CAO). This is an Officer who has received additional training on procedures and methods of interrogating computerised accounting systems. The CAO may, for example, ask for special prints to be produced or interrogation software to be run against the business accounts, or for tapes/disks of data to be stripped off for interrogation off site. If interrogation software is loaded on the business's computers it is imperative that HMRC are denied running the checks against the on-line data since this could corrupt current data. It is always advisable to run interrogation checks off-line. If HMRC ask for data to be copied and downloaded for removal, it is important to take a copy of the data for checking by the business. It must be appreciated that when HMRC remove data they can then 'play with' that information to their hearts' content!

3.24 Again, depending on the sophistication of the system, the CAO may flowchart the procedures and processes conducted by the computer. These flowcharts will highlight, from a VAT perspective, the key controls and weaknesses in the system. Subsequent assurance visits will check to see, in particular, whether the key controls are still in place. The removal of a key control could mean that the VAT accounting of that system has been flawed and weakened in some manner.

3.25 Whether a business is visited by an Officer, a Senior Officer, a CAO or a team of Officers is generally dictated by its size and complexity. In addition to providing information about the checks conducted on a business, the VAT465 S or B also requires the Officer to provide information about the complexity of the business. This is done by requiring the Officer to allocate points for certain aspects of the business following his review, including:

1 Accounts – how complex is the accounting system, ie does the business have a simple cash book or does it use a multi-locational computerised system?

2 Organisation – is the business a single shop or a multi-national company?

3 Tax features – does the business sell goods or services attracting VAT at a single rate of VAT or does it supply goods and services at all rates including imports, exports, etc?

4 Compliance – were any assessments issued and, if so, at what value?

3.26 The points allocated by an Officer can be influenced by the way the Officer was treated during his visit and any suspicions he felt. The combination of the various points allocated by the Officer are fed into the Electronic Folder system. These points are then used by the centralised risk team to determine when the next assurance visit should be conducted. The more points, the more frequent the visits are likely to be.

3.27 Businesses that are registered for VAT purposes as a VAT group, will generally be controlled by the same team. However, where individual companies within the group registration are remote from the main site and are self-accounting these may, if their size and complexity merits it, be controlled by a different team from their local VAT office. Likewise, a company may have self-accounting branches which could be controlled on a remote basis. Companies registered on a divisional basis will invariably be controlled by different teams from their regional office as opposed to being centrally controlled.

3.28 Large and complex businesses are removed from the normal routine. This type of business is known as a 999 trader and will be either a category 1 or 2 999 trader, depending on the size of the business, the level of tax declared and the complexity of the particular VAT liabilities involved. Unlike businesses within the regular routine, large traders are allocated to a particular Officer or 'Client Relationship Manager'. The rationale for this approach is that the bulk of VAT is collected from relatively few very large businesses. VAT receipts from businesses handled by the Large Business Service represent just over 33% of total VAT receipts (excluding import VAT). HMRC therefore, have determined that they need to control these large traders with a systematic approach on a regular basis to ensure that the revenue take is maintained. Simple errors at large businesses can generate significant under-declarations of VAT. These businesses are often complex in organisation and use several computer systems to produce data for the VAT return.

3.29 The Large Business Service ('LBS') located within the newly organised Operations Business Stream has replaced the former Large Trader Business Group. New 'Client Relationship Managers' will co-ordinate dealings with large traders with a 'Sector Leader' responsible for compliance in that 'sector'.

3.30 The scheme of control for these businesses may necessitate VAT Officers being permanently at the business and possibly at more than one location. For businesses subject to LBS control it will usually mean that all UK subsidiaries and branches of the business are controlled by the same team. This allows the LBS team to learn a tremendous amount about the business and how it operates. By allocating Sector Leaders a common approach can be adopted by HMRC, but it also allows HMRC to learn a lot about the industry generally and to exploit common problems.

CREDIBILITY VISITS

3.31 You may not just see the VAT Officer on assurance visits. The VCU computer system conducts routine checks on each VAT return submitted. The credibility routine, for example, not only checks that the figure shown in box 1 (VAT due in this period on sales and other outputs) is not significantly greater than 17.5% of the box 6 figure (total value of sales and other outputs excluding any VAT), but it also conducts a series of comparison exercises.

3.32 When a business completes a VAT1 (Application for registration), it is required to describe its main business activity. This allows HMRC to assign a trade classification to the business. For example, all petrol filling stations will be allocated to the same classification. Thus, when each filling station puts in its VAT return, the VCU can compare any single VAT return for a petrol filling station with all other filling stations submitting VAT returns for that period. Trends can, therefore, be detected. If all petrol filling stations are showing an upturn in trade in any particular period and one filling station in Birmingham is claiming a repayment then, depending on the tax considered to be at risk, the VCU may send that VAT return to the nearest VAT office for verification prior to the repayment being made.

3.33 Often this type of verification will simply be a phone call to the business asking why an unusual VAT return was submitted. It may, for example, simply be that the business is stocking up or has incurred significant refurbishment costs for a building, etc. However, if the amount is large, the Officer may decide to visit. The Officer should agree the visit in advance, but it is usual to arrange the visit soon after the initial telephone call, particularly when it is a repayment return. This will usually simply be to verify the single queried VAT return and the checks will just be to satisfy the Officer that the return is credible in the circumstances. It is worth noting that whilst the return is being queried, the clock for a repayment supplement is stopped. Thus, it is in the interests of the business to ensure that such credibility queries are dealt with and agreed with HMRC as soon as possible.

INTRASTAT VISITS

3.34 Businesses involved in the sale and movement of goods to other member states are required to prepare and submit European Sales Listings ('ESL') supplementary statistical declaration (supplementary declaration). The ESL is used by all EU VAT administrations as a control document to monitor and check on the movement of goods across EU borders. The information contained on the supplementary declaration is used by HMRC to build up the statistical data on what goods have been 'dispatched' from the UK and the 'arrivals' of goods in the UK from other member states. The Intrastat information, as it is called, is compiled from two sources. First, boxes 8 and 9 of the VAT return and secondly the supplementary declaration.

3.35 Supplementary declarations must be submitted each calendar month when the level of dispatches (form C1501) and arrivals (form C1500) exceed a prescribed minimum threshold, currently this annual threshold is £260,000. These forms can now be submitted and amended on-line, via the HMRC website. Depending on the level of activity businesses may only be required to submit returns for dispatches or arrivals or both. The information required to be gathered and declared on the supplementary declaration by each member state can be different. However, the core information is always required.

3.36 Besides the header information (VAT registration number, number of items, period covered, etc) the statistical information required on a supplementary declaration in the UK is:

1 commodity code;

2 value;

3 delivery terms;

4 nature of transaction;

5 net mass;

6 supplementary units;

7 member state to which/from which consigned;

8 trader's reference (optional).

3.37 The above information is invariably not contained on the main accounting system. This can, therefore, lead to time delays in submitting the supplementary declarations and the date can slip through lack of time being spent on capturing accurate information. As a basic check, it is always worth comparing the values declared on the monthly supplementary declarations against the monthly/quarterly VAT returns for the same period. If the figures do not agree, a problem may have arisen in capturing the data.

3.38 VAT Officers will usually inspect and check supplementary declarations as part of an assurance visit. However, for large businesses (999 traders) a day each year may be set aside to verify the data supplied on the supplementary declarations. HMRC will also visit when supplementary declarations have not been completed in order to ascertain why the returns have not been submitted.

MUTUAL ASSISTANCE THROUGH EXCHANGE OF INFORMATION

3.39 The continuing moves toward a single European market without border controls involving the liberalisation of capital movement and of payments is not only promoting intra-community trade, but undoubtedly encouraging tax dodgers. Missing Trader Inter Community ('MTIC') fraud represents one of the most high profile and serious attacks on the tax system and has prompted HMRC and the tax authorities in other member states to work closely together to combat this.

3.40 Member states are obliged to exchange information that might enable them to effect a correct assessment of taxes on income and capital under a Mutual Assistance Directive, which has been amended to include VAT. In 2005

HMRC received nearly 700 requests for information from other member states and the extent of this co-operation seems set to increase if the current climate persists regarding the need to combat not only MTIC, but other more sophisticated VAT avoidance schemes which may exist.

3.41 A number of multilateral VAT control visits have been carried out over the past few years on the joint control of multi-national companies. The object of these visits has been to test the effectiveness of the tools provided by the EU legislative framework for administrative cooperation in controlling multinationals.

3.42 However, the national legislation of some member states has prohibited this type of exercise even though EU legislation permits it. The EU Commission believe that these EU-wide controls should become a common part of each member state's national control strategies.

3.43 Further proposals to cover mutual assistance in the recovery of VAT across member states, together with an existing exchange programme to enable indirect tax officials to visit other member states, suggest that EU- wide controls may become commonplace over the next few years.

OTHER VISITS

3.44 Many businesses registered for VAT may also be involved with other aspects of the department's work. Often these other activities will involve visits from Officers trained in HMRC matters. The information gleaned about the business from the department's involvement in these activities can also be expected to find its way on to the VAT Officers' records. Recently there has been a move by HMRC to conduct joint VAT and excise visits at particular businesses, for example, exporters. The degree of liaison by Officers involved in the various aspects of the department's work has increased greatly over the last few years and allows HMRC better control over the various taxes and duties for which they are responsible.

PREPARING FOR VISITS

3.45 An assurance visit from HMRC must not be treated as a routine meeting. Most businesses would prepare and plan a meeting with the former IR, the same preparation and planning should also be applied to a VAT visit with HMRC.

3.46 Preparation for assurance visits must start well before the visit. Any business registering for VAT must accept that they will be visited by VAT

Officers and the more complex the business, the more regular the visits. When establishing accounting systems, the following points should, therefore, be borne in mind:

1 establish documented procedures for all accounts staff;

2 prepare guidance manuals for staff dealing with VAT;

3 define default procedures should system failures occur; and

4 ensure that staff dealing with VAT are trained.

3.47 Before the visit, try to arrange an office for the VAT Officer away from the normal office routine but in a position where he can be 'controlled'. This prevents the Officer from overhearing conversations which may be misinterpreted. The office should be comfortable and tidy. Any confidential documents should be locked securely away. The following points should also be considered:

1 upon arrival, check the Officer's identity;

2 give clear instructions to all staff that HMRC Officers are on the premises;

3 make notes of the meeting with the HMRC Officer, noting checks performed and documents inspected;

4 write to confirm rulings given verbally by HMRC;

5 use HMRC's own controls – flowcharts/interrogation software;

6 be polite but firm in your dealings with HMRC; and

7 do not allow the Officer free run of the premises.

3.48 Preparation for any visit from HMRC should also be part of the ongoing routine for any business. If any business ignores good accounting practice, a period of, say, two weeks notice of a visit would not be enough to get accounts into good order. As indicated above, good accounting routines should always be established. It is also important that, wherever possible, the accounting procedures should be known by more than one person. There have been a myriad of appeals to the VAT Tribunals against a default surcharge in which the business has argued that the director was 'on holiday' or the accounts manager was 'sick'. Some of these cases have been won, but only where it has been established that the missing person was away unexpectedly. Good accounting practices allow a business to be prepared for the unexpected!

3.49 It is worth taking time to establish a period end routine when completing VAT returns – a best practice approach to VAT. A key objective of HMRC is to 'direct resources away from the majority of compliant traders and to focus attention on the high-risk businesses'. In the 2006 Spring Departmental Report,

HMRC pointed to a Risk Blueprint focusing assurance activity within small and medium enterprises as the highest risk businesses. This resulted in the identification of a net VAT liability of over £600 million. A new Anti-Avoidance Group was set up to identify those taxpayers who are more likely to avoid paying tax. HMRC look set to continue in this vein focusing resources and identifying those who present the greatest threat of non compliance. The more that a business can demonstrate, therefore, that it is managing its VAT affairs correctly, the less time HMRC are likely to spend inspecting that business – and that can only be good news.

3.50 A business should always seek to establish two criteria. First, to minimise its VAT costs and secondly to maximise its cashflow. Effective planning for VAT can assist in achieving both of these criteria. Period-end routines can assist in recognising differences from the norm and serve to identify under or over-declarations of VAT. Whilst HMRC officers are obliged to adjust for errors they discover that are in the taxpayers favour, the checks undertaken during visits are generally aimed at identifying under-declarations. HMRC officers are unlikely to undertake checks designed to ascertain whether a business has failed to take credit for the tax or if it has been taken late. It is therefore important that each business has its own checks and procedures in place to ensure that it is not over-declaring its VAT liability. When VAT is under-declared, HMRC can impose interest and, depending on the amounts involved, penalties. The art, therefore, is to identify under-declarations before HMRC do.

3.51 The concept of the credibility visit which, from HMRC's perspective, often identifies the one-off error made by a business has already been explained. Simply having a second person to check the figures for a VAT return and making sure that the figures shown in box 4 (VAT reclaimed in this period on purchases and other inputs including acquisitions from the EU) is not greater than 17.5% of box 7 (total value of purchases and all other inputs excluding any VAT) is a start. Businesses can also develop a bespoke package of internal documents or spreadsheets which serve to compile the VAT return data. Various checks can be built into these processes. It is also a good idea not to have the same person both preparing and signing the VAT return.

3.52 A common criticism from HMRC is that the signatory to the VAT return is often at too low a level within a large business. A routine period-end procedure is an ideal way to get VAT taken more seriously within a business, especially if the finance director is required to sign the VAT return.

SEARCH AND ENTRY

3.53 Former Officers of HMCE have some of the widest powers in UK law enforcement, with commentators often making the point that HMCE have, in certain respects, wider powers than the police. Many of these rights and powers have been bestowed on HMCE over their hundreds of years of history and are rigorously defended. The fact that some of these old rights were retained is a testament to the generally judicious and appropriate use of their powers.

3.54 The Commissioners for Revenue and Customs Act 2005 (CRCA) which established HMRC transferred the powers of the former IR and HMCE to the new department. As a short-term measure, however, these powers have been 'ring fenced' so they can only be used for their original purpose. This means powers bestowed to HMCE can still only be used for administering VAT. This may seem like good news in that HMCE cannot use powers that relate to VAT to obtain information about another matter. It must be remembered, however, that information was shared between HMCE and the IR before the formation of HMRC and that the merging of the two departments can only have improved the internal communication network.

3.55 During the Parliamentary process for the CRCA, a major review of the powers, deterrents and safeguards for HMRC was announced. This review will aim to address the issues of aligning and modernising the existing powers and safeguards of the newly formed department.

3.56 It is interesting to note that former Customs Officers, besides carrying an identity card, also used to carry an 'Officer's Commission'. This document, signed by a Commissioner of Customs and Excise, confirmed the appointment of the named person as an Officer of Customs and Excise. This document confirmed the Officer's powers under the law to 'perform all such matters and things as are by any Act of Parliament in force relating to the Revenues of Customs and Excise … and to enforce all laws, regulations, penalties and forfeitures as directed by the Commissioners of Her Majesty's Customs and Excise'. The Commission went on to require 'every Constable and member of Her Majesty's armed forces or coastguard and all other whom it may concern' to assist the Officer in the performance of his duties, although the armed forces are not generally required at VAT assurance visits! Whilst the principles and powers that were outlined in the document are still applicable to current Officers, the document itself has been withdrawn from use.

3.57 Officers' of HMRC have very wide ranging powers at their disposal. As regards VAT, former HMCE powers are principally contained in The Customs and Excise Management Act 1979 (CEMA 1979) and The Value Added Tax Act 1994 (VATA 1994). For Intrastat purposes, the powers of Customs are contained in the Statistics of Trade (Customs and Excise) Regulations 1992. All that will be dealt with here are the powers generally exercised during a routine VAT inspection.

3.58 VATA 1994, Sch 11 deals with the administration, collection and enforcement of the tax. Paragraph 6 requires a business to keep records; para 7 requires a business to submit VAT returns, supplementary declarations, European sales listings, etc and to provide, on demand, 'any documents relating to the goods or services or to the supply, acquisition or importation'. Paragraph 11 gives an Officer the right to enter at any reasonable time premises used in connection with the carrying on of a business. This paragraph also permits an Officer the right to inspect any goods located on any premises when he has reasonable cause to believe that those goods have been the subject of an acquisition or will be used to make a taxable supply. These paragraphs contain the basic powers that permit an Officer to enter buildings, inspect goods and to inspect the books and records of a business.

3.59 As mentioned earlier, VATA 1994, Sch 11, para 7 requires that all documents relating to a supply be produced to an Officer on demand. This will usually relate to, but is not restricted to, invoices (purchases and sales), delivery notes, ledgers, computer printouts of sales and purchases, control accounts, bank statements, etc. Paragraph 7 also requires the production of any profit and loss account and balance sheet relating to the business. It should be borne in mind that this only requires production of the statutory accounts. It is important to recognise, therefore, that this requirement does not immediately relate to the provision of management accounts produced by the business itself. Similarly, the statutory powers of the former HMCE concerning the provision of information do not mean that Officers can immediately demand sight of confidential advice provided to a business by their tax advisers.

3.60 Following consultation with the ICAEW and the Institute of Taxation, HMCE issued VAT Leaflet 700/47/93 'Confidentiality in VAT matters (Tax Advisers) – Statement of practice'. This leaflet acknowledges the confidential nature of such tax advice and recognises that tax advisers have a duty of confidentiality to their clients. The former HMCE policy in this area, therefore, is not normally to request the business to produce confidential opinion letters. This will typically include auditors' working papers and management letters, except to the extent that they contain information relating to a supply of goods or services. Where advice letters contain mixed information, ie general advice and guidance and advice relating to a supply of goods or services, HMRC will normally accept an extract from the document supported by a written statement from the tax adviser or business that in his opinion HMRC do not have the power to see the other part(s) of the document.

3.61 In practice, Officers will ask for everything and anything on the basis that there is no harm in trying! If any business is in doubt as to whether to give any documents to HMRC they should consult their advisers. If documents of a confidential nature are given to HMRC – which should be resisted – ensure, as far as possible, that no copies are taken.

SURVEILLANCE OPERATIONS

3.62 In general terms, surveillance operations cover two types of activity. First, test purchases and second, observation of premises and/or people. If VAT Officers have reason to believe that a business is suppressing the value of its sales, one device that can be used to good effect is to conduct a test purchase operation. This is a low-key investigation technique typically employed against suspicious retailers, particularly restaurants and hairdressers. A small team of VAT Officers, are sent to the target premises to, for example, purchase a meal and to observe the waiters and other staff to see what happens to the money, ie what procedures are operated.

3.63 The Officers will complete a report (sometimes a witness statement) which typically details:

1 what they purchased (a receipt is an essential feature);

2 what the cash-taking routine is for the business, ie what does the waiter do with the cash or credit card slips, etc;

3 the number of diners in the restaurant between certain times; and

4 the general atmosphere in the restaurant.

3.64 This type of activity may go on for several days, or if the business is large enough, over a period of weeks. The output from this type of activity gives a rough idea of the level of takings for the restaurant for a given period. By extrapolation, an idea of the actual level of takings for a VAT period or year can be ascertained.

3.65 The 'test meal' will be followed fairly quickly by a routine assurance visit. The VAT Officer, armed with the intelligence gained from the test meal operation, can compare known takings against the takings declared in the record of daily gross takings that must be maintained by every retailer. Clearly, if the test meal operation identifies a significant difference between declared and actual takings, the assurance visit is likely to turn very swiftly into an investigation.

3.66 If HMRC want to obtain information about premises and/or people they will, on occasion, mount an exercise to observe those premises or people (known colloquially as 'obs'). This procedure does demand considerable skills which would not normally be expected of a VAT Officer. These techniques, because of the level of expertise required and the manpower needed to conduct this type of operation, are usually only employed by trained investigators.

INVESTIGATIONS

3.67 Roughly coinciding with the formation of HMRC, two other agencies were formed to take over some of the responsibilities which were previously dealt with by HMCE. These are the Revenue and Customs Prosecutions Office ('RCPO') and the Serious Organised Crime Agency ('SOCA').

3.68 The RCPO now deals with prosecuting all tax fraud cases in England and Wales as an independent agency, while SOCA has now taken over responsibility for former HMCE investigation and intelligence work on serious drug trafficking and related criminal finances.

3.69 However, HMRC retain the responsibility for protecting the UK's borders, including the enforcement of all prohibitions and restrictions at the frontier, and their law-enforcement role on tackling highly damaging fiscal crimes.

3.70 Furthermore, some areas involving investigations have been centralised. Within the Operations Business Stream a centralised Intelligence Unit has been created, as has a Detection Unit dealing with anti-fraud and smuggling operations. The Special Civil Investigations Unit has also been created to deal with serious acts of evasion using civil powers. Due to its cost efficiency this remains the procedure of choice but HMRC reserve the right to pursue a criminal investigation where they deem appropriate.

ROLE OF THE PROFESSIONAL ADVISER

Business review

3.71 A professional adviser can, of course, take many roles and provide a variety of services. In an ideal world every accounting system should have rigorous procedures all of which are documented and involve staff having split responsibilities. However, in practice this utopian ideal may not always translate to the real world. It should also be remembered that professional advice is not cheap. A business invariably strikes a balance between the perceived risks and the cost of implementing a rock-solid accounting system.

3.72 Although the vast majority of businesses are subject to an annual audit, VAT errors or mistakes are rarely material to the accounts and VAT does not, therefore, form a large part of an audit. The role of the professional VAT adviser is something beyond the scope of an audit.

3.73 A typical role for a professional adviser can be to conduct an overview of the system operated by a business to determine key weaknesses and controls and to ensure that the systems suit that particular business. This type of VAT review is often likened to an assurance visit; the question then posed by the business is 'why do we pay an adviser to do that, when HMRC do it for free?'. There are two fundamental reasons why a separate review should be considered by a business. First, HMRC's role, however they like to present it, is to maximise revenue. This means that HMRC will be looking mainly for errors where VAT has been under-declared or over-recovered. If such errors are found by HMRC, as stated earlier, this will result in an interest charge and, depending on the significance of the error, a monetary penalty. Secondly, HMRC are not in the business of giving bespoke tax advice. Planning opportunities will not be drawn to the business's attention by a visiting VAT Officer!

Assessments

3.74 I suspect that many businesses when they receive an assessment from HMRC following a visit, simply pay it. A significant number of assessments issued by HMRC are, in my experience, unenforceable. The first thing a professional adviser will do on reviewing an assessment issued to a client is to ensure that it is not out of time. Simply paying assessments in these circumstances is throwing money away. It is also important to recognise that VAT Officers are trained to use departmental instructions, public notices and leaflets – not all Officers have the legislation, let alone read and understand it. This is not a criticism of VAT Officers, but training a large number of staff and requiring them to treat transactions on the same basis does mean a standardised approach – hence a heavy reliance on the public notices, etc.

3.75 It must be remembered that most public notices and leaflets are simply HMRC's interpretation of the law. The number of successful appeals against HMRC's view stand as a testament to the fact that HMRC's interpretation can and should, where appropriate, be challenged. It should also be appreciated that UK VAT legislation must reflect the provisions of EU VAT legislation. A business has the right, on appeal, to challenge HMRC's interpretation on both UK and EU law – HMRC can only argue from UK legislation. A professional adviser is aware of the vast amount of UK and EU legislation and legal precedent and has far greater resources available than a normal business.

Appeals

3.76 This can be a daunting thought for many businesses. The tribunal procedures can be obscure for the uninitiated as can the idea of building the legal arguments and giving evidence at the tribunal. A professional adviser can put the case together and remove a lot of the concerns usually experienced by a business going to a tribunal for the first time. Although a business can take a case on its own, with the complexity of today's legislation, particularly if a case involves VAT liability, a business is well advised to seek professional guidance. It should be remembered that if the business is successful in its appeal, the Crown pays the costs – albeit taxed costs.

The Revenue & Customs Adjudicator

3.77 If a business has a grievance about the way it has been dealt with by HMRC, the business may be able to complain to the HMRC Adjudicator. Appropriate complaints concern the way in which HMRC have conducted themselves in relation to a business's affairs and may include, for example:

- situations where HMRC have been excessively slow in dealing with a particular matter;
- an Officer being discourteous;
- a case where HMRC have made a mistake which they have failed to remedy; or
- situations where HMRC have used their discretion or their powers inappropriately.

The Adjudicator may award costs but can also require HMRC to make a consolatory payment, order things to be done to a particular time scale or recommend that the Officer is changed.

Investigation

3.78 If an assurance visit becomes uncomfortable or an investigation team arrives at the business, the business advisers should be contacted immediately. Trying to handle situations where interviews are being conducted under caution can be fraught and create a high degree of distress. The following are points to remember:

1. phone the professional adviser immediately to seek specific advice;
2. be polite and helpful at all times, as it is an offence to obstruct an Officer in the course of his duties;
3. politely but firmly refuse to give interviews under caution, whether taped or written;
4. say something to the effect that 'we are happy to answer your questions, however, could you please outline your areas of concern so that due consideration can be given to providing the correct answer'; and
5. always remember that when an investigation is instigated, it is an indication that the Officer believes that offences may have been committed! If a comment is made under caution, it cannot be retracted. Trying to persuade HMRC that something said in a statement was wrong or inaccurate can be very difficult and expensive.

Chapter 4

National Insurance visits and investigations

Peter Arrowsmith FCA, National Insurance Consultant

4.1 With around £105 billion of National Insurance contributions due to be collected in a year (of which over £100 billion are Class 1 contributions) there is a clear duty on the National Insurance Contributions Office and HMRC generally to ensure that employers and the self-employed pay what is due and otherwise comply with the many NIC legislative requirements. The policing of the NIC systems largely, but not entirely, falls to HMRC employer compliance officers.

INSPECTORATE POWERS

4.2 Previous, and arguably heavier, powers available to employer compliance officers dealing with NIC matters were changed with effect from 6 April 2005 when SSCBA 1992, s 110ZA was rewritten by the National Insurance Contributions and Statutory Payments Act 2004. From that date, the tax and National Insurance powers of what are now HM Revenue and Customs officers to inspect records and obtain information have been aligned and Taxes Management Act 1970, ss 20, 20B and 20BB – with appropriate modifications – applies to NIC. The rewritten section 110ZA does not deal with Class 3 contributions as they are entirely voluntary, and Class 4 contributions were already within the TMA regime in any event.

4.3 All employer compliance officers carry a warrant card setting out their powers in addition to a standard identification card. Employers should ask to see such warrants if they are unsure of what rights the employer compliance officers have.

Reasons for visit

4.4 There are many reasons why an employer compliance officer would want to visit an employer. It could be because he is a new employer and the employer compliance officer wants to introduce himself and check that the employer is familiar with the basic rules for NIC, Statutory Sick Pay (SSP),

Statutory Maternity Pay (SMP), Statutory Paternity Pay (SPP) and Statutory Adoption Pay (SAP) – collectively known as 'Statutory Payments'). There could be a small discrepancy in the year-end reporting forms and the employer compliance officer needs a quick look at the employer's records. It could be that there is a special check being made of specific industry type or an employer has been selected for a more in-depth examination. Given that most visits are fairly routine and will cause employers little or no trouble, the rest of this chapter will focus on how employer compliance officers carry out a full-scale investigation.

Which employers are chosen for investigation?

4.5 Although random visits continue to be made, employer compliance officers are likely to have done a little bit of homework to identify employers worthy of a visit. They are under some pressure to collect additional NICs (and tax too) and so they will not want to waste time visiting employers who are unlikely to have underpaid or made other serious errors. Employer profiling is used to identify suitable targets and factors taken into account include size, geographical location, industry type and make-up of workforce etc. Computer programs are regularly used to identify such targets.

Purpose of visit

4.6 Protecting the National Insurance Fund is the primary purpose of the NIC element of any visit but another very important purpose is ensuring that employee benefit rights are fully maintained by confirming that the correct amount of NIC has been paid. Other reasons for a visit are to identify instances where too little or too much NIC has been paid and to correct any errors, and to check that the Statutory Payments are being correctly and timeously paid out to employees when due.

Timing

4.7 Employer compliance officers will not want to visit too often and so they try to work on a five-year cycle although where serious errors have been found or significant NICs collected check visits will be made in the interim period. Following the 1999 merger of the former Inland Revenue and the former Contributions Agency all inspection visits now deal with both tax and NIC (including the related Statutory Payments issues) at the same time. This continues to be the case following the subsequent 2005 merger between HM Customs & Excise and the Inland Revenue.

Notification of visit

4.8 It is extremely rare these days for employer compliance officers to make unannounced visits. Employers are more likely to receive a telephone call or letter at least two weeks in advance. Employers should not hesitate to seek to delay or defer a visit if there are work pressures caused by, for example, being at or near the end of the financial or trading year or because of staff shortages. However, the authorities are aware that sometimes requests for later dates are attempts to avoid a visit at all costs. Deliberately attempting to avoid being audited is severely frowned upon and appropriate measures will be taken if necessary.

4.9 Employer compliance officers may want to make a preliminary visit to explain how they see the inspection progressing whilst at the same time obtaining some background information such as who will be able to deal with the queries, the form in which the various records are kept and for how long the records are held and whether there is suitable accommodation for them to use. At that preliminary meeting the employer is likely to find out how many employer compliance officers and support staff will be involved in the inspection, how long it is likely to take and any specific areas in which the employer compliance officers are interested.

4.10 Equally, the visiting officer may well have used an internal computerised audit programme called 'IDEA' which – in advance of the visit – performs certain checks and procedures on the submitted P35 and P14 data and highlights key areas (down to individual employee level) for detailed examination and consideration at the visit.

Length of visit

4.11 It is virtually impossible to estimate in advance just how long an inspection will take and they will range from an hour to several weeks. It is safe to say that where there are, say, at least 1,000 employees the inspection will last for at least two weeks. It may well be that employer compliance officers are not on the premises for a continuous period but will simply check an aspect at a time, go away and put together their findings and then return and check something else.

Place of visit

4.12 Employer compliance officers will generally want to carry out their inspection at the employer's place of business and if the records are not readily available there they are likely to ask for the records to be brought to the place of business. Sometimes employer compliance officers can be persuaded to visit another location such as a payroll bureau or an accountant but that is the exception rather than the rule. Employer compliance officers will, however, want to visit other work locations to check paperwork held locally and maybe even to count the number of heads to make sure that they are all on the payroll.

Preparation for the visit

4.13 There is a lot an employer can do beforehand to make sure that the inspection runs smoothly. He should, for example, make sure that all the records requested by the employer compliance officer are readily available and that someone with knowledge of the employer's system and procedures is available to deal with any queries. That person should be senior enough to be able to answer queries without needing to refer matters elsewhere. An employer should also ensure that accommodation is made available for the employer compliance officers and it would be courteous to ensure that the room is lockable, that there is access to a telephone and that there are tea, coffee and toilet facilities.

Commencement of the visit

4.14 At the beginning of the visit the employer compliance officer(s) should make the necessary introductions and explain the process of conducting the examination of the records. This is the time for both the employer compliance officer and the employer to ask any questions and also to ensure that all the required records (listed below) are available. The employer compliance officer should also establish who should be contacted in the event of queries and questions. During the course of the audit the records of all employees and directors will be checked to ensure that contributions (including Class 1A, Class 1B and, in the case of unincorporated businesses, Class 2) are being correctly assessed and paid and also that SSP, SMP, SPP and SAP is being paid to employees who qualify and that only the correct recoveries are being made from the employer's monthly (or quarterly) remittances. While they will start with the current year they will usually check back into the preceding year and earlier years if they feel it is necessary.

Records to be made available

4.15 Employer compliance officers need to be able to examine any of the employer's records that could involve a liability for National Insurance contributions. The list of documents that may be required for examination is extensive and, while not exhaustive, includes:

- *Accident Book* – where there is a legal requirement to keep such a book employer compliance officers will want to ensure that it is held and that it is being correctly completed.
- *Bank Statements* – employer compliance officers will want to identify payments which do not go through the payroll and which could attract an NIC liability.
- *Cash Book* – employer compliance officers will want to confirm that payments subject to NIC have been transferred to the payroll and have been correctly treated.
- *Certificates of Deferment* – the visiting officers will want to ensure that these certificates are actually held.
- *Certificates of Exemption* – employer compliance officers will want to ensure that these certificates are valid and have been correctly used.
- *Certificates of Election for married women paying reduced rate National Insurance* – again employer compliance officers will want to ensure that these certificates continue to be valid.
- *Cheque Stubs* – employer compliance officers will want to identify payments that should have gone through the payroll for NIC purposes.
- *Company Accounts* – employer compliance officers will want to examine these as there are various clues to the NIC position. For example, does the employer NIC on the P35 broadly equal 11% or 12% of the total employee remuneration shown in the accounts and has all the remuneration paid to directors been considered for NIC purposes?
- *Contracting-out Certificate* – is this valid and has the employer correctly identified those employees covered by the contracting-out arrangements?
- *Deduction Working Sheets (P11s)* – very few employers will use the standard P11s but they will have equivalent documentation (whether on paper or held electronically) and employer compliance officers will check a number of calculations to ensure that the correct NIC figures have been reached, often downloading electronic records onto their own computerised audit program 'IDEA' for further analysis work off the premises.
- *Sick Absence Records* – employer compliance officers will look to see if employers have correctly dealt with sick absences and in the main this will be to ensure that employees have received the equivalent of Statutory Sick Pay.
- *Maternity Absence Records* – employer compliance officers will want to check a few SMP calculations and confirm that employers are holding the correct evidence of pregnancy.

- *Paternity and Adoption Pay Records* – employer compliance officers will look to see if employers have correctly dealt with such absences and in the main this will be to ensure that employees have received the correct payments and the employer holds the appropriate certification from the employee(s) in question.
- *Minute Book* – this is where employer compliance officers will identify additional payments to company directors and senior executives (this may include the awarding of shares, share options and other similar securities).
- *P30 BC Paying-in Book/P32* (*or equivalent electronic records*) – employer compliance officers will want to ensure that monies have been paid over to HMRC when due.
- *Petty Cash Book* – again employer compliance officers will be looking to identify payments that should have gone through payroll for NIC purposes.
- *Petty Cash Vouchers* – this is another area where employer compliance officers will be looking for payments liable for NIC which have not gone through the payroll arrangements.
- *Wage Book/Payroll* – this is where employer compliance officers will pay close attention and they will take a sample of entries to ensure that NIC liabilities have been fully met and that the correct reporting mechanisms are in place.
- *Dispensation* – employer compliance officers will want to ensure that where NIC liabilities have not been met that this is because the terms of a dispensation granted by HMRC have been fully complied with. In appropriate cases HMRC can, and will, withdraw dispensations retrospectively if the terms on which they were issued have ceased to apply or if the circumstances were misrepresented in the original application.

4.16 When checking the above documentation employer compliance officers will pay close attention to the following aspects:

- *Basic Pay* – they will want to ensure that NI has been paid on the full amount and that the correct contribution category letter and earnings period have been used.
- *Bonuses* – employer compliance officers will want to ensure that this has been added to the basic pay in the correct earnings period and that NIC has been assessed on the total. Employer compliance officers will pay very close attention to any bonus arrangements that have avoided NIC liabilities.
- *Company Cars, Fuel Expenses and other benefits in kind* – employer compliance officers are likely to carry out an in-depth examination of Class 1A contribution liabilities. They will also look to identify fuel used

for private motoring and to ensure that all NIC liabilities are met. They will also look at mileage rates and allowances paid by employers to ensure that there is no profit element, as well as considering all other benefits in depth.

- *Other Payments in Kind* – employer compliance officers will want to satisfy themselves that payments in kind are genuine, that if they have not been subjected to NIC liabilities that such payments fall within the general Class 1 NIC exclusion provisions and, where appropriate, Class 1A accounted for nonetheless.
- *Casual and Part-time Workers* – they will want to ensure that they go through the payroll when earnings reach the NIC lower limit and that National Insurance numbers (NINOs) are held.
- *Directors* – employer compliance officers will want to identify all individuals who fall within the definition of a company director for NIC purposes and verify that an annual earnings period (or pro-rata in the year of appointment) has been used. They will also look closely at any arrangements that are shown to avoid NIC liabilities.
- *Employees with Appropriate Scheme Contracted-out Number* (*including directors*) – employer compliance officers will want to confirm that the correct category letter has been used and that the scheme numbers go on the end-of-year returns.
- *Expenses Payments* – this is an area where employer compliance officers will pay very close attention and they will be seeking to identify profit elements within payments as well as entirely non-business payments so that NIC liabilities can be assessed. They will look closely at what expenses employees are allowed to claim and the steps that employers have put in place for authorising such expenses.
- *Fees/Commissions* – employer compliance officers will want to make sure that such payments are added to the basic salary in the correct earnings period and that full NIC liabilities are met.
- *Overtime* – employer compliance officers will again check that this has been added to basic pay.
- *Self-employed Workers* – this is always an area which excites employer compliance officers simply because of the likely additional NIC yield if the individuals are in fact employees. They will look closely at the employment arrangements and in particular at any supervision, control or direction that is evident.
- *Workers exempt from payment of National Insurance/paying reduced rate National Insurance/not liable to pay National Insurance* – employer compliance officers will be looking for documentation to support the NIC position. This may involve employers in having to provide certificates of

reduced rate authority, deferment certificates, age exemption certificates and certificates of coverage issued by foreign Social Security authorities.

- *Shares and other Securities, including Options* – employer compliance officers will examine all arrangements carefully including those in relation to approved schemes where transactions outside normal rules may give rise to liability.

More generally, the officers will also want to ensure that none of the business activities are such that either the personal service companies ('IR35') or management service companies provisions are applicable.

RECORD KEEPING

4.17 The legislation requires employers to keep records for the current tax year and the three previous years. It is likely that employer compliance officers will restrict their initial action to the current year and the last closed tax year. If errors are found they will go back further. If employers have records going back more than three years employer compliance officers are likely to look at the last six years. It is arguable, however, that if an employer only holds records for the three years the wording of the social security legislation precludes an employer compliance officer from going back any further simply because he would be unable to identify a named employee who received a payment of earnings on a specific date. However, in practice, employer compliance officers will normally seek six years arrears in all cases.

4.18 It is the employer's responsibility to make sure that the relevant records are made available to employer compliance officers. If the records are going to take a time to put together or to collect from different locations then employer compliance officers are usually agreeable to delay the inspection for a short time. Employers who do not make the relevant records available to the officers within a reasonable time may find that the employer compliance officer will take criminal proceedings.

4.19 It is always open to an employer compliance officer to take records away from the business premises but he will generally return them as quickly as possible. If an employer needs the records for his business purposes then the employer compliance officer will arrange for copies to be supplied to him.

ERRORS AND OMISSIONS

4.20 One of the main purposes of an inspection is to ensure that employers are not making errors. Yet with such a complicated scheme to operate it is inevitable that employers will make mistakes. The opportunities to get it wrong are wide and varied – some of the common areas include:

1 accepting a person as being self-employed when the facts do not support the decision;

2 using the wrong year's NI tables – whether hard-copy tables or through not having updated software either at all or on time;

3 having incomplete identity details – usually the lack of NI numbers;

4 deducting reduced rate contributions without holding the appropriate certificate;

5 continuing to deduct reduced rate contributions when a woman has been divorced;

6 directors' annual earnings periods;

7 errors with Statutory Payments;

8 failing to account for employees' contributions without the required proof of age exemption or failing to account for any National Insurance contributions without the appropriate international coverage certification.

4.21 Items 2 and 3 above – at least – will cause PAYE Schemes filed electronically for 2005/06 onwards to be immediately rejected upon submission. Paper, etc returns containing such errors will also be returned in due course for correction by the employer. In either situation, the P35 is not then treated as having been submitted until the errors are successfully corrected.

4.22 Very few employers make mistakes deliberately. During visits employer compliance officers try to ensure that employers both understand and can operate the system. Where errors are found then the employer compliance officer will draw it to the employer's attention with guidance as to how the position should be rectified and how it should be avoided in future. Where the error results in an overpayment or underpayment of NIC then the employer compliance officer will again give guidance as to how this should be rectified. In simple terms if the error is in the current tax year then an adjustment can be made, but if it is in a closed tax year then either a refund application can be made or the employer compliance officer will issue a demand for arrears.

INSPECTION REPORT

4.23 At the end of the inspection, the employer compliance officer will explain, in some detail, what has been discovered, answer questions, try to ensure that the employer (and staff) will be able to deal with problems in the future and know who to contact when faced with difficulties. Afterwards the employer will usually receive a written report of some kind, and will definitely do so, along with calculations, if arrears of NIC (and/or tax) are being demanded. It could merely be a letter or it could be a much more formal document. Whatever is issued will highlight the officer's findings and contain his recommendations to improve the record keeping. What employers will really be interested in is the usual demand for NIC arrears. Such demands will almost certainly accompany the inspection report with a request for payment. It is likely that some interest charge will also be levied, and in some cases penalties too. It is up to employers to pay over what is due or if they consider that there is no liability to set out in writing why they believe that is the case. This is often when advisers become involved and they will take the matter forward on behalf of the employer. The bigger the employer the more likely it is that employer compliance officers will want to have a formal meeting at the end of the inspection to discuss all the findings.

4.24 When assessing any arrears the employer compliance officers will also advise the employer of the implications of interest charges on contributions (and tax) that have not been paid by 19 April (22 April where the payment is made electronically for 2004/05 onwards) in the tax year following that in which they were due.

FUTURE VISITS

4.25 When the employer compliance officer decides to make a further visit will depend greatly on what he finds at the inspection. If there is little of concern then it is likely to be five years or more before he returns. If, however, there are a large number of errors or significant NIC due then he may very well make a check visit within 12 months or so.

CONCLUSION

4.26 With employer compliance officers' growing ability to target firms for audit with greater effectiveness, the potential for discovering financial irregularities is greater and the accent is now firmly on yield discovered rather than the number of visits carried out.

4.27 Targeting, by its very nature, involves the selection of businesses where experience indicates that there is more likelihood of employers making mistakes. Coming into this area are companies with a high turnover of staff, companies who employ large numbers of casual staff, companies with numerous widespread sites with consequential long lines of communication, companies who make large numbers of mistakes in their end of year returns. However, while being able progressively to identify such businesses employer compliance officers also have a duty to protect the NIC records of all types of employers. There must therefore be a balance between concentrating purely upon yield with the need to demonstrate that it is protecting employees in all types of employers.

4.28 From the above comments, it will be appreciated that there is not a lot that employers can do to avoid inspection visits. They will be selected as a target for any number of reasons and the employer compliance officer will follow that through. What employers can do, however, is check their procedures and ensure that they are following the legislative requirements. They could, in fact, mirror the type of checks that employer compliance officers carry out on a regular basis and ensure that all is in order.

Chapter 5

National insurance: fines, penalties and appeals

Peter Arrowsmith, FCA, National Insurance Consultant

OFFENCES AND PENALTIES

General

5.1 In December 2006, HMRC issued a consultation document 'Modernising Powers, Deterrents and Safeguards' which proposed a new approach to the imposition of penalties. Starting from 2009 and following Finance Act 2007, some of the penalties detailed throughout this chapter will be superseded – see para **5.24**.

False information, delays and obstruction

5.2 The criminal penalties which once applied are dealt with as civil offences from 1 April 1999, following the transfer of responsibility from the former Contributions Agency to what was then the Inland Revenue and which merged with HM Customs & Excise in April 2005 to become HMRC.

Contravention of regulations

5.3 The previous criminal offences under SSAA 1992, s 113 are replaced with effect from 6 April 1999 by new s 113 inserted by Social Security Act 1998, s 60. This provides for regulations to be made setting out a scheme of civil penalties. It should be noted that, in the case of Class 1 NICs, it is the employer who is guilty of an offence, even if he delegated his duties of compliance to another (*Godman v Crofton* [1913] 110 LT 387). There is an extensive scheme of penalties applying to employers' failures in relation to Statutory Sick Pay, Statutory Maternity Pay, Statutory Paternity Pay and Statutory Adoption Pay (SSAA 1992, ss 113A, 113B, Employment Act 2002, ss 11, 12, Sch 1). These include:

- failure to produce documents or records or to provide information – up to £300, and for continuing failure a possible penalty of up to £60 per day;
- failing to maintain records – up to £3,000;
- repeated failure to make payments to employees – up to £3,000;
- incorrect payments due to fraud or neglect – up to £3,000;
- excessive advance funding by reason of fraud or neglect – up to £3,000.

These penalties will also be reformed in due course, but not as soon as April 2009. A consultation document was issued in January 2008.

Offences relating to contributions

5.4 If an employer deducts or tries to deduct all or part of the employer's Class 1 secondary liability from the employee's pay he is guilty of an offence (SSCBA 1993, Sch 1, para 3A and SI 2001/1004, Sch 4, para 6(2), (3)).

5.5 The Social Security Act 1998 imposed a new *criminal* offence of fraudulent evasion and being knowingly involved in fraudulent evasion of contributions. The offence is brought to trial summarily or on indictment. When tried summarily the maximum fine is level 5 (£5,000) on the standard scale. When tried on indictment the maximum penalty is seven years' imprisonment and/or an unlimited fine (SSCBA 1992, s 114 inserted by Social Security Act 1998, s 61). It should be noted that this offence relates to 'any person' and so may extend to an accountant, tax advisor or junior payroll clerk.

Offences by bodies corporate

5.6 Where a company commits an offence by failing to pay a contribution, and it is proved that the offence was committed with the consent or connivance of, or to be attributable to any neglect on the part of a director, manager, secretary or other similar officer of the company, proceedings may also be taken against that individual (SSAA 1992, s 115 (1)). This applies equally to a company which is managed by its members (SSAA 1992, s 115 (2)).

5.7 The former Contributions Agency (CA) successfully prosecuted a director of two 'phoenix' companies under s 115 in 1995. Directors of such companies typically incur large debts through the non-payment of creditors and then liquidate the company, relying on its limited liability status to protect themselves. NICs are often deducted correctly from employees' wages, but are not passed on to what is now HMRC. This was the first criminal case of its kind (CA Press Release of 27 September 1995).

Employer failing to pay Class 1 and Class 1A contributions

Notice of amount due

5.8 If within 17 days of the end of any income tax period an employer has either failed to pay, or paid insufficient Class 1 or Class 1A contributions and HMRC's Debt Management and Banking service believes that contributions are due, he may issue a notice to the employer instructing him to make a return within 14 days, showing the amount of contributions which he is liable to pay in respect of the period in question (SI 2001/1004, Sch 4, para 14 (1)(3)).

5.9 The Debt Management and Banking service may alternatively, upon consideration of the employer's record of past payments, to the best of their judgment, specify the amount of contributions which they consider the employer is liable to pay and give notice of the amount (SI 2001/1004, Sch 4, para 15(1)).

Evidence of non-payment of contributions

5.10 If the employer has not paid either the estimated liability or the actual amount due within the seven days allowed in the notice, Debt Management and Banking's certificate of the amount due is, until the contrary is proved, sufficient evidence in any proceedings before the courts that the sum mentioned in the certificate is unpaid and due (SSAA 1992, s 118(1); SI 2001/1004, Sch 4, para 15(4)). A document purporting to be such a certificate is deemed to be such a certificate until the contrary is proved (SSAA 1992, s 118(3) and SI 2001/1004, Sch 4, para 15(4)). The Social Security Act 1998 broadens these arrangements to provide that a certificate of an authorised officer of HMRC confirming the non-payment of contributions, interest or penalty may be provided to court as evidence of non-payment of debt until the contrary is proved (SSAA 1992, s 118(1), substituted by Social Security Act 1998, s 62). The Social Security Act 1998 also provides for distraint action to be taken in England and Wales where a person served with a certificate confirming their debt, fails to make payment within seven days. A magistrate's warrant is required for forced entry to premises and, where necessary, the assistance of a constable may also be secured. Any goods distrained will be held for a five-day period and then sold by auction. After recovery of the debt the balance of the proceeds, if any, are to be paid to the debtor (SSAA 1992, s 121A inserted by Social Security Act 1998, s 63). Premises does not include a private dwelling house unless an authorised officer has reasonable grounds to believe that a trade or business is being carried on from those premises (SSAA 1992, s 121A(10)). In Scotland, poinding proceedings under Debtors (Scotland) Act 1987, Sch 5 can be instituted where a person has been served with a certificate confirming the debt (s 118(1) above) but fails to make payment within 14 days. A sheriff's summary warrant is required for recovery and sale by way of poinding. Applications must be accompanied by the certificate of debt and a certificate stating that the certificate of debt was served on the person in question and the debt remains unpaid (SSAA 1992, s 121B inserted by Social Security Act 1998, s 63).

Recovery of Class 1 contributions

5.11 The provisions of ITEPA 2003 and PAYE Regulations relating to the recovery of tax apply also to Class 1 contributions which an employer is liable to pay to the Debt Management and Banking service, as if they had been tax charged by way of an assessment on the employer as 'general earnings' (ITEPA 2003, s 684 and SI 2001/1004, reg 67(1)).

5.12 Proceedings may be brought for recovery of Class 1 and Class 1A contributions in the same way as they are for income tax charged on 'general earnings' (TMA 1970, s 65(3)).

Class 1, Class 1A and PAYE penalties

5.13 FA 1989 introduced significant changes to the penalty regime for PAYE failures, including the penalty in respect of late and incorrect year end returns (forms P14 and P35) (TMA 1970, s 98A). With effect from 22 October 1990, these penalties also apply in relation to returns required under NI regulations of Class 1 and Class 1A contributions. For NIC purposes, the Social Security Contributions and Benefits Act 1992 (SSCBA 1992), Sch 1, para 7 mirrors the PAYE penalty provisions in TMA 1970, s 98A subject to the following modifications:

1 Where a person has failed to render a tax return for a particular tax year within the time prescribed and is thus liable for (has been required to pay) a penalty for a default in the first 12 months, he is not liable for a similar penalty in respect of the associated contributions return (SSCBA 1992, Sch 1, para 7(3)).

2 Where a person has failed to render a tax return and an associated contributions return for a particular tax year and the failure has continued beyond 12 months, a single penalty may apply of up to the sum of any tax and contributions remaining unpaid at the end of 19 April following the end of the tax year to which the return relates. An authorised officer must determine that a penalty is to be imposed in respect of both returns (SSCBA 1992, Sch 1, para 7(4)(5)).

3 Where a person has fraudulently or negligently made an incorrect tax return and an associated contributions return for a particular tax year, a single penalty may apply of up to the sum of any tax and contributions

remaining unpaid at the end of 19 April following the end of the tax year to which the return relates. Again, an authorised officer must determine that a penalty is to be imposed in respect of both returns (SSCBA 1992, Sch 1, para 7(4)(5)).

5.14 Any penalties collected by HMRC in respect of NICs are, after the deduction of the collection costs, paid to the National Insurance Fund (SSCBA 1992, Sch 1, para 7(6)(8)).

Personal liability notices

5.15 With effect from 6 April 1999, officers of bodies corporate may be issued with a personal liability notice where the business has failed to pay the correct contributions at the correct time and the failure *appears* to be attributable to fraud or neglect on the part of one or more individuals (SSAA 1999, s 121C inserted by Social Security Act 1999, s 64).

5.16 The personal liability notice will transfer the whole or a specified part of the company's NIC debt to the director or company secretary as a personal debt of the individual, including the associated interest accrued to date. Further interest will accrue until payment is made. Appeals may be made against such notices and will always be heard by the Special Commissioners in the first instance (SSAA 1999, s 121D(2) inserted by Social Security Act 1999, s 64).

Penalties for late returns

5.17 For 1994/95 and subsequent years, an employer who has not filed his end of year return of tax and NICs by the due date (19 May following the year of assessment) is liable to an automatic penalty of £100 for each month or part month it is delayed, in respect of every 50 employees (or part thereof) who should be on the return. For example, a return for 51 employees which is late by one day would attract an automatic penalty of £200 (TMA 1970, s 98A). Where the delay continues beyond 12 months, an additional penalty is due, equal to the amount of tax and NICs unpaid at 19 April following the end of the year to which the return relates.

5.18 Until the automatic penalties were imposed, an interim scheme, which was intended gradually to tighten up on PAYE compliance, applied in respect of late end of year returns for the years 1989/90 to 1993/94 – see para **5.76**. Where an employer failed to make a return by the due date, the initial maximum penalty was £1,200 per 50 employees. Once the initial penalty had been imposed by formal proceedings before the Commissioners, there was a continuing penalty of £100 per 50 employees for each further month that the failure continued up to 12 months. The interim scheme was introduced gradually and penalty action was only taken against a proportion of defaulting employers.

Penalties for incorrect returns

5.19 The penalty for an incorrect return, fraudulently or negligently made, is an amount up to the difference between the amount paid for the year of assessment to which the return relates and the amount which would have been payable if it had been correct (TMA 1970, s 98A (4) and SSCBA 1992, Sch 1, para 7(2)).

Penalties for incorrect manner of payment

5.20 In respect of Class 1 NIC and PAYE liabilities for 2004/05 et seq, large PAYE schemes (those with 250 or more employees) must make their monthly remittances by electronic means. Where the full amount due is not paid electronically then the employer is in default. The only ground for an appeal against a default notice is that there was no default. A surcharge is imposed for defaults on an increasing scale that will, if there are sufficient defaults, reach 10% of the annual amount due. This remains the case even where all payments were on time and complete but paid by cheque. There are three extra days to pay if doing so electronically, though cleared funds must be received within those extra three days (SI 2001/1004, regs 90F–90L).

Class 1A contributions

5.21 For 2000/01 onwards there is a penalty of up to the amount of contributions underpaid where there is fraud or neglect (SI 2001/1004, reg 81(1)), otherwise £100 per 50 earners per part or full calendar month for the first 12 months, or the amount of contributions underpaid if the failure extends beyond 12 months (SI 2001/1004, reg 81(2), (3) and (4)).

5.22 Where Class 1A contributions were paid through Forms P14 and P35 for years up to and including 1999/2000 the same penalties and interest consequences ensued as if the Class 1A NIC was Class 1 NIC for the year to which the P14/P35 relates, eg 1997/98 Class 1A NIC entered on Form P14 in July 1998 and 1998/99 P35 in April/May 1999, will be subject to interest from 19 April 1999 and to the 19 May 1999 P35 submission date. Previously, no interest charge or penalty could arise if the employer had applied to use the 'Alternative Payment Method'. This anomaly was rectified from 20 April 1999, ie in effect, for 1998/99 Class 1A onwards, by the Social Security (Contributions) Amendment (No. 3) Regulations 1999 (SI 1999/975). However, interest and penalty charges arise from the due date for payment, eg 19 July 1999 for 1998/99 Class 1A NIC, whereas failure to pay will not, using the P14/P35 mechanism, attract interest until 19 April 2000 nor require the return to be rendered until 19 May 2000. This anomaly disappeared from 6 April 2000 as the former 'Alternative Payment Method' formed the basis of the current Class 1A return structure – now using Forms P11D and P11D(b).

Class 4 contributions

5.23 The penalty provisions of TMA 1970, Part X apply to Class 4 contributions which are payable by way of assessment made in accordance with income tax legislation (SSCBA 1992, s 16).

5.24 For returns due to be made from April 2009 onwards a new penalty regime set by Finance Act 2007, Sch 24 will apply. It is expected that additional National Insurance legislation will be required in the meantime to mirror the application of Sch 24 to PAYE returns, etc.

5.25 The new penalties will be determined by reference to the amount of tax/NIC understated, the nature of the behaviour that gives rise to the understatement and the extent of disclosure made by the 'taxpayer'.

5.26 The penalty will be zero for mistakes made despite 'reasonable care' having been taken, 0–30% where there has been failure to take reasonable care (with a minimum of 15% where disclosure was prompted by HMRC), 20–70% where there has been deliberate understatement (with a minimum of 35% where disclosure was prompted by HMRC) and 30–100% where there has been deliberate understatement with concealment (with a minimum of 50% where disclosure was prompted by HMRC).

5.27 In some cases penalties may be suspended for up to two years, eg if the error is due to systems or record-keeping failure.

5.28 Where an inaccuracy does not result in tax/NIC being lost altogether but being declared in a later period than it should have been, the penalty is 5% for each year of delay.

5.29 There is a right of appeal against the imposition and amount of a penalty. The onus of proof is on HMRC.

INTEREST

Overdue contributions

5.30 With effect from 1992/93, interest applies automatically to payments of PAYE and subcontractors' deductions outstanding at 19 April after the end of the tax year, eg 19 April 2003 for the 2002/03 tax year. Before this, and only from April 1988, interest arose in cases where tax, which the employer had failed to deduct under PAYE, was formally determined under what was then the Income Tax (Employments) Regulations 1993, reg 49. A similar charge did not apply for NIC purposes prior to 1992/93.

5.31 For 1992/93 and subsequent years, interest is automatically charged on primary and secondary Class 1 contributions paid more than 14 days after the end of the year in respect of which the contributions were due, eg 19 April 2008 for 2007/08 Class 1 contributions, or paid more than 17 days after the end of the year if payment is made electronically for 2004/05 onwards (SI 2001/1004 Sch 4, para 17). The same also applies to Class 1B contributions not paid by the due date.

5.32 Interest on late paid Class 1A contributions is automatically charged for 1991/92 and subsequent years. In respect of 2000/01 onwards, interest on overdue Class 1A runs from the due date (normally 19 July) (SI 2001/1004, reg 76). The due day is extended by three days if payment in respect of 2004/05 onwards is made electronically (SI 2001/1004, reg 71).

5.33 Until 6 April 2000 it accrued from the fourteenth day after the end of the year in which it was due to be paid, eg 19 April 1999 for 1997/98 Class 1A contributions (former SI 1979/591 Sch 1, reg 28B).

5.34 If, however, Class 1A contributions were paid by the 'Alternative Payment Method' (APM) up to 1999/2000 interest will run from the due date itself following a change in legislation effective from 20 April 1999, eg under the APM, interest for 1998/99 contributions will accrue from 20 July 1999. In earlier years, no interest could be charged under the APM.

5.35 In all cases, the rate of interest charged is the same as for late paid income tax as set by FA 1989, s 178 (SSCBA 1992 Sch 1, para 6(3)).

Repaid contributions

5.36 With effect from 19 April 1993, Class 1 and 1A contributions which are repaid after the 'relevant date' carry interest. The relevant date for 1999/2000 and subsequent years is:

1 for Class 1 contributions, 14 days after the end of the tax year in respect of which the contribution is payable, for Class 1A contributions, 14 days after the end of the tax year in which the contribution is payable, for Class 1B contributions, 19 October after the end of the tax year to which the contribution relates; or

2 if later, the date of payment,

and in the case of years up to and including 1998/99 the relevant date is:

1 for contributions paid more than 12 months after the end of the year in respect of which the payment was made, the last day of the year in which it was paid; or

2 in any other case, the last day of the year after the year in respect of which the contribution in question was paid

(SI 2001/1004, Sch 4, para 18).

Repayment and remission of interest

5.37 Where an employer has paid interest on late paid Class 1, Class 1A or Class 1B contributions which is subsequently found not to have been due, the interest will be repaid (SI 2001/1004, Sch 4, reg 19).

Interest will be remitted if the contribution in respect of which it was charged was paid late as a result of an official error on the part of HMRC or its predecessor bodies where the employer or his agent did not cause or materially contribute to the mistake or omission (SI 2001/1004, Sch 4, para 20).

Interest on Class 4 and 2 contributions

5.38 With effect from 19 April 1993, Class 4 contributions collected by assessment may attract an interest charge under TMA 1970, s 86. Prior to that date interest could only be charged in accordance with the former s 88, where an assessment was made for the purpose of making good to the Crown a loss of tax wholly or partly attributable to a failure or an error on the part of the taxpayer (SSCBA 1992, Sch 2, para 6).

5.39 The Social Security Act 1998 amends SSCBA 1992, Sch 2, para 6 so that references to TMA 1970, s 88 in that section are repealed (SSCBA 1992, Sch 2, para 6(1) as repealed by Social Security Act 1998, s 59).

5.40 Interest is not chargeable in respect of Class 2 contributions that are paid late, although a 'penalty rate' currently applies instead. This ensures that where payment is made later than one tax year after the end of the year to which the contributions relate they may be charged at the highest rate in force from the time payment was due to the time it was made (inclusive).

APPEALS

5.41 Until April 1999 there was, in the Social Security Acts, no provision for appeals in connection with contribution matters and the appellate bodies which operate in connection with state benefits had no jurisdiction so far as the contribution side of the state scheme is concerned. Although, there was *effectively* an appeal procedure in connection with contributions it was not widely known or understood and entailed asking a 'Question' of the Secretary of State for Social Security, who then determined the matter in a quasi-judicial capacity. A decision of the Secretary of State in favour of a contributor or employer could not be further appealed by the authorities, but an employer or contributor could appeal against a decision unsatisfactory to them although only to the High Court (and no further) and only on a point of law (see paras **5.103–5.110**).

5.42 However, with the transfer of the former Contributions Agency to the then Inland Revenue with effect from 1 April 1999 and the transfer of Contributions Policy functions from DSS to the Treasury from the same date, the opportunity was taken to modernise the appeals system, such as it was. It is now brought almost entirely into line with those procedures encountered in dealing with most other imposts for which what is now HMRC is responsible.

5.43 The fact that there remain some small differences, and the previous absence of a formal appeal system in relation to contributions, is explained by the fact that the Social Security Acts (unlike the Taxes Acts) make no provision for formal assessments of their levies – other than Class 4 contributions, appeals against which have always been heard by the Tax Commissioners. The liability is either self-assessed at a fixed rate or employer-assessed by reference to earnings paid (eg Class 1 contributions) or to company cars, fuel and – from 6 April 2000 – other taxable benefits made available to employees (ie Class 1A contributions) or, from 6 April 1999, in respect of minor payments made to employees (ie Class 1B contributions).

5.44 The current system has operated from 1 April 1999 and is largely regulated by Social Security Contributions (Transfer of Functions, etc) Act 1999 (SSCTA 1999) and Social Security Contributions (Decisions and Appeals) Regulations 1999 (SI 1999/1027). In due course – probably from April 2009 – the procedures outlined in the remainder of this chapter will be replaced once the Tribunals, Courts and Enforcement Act 2007 comes into force. However, changes to appeals in respect of social security matters (which will include Home Responsibilities Protection and contracting out matters) are likely to be made in late 2008.

Decisions of Officers of HMRC

5.45 Where a contributor or his employer is faced with a demand for payment that is considered to be wrong or excessive, the matter will first be considered informally. If the dispute cannot be resolved in this way, it will then be for an Officer of HMRC to issue a formal 'decision' under SSCTA 1999, s 8.

5.46 The formal decision is then appealable in much the same way as an old style tax assessment or an amendment to a self-assessment.

The subject matter of a decision

5.47 An Officer may decide:

- whether a person is or was an earner and, if he is or was, in which category of earners he should be included;
- whether a person is or was employed in employed earner's employment for industrial injuries purposes (SSCBA 1992, Part V);
- whether a person is or was liable to pay any contributions of any class and the amount of the liability;
- whether a person is or was entitled to pay contributions, notwithstanding that there is no liability to pay, eg payment of voluntary contributions;
- whether contributions of a particular class have been paid for any period;
- on any issue in connection with Statutory Sick Pay, Statutory Maternity Pay, Statutory Paternity Pay or Statutory Adoption Pay;
- on matters concerning the issue or content of any notice under SSCBA 1999, s 121C (notices of company officer's personal liability for unpaid contributions);
- any issue arising under Jobseekers Act 1995, s 27 (Back To Work schemes for long-term unemployed);
- whether to give or withdraw approval for the transfer to the employee of the employer's Class 1 liability in respect of certain unapproved share options;
- whether a person is liable to a penalty and the amount;
- other issues as may be prescribed by regulations made by the Commissioners of HMRC.

(SSCTA 1999, s 8(1))

5.48 The third and fifth items above do not include decisions relating to Class 4 contributions which have, because they are invariably collected along with income tax, always been dealt with under tax appeal procedures (SSCTA 1999, s 8(2)).

5.49 The sixth item above does not extend to any decision as to the making of subordinate legislation since policy for Statutory Sick Pay and Statutory Maternity Pay remains with the Secretary of State for Work and Pensions (formerly the Secretary of State for Social Security), even though it is now administered by HMRC. Nor does it extend to any decision as to whether the liability to pay Statutory Sick Pay, Statutory Maternity Pay, Statutory Paternity Pay or Statutory Adoption Pay is that of HMRC or the employer. Likewise policy responsibility for Statutory Paternity Pay and Statutory Adoption Pay lies with the Secretary of State for Business, Enterprise and Regulatory Reform (SSCTA 1999, s 8(3)).

5.50 With regard to the final item in the above list, further matters have been prescribed (with effect from 8 October 2002 except where stated) as follows:

- whether a notice should be given under SI 2001/1004, reg 3(2B) and if so the terms of such notice;
- whether a notice given under SI 2001/1004, reg 3(2B) should cease to have effect;
- whether a direction should be given under SI 2001/1004, reg 31 and if so the terms of the direction;
- whether the condition in SI 2001/1004, reg 50(2) is satisfied;
- whether late applications under SI 2001/1004, reg 52(8), reg 54(3) or reg 55(3) for the refund of (respectively) contributions generally, Class 1 contributions paid at the wrong rate or Class 1A contributions should be admitted;
- whether, where a secondary contributor has failed to pay primary contributions that failure was with the consent or connivance of the primary contributor, as is mentioned in SI 2001/1004, reg 60;
- whether the condition in SI 2001/1004, reg 61(2) is satisfied;
- whether in the case of Class 2 contributions remaining unpaid at the due date, the reason for non-payment is the contributor's ignorance or error, and if so whether that is due to failure to exercise due care and diligence (SI 2001/1004, reg 65(2));
- whether the reason for non-payment of Class 3 within the prescribed period is the contributor's ignorance or error, and if so whether that is due to failure to exercise due care and diligence (SI 2001/1004, reg 65(3));
- whether the reason for non-payment of Class 3 within two years of the end of the year to which the contributions relate is the contributor's ignorance or error, and if so whether that is due to failure to exercise due care and diligence (SI 2001/1004, reg 65(4));

- whether a late application under SI 2001/1004, reg 110(3) for the return of a special Class 4 contribution should be admitted;
- whether a contribution (other than a Class 4 contribution) has been paid in error (SI 2001/1004, reg 52(1)(a));
- whether there has been a payment of contributions in excess of the amount specified in SI 2001/1004, reg 21 (SI 2001/1004, reg 52(1)(b));
- whether certain delays mentioned in the now superseded National Insurance (Contributions) Regulations 1969 are reasonable, etc;
- whether the delay in making payment of primary Class 1 contributions was neither with the consent or connivance of the primary contributor (Social Security (Crediting and Treatment of Contributions, and National Insurance Numbers) Regulations 2001, reg 5);
- whether in the case of a contribution paid after the due date, the failure was due to ignorance or error and not failure to exercise due care and diligence (Social Security (Crediting and Treatment of Contributions, and National Insurance Numbers) Regulations 2001, reg 6);
- from 6 August 2007, whether the circumstances are such that the managed service company provisions apply.

5.51 The Board may make regulations with regard to the making of decisions and Officers may direct that he shall have the assistance of an 'expert' where it appears that a question of fact requires special expertise (SSCTA 1999, s 9(1)(2)). 'Expert' means a person appearing to the Officer of the Board to have knowledge or experience which would be relevant in determining the question of fact (SSCTA 1999, s 9(3)).

5.52 The Board may make regulations enabling decisions under s 8 to be varied or superseded (SSCTA 1999, s 10) and have done so.

5.53 A decision must be made to the best of the Officer's information and belief and must state:

- the name of every person in respect of whom it is made, and
- the date from which it has effect, or
- the period for which it has effect.

(Social Security Contributions (Decisions and Appeals) Regulations 1999, reg 3(1)).

5.54 An Officer may entrust responsibility for completing procedures to some other Officer, whether by means involving the use of a computer or not, including the responsibility for serving the notice on any person named in it (Social Security Contributions (Decisions and Appeals) Regulations 1999, reg 3(2)).

Giving notice of the decision

5.55 Notice of a decision must be given to every person named in it or, in the case of a decision relating to entitlement to Statutory Sick Pay, Statutory Maternity Pay, Statutory Paternity Pay or Statutory Adoption Pay to the employee and employer concerned (Social Security Contributions (Decisions and Appeals) Regulations 1999, reg 4(1)).

5.56 In the case of Class 1 contributions the notice will name the employer and each affected employee. Where the number of employees exceeds six HMRC will normally seek to agree a representative sample of employees with the employer or the agent and will name only those selected employees (as well as the employer) in the Notice. This is an extra-statutory arrangement, there being no legal basis for the selection of six employees as the number beyond which not to look at each case individually.

5.57 In *Westek v HMRC Commissioners* (Sp C 629), a notice of decision sent to the employer had merely referred to 'earnings of employees' without naming the employees in question. W, inter alia, challenged the validity of the notices. The Special Commissioner upheld the view of HMRC that the decisions had been made under Social Security Contributions (Transfer of Functions, etc) Act 1999, s 8(1)(c) and it was only the employer that in the first instance was liable to pay both the primary and the secondary contributions. Accordingly, the notice needed only to name, as it did, the employer and it was therefore only the employer who had to be sent a copy of the decision notice (Social Security Contributions (Decisions and Appeals) Regs 1999, reg 4). In 1999 the then Inland Revenue had stated that the affected employees would always be named in notices of decision. Following Sp C 629 in 2007 it must therefore be expected that this policy will no longer be followed consistently.

5.58 Where the dispute relates to Class 1A contributions only the employer is affected as no employee's contribution arises. However, whilst there is therefore no obligation on the part of HMRC to name employees in the notice, it will usually do so where the decision concerns the provision of particular benefits. Similar procedures apply, as far as possible, in the case of disputed Class 1B liability.

5.59 In the case of Class 2, Class 3 or Class 4 decisions (the latter relating only to cases where Class 4 is not collected through the self-assessment tax return, eg deferment cases), there will invariably be only one person named in the notice.

5.60 The notice must state the date on which it is issued and may be served by post addressed to any person at his usual or last known place of residence or his place of business or employment. Notice to a company may be addressed to its registered office or its principal place of business (Social Security Contributions (Decisions and Appeals) Regulations 1999, reg 4(2)(3)).

5.61 A decision may be varied by an Officer if he has reason to believe that it was incorrect at the time it was made. Notice of such variation must be given to the same persons and in the same manner as the original decision (Social Security Contributions (Decisions and Appeals) Regulations 1999, reg 5(1)(2)).

5.62 If a decision is under appeal, it may be varied at any time before the Tax Commissioners determine the appeal (Social Security Contributions (Decisions and Appeals) Regulations 1999, reg 5(4)).

5.63 A decision may be made superseding an earlier decision, including a varied decision, which has become inappropriate *for any reason*. A superseding decision will have effect from the date of the change in circumstances which rendered the previous decision (or varied decision) inappropriate. The previous decision ceases to have effect immediately the superseding decision comes into effect (Social Security Contributions (Decisions and Appeals) Regulations 1999, reg 6(1)(2)).

5.64 Decisions are issued on Form DAA1 (A) which tells the recipient to let their professional advisor or agent, if they have one, see it. Copies will be issued direct to agents, if acting. Where copies are sent to more than one person, the notes on the face of the notice will be varied on each copy to reflect the differing effects of the decision on different categories of people affected, eg where copies are sent to employers and one or more employees. The Notice of Decision also includes a payslip for making payment of the National Insurance contributions in question and will be sent with a letter of explanation which will, in practice, usually be a summary of what has been established in previous correspondence. A guide, DAA2 'A Guide to Your Notice of Decision' will also be sent to every recipient.

Appeals against Officer's decisions

5.65 Any person named in a notice of decision has the right of appeal to the Tax Commissioners. The same right also extends to personal liability notices issued to company officers in respect of company contribution debts (SSCTA 1999, s 11(1)(2)(4); SSAA 1992, s 121D, as inserted by Social Security Act 1998, s 64).

Manner of making an appeal

5.66 An appeal must be made in writing within 30 days after the date on which the notice of decision was issued and must be made to the Officer who gave notice of the decision. The Guide DAA2, sent with every notice of decision, contains a tear-off appeal form (DAA3) which may be used, but an appeal made in any format – provided it is in writing and made within the specified 30 days – is legally valid (SSCTA 1999, s 12(1)(2)).

5.67 The notice of appeal must specify the grounds of appeal, but on hearing by the Commissioners they may allow additional grounds, not stated in the notice of appeal, to be put forward if satisfied that the omission was neither wilful nor unreasonable (SSCTA 1999, s 12(3)).

5.68 By law, appeals will be heard by the General Commissioners unless the appellant elects under TMA 1970, s 46(1), at the time of making the appeal, that the hearing shall be before the Special Commissioners. TMA 1970, s 31(5A) to (5E) have effect in relation to such an election (SSCTA 1999, s 12(4)(5)).

5.69 Appeals against notices issued under SSAA 1992, s 121C will always be heard by the Special Commissioners.

5.70 However, in practice, HMRC ensures that all NIC appeals (including those pertaining to Statutory Sick Pay, Statutory Maternity Pay, Statutory Paternity Pay and Statutory Adoption Pay) are heard by the Special Commissioners as the Inland Revenue, as it was then, decided in summer 2004 that all such appeals shall be automatically deemed to be 'complex'.

5.71 The Board have the power to make regulations, with the concurrence of the Lord Chancellor and the Lord Advocate, in respect of contributions, Statutory Sick Pay, Statutory Maternity Pay, Statutory Paternity Pay and Statutory Adoption Pay appeals and may also make regulations regarding matters arising pending a decision of an Officer under s 8, pending the determination by the tax appeal Commissioners, out of the variation of a decision or out of the superseding of a decision (SSCTA 1999, ss 13, 14).

Place of hearing of appeal

5.72 If, exceptionally, an appeal is heard by the General Commissioners it shall be heard in the division in which one of the following places, specified by election made by the appellant, is situated:

- the appellant's usual place of residence in the United Kingdom at the time the election is made;
- if any, the appellant's place of business in the United Kingdom at the time the election is made;

- if any, the appellant's place of employment in the United Kingdom at the time the election is made.

5.73 'Place of business' means the place where the trade, profession or vocation is carried on and, if it is carried on at more than one place, the head office or the place where it is mainly carried on.

5.74 The division covering the place of employment may be the subject of an election whether or not the subject matter of the appeal relates to matters connected with the employment (Social Security Contributions (Decisions and Appeals) Regulations 1999, reg 7(1), (2), (3), (8), (9)).

5.75 The election must be made at the time that the appeal against the decision of the Officer is made or else before such later date as the Board may allow and it is irrevocable (Social Security Contributions (Decisions and Appeals) Regulations 1999, reg 7(5)).

5.76 Where no election is made, or is not made in time, an Officer of the Board may make an election specifying one of the above three locations. If there is no such location, an Officer of the Board may give directions to determine a place for the appeal to be heard, but such direction does not have effect unless the Officer notifies the appellant of his direction (Social Security Contributions (Decisions and Appeals) Regulations 1999, reg 7(4), (6), (7)).

Multiple appeals

5.77 Where more than one appeal is made to the General Commissioners in respect of the same decision (eg both employer and employee, or more than one affected employee), all such appeals must be heard at the same time and, where none of the appellants has made an election concerning the division of the General Commissioners which is to hear the appeal, an Officer may give directions for determining the location (Social Security Contributions (Decisions and Appeals) Regulations 1999, reg 8(1), (2)).

5.78 Where more than one appeal has been made and, collectively, more than one location for hearing has been specified for the hearing, then any such election made by the employer shall be ignored – whether the appeal relates directly to contributions or to entitlement to Statutory Sick Pay, Statutory Maternity Pay, Statutory Paternity Pay or Statutory Adoption Pay (Social Security Contributions (Decisions and Appeals) Regulations 1999, reg 8(3), (4)).

5.79 If there then remains only one division which is the subject of an election, an Officer may direct that the General Commissioners for that division shall determine the division of General Commissioners that shall hear the appeal. In determining the matter, the Commissioners shall consider any representations made orally or in writing by any of the appellants (ie including the employer) (Social Security Contributions (Decisions and Appeals) Regulations 1999, reg 8(3), (5)).

5.80 If there is, however, more than one division which is the subject of an election, an Officer may give directions as to the division of General Commissioners which shall determine the division of General Commissioners that shall hear the appeal. In determining the matter, the Commissioners shall consider any representations made orally or in writing by any of the appellants (ie including the employer) (Social Security Contributions (Decisions and Appeals) Regulations 1999, reg 8(3), (6)).

5.81 If there is no election made by any appellant, an Officer may give directions for determining the division of General Commissioners that shall hear the appeal, taking into account factors which appear to him to be relevant (Social Security Contributions (Decisions and Appeals) Regulations 1999, reg 8(3), (7)).

5.82 No such directions as are mentioned above shall have effect in relation to any appeal unless the Officer serves on each appellant a notice stating the effect of the directions made (Social Security Contributions (Decisions and Appeals) Regulations 1999, reg 8(8)).

Late appeals

5.83 Late appeals may be admitted if the Officer of the Board is satisfied that there was a reasonable excuse for not bringing the appeal within the normal time limit, provided that application is made without undue delay thereafter (Social Security Contributions (Decisions and Appeals) Regulations 1999, reg 9, applying the provisions of TMA 1970, s 49).

Determination by Commissioners

5.84 A notice giving the time, date and place of hearing will be sent to the appellant(s) and any agent or professional advisor, normally at least 28 days before the hearing (Inland Revenue Tax Bulletin, June 1999, p 664).

5.85 The Commissioners may decide by a majority of those present at the hearing that the decision shall be varied in any manner or that it shall stand good. The Commissioners may examine the appellant on oath or affirmation or take other evidence (Social Security Contributions (Decisions and Appeals) Regulations 1999, reg 10).

Settling appeals by agreement

5.86 Appellants may, before an appeal is heard by the Tax Commissioners, come to an agreement with an Officer that the decision under appeal should be treated as:

– upheld without variation, or

– varied in a particular manner, or

– superseded by a further decision,

and the same consequences will then ensue as would have ensued if the Officer had made a decision in the same terms as that under appeal, had varied the decision or made a superseding decision, as the case may be. In any of these circumstances, all appeals against the original decision shall lapse and notice of the agreement must be given by the Officer to all persons named in the decision who did not appeal against it (Social Security Contributions (Decisions and Appeals) Regulations 1999, reg 11(1), (2), (3)).

5.87 If such an agreement is not made in writing it is necessary for the Officer to confirm by written notice to every appellant the fact that an agreement was come to and details of its terms (Social Security Contributions (Decisions and Appeals) Regulations 1999, reg 11(4)).

5.88 An appellant may, before an appeal is heard by the Tax Commissioners, notify the Officer and every other person named in the decision, either orally or in writing, that he does not wish to proceed with the appeal. Unless, within 30 days, any person to whom that notice is given indicates that he is unwilling that the appeal should be treated as withdrawn then the appellant, the Officer and every person named in the decision are treated as having reached an agreement that the decision should be upheld without variation (Social Security Contributions (Decisions and Appeals) Regulations 1999, reg 11(5)).

5.89 Where an appeal is to be settled by agreement in any manner mentioned above, the agreement may be made with any person acting on behalf of an appellant or any other person named in the decision and notices may be validly given to such persons (Social Security Contributions (Decisions and Appeals) Regulations 1999, reg 11(6)).

Dissatisfaction with Commissioners' determination

5.90 If HMRC, the appellant or another party to the proceedings think that the Commissioners' decision is wrong on a point of law, then the appeal can be taken further through the courts. At this stage, the contributions in dispute must, if that is not already the case, be paid. If the appellant is successful, the amount will be repaid. If the hearing is with regard to Statutory Sick Pay, Statutory Maternity Pay, Statutory Paternity Pay or Statutory Adoption Pay employers do not have to pay such amounts until the courts have settled the appeal.

5.91 In the case of a decision by the General Commissioners, within 30 days the Clerk to the Commissioners must be requested in writing to provide a case to be stated for the opinion of the High Court (the Court of Session in Scotland, or the Court of Appeal (Northern Ireland) in Northern Ireland). The statutory fee (currently £25) must be enclosed. The Clerk must prepare a draft within 56 days, and there is then 56 days from receipt to make representations, which must be copied to HMRC. HMRC may also make representations within the same period, which must be copied to the appellant, who then has a further 28 days to make further representations in response to those of HMRC. Any such further representations must again be copied to HMRC. The Commissioners then sign the case in its final form and send it to the appellant. If the case is to be taken further, it must be sent to the High Court, etc, within 30 days of receipt (and a copy sent to HMRC). This time limit cannot be extended.

5.92 Appeal from the High Court may be made to the Court of Appeal and then the House of Lords (Social Security Contributions (Decisions and Appeals) Regulations 1999, reg 12, applying the provisions of TMA 1970, s 56).

5.93 Where, as is usually the case, the Special Commissioners heard the appeal, they will issue a written decision. If the decision is to be contested, notice must be sent direct to the High Court within 56 days stating the grounds of appeal. Copies of the notice must be sent to HMRC and the Special Commissioners.

5.94 Appeal from the High Court may be made to the Court of Appeal and then the House of Lords. Alternatively, the case may be heard initially by the Court of Appeal, with the leave of the Court of Appeal (Social Security Contributions (Decisions and Appeals) Regulations 1999, reg 12, applying the provisions of TMA 1970, s 56A).

Decisions under the Pension Schemes Act 1993 and in respect of the award of credits, etc

5.95 An Officer is to make decisions in relation to questions referred to in Pension Schemes Act 1993, s 170(1) (SSCTA 1999, s 16(1)).

5.96 A dissatisfied party will not, however, appeal to the Tax Commissioners but has the right of appeal to the Appeals Service (which deals with State benefit disputes) (Social Security Act 1998, s 12, as amended by SSCTA 1999, s 16(6)).

5.97 The current benefit appeals route has three layers:

- appeal tribunal;
- Social Security Commissioners;
- Court of Appeal

(Social Security Act 1998, ss 12–18).

5.98 The same procedure applies in the case of appeals against decisions of Officers concerning the award of National Insurance credits or Home Responsibilities Protection. However, changes to these procedures are likely to be made before the end of 2008.

Class 4 appeals

5.99 Because Class 4 contributions are payable in accordance with assessments made under the Taxes Acts, the provisions of Taxes Management Act 1970, Pt V have always applied with necessary modifications in relation to such contributions as they apply in relation to income tax and this continues to be the case after 31 March 1999 (SSCBA 1992, s 15(1), (2), (5), Sch 8). The effect of this is that an appeal against any Class 4 assessment must be made in writing within 30 days of the issue of the notice of assessment, must state the grounds on which it is based and must be to the General Commissioners, unless the appellant elects for it to be taken before the Special Commissioners. An appeal may be brought out of time if there is a reasonable excuse for the delay. An appeal against the decision of the Commissioners may be made to the High Court by way of Stated Case on a point of law and thence to the Court of Appeal and the House of Lords (see, for example, *Martin v O'Sullivan* [1982] STC 416) (TMA 1970, ss 31(1), (4), (5), 49(1), 56).

5.100 Under 'self-assessment' from 6 April 1996, there will be few assessments issued now. However, in the case of a dispute, whether for income tax, Class 4 contributions or both, it will be necessary for HMRC, exceptionally, to issue an assessment in order to enable an appeal to be made by the taxpayer/contributor.

5.101 The only questions concerning Class 4 contributions which are excluded from this jurisdiction are:

(a) whether by regulations made under SSCBA 1992, s 17(1) a person is excepted from Class 4 liability or his liability is deferred; and/or

(b) whether he is liable for Class 4 contributions that may be collected directly by the NICO under SSCBA 1992, ss 17(3)–(6), 18.

5.102 These two matters previously fell within the Secretary of State's remit. However, from 1 April 1999, they become matters for a decision of an Officer of the Board under SSCTA 1999, s 8 and then, only by those means, will the matter now fall to be put before the Tax Commissioners.

Questions put to the Secretary of State before 1 April 1999

5.103 Where a person had made an application before 1 April 1999 for a question to be determined by what was then the Secretary of State for Social Security (renamed Secretary of State for Work and Pensions in summer 2001) but, as at that date, the question had not been determined, the matter is thereafter treated as being one for a decision of an Officer of HMRC (Social Security Contributions (Decisions and Appeals) Regulations 1999, reg 4).

5.104 It will now therefore be necessary in such cases for a formal decision to be issued under SSCTA 1999, s 8 so that an appeal may then be made, within 30 days, to the Tax Commissioners. Affected parties may feel aggrieved that delay by the DSS/CA/Secretary of State in dealing with the 'appeal' (such as it was) under the old system results in them now having to follow what is, in some respects at least, a less favourable route. Whilst the old system was little known and had fallen into disrepute, it had the advantage that the DSS/CA could not counter-appeal if the determination was in the contributor's favour. For cases dealt with by correspondence, rather than an oral hearing, it was also relatively inexpensive.

5.105 The then Inland Revenue issued, in May 1999, a temporary extra-statutory concession as regards interest on amounts of National Insurance contributions disputed by employers and others before 1 April 1999. Under the new arrangements, the disputed NIC and the interest on it need not currently be paid while an appeal to the General or Special Commissioners is pending (although the Transfer Act does enable regulations to be introduced to require payment before an appeal may be heard). But, if the liability is confirmed, interest runs under the usual rules, eg for Class 1, from 14 days after the end of the tax year to which the contributions relate.

5.106 The Secretary of State's Question procedure provided that interest did not accrue from, broadly, the time the dispute arose and the time the question 'was disposed of'. Where an application had been submitted before 1 April 1999 for a determination by the Secretary of State but no determination had been made by that time, then interest will, under the extra-statutory concession, continue to be remitted until 1 August 1999 or the date the s 8 decision is made – whichever is the later. If, before 1 April 1999, a contributor had advised the Contributions Agency that they disputed liability, but it had been agreed that no formal application would be made pending the outcome of a lead case, then interest will also be remitted until the later of 1 August 1999 and a s 8 decision on the individual case (not the lead case). Where a determination was made before 1 April 1999, but a Statement of Grounds (needed before making an appeal to the High Court) was requested but not received until after that date, then interest will be remitted until the later of 1 August 1999 or 14 days after the issue of the Statement of Grounds.

5.107 This ESC was said to apply to about 100 formal cases and about another 2,300 cases where the same points arose and it had been agreed with Contributions Agency before 1 April 1999 that the outcome would await the result of a lead case. It also affected about 40 cases where the Secretary of State had confirmed liability but the matter was likely to go to the High Court.

5.108 The former regulation 28D, which provided for the 'freezing' of interest under the pre-1 April regime has now been largely repealed, but the amended provision continues to provide for the remission of interest in cases of official error (Inland Revenue Press Release 100/133, 9 July 1999) (SI 2001/1004, Sch 4, para 20).

Publication of decisions

5.109 SI 1986/2218, reg 16(1) gave the Secretary of State the authority to publish decisions 'in such manner as he thinks fit'. A decision is specific to an individual's contribution position and, while it was binding on the CA, Benefits Agency, Social Security Commissioners, social security appeals tribunals and the courts, in respect of the person (or persons) named in the decision, it had no wider application. Between 1950 and 1958 'Selected Decisions of the Minister on Questions of Classification and Insurability' were published but are now out of print. Subsequently, the Secretary of State, for reasons of cost and confidentiality, chose not to publish them.

5.110 As with other types of cases, National Insurance appeals heard by the Special Commissioners are published – anonymised where appropriate.

Chapter 6

NIC investigation trigger points

Peter Arrowsmith FCA, National Insurance Consultant

INTRODUCTION

6.1 Over a number of years employer compliance officers have adopted a much higher profile and there is clear evidence that considerably more thought is going into deciding which employers will be selected for a visit or investigation. In very simple terms HM Revenue and Customs (HMRC) is making the best use of the resources it has for visiting duties and it is clearly seeking value for money. To help it achieve this aim it has sought help from accountancy firms and management consultants and, from the way in which it now conducts investigations, that was clearly money well spent.

6.2 Following the merger between the IR and Contributions Agency on 1 April 1999 inspections are now, almost without exception, made into both tax and NIC – including Statutory Sick Pay (SSP), Statutory Maternity Pay (SMP), Statutory Paternity Pay (SPP) and Statutory Adoption Pay (SAP) at the same time in a single visit. Another significant factor is the attitude of the current government where the perfectly legal use of legislation to avoid or reduce National Insurance contributions is regarded as evasion. With such a prevailing attitude many employers are likely to suffer an investigation which is not really justified. Such activity is now also affected by the application of the disclosure of tax avoidance schemes regime to any National Insurance contributions avoidance schemes that are not already reportable due to a tax saving too – the extension to National Insurance took effect from 1 May 2007.

6.3 There is no disputing that a certain amount of check visiting is necessary. The amount of public money involved makes this mandatory, although the number of employers visited (out of a total of around 1.2 million) was only around 18,000 in a recent year. However, with substantial staff reductions ordered by the government by the end of the decade the likelihood of visits must inevitably reduce. It can be expected, however, that penalties will be applied with ever-decreasing laxity and the review of HMRC's powers that took place during 2006 and 2007 also provides from April 2009 a harsher regime to encourage compliance without the need for too much human intervention (see Chapter 5).

6.4 Before looking at what can trigger a National Insurance investigation, it is worthwhile looking at the overall National Insurance funding position.

National Insurance funding

6.5 National Insurance contributions (NIC) are no longer cheap – the abolition of the employer's upper earnings limit in October 1985 and the extension of employee liability from April 2003 have seen to that. In the 2008/09 tax year HMRC expects to collect around £105 billion in NIC. This amount vies with VAT as the second largest source of government revenue after income tax. Of the money collected, nearly 96% comes in the shape of Class 1 contributions, ie from employees and employers. Estimated social security expenditure for 2008/09 is around £70 billion on the contributory benefits alone. There are in addition other benefits such as Income Support, Tax Credits and Child Benefit which are funded from general taxation. Even allowing for the fact that National Insurance contributions also make a contribution to the running of the National Health Service (around £22.3 billion in 2008/09) the National Insurance Fund has in recent years started to accumulate surpluses. By 5 April 2013 it is estimated that there will be a surplus of over £136 billion. Since the Government Actuary recommends a working balance of only one-sixth of annual benefit expenditure, this suggests that there is an excess surplus of over £120 billion – equivalent to a basic rate income tax reduction of over 10% a year for the lifetime of a parliament. It would seem that National Insurance rates are higher than they need to be!

6.6 The UK social security system is based on a pay-as-you-go principle – the contributions now being paid are used to fund the current payment of social security benefits. The money collected should be enough to cover HMRC's administrative costs and to pay all contributory benefits in the year. For a few years from 1985 the Government Actuary consistently underestimated the NIC yield mainly because earnings grew at a faster rate than expected. The result was an embarrassing surplus in the National Insurance Fund and one Government Minister actually described the Fund as being awash with money. In contrast, the twenty-first century surplus in the Fund appears to be a matter of pride for the government rather than embarrassment.

6.7 Furthermore, the current surplus continues to increase year on year despite the fact that for a number of years early in the millennium the retirement pension increased at a rate higher than inflation (and in some years higher than earnings – even though the government states that it cannot afford to restore until later in this Parliament the 'earnings link' that was abolished in the 1980s). In addition, National Insurance rates for employers were reduced (thus reducing the income into the National Insurance Fund) to counterbalance the imposition of the climate change levy and aggregates tax – yet the proceeds from these duties go to the Treasury, not the National Insurance Fund. But for these factors, the National Insurance Fund surplus would be even greater.

6.8 The most far-reaching measure, however, has been a change in the attitude of what is now HMRC. Employer compliance officers will no longer waste time visiting back-street garages or corner shops to confirm that the basic NIC rules are being complied with, but will visit large employers and investigate all aspects of social security going back as far as six years (as well as tax, of course). They will pay particular attention to those employers who have used structured NIC mitigation schemes and to those with an international exposure because that is where significant contributions are thought, often correctly, to be underpaid.

REASONS FOR INVESTIGATIONS

6.9 With virtually the whole social security system to police, employer compliance officers could realistically pop up anywhere and look at anything. In reality, however, there are a few specific instances where they are likely to show most interest.

6.10 As regards National Insurance contributions and related matters, they include:

- errors in an employee's end of year return;
- a complaint from an employee;
- a local HMRC initiative, though becoming less common since regionalisation;
- a national drive against a specific industry;
- a routine audit visit;
- an employer failing to reply to correspondence;
- a large employer;
- an employer with an international exposure.

End-of-year returns

6.11 Every employee who earns an amount equal to the National Insurance lower earnings limit in any week in a tax year must have submitted at the end of the year a P14 on his behalf. This is so even though no actual contributions may be payable – if earnings are below the earnings threshold – because it is earnings at or above the lower earnings limit that gives rise to benefit entitlement. That P14 is the only real contact the National Insurance Contributions Office (NICO) of HMRC has with most employees and it is not surprising that the form is subjected to a number of checks both immediately upon electronic submission and then at Newcastle using various computer routines which have been developed over the years. The very first check at Newcastle is to ensure that there is enough information to match the contributions paid against an individual's record on the NIRS2 computer system. Does the National Insurance number match with the identity details held for that number?

6.12 Where there is no match or a number is missing HMRC will attempt to trace the individual from the other information supplied. However, if it is a common name and no meaningful date of birth or address is supplied on the P14, then there is little chance of HMRC making a successful trace and they would have no option but to come back and ask further questions of the employer who submitted the P14. If there are too many enquiries for a single employer then that may be enough to trigger some form of investigation on the grounds that if an employer cannot be bothered getting numbers correct he is probably making other errors. Obtaining the correct National Insurance number is no longer an onerous task.

6.13 The former Contributions Agency identified that they were spending an inordinate amount of time sorting out missing numbers and so they introduced procedures to help employers. This includes extra information on form P46, the introduction of a separate enquiry form which can be sent to NICO and the ability to contact NICO by telephone. These various measures reduce the number of enquiries coming from Newcastle and employers should supply the additional information where it is easy to do so.

6.14 Once sufficient identity details have been established, then HMRC has two separate types of checks. The first concerns matching the contributions paid against those expected. For instance if contracted-out contributions have been paid and HMRC has no record of an individual joining a company pension scheme then questions will be asked. The same happens in reverse where they are expecting contracted-out, but they receive full-rate contributions. When did the individual leave the pension plan and how have his pension rights been secured are obvious questions that need to be answered.

6.15 It is this type of checking, called compatibility checking, which raises queries regarding individuals who have paid a lower rate of contribution and there is no evidence to support that level of contribution. Examples will include married women paying the reduced rate of contribution where no valid certificate is held, individuals paying the pensioners' rate when they have not yet reached state pension age and so on. Millions of enquiries are raised each year on this front and thousands of man-hours are wasted by the authorities. They are showing less and less patience with employers who make regular errors and to bring these employers into line a check visit of some sort is likely to be made.

6.16 The second type of checking is called ratio checking and this is a consideration of the financial aspects of the payments. For example, has the employer paid roughly 12–12.5% of the taxable pay by way of employer NIC? Except for a married woman paying the reduced rate, does the employer portion come out as more than the employee share? Do the total contributions exceed the employee contribution liability? If not there is likely to be something wrong. Has SSP been paid beyond a certain acceptable level? A similar sort of check is carried out for SMP although here it is much more difficult because there is no maximum rate payable for the first six weeks. Where the SMP paid looks excessive, however, or exceeds a certain amount NICO may very well ask an employer compliance officer to check the validity of the figures. Among other issues he will want to satisfy himself that any bonus payment used to calculate the entitlement has been treated properly.

6.17 Other checks carried out at Newcastle include an arithmetical check on the amounts on the individual P14 forms to ensure that the total agrees with that shown on the summary form P35. The checks will also confirm that the correct year's rates and limits have been used along with confirmation that the appropriate contributions have been paid on earnings that exceed the employee upper limit. A number of checks will be automatically included where electronic filing is undertaken. Where the data is not satisfactory the return(s) will be rejected. If correct and valid data is not resubmitted in time and/or electronically (if required), then standard penalties will be imposed.

Category X notations

6.18 One important area where employer compliance officers show an interest is in the area of Category X – the contribution category letter which signifies that no contributions are payable. This creates some difficulty for HMRC simply because they have no earnings or contributions on which to base their validation checks. The Newcastle computer is simply programmed to accept the validity of such entries, but it would be a bit of a nonsense for NICO to accept these returns without question. It would only be a matter of time before unscrupulous employers made fraudulent use of the X notation. In the past checking has been restricted to a sample of returns every few years, but the additional contribution yield from those checks has encouraged the authorities to instigate an annual check and so employers can now expect to see a considerable amount of activity on this front.

6.19 Because of this increased activity, employers should be aware of when it is in order to use Category X. The following uses will be accepted by employer compliance officers although they may well investigate the matter before giving approval:

- The employee is under age 16 at the time the payment of earnings is made. Employers should ensure that they have a record of when the employee reaches 16 so that liability begins with the correct payment.

- The earnings are below the relevant earnings limit. Care needs to be taken to ensure that the earnings fall below the lower earnings limit in each earnings period. Unless a company director (or other employee in respect of whom an annual earnings period has been imposed by a directive) is involved it is wrong to look at the total earnings at the end of the year and compare the amount paid with the annual limits. Another common mistake is the assumption that if an employee is given a weekly or monthly payment which is equal to the appropriate lower earnings limit then no NIC entries are required. This is incorrect because benefit entitlement starts at the lower earnings limit itself and not at a penny over it. This mistake is common where a spouse helps out in the family business and the wage/salary payments are made to make use of tax allowances.
- The only payment being made is a pension. Employer compliance officers are a bit wary of payments made in the form of pensions and are likely to want to satisfy themselves that the pension is genuine and not some other payment wrongly described. Special attention will also be paid where there are contributions into or benefits from unapproved pension arrangements.
- The employee is working temporarily in the UK and is paying contributions to another country's social security scheme. All will be well if the employee has come from a treaty or EC/EEA country and holds the appropriate certificate of coverage. Employers should check every so often to ensure that certificates have not expired and that the employment details quoted on the certificate have not changed in any material way.
- The employee has been sent from a non-treaty country by his overseas employer to work temporarily in the UK. In such instances there is no contribution liability for the first 52 weeks in the UK. To avoid difficulties employers should ensure that they have a workable system whereby they identify when the contribution liability begins.
- The employee has been sent to a treaty country and the appropriate certificate of coverage issued by the UK authorities has expired. If any earnings were still paid in the UK no contribution liability would arise.
- The employee is working abroad in a non-treaty country and has been out of the UK for more than 52 weeks.

6.20 Whilst the above circumstances are perfectly acceptable to HMRC, many employers continue to use Category X in other situations and so incur the wrath of an employer compliance officer when the matter finally comes up for investigation. The following are the more common examples of where employers incorrectly use Category X:

- no P14 entries are made where earnings are below the earnings threshold, even though they exceed the lower earnings limit;

- a non-working director, etc has some earnings in the form of fees or bonuses which reach or exceed the relevant limit;
- an employee from a non-treaty country has been in the UK for more than the exempt first 52 weeks;
- an employee from a treaty country holds a certificate of coverage which is either invalid or out of date;
- the earnings are thought to be exempt from NIC liability, eg paid via some avoidance scheme which is flawed. This is an area almost certain to provoke an investigation because officials believe that few avoidance schemes now work on account of the many changes to the exemptions in the Contributions Regulations.

6.21 Employers should not be surprised to hear that when an employer compliance officer investigates matters and finds something amiss he will not restrict his actions to recovery of outstanding contributions to the year in question. In fact employer compliance officers are likely to try to collect arrears for as far back as the particular circumstances have existed. Since the merger in 1999, requests for more than six years' arrears are now almost unheard of, but should still be resisted where they occur.

6.22 Although HMRC cannot be expected to issue any guidance on this matter, it would be reasonable for them to restrict the cases they select for investigation. There will always be times when the Category X notation is quite correct and allowance will have to be made for this. Employer compliance officers will not want to waste time investigating matters which are unlikely to throw up additional contributions. For instance, it is unlikely that employer compliance officers would want to look at cases where an employee is out of the UK or has been out of the country for part of the year. They are also unlikely to be very keen spending time looking at cases where the employee is dead or where it is likely that the payment could be some sort of occupational pension and the introduction of an internal age limit is probable with employer compliance officers not looking at cases where the employee is, say, 55 or over. A (P14) return with Category X contributions shown along with some other category of contributions would also be less likely to be examined on the reasoning that if an employer has shown at least one category letter in addition to Category X then he would seem to know what he is doing.

6.23 Investigation of Category X cases now features strongly in an employer compliance officer's regular routine work and any irregularities found in this area may well provoke a more detailed investigation.

Complaints from employees

6.24 From time to time complaints are received from employees alleging that:

- contributions are being deducted but not sent on to HMRC;
- too much is being deducted as employee contributions;
- the employee has to pay the employer's share;
- the individual is being made to work on a self-employed basis;
- the individual is not being paid the National Minimum Wage (NMW).

6.25 Whilst a single complaint will not be ignored it may not generate any activity other than a phone call or a letter to the employer, but it is reasonable to assume that a series of complaints will result in some sort of investigation. Such matters should never be taken lightly and steps should be taken to allay employee fears. Indeed, HMRC now actively solicits calls from 'people who have information relating to businesses or individuals that are not paying tax and/or National Insurance' on the Tax Evasion Hotline 0800 788 887.

6.26 Separate staff in HMRC deal with all NMW matters. However, these employees are now allowed freely to exchange information with colleagues in other sections of the organisation.

Regional initiatives

6.27 It is entirely up to regional HMRC managers to decide whether they want to set up any local investigations. For example, a specific industry may be based in a particular area and bad habits creep in particularly where one employer obtains a commercial advantage and others follow. It is not uncommon for employer compliance officers to be sent in to tidy up matters. It is also quite common for personal prejudices to creep in and perhaps public houses, market traders and mini-cab drivers are singled out for investigation. More often than not the purpose behind a local initiative is to check that employees at a specific location are not working and claiming benefits at the same time. If employees at a particular location are prone to defraud the Department for Work and Pensions (DWP), then some thought will be given to whether the employer has been in collusion with the employee.

National programme

6.28 It has long been recognised that employers with operations at many locations create problems for employer compliance officers. At one time, employer compliance officers usually had to remain in their specific geographical area and so the larger employers often slipped through the net. Nowadays teams of employer compliance officers from the Large Business Service will assume responsibility for visiting all the branches irrespective of where they are located.

6.29 Specific industries or employment groups will sometimes be targeted for some form of investigation and, when that happens, control will be exercised from some central point to ensure continuity of action and equity of treatment.

Routine visits

6.30 Employer compliance officers have a theoretical and underlying objective to visit every employer via a five-year rolling programme but, given the more sophisticated targeting arrangements now in place along with the quest for additional contributions combined with significant planned staff reductions, this programme invariably falls by the wayside. Employer compliance officers, however, will still be responsible for policing their own geographical area and can decide to make a visit whenever they deem it to be necessary. A surprise visit especially where the findings are publicised will often have the result of making many others fall into line and so the value of such visits should never be underestimated and equally, small employers should never assume that they are exempt from investigation.

Failing to reply to correspondence

6.31 Most of the sections that make up HMRC will have to write to employers from time to time. The most common reason for them getting in touch is that their records are not complete enough to allow a benefit claim to be decided (HMRC at NICO operates the NIRS2 computer on behalf of itself and DWP). Because a benefit claim is involved there is a fair degree of urgency, and if there is a delay in replying the papers are likely to be referred to an employer compliance officer to visit and collect what is needed. Such visits might then not be restricted to collecting purely what is needed, and a full check of the other National Insurance and perhaps tax issues may well be carried out. To avoid such an investigation is simple – reply quickly, but if that is not possible then tell the writer accordingly and indicate when a reply will be sent.

Large employers

6.32 As already mentioned above, large employers were historically left well alone simply because of the effort needed to carry out an investigation coupled with the fact that a number of different locations may be involved. The former Contributions Agency worked out that the bigger the employer the bigger the potential yield and so matters changed. Special teams of Inspectors began to work together to investigate these larger employers. This approach has continued since the merger, these special teams being subsumed at first into what was the Large Business Office and, since the merger with the former HM

Customs and Excise, has now become the Large Business Service dealing with all indirect taxes as well. The name of the game is additional contributions and as long as they are likely to be collected an investigation will continue. A large employer is generally one who has at least 1,000 employees either at a single location or spread all over the country. The employer compliance officers looking after the larger employers also have some responsibility for investigating the many structured National Insurance contribution avoidance schemes, irrespective of the size of the employer.

Employers with an international exposure

6.33 HMRC believes that employers who send employees abroad are significantly underpaying their National Insurance contributions and so in-depth investigations are likely to be carried out again by employer compliance officers from the Large Business Service. It is usually a simple task to identify the relevant employers because they need to hold certificates confirming the contribution position and they are only issued by a central point at NICO in Newcastle.

6.34 Employer compliance officers will want to satisfy themselves that where UK certificates are held contributions have been paid on the full remuneration package with particular emphasis placed on the various allowances linked to employment abroad, payments made at the foreign location and the local income tax position.

6.35 In summer 2003, a revised approach to handling enquiries in relation to inbound expatriates was outlined. HMRC recognises that enquiries are often easier if it has established a working relationship with the relevant in-house tax department or professional advisers. Given the complex issues that are usually involved, there will be situations where the apparent Exchequer risk means that HMRC may need to pursue enquiries that will have substantial compliance costs for the employer. They recognise, however, that:

- such enquiries often relate to individuals not familiar with the UK tax and NIC system;
- directors and employees on tax-neutralised packages can sometimes fail to understand the need for the UK tax authorities to make detailed enquiries into their financial affairs;
- there can be considerable compliance costs in retrieving documentation, especially from overseas.

6.36 The former Inland Revenue stated that it 'will be aware of these factors when handling … enquiries', and that these will increasingly be undertaken by specialist units. Such units will be able to develop greater expertise. However, some such enquiries will still be undertaken outside the specialist units. Where this is so, the section concerned may be Special Compliance Investigations (SCI). SCI will generally only undertake enquiries in relation to inward expatriates where there are additional features (such as suspected serious fraud, 'novel' avoidance or where SCI has a wider main interest). Both local area and also Large Business Service employer compliance teams will continue to carry out reviews of large employers and refer expatriate issues to the specialist units. The former may refer aspects relating to expatriates to specialist offices, such as the Centre for Non Residents (eg on residence and domicile issues).

Unlucky

6.37 Some employers may not have been selected for a visit but, nevertheless, an employer compliance officer appears. A good example of this happening is where it starts to rain and the employer compliance officer goes through the first doorway he sees. For this reason alone there is no room for complacency and all employers should keep in mind that a knock could come to their door at any time.

CONCLUSION

6.38 Despite the potential of up to 70,000 visits expected per year, in a recent year only 18,000 visits were conducted. Whether this number might yet revert to former levels remains to be seen but either way the arithmetic shows that there is less than a 1in 20 chance of any employer suffering an investigation and considerably less than that if staff resources remain constrained. These numbers, however, are not the real story and given that the smaller employers will generally be ignored the odds move quickly against larger employers.

6.39 Little can be done to avoid an investigation if an employer is deemed to be a large employer although it will usually be possible to delay the event. What employers should aim to do is keep a low profile by ensuring that their end-of-year returns are as complete and accurate as possible and that any enquiries from the authorities are dealt with as quickly as possible.

Chapter 7

Criminal investigations in relation to direct tax

Andrew S Watt, MAE, Managing Director, Tax Disputes and Investigations, Alvarez & Marsal Taxand UK LLP

BACKGROUND

7.1 Writing in his Association's journal in 1924 an Inspector of Taxes observed:

> 'The five or six years ending with 1920/21 will probably go down in our fiscal history as a period of maximum fraud and evasion. The weight of the tax burden in those years increased the temptation, the unavoidable relaxation of vigilance on the part of Inspectors and accountants under war conditions multiplied the opportunities, and as regards the methods of fraud the prevalence of abundant profits not needed as additional working capital, and therefore capable of being conveniently hidden away in secret hoards, greatly facilitated the practice of omitting transactions from trading books.'

7.2 It was in this climate that the Enquiry Branch – which became the Revenue's elite investigation unit – was set up to combat the evasion of excess profits duty which had been imposed to help fund the nation's efforts in the 1914–18 war.

7.3 Seventy years later the realisation that tax evasion was still rife despite the fact that rates of direct taxation were, and still are, at almost unprecedentedly low rates, persuaded the then Board of Inland Revenue (the Board) to carry out a major reconstruction of its head office investigative effort, the main focus of which effort had previously been the Enquiry Branch, Special Office and the Board's Investigation Office (BIO).

INVESTIGATION STATISTICS

7.4 Published statistics suggest that the scale of tax evasion has continued apparently unabated. The following table shows the yield from the Revenue's efforts to counter fraud and evasion as reported in the Board's annual reports.

Yield from counter evasion work (tax interest and penalties)

	2002 (£m)	**2003** (£m)	**2004** (£m)	**2005** (£m)	**2006** (£m)	**2007** (£m)
Network offices	1285.7	1333.0	1443.0	1571.8	1948.0	3094.5
Special Compliance Office	337.2	345.1	387.7	-	-	-
Special Civil Investigations	-	-	-	1035.0	1065.0	2618.0
Large Business Offices	1443.7	1763.0	1789.5	2368.5	2221.2	3194.9
International Division	196.6	285.9	335.0	-	-	-
Other Specialist Offices	445.1	570.0	627.7	258.4	422.9	259.7
	3708.3	4297.0	4582.9	5234.7(1)	5657.1	9167.1

Note: (1) For years 2005 onwards it is not possible to identify from the published figures the yield from International Business Tax and from some of the other specialist offices.

7.5 The overall increase in the yield over the period of at least 147% (probably greater, given that HMRC appear not to be reporting figures which were previously given) is symptomatic of non-compliance on a massive scale.

7.6 The yield from the Large Business Offices – now the Large Business Service – is surprising given that the offices deal with the tax affairs of some of the country's largest businesses from which one might reasonably have expected a higher standard of compliance.

7.7 The drive against serious tax fraud has produced a spectacular increase in yield over the period, admittedly from the enlarged department. That coupled with the fact that the yield:cost ration in Special Civil Investigations (SCI) in 2007 was 98:1 – by far the highest in the HMRC network – suggests that additional resources invested in this area would be amply justified.

7.8 It can, however, be seen from the criminal proceedings statistics (see para **7.9**) that despite the widespread evidence of serious fraud, the rate at which the Revenue have initiated prosecutions for false business accounts and tax returns, PAYE and subcontractor frauds has actually declined over recent years. With a view to speeding up the criminal investigation process, the Government gave the Revenue the power to require the production of documents under the authority of an order from a Circuit Judge (in England and Wales) (TMA 1970, s 20BA). Furthermore, following the report by Lord Grabiner QC entitled *The Informal Economy* published in March 2000, the Government introduced a new statutory offence of evading income tax. This is contained in FA 2000, s 144 which came into force on 1 January 2001. The new offence may be tried either summarily in the magistrates' court or on indictment in the Crown Court (and in the appropriate courts in Scotland and Northern Ireland). The new power was intended to facilitate joint prosecutions of those who defraud the Benefits Agency and the Inland Revenue at the same time, say for example, where wages are paid to employees 'cash in hand' to avoid income tax deductions and then suppressed in claims to income-related benefits. There were 193 successful prosecutions in 2005 of individuals who had infringed the Working Family Tax Credit provisions.

7.9 However, many will question whether this is the most appropriate use of Revenue investigative resources. The conclusions contained in the report of the House of Commons Committee of Public Accounts in December 2003 were particularly damning and are still relevant today:

> 'The Revenue should focus their work on making a reasonable estimate of the tax gap ie the difference between full and actual compliance with the tax rules so that they can judge the effort needed for a given reduction in losses.
>
> They should set a date for completing and publishing their revised compliance strategy including an explicit strategy for preventing, detecting, investigating and deterring fraud, and the performance measures by which they assess achievement.
>
> The low number of fraud investigations and prosecutions is not commensurate with the potential sums at stake in lost revenue …Investigation work on tax fraud appears to have reduced as work on tax credit fraud has increased, despite additional resources being provided.
>
> To date the results of work aimed at using the new offence of evading income tax, which is particularly relevant in tackling fraud in the shadow economy, have been limited.
>
> More prosecutions should also bring opportunities to make greater use of the confiscation and restraint powers to deprive fraudsters of the wider proceeds of their crime.
>
> The Revenue should also publicise their awareness of new forms of fraud and evasion schemes, as a deterrent to further use,……. drawing on the experience of their overseas counterparts such as the US Internal Revenue Service.'

Criminal proceedings (Number of persons convicted – acquittals shown in brackets)

	2000	2001	2002	2003	2004	2005
False accounts/returns	21(4)	14(4)	13(1)	6	9(1)	10(3)
False claims/deductions	1	–	–	1(4)	2(2)	7(2)
PAYE: false returns	4(1)	3	4	4	7	2
Sub-contractors exemption Certificate fraud	4(1)	10(1)	1(2)	–	–	2
Contrived liquidations	2	0(1)	3	–	1	–
Failure to notify chargeability	1(1)	–	–(1)	–	1	3
Tax credits	n/a	2	28	34(1)	56(1)	193(8)
Miscellaneous/ Grabiner	2(3)	3	–	5	8	26
Total	**35(10)**	**32(6)**	**49(4)**	**50(5)**	**84(4)**	**243(13)**

Note: From April 2005 HM Revenue & Customs ceased to be a prosecuting authority and statistics in the above form are no longer readily available from the Revenue and Customs Prosecutions Office. There are no figures available for 2005/06 – the first year of the merged Department. In 2006/07 there was a total of 206 prosecutions including 130 for Tax Credit fraud of which 13 resulted in acquittals. In 2007/08 there were 237 prosecutions including 125 relating to Tax Credits, 12 of which resulted in acquittals.

7.10 Although the number of prosecutions for false accounts and tax returns remained at a low level at least until 2004/05 – due in some measure it must be said to the time required to prepare a complex fraud case for criminal trial – there is some evidence in the total figures for 2007 and 2008 and in the increased yield from civil investigations of serious fraud, that the strictures by the Committee of Public Accounts have been taken to heart.

THE NEW REGIME

7.11 1 March 1995 became a landmark date in the history of the Revenue's efforts to counter serious tax fraud. On that date, the Enquiry Branch, Special Office and BIO ceased to exist as separate entities, thus completing the process of integration which had begun with the establishment of the Special Compliance Office (SCO) on 1 April 1992. The principal function of the BIO, until 1995, had been to police the proper operation of the subcontractor tax deduction scheme in the construction industry and the PAYE system run by all employers. In the press release announcing the changes, the Revenue expressed the hope that they would 'improve operational efficiency and give greater opportunity for team working'.

7.12 At the same time as these structural changes were put into effect, the SCO published new codes of practice (COPs). The first (COP 8) set out the basis on which investigations other than those involving suspected serious fraud were to be dealt with. The other (COP 9) governed the conduct of investigations involving serious fraud where it was likely that a monetary settlement would be appropriate, ie the Hansard procedure. There was no Revenue code of practice governing the working of cases for prosecution. These were subject to the codes of practice promulgated in accordance with the Police and Criminal Evidence Act 1984 s 66.

7.13 Following the merger of the Inland Revenue (IR) and HM Customs and Excise (C&E) in April 2005 to form HM Revenue and Customs (HMRC), it became obvious the Departments had been investigating serious tax fraud in diametrically different ways. From April 2002 C&E had been conducting VAT civil investigations under their 'new approach' without invoking the Police and Criminal Evidence Act 1984 (PACE) procedures and with the threat of prosecution only where false declarations were made. Conversely IR Hansard investigations had always carried the threat of prosecution for the original offence as well as for false disclosure. And since December 2003, as a result of the decision in the Court of Appeal in *Gill and Gill* 2003 STC 1229, such investigations had been conducted in accordance with PACE procedures. Clearly this difference in treatment was untenable given that VAT and direct tax investigators were working alongside each other. Accordingly, with effect from 1 September 2005, HMRC introduced a new Civil Investigation of Fraud (CIF) procedure. At the same time SCO was re-branded as Special Civil Investigations (SCI) and a new chain of CIF offices was established in various locations around the UK staffed in part by former SCI Officers. It is important to note that once a CIF investigation has been launched the taxpayer receives a written guarantee that there can be no criminal prosecution in respect of the original offence(s). However, the threat of prosecution still remains for the making of false statements in the course of the investigation. Local offices submit cases to the CIF teams for possible investigation where the tax at risk exceeds £75,000. Where the tax at risk exceeds £500,000 the case will be referred to SCI which also investigates using the CIF procedure.

As well as tackling complex evasion and marketed avoidance, SCI has from April 2008 become a Directorate in its own right and has assumed responsibility for –

- ensuring compliance with the National Minimum Wage
- labour providers
- VAT missing trader intra-community fraud
- inland protection duties taken over from the UK Border Agency (contraband smuggling and counterfeiting)
- policing the Tax Credit and Child Benefit systems

SCI is working closely with the Large Business Service and is proactively using insolvency intervention as a compliance tool including in some cases where a taxpayer refuses to cooperate with a CoP 9 investigation under CIF.

7.14 Over the years, other Revenue head office investigative units have been set up to attack the hydra of serious tax fraud and avoidance. These include the Special Trades Investigation Unit and the Special Investigations Section. Both of these units still exist but are not part of the SCI structure although they also apply the CIF procedure in some of their investigations.

7.15 Towards the middle of 2003, the Revenue launched the Offshore Arrangements Project. They acknowledged the legitimacy of many offshore arrangements, but claimed that there was evidence of their use as vehicles for avoidance and evasion. The launch document referred to the non-disclosure of beneficial shareholders and directors of offshore companies. It was said that companies in offshore centres controlled thousands of UK companies, whilst thousands more held minority shareholdings. In addition, a significant proportion of land and buildings in the UK was owned, or had been owned, by offshore companies.

7.16 As part of this initiative, the Revenue established the Offshore Fraud Projects Group (now disbanded), as part of what was then SCO Liverpool. This team compiled a database of UK residents with offshore bank accounts and British firms with offshore subsidiaries. Furthermore, enquiries were made of credit card companies using the power in TMA 1970, s 20(8A). This eventually culminated in HMRC serving notices on five major retail banks in the UK requiring them to provide details of customers – individual as well as corporate – with an address in the UK and a bank account offshore. In April 2007 HMRC launched the Offshore Disclosure Facility (ODF) which gave the opportunity for individuals and companies with undeclared offshore bank accounts to disclose the same and to pay the tax, interest and a 10% penalty. The time limit for making such disclosures expired in November 2007 and HMRC had until 30 April 2008 either to accept or reject the disclosures as made. Approximately 400,000 pieces of information were received from the 5 banks and some 60,000 disclosures were made under the ODF of which about 40% were from customers of banks other than those which had received disclosure notices. Without doubt the Criminal Investigation Directorate will have reviewed many of the cases reported by the banks in respect of which no disclosure has been made. As expected HMRC have moved against the customers of the next tier of the 500 or so banks which have an offshore connection and which trade in the UK.

7.17 Another interesting initiative has been the purchase by HMRC, from a former employee of a Liechtenstein bank, of a CD allegedly containing details of some 100 UK residents with bank accounts in Liechtenstein. If criminal prosecutions arise from this, it will be interesting to see whether the evidence taken from the CD will be admissible.

PROSECUTION POLICY

7.18 The Board of Inland Revenue's approach to prosecution was clearly stated in a paper entitled 'Prosecution Policy' published in September 1980 in which it was said:

> 'In the main … the Department deals with the tax evader not by prosecution but by money penalties graded according to the gravity of the offence … criminal prosecution for tax offences is undertaken only in a small minority of … the more serious cases of fraud.'

7.19 Underlying this policy of selectivity is a philosophy of deterrence. This was expressed in the same paper thus: '… to prosecute in some examples of all classes of tax fraud. This policy is essential because it is the possibility of prosecution which prevents the spread of tax fraud to unacceptable limits'. This ethos is still reflected in HMRC's approach to criminal investigations.

7.20 The Board of Inland Revenue's report for the year to 31 March 1999 reaffirmed the intention to continue the policy of selective prosecution. To date, challenges to this approach under the Human Rights Act, which became law in 1998, have been largely unsuccessful.

7.21 It is important to note that the offences which constitute tax evasion also constitute money laundering offences and this is dealt with in Chapter 8. Increasingly, HMRC are using the powers contained in the Criminal Justice Act 1988 to confiscate assets which are deemed to be the proceeds of criminal conduct. In addition, the Proceeds of Crime Act 2002 introduced radical new powers to deprive criminals of their assets.

7.22 While HMRC is responsible for investigating suspected criminality in relation to tax, the decision as to whether or not to prosecute in England and Wales is made by the Revenue and Customs Prosecutions Office (RCPO) established in 2005. In Northern Ireland this function is fulfilled by the Public Prosecution Service for Northern Ireland and in Scotland by the Crown Office and the Procurator Fiscal Service.

7.23 The RCPO is an independent government department and is answerable to the Attorney General. It was established in the wake of two judicial reports – Gower Hammond and Butterfield – both of which were critical of certain aspects of C&E's handling of its prosecution role. It has about 250 staff based in London and Manchester. RCPO determines which of the cases referred to it by HMRC should proceed to prosecution by applying the tests set out in the Code for Crown prosecutors.

FACTORS SUGGESTING THE LIKELIHOOD OF CRIMINAL INVESTIGATION

7.24 Beginning with their evidence in 1983 to the Committee on enforcement powers of the Revenue Departments (the Keith committee) HMRC have set out the indices of serious fraud regarded as heinous, the presence of any one of which in a case would make the possibility of prosecution more likely. These have been altered and modified over the years as the threats to the tax gathering system have changed. As an example, in recent years, significant losses were sustained as a result of massive frauds on the Tax Credit system perpetrated by organised criminal gangs.

7.25 HMRC reserve the right to conduct a criminal investigation in *any* case and to carry out these investigations across a range of offences and in all the areas for which they have responsibility. When considering whether a case should be investigated under the Civil Investigation of Fraud (CIF) procedure or should be the subject of a criminal investigation, one important factor to be considered will be whether the taxpayer has made a complete and unprompted disclosure of the offences committed. Professional advisors should have this in mind at all times. Apart from prosecution considerations, an unprompted, voluntary disclosure will attract significant mitigation of any civil penalties.

7.26 Clearly, HMRC simply do not have the resources to investigate with a view to prosecution more than a miniscule proportion of serious tax fraudsters, and the following are examples of the sorts of circumstances which might lead HMRC to consider using the most potent weapon at their disposal:

- In cases of organised criminal gangs attacking the tax system or systematic frauds where losses represent a serious threat to the tax base, including conspiracy.
- Where an individual holds a position of trust or responsibility. Where the suspected offender is a professional tax adviser, eg an accountant or a solicitor HMRC take a particularly stringent view. A dishonest accountant is particularly reprehensible in HMRC's eyes, being a source of 'infection' who is likely to have assisted a number of clients in the commission of serious fraud. However, the Board will not necessarily prosecute all the advisor's clients who may have been involved in fraudulent activities along with their advisor. This principle was tested in an application for judicial review *R v IRC, ex parte Mead and Cook* 1992 STC 482. In its judgment, the High Court upheld the Board's right to be selective in prosecuting persons alleged to have committed serious fraud.

  Another case (unreported) which highlights the dangers of prosecution for professional advisers is *R v Charlton* (see Taxation 4 January 1996). One of the defendants convicted on two counts of cheating the Revenue, for which he served a term in prison, was a barrister who had advised a corporate client on tax avoidance arrangements involving operations in a low tax jurisdiction. In the case of *R v Chipping*, a United Kingdom solicitor and a Jersey resident accountant were convicted of conspiracy to cheat the public revenue and received custodial sentences.
- Where materially false statements are made or materially false documents are provided in the course of a civil investigation. It is this determination which underpins the CIF procedure introduced in Septem-

ber 2005. In 1987, the case of *R v Piggott* culminated in a former British champion jockey receiving a three-year term of imprisonment after pleading guilty to serious tax fraud charges. One of the aggravating features of the case had been that the defendant had undergone two previous tax investigations, at the conclusion of which he had signed false statements of assets.

- Where, pursuing an avoidance scheme, reliance is placed on a false or altered document or such reliance or material facts are misrepresented to enhance the credibility of a scheme. This underlines the fact that although an avoidance scheme would normally be pursued under Code of Practice 8 – 'Cases where serious fraud is not suspected' – HMRC will not be inhibited from changing tack and initiating a prosecution in appropriate circumstances.
- Where deliberate concealment, deception, conspiracy or corruption is suspected. The siphoning off of profits into an offshore bank account in a false name would be one such example.
- In cases involving the use of false or forged documents. Modern day technology has brought this particular fraud within easy reach of anyone with access to a computer and printer. The use of false invoices or the keeping of a second set of books is likely to lead HMRC to at least consider applying the ultimate sanction.
- In cases involving importation or exportation breaching prohibitions and restrictions.
- In cases involving money laundering with particular focus on advisors, accountants, solicitors and others acting in a professional capacity who provide the means to put tainted money out of reach of law enforcement.
- Where the perpetrator has committed previous offences or there is a repeated course of unlawful conduct or previous civil action.
- In cases involving theft, or the misuse or unlawful destruction of HMRC documents.
- Where there is evidence of assault on, or threats to, or the impersonation of HMRC officials.
- Where there is a link to suspected wider criminality, whether domestic or international, involving offences not under the administration of HMRC.

7.27 HMRC have made absolutely clear their unbending attitude to certain offences which they will almost always seek to prosecute rather than offer the CIF approach. These are:

- VAT missing trader intra-community (MTIC) fraud – generally involving the importation and onward sale of small high value components such as mobile phones and computer chips;
- VAT bogus registration repayment fraud;

– organised Tax Credit fraud.

THE ORGANISATION OF CRIMINAL INVESTIGATION IN HMRC

7.28 HMRC Criminal Division is split into four directorates:

- Criminal Investigation: responsible for the bulk of the Department's criminal investigations. Following the creation of HMRC, responsibility for dealing with drug trafficking and associated criminal finance and organised immigration crime, was transferred along with a large number of C&E investigators, to the Serious Organised Crime Agency.
- Internal governance: handles civil and criminal internal investigations.
- Detection: looks for individuals and organisations bent on criminal activity whether at the border or inland. Where appropriate, responsibility for investigation is passed over to the criminal investigation directorate, the Serious Organised Crime Agency or the police.
- Risk and intelligence: uses criminal investigation powers to develop cases and highlight areas of potential criminal activity.

7.29 The maintenance of professional standards of criminal investigation within HMRC rests with a separate directorate in HMRC – Criminal Justice and Enforcement Standards – which was established no doubt at least partly in response to the criticisms made in the Gower Hammond and Butterfield reports.

HMRC'S CRIMINAL INVESTIGATION POWERS

7.30 The creation of the new department in 2005 brought into sharp focus the disparity between the respective powers of the former IR and C&E criminal investigators. The latter had historically always had significantly greater powers than their counterparts and it is understandable that this situation could not be allowed to continue. Following an extensive consultation process, Finance Act 2007 enacted a number of amendments to the Police and Criminal Evidence Act 1984 (PACE) aligning the powers of criminal investigators across the department. These mainly affect the powers of HMRC investigators to:

- Apply for production orders requiring information to be produced. Revenue Investigators had previously relied solely on the Taxes Management Act 1970 (TMA), s 20BA which remains on the Statute Book. However, HMRC are now required to use Sch 1, para 4 of PACE 1984 if they require the production of 'special procedure material' (see later).

- Apply for search warrants. TMA, s 20C has been repealed and all HMRC investigators will now normally rely on s 8 or Sch 1, para 12 of PACE or in certain circumstances s 66 of the Serious Organised Crime and Police Act 2005 (SOCPA).
- Make arrests. HMRC investigators had previously relied on the presence of police officers to carry out this function on their behalf.
- Search suspects and premises following arrest.

7.31 In Northern Ireland these powers derive from the Police and Criminal Evidence (Northern Ireland) Order 1989 which has also been amended. PACE does not apply in Scotland but similar powers have been introduced for HMRC investigators there.

7.32 Cross-border powers contained in FA 2007 enable HMRC's criminal investigation powers to be exercised in all parts of the UK. Thus a search warrant issued by a court in Scotland can be exercised in England if it is endorsed by an English court and vice versa. It may be possible to prosecute an offence in more than one part of the UK and guidance will be issued explaining how the prosecuting authorities determine in which UK country an offence is prosecuted.

7.33 Considerable concern was expressed during the consultation process especially about the extension of arrest powers to former Revenue investigators. In response, measures to control the use of the new powers have been introduced. They can only be used by officers who are authorised to use them that is by officers of HMRC who have been appropriately trained and are engaged on operational duties in the various Directorates mentioned above. PACE stipulates that certain powers can be exercised only by police officers of a particular rank. These ranks are converted to HMRC grades of an equivalent authority:

Sergeant	Officer
Inspector	Higher Officer
Chief Inspector	Higher Officer
Superintendent	Senior Officer

7.34 HMRC has set internal authorisation levels requiring an authorised officer to obtain the approval of a higher graded officer before using certain powers. The police are the primary user of PACE powers and the authority levels within HMRC are no lower than those set in the police force. Indeed, for applications to a magistrate or a court for a production order or a search warrant, HMRC has set the main authority level at a minimum of Senior Officer Grade. By contrast most authorities within the police force are held at the equivalent of a Higher Officer in HMRC.

7.35 Officers serving in the Criminal Investigation Directorate are trained in areas which include:

- custody time limits and procedures;
- powers to search persons;
- Powers to search persons following arrest;
- Transporting prisoners;
- Safety training including personal safety and the use of handcuffs;
- Responsibility for disclosure under the Criminal Procedures and Investigation Act 1996.

7.36 Over one and a half thousand officers in the Criminal Investigation Directorate have powers of arrest which can only be exercised for HMRC offences.

7.37 HMRC investigators also have assistance and advice available from HMRC criminal lawyers who may be assigned to work on the larger investigations and who will also consult the prosecuting authorities at an early stage on major prosecutions.

The Criminal Taxes Unit is a multi-disciplinary group within the Criminal Division. It has been set up to tackle cases where wider criminality is suspected. It works in partnership with other law enforcement agencies to ensure that taxation is fully utilised as a weapon against crime.

SEARCH WARRANTS AND PRODUCTION ORDERS

7.38 The clearest possible signal of the Revenue's intentions to investigate with a view to prosecution is a dawn raid carried out under s 8, or Sch 1, para 12 of PACE, when the HMRC invoke their powers to enter premises, by force if necessary, to search the premises and 'seize and retain anything for which a search has been authorised' (s 8(2), Sch 1, para 13 and s 22) notwithstanding the fact that the thing found is not evidence of an offence which relates to a matter in relation to which HMRC have functions.

7.39 'Premises' includes any place and in particular:

- any vehicle, vessel, aircraft or hovercraft;
- any offshore installation;
- any renewable energy installation;
- any tent or moveable structure (s 23).

7.40 Where an officer of HMRC is conducting a search under the authority of a PACE warrant, he may also carry out a 'same sex search of any person found on the premises where he has reasonable cause to believe that person to be in possession of material likely to be of substantial value (by itself or together with other material) to the investigation of the offence'.

7.41 In the past it was almost certain that not only would the suspect taxpayer's home be raided, but also his business premises and quite probably the offices of his professional advisers – both accountants and lawyers. This was so even if neither set of advisers was suspected of wrongdoing, since the Revenue wish to obtain documentary evidence at as early a stage as possible. This approach has changed significantly now that HMRC have a production order power available to them.

7.42 In some respects the amendments to PACE introduced by ss 82–s 87 of the FA 2007and as applied by Statutory Instrument 2007 No. 3175 (The Police and Criminal Evidence Act 1984 (Application to Revenue and Customs) Order 2000) have made life more difficult for those HMRC criminal investigators accustomed to dealing with direct tax investigations.

7.43 TMA, s 20C has been repealed and in future it is likely that all HMRC search warrants will be authorised under either s 8 of PACE or Sch 1, para 12 of PACE (but see below regarding SOCPA).

7.44 To obtain a search warrant under the now defunct s 20C of TMA, HMRC had to persuade a Circuit Judge in E&W (a sheriff in Scotland or a County Court judge in Northern Ireland) that there was 'reasonable ground for *suspecting* that an offence involving serious fraud in connection with … tax is being, has been or is about to be committed'".

7.45 Now HMRC have to surmount a higher hurdle by convincing a Justice of the Peace (JP) that 'there are reasonable grounds for *believing* that an indictable offence has been committed' (s 8(1)). A similar more stringent threshold applies to an application to a Circuit Judge under sch 1, para 12. On the other hand, whereas an application for a search warrant under s 20C had to be approved by the Board of Inland Revenue – in practice the head of SCI – an application under s 8 or Sch 1 of PACE can, it appears, be approved at a much lower level. The applications for search warrants are made ex parte and must be supported by information in writing. Various safeguards, mainly relating to the identification of the premises to be searched, are set out in s 15. Note: actions preparatory to committing a tax offence are now no longer grounds applying for a warrant to raid premises.

7.46 Evidential material which is likely to be relevant, and of substantial value, to the investigation can be seized (s 8(i)(b)(c)). However, there is a protection for items subject to legal privilege, excluded material and special procedure material (s 8(i)(d)). The search warrant application has to specify that there are no reasonable grounds for believing that the material on the premises to be searched consists of or includes items subject to legal privilege, excluded material or special procedure material. The JP also has to be satisfied that either it is not practicable to communicate with any person entitled to grant access to the evidence or that entry to the premises will not be granted without a warrant or that the purpose of the search is likely to be seriously prejudiced unless HMRC can gain instant access (s 8(3)). Computerised information must be provided in a form which can be taken away and in which it is visible and legible or from which it can readily be produced in a visible and legible form (s 20).

7.47 The legal privilege protection applicable to both s 8 and Sch 1 search warrants is defined in s 10 and is worded in the same way as it was in s 20C.

7.48 'Excluded material' is defined in s 11(1) as personal records which a person has acquired or created in the course of trade business profession or other occupation or for the purpose of any paid or unpaid office and which he holds in confidence. Also included are human tissue and the like. Material of such a description would clearly include a patient's records held by a GP or psychiatrist.

7.49 Excluded material also includes a journalist's notes or information obtained from a confidential source and held in confidence or records other than documents.

7.50 'Special procedure material' is defined in s 14(2) as meaning material, other than material subject to legal privilege, acquired or created in the course of any trade, business, profession or other occupation and held subject to an express or implied undertaking that it is to be held in confidence or under a legal obligation of secrecy or restriction on disclosure. This would include business records held, say for instance, by an accountant on a client's behalf and an accountant's working papers. Also included is journalistic material other than the type of journalistic material which is classed as 'excluded material'.

7.51 Where a search is likely to uncover special procedure material which may be required as evidence, HMRC will have to obtain a warrant signed by a Circuit Judge under Sch 1, para 12. As with s 8, material subject to legal privilege cannot be seized under a Sch 1, para 12 warrant. On the other hand, under the Criminal Justice and Police Act 2001, Officers faced with large volumes of material during a search under ans 8 warrant, may take it from the premises to be sifted and examined elsewhere. Legally privileged, excluded or special procedure material seized under a s 8 warrant and which cannot be retained must be returned as soon as practicable. Similarly, legally privileged and excluded material seized under a Sch 1 warrant must also be returned.

7.52 It should be noted that an officer of HMRC may, without a warrant, enter and search any premises occupied or controlled by a person who is under arrest for any relevant indictable offence if he has reasonable grounds for suspecting that there is on the premises evidence, other than items subject to legal privilege, that relates to that offence, or to some other indictable offence which is connected with or similar to that offence (s 18).

7.53 Following a PACE raid, HMRC must supply a record of what was seized within a reasonable time of being so requested (s 21(1)(2)). Unless any investigation or criminal proceedings would be prejudiced, HMRC are also required to allow access under supervision to, and provide copies of, documents seized (s 21(3)–(8)).

7.54 The introduction in 2000 of a production order power in the form of s 20BA of TMA 1970 was intended, at least in part, to obviate thc need to execute a s 20C raid on a professional firm, such as a lawyer or an accountant, or on a bank that were not viewed as being implicated in criminal activity but speedy access to information held by them was required. At the same time as s 20BA was enacted, s 20C was amended to state that the Board should not authorise an application for a search warrant unless they believed a request for a production order would seriously prejudice an investigation. HMRC are now bound by a similar provision in PACE. If, for instance, access to an accountant's working papers is required, and an application for a production order might seriously prejudice the investigation, HMRC may apply to circuit judge under Sch 1, para 12 of PACE for a search warrant. The application must make it clear why HMRC believe a production order may seriously prejudice the investigation.

7.55 Where HMRC require access to 'special procedure material' such as an accountant's working papers or a solicitor's conveyancing files and they do not wish to invoke their search powers they can seek leave of a circuit judge to serve a production order under Sch 1, para 4. The costs – internal and external – in responding to such an order are recoverable (unlike the costs in dealing with a s 20BA order).

7.56 The target of such an order is entitled to be present at the hearing before the judge. The material must be produced to HMRC within seven days from the date of the order or such longer period as is specified in the order and, if it is stored in any electronic form, must be produced in a form in which it is visible and legible.

7.57 A para 4 production order may be served on a person – whether an individual, company or any one of the partners in a partnership – either by delivering it to, or by leaving it at, the proper address or by sending it by registered post or recorded delivery. The proper address for a company is the registered or principal office and for a partnership it is it is the principal office of the firm and in any other case it is the last known address of the person concerned.

7.58 Any person in receipt of a notice of an application for a para 4 production order must not conceal, destroy, alter or dispose of the material without the leave of a judge or written permission of HMRC until either the application is dismissed or an order made following the application has been complied with. Failure to comply with an order will be treated as contempt of the Crown Court.

7.59 Where HMRC require production of documents which are not special procedure material, they must continue to use s 20BA of TMA 1970. Such documents will be those which, although acquired or created in the course of business, are not held under a duty of confidentiality. Copy sales invoices would be such a document.

ORDER FOR THE DELIVERY OF DOCUMENTS UNDER TMA 1970, S 20BA

7.60 Following the changes introduced in FA 2007, HMRC may only use s 20BA if the Officer thinks that an application under Sch 1, para 4 would not succeed because the material required does not consist of, or include, special procedure material. Section 20BA and Sch 1AA give HMRC authority to order the production of documents: 'which may be required as evidence for the purpose of any proceedings in respect of an offence … involving serious fraud in connection with, or in relation to, tax' (TMA, s 20BA(1)(a)(b)).

7.61 The Order for the Delivery of Documents (Procedure) Regulations SI 2000/2875 contains procedural rules governing the application for a production order and the resolution of disputes as to legal privilege. Finally, Code of Practice 22 (COP 22) explains how the power should be used.

7.62 An order to produce documents has to be made by 'the appropriate judicial authority' (a circuit judge in England and Wales) the person against whom the order is sought must be given not less than five working days' notice before the hearing of the application (SI 2000/2875, reg 4(2)).

7.63 Exceptionally, the right of the target of an order to appear and be heard at the hearing of the application can be waived if the appropriate judicial authority is satisfied that this would seriously prejudice the investigation of the offence (TMA 1970, Sch1AA, para 3(1)). It is difficult to imagine the circumstances in which a production order would be served on a professional firm in relation to a client of that firm without there being a simultaneous raid on the client. However, there are additional safeguards to protect the security of HMRC's investigation in the form of an anti-'tipping-off' provision on similar lines to that contained in the money laundering legislation.

Complying with a section 20BA production order

7.64 A person who has been given notice of the Revenue's intention to apply for an order must not, on pain of proceedings for contempt of Court: 'disclose to any other person information or any other matter likely to prejudice the investigation of the offence to which the application relates' (Sch. 1AA, para 4(1)(b)).

7.65 It is not difficult to envisage the dangers for HMRC's investigation when they are engaged in the delicate process of compiling a case against an unknowing suspect, say, by obtaining information from banks.

On the other hand, where the intended recipient of a notice is a 'professional legal adviser' there is no let or hindrance on him 'disclosing any information or other matter' to a client or his representative in connection with the giving of legal advice to the client or to any other person in contemplation of, or in connection with, legal proceedings and for the purpose of those proceedings (Sch 1AA, para 4(2), (3)). A lawyer's rights in this connection seem to be crystal clear, but where does the accountant stand? Is he a 'professional legal adviser'? The view of SCI is that he is not, but if so, why does the legislation not refer to 'barrister, advocate or solicitor'? HMRC's view may be open to challenge.

7.66 It is most strongly suggested that an accountant who finds himself in this dilemma should at least liaise closely with the investigator in charge of the investigation and possibly seek legal guidance on his own account. As has been indicated earlier, it is the writer's view that HMRC will in all probability solve the problem by simultaneously raiding a client where his accountant is to be the recipient of a production order! Needless to say, any permission to disclose information does not apply to anything disclosed with a view to furthering a criminal purpose.

7.67 The legislation envisages that the person who has the documents required by HMRC in his power or possession will be given ten working days to comply with the order or 'such shorter or longer period as may be specified' (s 20BA(2)(b)). The time limits for giving notice of the intention to apply for an order and for the recipient to comply, run from the day of receipt at the 'proper address' (usually the last known place of residence, or business, or employment or a company's registered office) or, where that day is not a working day, from the next working day. There is also provision for such notices to be delivered 'by facsimile …or other similar means' (but only by agreement of the intended recipient (COP 22), in which case the notice is deemed to have been given when 'the text is received in legible form' (SI 2000/2875, reg 5(1), (2), (3)). Readers will instantly recognise the scope for challenges against the validity of HMRC's operation of these procedures.

7.68 The order must specify or describe the documents which are the subject of the application, which will hopefully limit the scope for the over-zealous investigator to embark on an over-speculative enquiry. The order must also describe the suspected offence – 'serious fraud in connection with, or in relation to, tax' will no doubt suffice – and must also name the person suspected of having committed the suspected offence. It is an offence, punishable at worst by two years' imprisonment and a fine, to falsify, conceal, destroy or otherwise dispose of (or permit the same to happen) any document required by an s 20BA order.

7.69 The statutory instrument, possibly anticipating the almost inevitable challenges, goes into fairly minute detail in setting down the procedures for complying with an order. For example, the order is complied with if the documents (originals – not photocopies) are delivered to the officer of the Board specified in the order, either by delivering them to him directly, or by leaving them marked for his attention at the address specified in the order. Should compliance within the time specified cause a problem, the target should not hesitate to agree an extension with HMRC. But, of course, do not wait until the time limit is about to expire or, even worse, has already expired, before asking for an extension. Where documents are sent by post, they will be treated, in the absence of evidence to the contrary, as having been produced on the second working day after first class posting and on the fourth working day if posted second class (reg 6(1), (2), (3)). One can imagine that a production order, particularly on a sole practitioner where the documents may already be in storage, could impose an almost intolerable strain on the business. Again, there must be a very real possibility of a challenge being mounted under the Human Rights legislation.

7.70 There are two sets of conditions one of which must be satisfied before a Sch 1 search warrant can be authorised. First, the application must be supported by a signed written authority from a Higher Officer of HMRC. The Circuit Judge must have reasonable grounds for believing either that:

- an indictable offence has been committed;
- there is material which consists of or includes special procedure material, and does not also include excluded material, on premises specified in the application or on premises controlled by a person specified in the application;
- the material is likely to be of substantial value (on its own or together with other material) to the investigation;
- the material is likely to be relevant evidence;
- other methods of obtaining the material have to have been tried without success or have not been tried because it appeared that they were bound to fail;
- it is in the public interest that the material should be produced or that access should be given to it, having regard both to the benefit which is likely to accrue to the investigation if the material is obtained and the circumstances under which the person in possession of the material holds it.

or that :

- there is material on the premises which consists of or includes excluded material or special procedure material and that a search warrant under legislation passed prior to PACE 1984 (eg the Custom and Excise Management Act 1979) would have been appropriate were it not for the fact that such legislation no longer has effect in relation to search warrants for excluded and special procedure material.

7.71 Where the judge is satisfied that either set of conditions is satisfied and that:

- it is not practicable to communicate with any person entitled to grant entry to the premises;
- it is practicable to communicate with a person entitled to grant entry to the premises but not with any person entitled to grant access to the material;
- the material includes excluded material in the form of medical records held subject to a statutory obligation of secrecy which would be breached by disclosure other than as a result of a search under a Sch 1 warrant;
- service of an application for a production order might seriously prejudice the investigation.

Or that:

- the second set of conditions is satisfied and that a production order under para 4 has not been complied with

he may issue a search warrant

7.72 The judge may not issue an 'all premises warrant' unless he is satisfied:

- that there are reasonable grounds for believing that it is necessary to search premises occupied or controlled by the person in question which are not specified in the application, as well as those which are, in order to find the material in question; and
- that it is not reasonably practicable to specify all the premises which that person occupies or controls which might need to be searched.

7.73 It is unlikely that the transition to PACE powers will lead to an increase on raids on professional firms. However, Sch 1 does not contain a prohibition on 'tipping off', as does s 20BA ,so it is just possible that HMRC will be less willing to rely on production orders if they have any fear that their investigation is in any danger of being prejudiced.

7.74 Code of Practice B of PACE gives extensive guidance to those using or intending to invoke the PACE search and production order powers and should also be consulted by those whose clients are subject to a raid or are, or are themselves, in receipt of a production order.

7.75 As was said earlier, most HMRC raids are likely to be conducted under PACE. However, SOCPA created a number of new powers of investigation including the power to force witnesses to answer questions or to provide documents or information. These powers are to be exercised by, amongst others, the Director of the RCPO, who may delegate these powers to a Revenue and Customs prosecutor who is any one of a number of senior officials and lawyers in HMRC.

7.76 Where someone has been served with a disclosure notice to produce documents under s 62 of SOCPA and has not complied, or it is not practicable to give a disclosure notice or the giving of a disclosure notice might seriously prejudice the investigation, a JP may issue a warrant to enter premises and seize documents (including computer discs) (SOCPA, s 66). Such a warrant may be applied for where the prosecutors 'suspect' (as for the repealed s 20C – not 'believe' as for s 8) that, for instance, the common law offence of cheating the public revenue has been committed. A very low threshold of loss of revenue of not less than £5,000 is stipulated – not quite the 'substantial financial gain' according to which 'serious fraud' was defined in s 20C.

7.77 However, it is understood that RCPO will in fact exercise its powers under SOCPA only in cases involving serious fraud, that is where the fraud has in fact resulted in substantial loss to the public revenue. The areas envisaged are Tax Credit and MTIC fraud. In other cases where HMRC have an existing power, PACE will almost certainly be applied.

7.78 As with other search powers, there is a protection for privileged material, but apparently none for excluded or special procedure material. Accordingly, a search warrant obtained under s 66 of SOCPA on application to a JP might cover, say, an accountant's working papers. To gain access to these by a search under Sch 1, PACE would require an application to a Circuit Judge.

DEALING WITH A DAWN RAID

7.79 The adviser's role on learning that his client is the object of a dawn raid is clear. First he must immediately arrange for professionals with adequate knowledge of the search provisions to stand by his client both at his home and at the business premises. Without a doubt the client, his family and, possibly to a lesser extent his staff, will be in a state of some fear and trepidation when faced with a determined search crew of HMRC investigators possibly accompanied by a uniformed police constable whose presence is intended to deter any breach of the peace. (The adviser must also bear in mind that his own business premises may be being raided at the same time although there is now less likelihood of this happening.)

7.80 Arrests will frequently be carried out at a very early stage of the raid process. If that happens, arrangements must be put in hand immediately for clients to be represented by a suitably qualified solicitor since HMRC will be looking to conduct interviews under caution as soon as practicable. Certain

Officers of HMRC have been authorised to carry out arrests and to search and detain the persons arrested. Offices of Revenue and Customs may be designated as being suitable to be used for the purpose of detaining arrested persons. However, Officers are not empowered to charge a person with an offence, to release a person on bail or to detain or fingerprint a person after he has been charged with an offence. The Commissioners of HMRC are required to keep records relating to detentions and charges and to include the information in their annual reports.

7.81 Needless to say, nothing should or can be done physically to impede the search. However, that does not mean that the warrant itself must not be scrutinised in minute detail to ensure that the search is being conducted strictly in accordance with the terms on which it has been issued. Section 16 stipulates several requirements in relation to the execution of PACE search warrants:

1 a warrant is valid for three months from the date of issue;

2 a warrant may be executed by any officer of HMRC;

3 entry and search must be at a reasonable hour unless the purpose of the search might be frustrated on entry at a reasonable hour. Criticism of the early morning raid was considered by the Keith Committee. One expert, in evidence to the Committee, maintained that the hours between 4 am and 7 am were the only hours when the hardened criminal could be guaranteed to be found at home. Thus the Revenue continues with their practice of commencing such raids in the early hours of the morning – usually 7am;

4 the warrant may authorise persons to accompany the investigator. Such persons have the same power as the Officer they are accompanying but they may exercise these powers only in the company, and under the supervision, of an Officer. The presence during a raid of unauthorised persons has been successfully challenged in judicial review proceedings;

5 if the warrant is an all premises warrant, premises which are not specified may not be entered or searched unless a senior Officer has given written authority nor may premises may be entered or searched for a second or subsequent time under a warrant which authorises multiple entries unless a senior officer has given written authority;

6 the Officer must identify himself to the occupier of the premises if he is present at the time the warrant is executed, and if not, to any other who is present, and provide him with a copy of the warrant;

7 if no person is present a copy of the warrant must be left in a prominent place;

8 a search may only be carried out to the extent required for the purpose for which the warrant was issued;

9 the Officer must endorse the warrant stating whether the articles sought were found and whether any articles were seized other than articles which were sought;

10 on completion of the search, an s 8 warrant has to be returned to the designated officer for the local justice area and a Sch 1, para 12 warrant, to the appropriate officer of the court;

11 a returned warrant must be kept for 12 months from its return during which time it must be available for inspection by the occupier of the premises entered and searched.

The award of costs of any application under Sch 1 and of anything done in pursuance of an order are entirely at the discretion of the judge granting the order. By contrast there is no provision for the award of costs of complying with an s 20BA order.

INTRUSIVE SURVEILLANCE

7.82 HMRC are empowered to apply for authority to use surveillance powers in the Regulation of Investigatory Powers Act 2000 and the Police Act 1997. These principally are:

– the interception of post and tele-communications;

– intrusive surveillance;

– property interference;

– covert human intelligence.

7.83 These powers can only be used when investigating serious crime and even then only with the approval of certain members of senior management within the highest levels in the Criminal Investigation Directorate. The Home Secretary has personally to approve the interception pf communications. And use of the power is overseen by the independent Interception of Communications Commissioner. The most intrusive surveillance has to be approved by the Office of Surveillance Commissioners which also reviews all other cases of intrusive surveillance.

LEGAL PRIVILEGE

7.84 Potentially one of the most difficult areas of the legislation relates to items which may be considered to be protected from disclosure by legal privilege and it is worth repeating the appropriate paragraph in its entirety-.Schedule 1AA, para 5 states:

> '(1) Section 20BA does not apply to items subject to legal privilege.
>
> (2) For this purpose "items subject to legal privilege" means –

(a) communications between a professional legal adviser and his client or any person representing his client made in connection with the giving of legal advice to his client;

(b) communications between a professional legal adviser and his client or any person representing his client or between such an adviser or his client or any such representative and any other person made in connection with or in contemplation of legal proceedings and for the purposes of such proceedings; and

(c) items enclosed with or referred to in such communications and made –

(i) in connection with the giving of legal advice; or

(ii)in connection with or in contemplation of legal proceedings and for the purposes of such proceedings, when they are in possession of a person who is entitled to possession of them.

(3) Items held with the intention of furthering a criminal purpose are not subject to legal privilege.'

The definition of legal privilege in s 10 of PACE is identical.

7.85 Readers will immediately note that, as far as production orders are concerned, the first arbiter as to whether or not a document is subject to legal privilege is the recipient of the notice himself. SI 2000/2875, reg 7(1)–(7) contains detailed provisions aimed at resolving disputes as to legal privilege which are far from being weighted in the Revenue's favour (in contrast to the legislation in the Criminal Justice and Police Act 2001 which will allow investigators – including HMRC – to remove, in the course of a raid and in certain circumstances, privileged material from the premises for sifting). It is likely that these regulations will also apply to disputes over legal privilege arising out of orders under PACE. Where a dispute arises in a production order case, the person in receipt of the order can apply to the appropriate judicial authority to resolve the dispute. The disputed documents must be lodged with the court at the same time. Naturally, HMRC will have the right to be present and be heard at the hearing of the application and costs may be awarded against HMRC except where the court holds that no document, or no part of a document, is subject to legal privilege.

7.86 There is an alternative and less formal means of resolving disputes as to privilege suggested in COP 22. This envisages an independent Counsel (or exceptionally a Revenue solicitor) considering the disputed documents in the light of the information previously seen by the Judge who granted the order, to enable him to give a considered view on the claim to privilege and thus to enable the Revenue to decide whether to challenge that claim.

INTERVIEWS

7.87 Not every prosecution, of course, is preceded by the drama of a dawn raid. Frequently HMRC will feel that they already have sufficient evidence indicating the commission of serious fraud. The source of this material could be a spin-off from another investigation, information and possibly documents provided by an informer and by potential witnesses, or quite possibly documents supplied by the taxpayer during the course of an investigation whether voluntarily or in response to a notice under s 20(1) or in obedience to a precept issued under reg 10 of SI 1994/1811 or 1812 by the Appeal Commissioners or by a third party such as a bank under s 20(3). New information-gathering powers contained in Finance Act 2008 will come into force in due course and s 20 TMA 1970 will be repealed

7.88 In such circumstances as these the Revenue's evidential jigsaw may be all but complete. All that is required to complete the final piece and guarantee the required standard of proof to convince a jury beyond reasonable doubt may be the evidence obtainable under caution from the suspect's own mouth. The letter from the Revenue inviting the taxpayer to an interview will make it clear that the taxpayer is to be cautioned and indeed will suggest that he or she may wish to be legally represented. Until 9 April 1995, the caution which investigators were required to administer in accordance with para 10 of the code of practice for the detention, treatment and questioning of persons issued under PACE read as follows:'You are not obliged to say anything but anything you do say may be taken down in writing and given in evidence'. Since that date as a result of a change brought in by the Criminal Justice and Public Order Act 1994, s 34, the caution now reads: 'You do not have to say anything. But it may harm your defence if you do not mention when questioned something which you later rely on in court. Anything you do say may be given in evidence'. At the same time, if the person cautioned is not under arrest, he must be told that this is the case, that he is not obliged to remain with the investigator and that he may obtain legal advice (if he is not already legally represented).

7.89 This shift in the balance towards the investigative authorities requires careful consideration by the taxpayer and his advisers who must by this time include a specialist criminal solicitor and quite possibly a barrister. Whereas under the old caution, the taxpayer was well advised to exercise his right to remain silent, the same cannot be said of the new regime. However, before submitting to interview, HMRC, who have probably already had many months prior to the meeting to examine documents and speak to witnesses and generally to formulate the case, should be asked to provide details of the questions which they want to be answered and copies of the documents which they wish to put to the taxpayer for comment during the course of the interview under caution.

THE TRIAL

7.90 The preparation for any serious fraud trial can take many months and indeed can run into years. In such cases charges will generally be:

1 the common law charge of cheating the Revenue;

2 offences under the Theft Acts;

3 forgery, perjury or conspiracy; or

4 fraudulent evasion of income tax.

5 making false statements dourin a CoP 9 investigation

7.91 All criminal cases begin in the Magistrates Court. Whether a criminal case ends up being transferred to the Crown Court depends upon the offence being charged and its level of seriousness. RCPO will serve bundles on the defendant incorporating documentary evidence upon which the prosecution intend to rely including statements from witnesses. These can run to many thousands of pages and can be, and indeed frequently are, added to right up to the commencement of the trial in the Crown Court. Managing these bundles is of crucial importance, and the option of scanning them on to a computer should be considered since this process can greatly facilitate the constant referral to those documents which is usually necessary and the transfer of documents between the defence team.

7.92 Any opportunity to attack HMRC's case must not be overlooked and the services of a forensic accountant will frequently be invaluable. All this requires close cooperation between accountants and lawyers, and the concept of the team surrounding and supporting the taxpayer cannot be over-emphasised.

7.93 The conclusion of the trial, whatever the outcome, is not the end of the matter. First, HMRC will seek to recover any tax lost as a result of the fraud (even if the taxpayer has been acquitted of any criminal offence). The Board's policy as regards penalties, is set out in SP2/88, and is:

1 to refrain from taking steps to recover civil money penalties on the basis of fraud in respect of an offence which has been before the criminal courts;

2 to seek appropriate civil money penalties in respect of any offence which has not been brought before the courts; and

3 to reserve the right to seek, where there are grounds to do so, a civil penalty in respect of negligence by a taxpayer who has been acquitted of criminal intent in respect of a prosecution for fraud.

7.94 Where a tax evader has been found guilty of fraud HMRC may seek, in accordance with the Proceeds of Crime Act 2002, to recover assets the value of which frequently exceeds the amount of tax lost. If that fails, civil recovery proceedings can be pursued under the same Act and as a last resort there is a form f taxation power available even if the source of the income is not known.

Chapter 8

The nexus between tax evasion and money laundering

Martyn Bridges, Partner, Bridges & Partners LLP, London

INTRODUCTION

8.1 The purpose of this chapter is to give an appreciation of the relationship between tax evasion and money laundering. It is a widely held view that the money laundering legislation exists solely to deal with those involved in drug trafficking, terrorism or other 'serious crimes'. It is fair to say that this view is now more commonly held outside the UK than within. Whilst the original money laundering legislation applied only to offences related to drug trafficking and terrorism, since 1 April 1994 the net has been widened considerably to include all criminal conduct.

8.2 This chapter does not consider the history of anti-money laundering legislation and addresses only the regime imposed by the Proceeds of Crime Act 2002 (PoCA) as amended and The Money Laundering Regulations 2007.

8.3 The structure of the chapter is as follows:

(a) A brief history of tax evasion – considers tax evasion and the 'untaxed' economy.

(b) The money laundering legislation – details its applicability to the proceeds of domestic and foreign tax evasion.

(c) The view of government – briefly considers how the government's view of the tax evasion and money laundering issue has developed.

(d) Guidance for financial intermediaries and professional advisers – considers some of the existing guidance available.

(e) Role of the fiscal authorities – considers how the money laundering legislation is being and may be used by the fiscal authorities in enhancing tax compliance and in prosecutions for tax related money laundering offences.

(f) The risk to intermediaries and professionals – considers some of the risks posed to intermediaries by the tax evasion/money laundering issue.

(g) Conclusion.

A BRIEF HISTORY OF TAX EVASION

8.4 Taxation has been a curse of the human race since at least early Roman times. It would be fairly safe to assume that tax avoidance and evasion were invented within hours of the first tax being introduced. Most people dislike paying tax and many, given the choice, would prefer to avoid (or evade) payment, in whole or in part.

8.5 To some extent, the amount of taxes avoided or evaded will fluctuate in line with the level of applied taxation. However, while it is fair to say that tax avoidance and evasion will increase over whatever may be regarded as the norm when tax rates are high, it is unlikely that the level will decrease dramatically when tax rates are low. It is human nature to avoid or evade taxation whenever the opportunity arises, no matter what the level of taxation.

The most significant fraud

8.6 Tax evasion is the most significant fraud. Without doubt, losses to government from tax evasion far exceed the combined losses from all other forms of economic crime. This is inherent in the fact that few criminals believe in paying tax on the profits of their criminal enterprises. Indeed, it is almost impossible for them to do so without disclosing the nature and extent of their illegal activities which may lead to the fiscal authority disclosing such criminal activity to other law enforcement organisations. This is all the more true given the enhanced legal gateways now available which permit the fiscal authorities to exchange information with law enforcement and the introduction of the Assets Recovery Agency. The English civil courts have long held that the profits of most illegal trading activities are chargeable to tax and the fact that they are obtained illegally does not afford any relief. Any moral dilemma which may have existed has long been dismissed as irrelevant. In this context remember Al Capone!

The 'untaxed' economy

8.7 The 'untaxed' economy (also known, inter alia, as the informal, hidden, parallel, shadow, black or underground economy) is usually a term which applies to the non-taxpaying community rather than those involved in other forms of economic crime such as commercial fraud and drug trafficking.

8.8 While, obviously, no precise figures are available, it is thought that in the US the untaxed economy is equivalent to between 8% and 10% of the gross domestic product (GDP). In Germany that figure exceeds 10%, and Italy, Greece, Portugal and Spain are thought to have untaxed economies amounting to around 30% of GDP. In Russia and other former eastern bloc countries, it is thought that the untaxed economy may amount to as much as 50% of GDP.

8.9 In the UK the untaxed economy is equivalent to between 8% and 12% of GDP, somewhat over £100 billion. In the unlikely event that the untaxed economy in the UK amounted to as little as 5% of national income, it is estimated that the loss in tax revenue would exceed £10 billion per annum. Of this the fiscal authorities recover only a fraction.

8.10 It is the author's view that the total amount of tax evaded or avoided in the UK is between £25 billion and £35 billion and, calculated at present-day values, the cumulative amount evaded or avoided over the last 20 years would exceed £500 billion. The distinction between tax evasion (which involves the proceeds of crime) and avoidance (which does not) is significant. Such niceties are outside the scope of this chapter. Clearly, even where the fiscal authorities have highly sophisticated investigative facilities, the amounts of money involved in tax evasion are astronomical; hence the earlier statement that tax evasion is the most significant fraud in fiscal terms.

Increased awareness

8.11 In the mid-1970s the UK Government began to realise the magnitude of these losses and commenced an extensive programme to increase the investigative powers available to the fiscal authorities and to encourage them to become far more aggressive and proactive than had hitherto been the case. The result was a dramatic and progressive increase in the amounts of additional revenue raised.

8.12 Over the same period the judiciary noticeably changed their attitude to tax evaders coming before the criminal courts. In the mid-1970s a tax evader convicted in the criminal courts could expect a reasonably small fine or, if he was extremely unlucky, a short custodial sentence. Attitudes have hardened and today prison sentences are usually imposed, together with a confiscation order in respect of the 'benefit' derived from the crime.

8.13 Given the current budget deficits of most developed economies, including the UK, and fears about the demographic time bomb, electronic commerce and globalisation, governments are looking to achieve greater fiscal efficiency. There are few votes in increased levels of direct taxation. Governments are seeking to extract the maximum amount possible from a diminishing tax base. Enhanced compliance methodologies and intelligence sources are actively sought out.

Why tax evasion is a crime

8.14 A widely held view is that tax evasion itself is not a 'real' crime, but represents no more than 'fair game' on the Exchequer. However, the UK criminal law has difficulty in recognising this philosophy and there is a wide range of potential criminal offences available under both statute and common law.

8.15 In the UK anyone who wilfully misstates the truth of their financial position while rendering information to the fiscal authorities for the purposes of assessing their taxable status commits a common law criminal offence of cheating the Revenue. The actions of a person who creates false records to understate the amount of tax which they owe, or who provides misleading documentation, can constitute false accounting. These offences do not apply solely to income tax and VAT; for example, failing to make proper returns for the purpose of evading National Insurance contributions is a similar criminal offence, while making false claims for state benefits or for the payment of Government subsidies can be an offence of obtaining property by deception. All these offences can be prosecuted and punished under common law or the Theft Act 1968, and all of them carry penalties of long prison terms and/or unlimited fines. In addition the courts can order the confiscation of the benefit obtained from the crime. The measure used to calculate the quantum of benefit is usually disproportionate and punitive.

8.16 In the Court of Appeal's judgment in *Regina v Allen* [1999] STC 846 (an appeal against a confiscation order relating to tax evasion), Laws LJ concluded:

> 'In short, the fact that the tax remains due does not mean that its evasion did not confer a pecuniary advantage … by his crime the appellant evaded payment of £4 million tax. That sum constituted the proceeds of the offence. On the agreed figures, as we have indicated, he had realisable assets of £3.1 million. The fact that he remained in law liable to pay the tax, the fact even, were it so, that the Revenue might later recover it, does not, in our judgment, yield the proposition that the proceeds of his crime were one penny less than the whole of the tax evaded.'

THE MONEY LAUNDERING LEGISLATION

European Union Directives

8.17 The first Directive of the Council of the European Community dated 10 June 1991 on the prevention of the use of the financial system for the purpose of money laundering provides the foundation for the domestic money laundering legislation of the Member States.

8.18 Nowhere in the Directive is the issue of tax evasion specifically exempted from the list of prohibited activities. Nowhere in the first Directive are the activities of those professionals who most usually give advice on fiscal matters excluded from the list of persons subject thereto. On the contrary, the Second and Third Directives focused attention specifically on the professions.

8.19 UK domestic legislation on money laundering is based on the European Directives and, again, nowhere is the issue of tax evasion specifically exempted from those activities which are prohibited. The latest (2005 and Third Directive) entered into force in the UK on 15 December 2007 with the implementation of the Money Laundering Regulations 2007 ('MLR').

8.20 As with the First and subsequent Directives, criminal activity means 'any kind of criminal involvement in the commission of a serious crime'. Certain serious offences are specified. Beyond this, Member States may designate any other offence as a criminal activity for the purposes of the Directives (ie the Directives set a minimum standard). In the UK legislation such as the Criminal Justice Act 1993 (CJA 1993) has long since been extended to cover the proceeds of all crime (including tax offences) and PoCA closes many legal loopholes which may have existed previously.

The Proceeds of Crime Act 2002

8.21 Part 7 of PoCA consolidates, replaces and expands the previous anti-money laundering legislation contained in CJA 1993 and other legislation. There are three specific offences of money laundering.

Section 327 – Concealing

8.22 A person commits an offence if he: conceals; disguises; converts; transfers or removes criminal property from England and Wales or from Scotland or from Northern Ireland.

Section 328 – Arrangements

8.23 A person commits an offence if he enters into or becomes concerned in an arrangement which he knows or suspects facilitates (by whatever means) the acquisition, retention, use or control of criminal property by or on behalf of another person.

Section 329 – Acquisition, use and possession

8.24 A person commits an offence if he: acquires uses or has possession of criminal property.

Section 340 – Interpretation

8.25 Criminal conduct is conduct which: constitutes an offence in any part of the UK; or would constitute an offence in any part of the UK if it occurred there.

8.26 Money laundering is an act which:

(a) constitutes an offence under ss 327, 328 or 329;

(b) constitutes an attempt, conspiracy or inducement to commit an offence specified in paragraph (a);

(c) constitutes aiding, abetting, counselling or procuring the commission of an offence specified in paragraph (a); or

(d) would constitute an offence specified in paragraph (a), (b) or (c) if done in the UK.

8.27 SOCCA define money laundering as follows: 'Money laundering is any action taken to conceal, arrange, use or possess the proceeds of any criminal conduct. Criminals try to launder "dirty money" in an attempt to make it look "clean" in order to be able to use the proceeds without detection and to put them beyond the reach of law enforcement *and taxation agencies*' emphasis added. (Source SOCA website 8 April 2008).

8.28 It should be noted that this primary legislation is drafted in extremely wide terms sufficient to embrace the conduct of the person involved in the criminal conduct himself; PoCA is not directed solely at intermediaries. Similarly, the primary legislation fails to provide any *de minimis* limit in relation to criminal property and applies to all criminal conduct no matter how petty.

8.29 In relation to the regulated sector as defined by the MLR, PoCA s 330 creates a criminal offence for any person within the scope of the MLR if they do not report their knowledge, suspicion or information which gives reasonable grounds for knowing or suspecting that another person is laundering the proceeds of any criminal conduct, where the information comes to them in the course of a business in the regulated sector.

8.30 The legislation embraces all criminal conduct (including summary offences) which constitutes an offence in the UK or elsewhere if the offence would be recognised in the UK. In relation to criminal conduct there is no exception in relation to tax evasion, which is capable of being charged in a multitude of ways under common or statute law.

8.31 Similarly, the long and learned debate concerning the identity of funds representing the proceeds of crime under previous legislation (ie whether the proceeds represented the profits or gains not declared for tax purposes or a lesser amount, namely the tax due thereon) is now put to rest completely by the new statutory definition of criminal property referred to above. Any earlier doubt concerning the point at which funds became the proceeds of crime (ie before or after a tax return or other false account or document was submitted to the Revenue) are potentially overcome by the new definition of money laundering referred to in PoCA, s 340(11) and, in particular, paragraphs (b) and (c) thereof. It remains necessary for the Crown to demonstrate that an act of alleged money laundering involved both criminal conduct and the proceeds of crime.

Foreign tax evasion

8.32 PoCA, s 340(2)(b) extends the money laundering legislation to funds derived from criminal conduct in foreign jurisdictions to the extent that such conduct would constitute an offence in any part of the UK had it occurred there.

8.33 Historically, some have questioned whether the money laundering legislation applies to the proceeds of foreign tax evasion that pass through the UK.

8.34 There is case law to support the general principle that UK courts will not enforce foreign revenue law (*Government of India v Taylor* [1955] AC 491). It was therefore suggested that to bring the proceeds of foreign tax evasion within the ambit of the money laundering legislation would violate this principle. In many cases, evading foreign tax will involve conduct which breaches the general criminal law as well as specific revenue law. Obvious examples are false accounting, conspiracy to defraud and obtaining a pecuniary advantage by deception.

8.35 The offence of widest application is likely to be false accounting under Theft Act 1968, s 17. If an offence of false accounting is committed in a foreign jurisdiction (albeit as part of a wider scheme to defraud the foreign fiscal authority) PoCA, s 340(2)(b) treats this as having occurred in the UK. Hence it would seem difficult to argue that ss 327, 328 or 329 do not apply.

8.36 It is important to note that the test laid down by s 340(2)(b) is whether the criminal conduct would constitute an offence if it had taken place in any part of the UK. There is no need to enquire into the workings of foreign tax systems to determine whether a client's actions may amount to a criminal offence in the foreign jurisdiction. The only question which needs to be addressed when considering the applicability of s 340(2)(b) is 'If the conduct had taken place in the UK, would it constitute a criminal offence?'.

8.37 The Criminal Justice (International Cooperation) Act 1990, s 4 – which originally related to drug trafficking offences – gives the Serious Fraud Office the power to investigate UK aspects of foreign tax offences and to assist foreign fiscal/prosecuting authorities in this regard. These powers have been used with substantial effect.

What constitutes knowledge or suspicion?

8.38 Under PoCA, it is an offence for those in the regulated sector to fail to report where, inter alia, they have reasonable grounds to suspect someone has committed a money laundering offence.

8.39 What would constitute the requisite degree of 'knowledge or suspicion' for these purposes given the new objective test imposed on the regulated sector? For example, is anecdotal evidence that the vast majority of a country's inhabitants routinely evade tax sufficient to sustain the argument that the individual should have 'known or suspected' that the foreign national seeking help with a transaction or advice was guilty of an offence? If the individual is aware of such anecdotal evidence, does this equate with 'knowledge or suspicion' based on the objective standard now imposed on the regulated sector. Certainly not; however, this may indicate a need for enhanced due diligence following the MLR, regulation 14.

THE VIEW OF THE GOVERNMENT

8.40 This section considers how the UK Government's view of the tax evasion and money laundering issue has developed over time.

Speech by Kenneth Clarke (Chancellor of the Exchequer), 5 October 1995

8.41 The link between money laundering and tax evasion was strengthened in a speech made by the Chancellor of Exchequer at the Commonwealth Finance Ministers' meeting held in Jamaica on 5 October 1995. In discussing the definition of criminal conduct, the Minister said:

> 'We must recognise that money laundering is associated with all types of crime – from fraud to extortion, arms smuggling to kidnapping. It is quite artificial to draw a distinction between drug related crimes and other crimes. In Britain we have responded to the shifting threat by passing legislation to cover the proceeds of all indictable offences. There is no moral difference between drug trafficking and other serious offences, and the risks from both are great, and this applies as much to fiscal offences as any other crime. All crimes

should mean all crimes. Who is the victim is irrelevant. Tax crimes make the law abiding suffer. It is they who make up the shortfall caused by those who cheat.'

Speech by Helen Liddell (Economic Secretary to the Treasury), 6 November 1997

8.42 Speaking at a conference on financial crime, the Minister said:

> 'There are international businessmen of intelligence and tact who require financial services. They trade in drugs, prostitutes and child pornography. They equip terrorists. They defraud the innocent or ill-informed. They bribe, forge and corrupt their way to greater market share.
>
> They have discovered that there are private bankers, brokers, accountants and other financial advisers who are comfortable providing services which help to obscure the relationship between the money and the man. But only if it is presented as "just a little problem with tax". They do not put their advisers in an awkward position by declaring the nature of their trade ... These people are money launderers and they sleep easy with the aid of their commissions and their self deception; just helping out with a little tax problem.
>
> Their laundering supplies the financial lifeblood of international organised crime and in my book (and in the eyes of the law and for that matter the Criminal Justice Act 1988) people who assist criminals are criminals.'

8.43 This view is fully supported by the present Government; indeed, since gaining power, they have both declared and demonstrated their intention to devote significant resources to tackling tax evasion. There is also evidence that this approach is gaining support in mainland Europe as governments seek to tackle their budget deficits.

G7 Initiative on Harmful Tax Competition, May 1998

8.44 Those who still doubt the Government's resolve to utilise the money laundering legislation to tackle tax evasion should consider the May 1998 G7 Initiative aimed at tackling the problem of harmful tax competition. As part of this UK-inspired Initiative, the G7 members (US, Japan, Germany, Italy, France, Canada and the UK) agreed that financial institutions should be required to report suspicions about the movement of criminal assets irrespective of whether the suspected criminality is tax related.

8.45 The Initiative also stated that the 'money laundering authorities' should be permitted to make information available to those investigating tax-related crimes domestically or overseas. In a speech given on 1 June 1998 to the Joint Meeting of Commonwealth Finance and Law Officials on Money Laundering, Helen Liddell stated:

> 'The [G7] Initiative is designed to ensure that financial institutions report suspicions of tax-related crime and that this information is shared both domestically and internationally. This work will begin to address the potential loophole which allows criminals to masquerade as tax-dodgers in order to avoid the reporting obligations of our money laundering systems.'

8.46 Whilst the G7 Initiative has no legislative force, many of its policy recommendations are implemented, and not solely in the member countries. In this instance, given the fact that the Initiative was inspired by the UK, the Government will seek to implement them.

8.47 The UK's immediate response was to announce the attachment of an officer from the Inland Revenue's Special Compliance Office (SCO now Special Civil Investigations (SCI)) to the Economic Crimes Unit of the National Criminal Intelligence Service (NCIS). NCIS (now SOCA) is the body responsible for analysing and allocating reports of suspected money laundering. SCO is responsible for investigating the most serious cases of tax evasion and avoidance; in appropriate cases, SCO will institute criminal proceedings. Customs and Excise have been represented at NCIS since the service was formed.

8.48 HM Treasury has acknowledged that the result of this will be that, for the first time, domestic and international intelligence on money laundering will flow to the Revenue. The assignment of a representative from a fiscal authority to the body which receives reports of suspected money laundering is likely to be mirrored in other countries.

8.49 Since UK banks are required to report suspicious transactions, and given that such reports are made to SOCA, a report is now also *effectively* made to HMRC (although HMRC do not see the reports themselves but rather a synopsis of material facts). Indeed, a report of a non-tax related suspicion which is dismissed by SOCA as not indicating 'traditional' criminality may now be investigated by HMRC if there is a suspicion of tax evasion.

8.50 Given the extant statutory 'information gateways', the HMRC officers at SOCA will also serve as a formal conduit for the delivery to other authorities of intelligence regarding possible fiscal offences. Certainly there are significant flows of intelligence within the EU and to or from Australia, Canada, New Zealand and the USA.

8.51 This is an enormously valuable source of information for the fiscal authorities. The traditional focus and expertise of SOCA has been predicated upon identifying evidence of drug trafficking and terrorist-related offences since this was the basis for the original money laundering legislation. There was little or no expertise at SOCA when it came to the detection and investigation of fiscal offences. However, this is no longer the case since, following the initial trial of one person on secondment from HMRC; the presence has been expanded considerably.

Foreign tax evasion

8.52 The following is an extract from Hansard, 12 July 1999, Vol 335, No. 121, Col 82:

> 'Mr Flight: "To ask the Chancellor of the Exchequer if he has agreed, with the relevant professionals, guidance on the conduct by corporate clients which they should regard as evidence of overseas tax evasion in cases where they are obliged to report suspicion thereof to the NICS [sic]".
>
> Reply given by Patricia Hewitt, Economic Secretary to the Treasury:
>
> "Under the Criminal Justice Act 1993, financial institutions should report to the National Criminal Intelligence Service all transactions which they suspect involve the proceeds of criminal conduct. This obligation is a central element of our defence against money laundering, and provides valuable intelligence in the fight against crime.
>
> The obligation applies equally to the proceeds of overseas offences (including overseas tax offences), where the conduct would have been criminal if it had occurred in the UK. 'Evidence' is not required; the obligation applies where there is knowledge or suspicion that the relevant conduct has occurred or is occurring." '

GUIDANCE FOR FINANCIAL INTERMEDIARIES AND PROFESSIONAL ADVISERS

Institute of Chartered Accountants in England and Wales

8.53 Section 7.3 of the ICAEW Members' Handbook relates to 'Professional Conduct in Relation to Taxation' and paras 2.43–2.48 specifically deal with 'Fiscal Offences and Money Laundering' as follows:

'Fiscal offences and money laundering

2.43 Where members become aware of tax irregularities, they should also bear in mind that under the money laundering legislation, fiscal offences can amount to money laundering.

2.44 Tax-related offences involve evasion and not avoidance and are not in a special category. Tax evasion is a crime, the proceeds of which have to be treated in exactly the same way as those from drug trafficking, terrorist activity, theft, fraud, etc. Offences may relate to direct tax such as income tax or corporation tax, or they may relate to indirect tax such as VAT. Whilst not all tax-related offences are indictable, most are, including frauds against the Revenue or Customs. (*Note: there can be no money laundering until there are proceeds of crime, in other words, in respect of tax evasion, until the tax has become due and has not been paid.*)

2.45 A member who has knowledge of or reasonable grounds for suspecting money laundering should consider whether he has an obligation to make a report to the appropriate authorities (the Money Laundering Reporting Officer in his organisation or the Serious Organised Crime Agency). (*Note: formerly reports were made to the National Criminal Intelligence Service; NCIS has been absorbed into SOCA.*)

2.46 Where a report has been made to SOCA, the client should not be informed where this would be considered tipping off under the terms of the Money Laundering legislation. (*Note: advice on tax matters to a client to persuade him to stop breaking the law by evading tax is not tipping off.*) Members should also note that a report made to NCIS is not a substitute for a proper disclosure to the tax authorities.

2.47 This is an important subject and can involve the member in criminal penalties. There have been recent changes in EU and UK law. Members should familiarise themselves with the required rules and procedures in Part 7 of POCA 2002 and the Money Laundering Regulations 2003 (SI 2003/3075) (*Note: both as amended, for example, with effect from 21st February 2006, s. 330(6) POCA 2002 was amended by The Proceeds of Crime Act 2002 and Money Laundering Regulations 2003 (Amendment) Order 2006 (SI 2006/308) to extend exemption from reporting knowledge or suspicion of money laundering formed in privileged circumstances to a new but limited category of 'other relevant professional advisers' – see TECH 2/06 at* http://www.icaew.co.uk/index.cfm?route=125055) and should read carefully the current professional guidance on the avoidance, recognition and reporting of money laundering (see Section 7.2 'Anti-money

> laundering (Proceeds of Crime and Terrorism): second interim guidance for accountants' at www.icaew.co.uk/membershandbook (currently being updated) and CCAB and ICAEW Advisory Service and Tax Faculty guidance at www.icaew.co.uk/moneylaundering). Members who are in any doubt about their responsibilities in this area should seek appropriate advice (for example from the Institute's money laundering helpline).
>
> **Members in employment**
> **2.48** Whilst these guidelines are addressed primarily to members in practice, they apply equally to members employed in professional practice and in business. Additional assistance for such members will be found in Section 7.1 'Professional conduct and disclosure in relation to defaults and unlawful acts'; see www.icaew.co.uk/membershandbook/.'

Reference to these paragraphs is made in the section dealing with 'Acquiring Knowledge of Direct Tax Irregularities' at para **4.7**, and para **5.22** in the section dealing with 'Inland Revenue Errors' and at para **8.6** in the section dealing with 'Acquiring Knowledge of VAT Errors and Irregularities'.

8.54 Members who are in any doubt about their responsibilities in this area should seek appropriate advice (for example from the Institute's money laundering helpline). Members seeking guidance from their professional body should note that the professional body as a Supervisory Authority under the MLR may be obliged to make a report to SOCA independently of the member himself. Professional advisers may be concerned that a report to SOCA may breach their duty of confidentiality and result in civil proceedings being instigated by their client (or former client!). For example, it is possible to imagine a situation where a report to SOCA leads to bank accounts being frozen causing significant losses to the client. Should the original suspicions prove to be ill-founded; the client may feel understandably aggrieved and may seek legal redress although there are a number of authorities which indicate a claim is unlikely to succeed.

8.55 PoCA, s 337 on protected disclosures exempts a person who receives information in the course of his trade, profession, business or employment from any legal or other obligations (ie professional) that would otherwise prevent him from making disclosures to the authorities. There are however three conditions:

(1) that the information came to the attention of the discloser in the course of his trade, profession, business or employment;

(2) that the information:

  (a) causes the discloser to know or suspect; or

(b) gives him reasonable grounds for knowing or suspecting, that another person is engaged in money laundering; and

(c) the disclosure was made as soon as is practicable after the information comes to the discloser.

8.56 The disclosure must be made in good faith and as soon as practicable. It is possible that illconsidered disclosures would not be protected from suit. The potential for civil litigation must not be overlooked; for example, there may be exposure to claims predicated upon constructive trusteeship – knowing receipt or knowing assistance. However, a detailed consideration of the risk of civil liability is beyond the scope of this chapter. Professional advisers who are considering a report to SOCA and are concerned about the risk of litigation should seek specialist advice.

Chartered Institute of Taxation

8.57 The Chartered Institute of Taxation (CIOT), in conjunction with the Association of Taxation Technicians (ATT), issued interim guidance for practitioners in March 2004 concerning 'Anti Money Laundering (Proceeds of Crime and Terrorism)'. The guidance in relation to tax offences is contained in Sections 5–10. The guidance was unchanged at 31 March 2008.

Auditing Practices Board

8.58 The Auditing Practices Board (APB) issued Practice Note 12 (Revised) 'Money Laundering – Interim Guidance for Auditors in the United Kingdom)' in March 2008. The purpose of the Practice Note is to provide auditors with information on the money laundering legislation and guidance on its relationship with their responsibilities as auditors. The Practice Note offers some extremely useful guidance on money laundering legislation, but is now silent on the subject of tax offences. The guidance generally is intended to reflect that given by the CCAB referred to above.

Joint Money Laundering Steering Group

8.59 Joint Money Laundering Steering Group Guidance Notes (revised in December 2003) on the subject of money laundering recognise that there is a relationship between fiscal offences and money laundering. The Guidance Notes were revised in December 2007 and no longer deal with specific offences. It is perhaps relevant to refer to the earlier guidance on the subject of tax offences and this is reproduced below. The following is an extract from the notes as they related to this issue:

'2.3 The term "criminal conduct" includes any conduct, wherever it takes place, that would constitute an criminal offence if committed in the UK, i.e. regardless of whether the conduct would also be an offence in the jurisdiction in which is was committed. This not only includes serious criminal conduct, e.g. drug trafficking offences, terrorist activity, corruption, tax evasion, burglary and theft, fraud, forgery and counterfeiting, product piracy, illegal deposit taking, blackmail and extortion. But also, any other offence which is committed and where benefit is gained of whatever size, for any person.

…

2.12 As with other criminal conduct, tax-related offences, where a benefit has been gained by any person, are reportable offences under the money laundering legislation. This includes tax offences committed outside the UK:

- that would amount to an offence if committed in the UK; and
- where the knowledge or suspicion came to a person in the course of his/her business within the UK regulated sector; and
- where there is a UK link, e.g. the "taxpayer" is resident in the UK, or where the proceeds of the foreign tax fraud have entered or passed through the UK institution (see paragraphs 5.76–5.77). The issues involved are set out in greater detail in Appendix C.

…

Appendix C

Reporting tax-related offences

Tax-related offences are not in a special category: the proceeds of a tax-related offence may, like the proceeds of a robbery or burglary, be the subject of money laundering offences, under the Proceeds of Crime Act 2002. Offences may relate to direct tax (such as income tax and corporation tax) or indirect tax (such as VAT or excise duty). As stated in Section 2 paragraph 2.12, most tax-related offences are triable on indictment and are therefore reportable offences under the money laundering legislation (*in fact 2.12 no longer states this*). This includes a tax offence committed abroad where the conduct would have been an offence if committed in the UK and where the proceeds have been received by, or passed through, a UK financial institution. Suspected tax evasion should be treated no differently to any other crime that is covered by the money laundering legislation.

However, as stated in Section 2 paragraph 2.4 there is no requirement for any financial institution to have knowledge of other countries' laws, including their tax laws. The issue under the money laundering legislation, for tax offences as for any other offences, is whether the conduct abroad would constitute an offence in this country. If, for example, it is known or suspected that an offence of fraud or false accounting has been committed by the customer against a foreign revenue authority, and the proceeds have entered or passed through the UK, then it should be reported to NCIS (*now SOCA*).

Financial institutions may reasonably assume that customers will meet their tax liabilities unless there is some reason to suspect otherwise, although they should not be taken in too easily by the tax avoidance excuse. Money launderers involved in other crimes may seek to explain transactions that might appear to be suspicious as being for the purposes of legal tax avoidance and financial institutions should remain on their guard. Such statements should not necessarily be taken at face value. If criminal conduct is suspected, then the normal reporting obligations apply.'

8.60 The former Guidance Notes were approved by HM Treasury for the purpose of PoCA on 17 July 2002.

Knowledge or suspicion of an offence

8.61 As with other offences, there is no requirement under the money laundering legislation for a UK financial institution, or a professional adviser, to investigate the affairs of its customers or clients to ascertain whether an offence has been committed. Financial institutions may not be in a position to judge whether a customer has paid tax due in the UK or in any other country. The money laundering legislation does not require a report to SOCA where there is a suspicion that a customer may be considering evading tax in the future. There has to be knowledge or suspicion that the conduct which has generated the proceeds of tax evasion has already occurred or is continuing. If knowledge or a suspicion does arise that the relevant conduct has taken place, then a report should be made to SOCA unless the client enjoys the benefit of legal professional privilege of the more limited benefits of the regulations relating to accountants. In these cases specialist advice should be obtained where necessary as these exceptions are limited in their application and certainly will not apply at all where conduct is capable of furthering a crime (the crime exception).

Procedures for processing the reports

8.62 It is possible that a special form will be prescribed for reporting suspicions of tax evasion. For the time being SOCA request that one of the two general forms in issue be used. SOCA will consider the disclosures received and will pass all or some of the intelligence contained in the suspicious transaction report to the enforcement agency with the power to investigate further. Disclosures which appear to provide evidence of a tax-related crime will be passed to HMRC. Each case will be judged on its merits and not necessarily on the amount of tax at risk.

8.63 Where the intelligence relates to offences committed overseas, SOCA will have the power to disclose the intelligence to Financial Intelligence Units overseas, subject to ensuring suitable safeguards. HMRC may also pass information to an overseas tax authority under provisions, for example under double taxation agreements or the EU Mutual Assistance Directive.

THE ROLE OF THE FISCAL AUTHORITIES

8.64 Historically, whereas HM Customs & Excise have charged money laundering offences in addition to predicate tax offences, the Revenue did not.

8.65 The quality of the intelligence flowing to the Revenue from 1998, and the results that quickly followed there from, led to a change of attitude which broadly coincided with the PCA entering into force. The Revenue Publication 'Working Together' Issue 13 commented on the PCA both generally and specifically where there was an impact from the tax perspective. The following extracts are of interest:

> ***'Requirement for Professional Advisers to Report Knowledge or Suspicion of Tax Evasion***
>
> All SAR forms must be submitted direct to NCIS. This is the case whether the report concerns the proceeds of tax evasion or any other form of criminal activity. NCIS is the government body to receive these reports as only they have the information to check whether there are links to wider criminality.
>
> The Inland Revenue is not a receiving body for these reports. Where a voluntary disclosure about unpaid liabilities due to tax evasion is intended to be made to the Revenue the professional adviser is still required to make a SAR to NCIS at the earliest opportunity.
>
> ***Reports that Concern Tax Evasion***
>
> Reports that relate to tax evasion will be referred within NCIS to an Inland Revenue team who will analyse and evaluate them. Where the only criminality identified from this analysis is tax evasion, the reports will be forwarded by NCIS to the Inland Revenue or HM Customs & Excise as appropriate. For offences of evading direct

taxes or NICs the Inland Revenue will be the investigating body and, in England and Wales, the prosecuting body for these offences. In Scotland the Procurator Fiscal and in Northern Ireland the Director of Public Prosecutions are the prosecuting bodies. Reports forwarded by NCIS to the Revenue will be received by Special Compliance Office (SCO).

…

Effect on Inland Revenue Enquiries and Hansard

Any Inland Revenue enquiries that result from or are informed by disclosures forwarded by NCIS will be carried out in the same manner as any other Inland Revenue enquiry.

In particular reporting a case to NCIS ahead of notifying the Revenue will have no bearing on how the Revenue may treat a case, if the taxpayer is actively seeking to set their affairs straight. This also applies to cases dealt with under the Inland Revenue approach to civil settlements known as "Hansard".

Confidentiality of information received by the Inland Revenue will of course remain of uppermost importance. In cases other than criminal investigations by SCO, procedures are in place such that investigators receive only the factual information from a SAR with no knowledge of who made the original disclosure.

…

Tipping Off

Approaching the Inland Revenue to make a disclosure on behalf of a client about unpaid tax liabilities after the SAR has been sent to SOCA does not constitute tipping off.'

8.66 Commentary regarding the Hansard Practice may be found later in this chapter. In November 2003 the (then) Inland Revenue Special Compliance Office provided further insight to the matter.

Flow of intelligence

8.67 The number of reports disseminated by the Revenue team within NCIS were:

2000/2001	2149
2001/2002	287
2002/2003	227
April 2003–20 October 2004	667

Whereas the trend was down, following the initial bonanza, the trend is upward and this is expected to continue, probably dramatically, following the first extension of the Regulated Sector on 1 March 2004 and the second on 15 December 2007.

8.68 The number of consent applications in cases of suspected tax evasion was 594 (to October 2003). Consent will be given or refused by NCIS (now SOCA) after taking advice from HMRC. It is relevant to note that the actual STR's (now SAR's) are not disclosed, but rather the intelligence derived from them using the 5x5 model. Thus the name of the reporter is not revealed although this may be capable or being inferred. HMRC also has access to overseas money laundering intelligence reports, including those received by SOCA from FIU's within the Crown Dependencies (eg Jersey, Guernsey and the Isle of Man).

HMRC's strategy

8.69 Clearly this fresh source of intelligence has served as a new source of investigation cases and will enhance existing investigations. The flow of intelligences will also inform the Revenue's risk assessment processes which are used as a basis for case selection. HMRC has stated in unequivocal terms that their first consideration in receiving intelligence will be to identity targets for criminal proceedings.

8.70 In their statement of Criminal Investigation Policy HMRC note that they will consider a criminal investigation 'In cases involving money laundering with particular focus on advisors, accountants, solicitors and others acting in a professional capacity who provide the means to put tainted money out of reach of law enforcement'.

8.71 HMRC has responsibility for investigating money laundering cases where tax evasion is the predicate crime and will operate a selective prosecution policy. To this end a specialist unit has been established (the Criminal Taxes Unit). Officers within the unit will use powers under PoCA and will work closely with other law enforcement agencies exchanging information under the legal gateways available. The prosecution of tax related money laundering offences is now the responsibility of the Revenue and Customs Prosecutions Office.

8.72 In 2004 SOCA stated:

> 'the Inland Revenue indicates that around a fifth of disclosures received from SOCA identify a new target and a quarter lead to new enquiries'.

8.73 In November 2004 the Revenue published a press release concerning the Proceeds of Crime Act and Money Laundering. This document also contained a statement of the Revenue's Anti Money Laundering Strategy. The statement expands on the principles outlined above and is a significant document worthy of being read in full. Consequently the strategy is reproduced in full in Appendix 2 to this book.

THE RISK TO FINANCIAL INTERMEDIARIES AND PROFESSIONALS

8.74 Historically, UK professionals involved in giving tax advice should always have considered the subtle difference between (legal) tax avoidance and (illegal) tax evasion. Recently the concept has widened to include a further category, tax mitigation, which relates to very simple statutory relief which is available to reduce tax liabilities (personal allowances etc).

8.75 However, tax avoidance can involve an artificial series of apparently commercial transactions which may have little or no substance, and which are designed merely to avoid taxation. Conversely tax evasion is where someone deliberately sets out to defraud the fiscal authorities. This can represent an act of commission, or one of omission. An offence may be committed where information is deliberately withheld or misrepresented to the fiscal authorities ie there is an inadequate disclosure of material facts that prevents a properly informed decision from being taken.

8.76 The dividing line between avoidance and evasion is becoming both thinner and more dangerous to cross. Professional advisers have taken the view that tax avoidance is capable of being recognised by the civil courts (or even in some circumstances, condoned by the Revenue) and is therefore legitimate, safe from the dangers of criminal litigation.

8.77 However, criminal law has difficulty in recognising the distinction, and when avoidance schemes are put before the criminal courts the court is likely to take a significant interest in the *bona fides* of the scheme and whether the transactions involved have any commercial substance or purpose. Should such transactions not pass the test of commerciality (reality), a criminal court, which will have little or no concept of the civil law distinction between avoidance and evasion, is unlikely to be sympathetic to the accused. A judge is reported to have commented that 'the distinction between tax avoidance and tax evasion is the thickness of a prison cell wall'.

8.78 This lack of distinction became apparent in a case in the criminal courts, *Regina v Charlton* [1996] STC 1418, which challenged an offshore invoicing scheme which had always been regarded (by some) as tax avoidance rather than evasion. The jury disagreed and some of the professional advisers were duly convicted and imprisoned.

8.79 How then does the layman distinguish between lawful tax mitigation or tax avoidance and unlawful tax evasion which may involve the proceeds of crime? Generally speaking, the more aggressive a 'tax planning' arrangement or scheme, particularly when accompanied by a reluctance to make a full and transparent disclosure of documents or facts to the fiscal authorities (either in filing a tax return, or on subsequent enquiry), the greater the risk of a criminal offence.

8.80 Consideration should be given to the activities with which professional advisers are often associated, namely:

(a) establishing and administering offshore corporate structures and trusts;

(b) handling cash for clients and/or the provision of client account facilities;

(c) the provision of investment advice.

Such activities are capable of being involved in laundering the proceeds of crime (including tax crime) and therefore potentially expose the professional adviser concerned to prosecution under the money laundering legislation.

8.81 In the UK the fiscal authorities have always regarded suspect tax practitioners as desirable targets for criminal proceedings because they occupy a position of trust in relation to the fiscal authorities (and also because they tend to produce high-profile criminal prosecutions). However, one problem for the fiscal authorities has always been proving (to criminal standards) that there has been a conspiracy between a taxpayer and his professional adviser. Informed application of the money laundering legislation to tax evasion may make it easier to bring criminal charges against financial intermediaries and professional advisers.

Developments in law and practice

8.82 There is little doubt that the European Directives on money laundering and the UK domestic legislation has imposed a huge burden on the financial community, both in terms of management time and the direct cost of compliance.

8.83 Ostensibly, these burdens and costs were introduced in order to make it impossible for those involved in organised crime to launder their profits and acquire a cloak of respectability. However, some cynics will assert that the underlying purpose of the money laundering legislation is to flush out the 'untaxed' rather than the criminal economy with a view to reducing losses to the Exchequer relating to tax evasion.

8.84 In the UK there is little evidence that the introduction of the legislation has had any material effect on organised crime. The fact is that since the 1930s organised crime has developed highly sophisticated money laundering techniques and, while the new legislation may make things slightly more difficult, it also creates a greater degree of awareness of risk, which will tend to drive the activities further underground.

8.85 It is also a fact that since the anti-money laundering legislation was introduced in the UK, there have been very few successful prosecutions (the exceptions have been mainly for drugs related transactions), although this is by no means the only measure of success. It will be interesting to see whether this situation changes in the future following the current HMRC strategy. The jury is definitely out!

8.86 Certainly the authorities intend to target the professional services sector, from which there have been comparatively few disclosures of suspicious transactions. Until now it is doubtful whether life has been made much more difficult for the 'respectable' tax evader, particularly where he has been established in business for some time. Where such a person has established connections with financial institutions, it seems that he can continue to use them with little personal risk. Should he not wish to take that risk, he can either retain his 'profits' in cash or continue to exploit tax havens such as Switzerland (and certain EU member states) which still enjoy a strong degree of banking secrecy, certainly in relation to fiscal matters.

8.87 For the legislation to become an effective deterrent there must be successful and high profile prosecutions. The legal framework and public interest policy is now in place to enable this. Certainly in this climate it would be foolhardy for a financial intermediary or professional adviser to claim a statutory defence based on the assertion that tax evasion does not constitute 'criminal conduct' for the purposes of money laundering legislation.

8.88 Consider a taxpayer under investigation by HMRC Special Civil Investigations Office where the 'Hansard' (Code of Practice 9) procedure is used. The Hansard procedure is dealt with elsewhere in this publication.

8.89 The fact that the tax authorities decide to accept a monetary settlement rather than instituting criminal proceedings is purely a matter of administrative convenience. The monetary settlement does not in itself 'make good' the underlying criminal conduct.

8.90 One crumb of comfort which is capable of being drawn from the practice is that the Revenue cannot accept a monetary settlement *and* institute criminal proceedings. However, there was a potentially worrying development. The case of *Regina v W* [1998] STC 550 (Court of Appeal) established that a pecuniary settlement negotiated by the Revenue in relation to tax liability did not preclude the Crown Prosecution Service (CPS) from instituting proceedings for false accounting.

8.91 Essentially, one part of the Crown does not bind another. In this case the charge of false accounting was severed from an indictment alleging conspiracy to defraud and was ordered to be tried first. The author understands that the alleged false accounting arose solely in relation to a scheme designed to facilitate tax evasion and was not part of separate alleged criminal conduct by the defendants which was the subject of the conspiracy counts.

8.92 The decision has potentially serious ramifications. Say, for reasons of public interest, the CPS chose to institute proceedings against a taxpayer who had already reached a monetary settlement with the Revenue. If the CPS were able to gain access to statements and documents produced in connection with the tax investigation, they might have little difficulty in bringing a successful prosecution for non-tax related predicate offences or money laundering.

8.93 In theory, this could lead to cases where, as a result of a monetary settlement reached with HMRC in respect of tax evasion, sufficient admissible evidence is generated to enable a money laundering charge to be brought by the CPS (or any other prosecuting authority such as the Serious Fraud Office, the Department of Trade and Industry) where the predicate crime upon which the money laundering charge is based was related to tax evasion.

8.94 Thus, a tax evader may find that having paid a sizeable amount of tax, interest and penalties to HMRC, he is charged with false accounting under Theft Act 1968, s 17 and a money laundering offence under PoCA. A money laundering charge would mean that the taxpayer is faced with the possibility of 14 years imprisonment and/or an unlimited fine (interestingly, the charge of false accounting carries a maximum sentence of only 7 years).

8.95 A trial in Scotland in July 1998 (not reported) should also serve to increase the likelihood of the tax evasion-money laundering link being utilised in what are ostensibly non-tax related criminal prosecutions. A man accused of being one of the financiers of a huge drug trafficking operation had a majority verdict of 'not proven' returned by the jury. It was reported that defence counsel advanced the argument that he was an 'Arthur Daley' figure, 'ducking and diving' in the black economy, 'doing a bit of this and a bit of that' and not paying income tax or VAT. Coupled with his legitimate business activities, his objection to paying tax was advanced in order to explain why he was in possession of huge sums of money.

8.96 Should the report be correct, no doubt HMRC would have viewed the proceedings with interest and acted accordingly. However, consider the position if the defendant had also been charged with offences relating to the evasion of direct and/or indirect taxation, coupled with money laundering charges. A failure to convict on the drug related charges would have been a pyrrhic victory had there been a conviction on charges relating to tax evasion; this would almost certainly have resulted in conviction on the money laundering charges.

8.97 Life for the alleged tax evader who enjoys a criminal lifestyle will be made more difficult by other provisions of POCA 2002 (ie the Civil Recovery Process or Revenue Functions of the Asset Recovery Agency).

8.98 It is now clear that HMRC will make use of the money laundering legislation. HMRC will be tempted to utilise the money laundering legislation in the most serious cases where financial institutions and/or professional advisers have assisted in or have otherwise facilitated tax evasion.

8.99 In the US the Internal Revenue Service will bring money laundering charges in relation to tax offences only where under declared income emanates from a criminal source. Where profits arise from a legitimate business, tax evasion, though remaining in a criminal offence, is not a predicate crime for money laundering purposes.

CONCLUSION

8.100 It is to be hoped that this chapter assists in dispelling the myth that tax evasion, or offences related to it, are not predicate crimes for money laundering purposes. Financial intermediaries and professional advisers must acquaint themselves with the relevant legislation and establish procedures to deal with situations where they suspect their clients are involved in tax evasion (and hence, potentially, money laundering). It is also vital that professional advisers ensure that their action or inaction, once they know or suspect money laundering is taking place, does not risk implicating them in any criminality.

8.101 Professional advisers should note that the money laundering legislation does not prevent them from acting on behalf of a client seeking to make a full disclosure of irregularities to one or more of the fiscal authorities. However, advisers acting for such clients should ensure that they do not give any 'transactional advice' which may implicate them in an 'arrangement' for the purposes of PoCA, s 328. In this context, consider a professional adviser representing a client seeking to make a disclosure to HMRC whilst at the same time offering the client some hypothetical advice on how to 'ring fence' certain assets from the fiscal authorities. In thc author's opinion, this is unlawful.

8.102 A former version of ICAEW's 'Professional Conduct in Relation to Taxation' points out at paragraph 2.32:

> 'The money-laundering legislation does not prevent a member from advising clients on negotiations with the tax authorities in respect of evaded tax liabilities, *on a bona fide basis of full disclosure* in accordance with the guidelines' (emphasis added).

8.103 As the line between tax avoidance and tax evasion becomes increasingly important, the money laundering legislation adds a 'double jeopardy' for those who either cross the line or assist another to do so. Professional advisers involved in devising and/or implementing aggressive tax avoidance schemes would be well advised to ensure that they genuinely deserve the 'avoidance' label – although this label is becoming far less comforting than it once was. Perhaps the test for any scheme should be whether a credible explanation could be provided to a Crown Court Judge and a jury of 12 lay people. If in doubt, it may be prudent to seek counsel from a member of the criminal bar.

Chapter 9

Meetings with HMRC

Chris Chadburn BSc (Econ), Independent Tax Investigations Consultant

INTRODUCTION

9.1 Meetings with HMRC arise in many circumstances. This chapter focuses on meetings between advisers, their clients and HMRC officers relating to direct tax business return enquiries and employer compliance reviews. Ensuring you have a 'good' meeting will often be crucial to getting the results both you and your client are looking for at the end of the enquiry process.

9.2 These notes refer to the current position on meetings. On 29 October 2007 HMRC announced that a different approach to enquiries would be trialed between November 2007 and April 2008. See http://www.hmrc.gov.uk/ctsa/openness-early-dialogue-enquiries.htm. This involves an explicit but flexible timescale for:

- an initial discussion;
- the production of information and documents;
- a records examination; and
- a discussion of the findings.

9.3 It is envisaged that the initial discussion will help the inspector understand:

  - the nature of the business;
  - the circumstances of the individual;
  - the records kept and the work done by the accountant;

PURPOSE OF THE MEETING

9.4 Detailed notes on meetings relating to enquiries are at HMRC's Enquiry Manual (EM) 1820 et seq. Meetings are described as a vital part in full enquiries and appropriate in aspect enquiries of substance. Explanations will invariably be needed from the taxpayer and it is suggested that these are best obtained directly at an early stage rather than by correspondence (EM 1821).

9.5 Inspectors are told that they should know exactly why they are holding the meeting; what they want to achieve and what information they want to obtain. Meetings are considered the best way to:

- explain the purpose of the enquiry;
- obtain facts about how the business is run and the records kept;
- establish whether the taxpayer wishes to make a disclosure;
- explain the position on interest and penalties where omissions are established;
- agree the action needed to move the enquiry forward;
- quantify the omissions;
- settle the enquiry.

This list is from EM 1822 which for some reason fails to mention a key point. That is obtaining the facts about the taxpayer's private finances.

9.6 Although some full enquiries are randomly selected the vast majority are taken up because it is considered by HMRC that tax is at risk. When tackling non-compliance HMRC is under increasing pressure to deliver results in terms of yield. This is resulting in much more careful consideration of the risk of something being wrong with the return and the likely scale of the problem.

9.7 The typical opening letter will involve a request for books and records and some additional information. This will normally relate solely to the business rather than the finances of the proprietors. There is no compulsion on the Inspector to say why the enquiry has been started and it would be very unusual for reasons to be given at this stage. In larger cases there may be a request for a meeting at the outset but this will typically be with the firm's accountant and the adviser to agree on how the records can most effectively be examined by HMRC.

9.8 In examining the books etc the Inspector is seeking to establish whether there is evidence to indicate whether or not the initial doubts on the accuracy of the return have been validated. Unless the review shows there to be no problem or is inconclusive the Inspector will usually proceed by requesting a meeting with the client.

9.9 In advising on how to overcome objections to a meeting EM 1861 confirms that the inspector should say why they want to meet the taxpayer. EM 1827 says that 'an agenda covering the main areas for discussion ..should always be provided. This should enable the agent to carry out any necessary preparation or research in advance'. In practice at the outset there is usually little by way of explanation of the need for a meeting beyond the assertion that experience shows this is the most cost effective way of dealing with the Inspector's concerns. Comment on what the Inspector wants to talk about is often restricted to general comment on the need to know more about the business or the client's personal finances or whatever.

9.10 EM 1861 concludes by saying that 'ultimately you do not have a power to compel a taxpayer or accountant to attend a meeting'. The relevant Codes of Practice (COPs 11 and 14) also make that clear. You will need to deal with the enquiry in a cost effective manner and this will be very difficult if you have little or no idea where the Inspector's attack is coming from. Clearly you need to discuss the meeting request with the client but invariably every effort should be made to establish with the Inspector why a meeting is considered necessary and the aspects to be covered. If the Inspector considers the quality of the records to be at best indifferent then this will be a principal reason to say they need to look at the business and private finances in more detail to validate the figures returned. Inspectors tend to talk in generalities at this point and keep specifics to themselves until after the taxpayer has provided explanations without prior notice of the questions.

9.11 If you are not convinced that a meeting at this stage is the best way forward for your client you can suggest to the Inspector that you are sure that many of the questions can be dealt with perfectly adequately by correspondence. Usually at this stage the Inspector will not have a convincing case and will probably take you up on your offer. It is a fact that you can provide considerable detail in this way that will take the enquiry forward. Your client has the benefit of giving answers after deliberation and research and you should be in a position to take a much firmer view on where the Inspector's interest really lies and whether a meeting is appropriate at that stage.

9.12 It is interesting to note that the old Enquiry Handbook, when looking at how to overcome objections to a meeting, said that the Inspector 'should be as open as possible in explaining your grounds for concern at this stage'. The EM contains no such reference.

9.13 The Inspector may point out that not agreeing to a meeting may be regarded as a lack of cooperation if penalties arise and this will affect the abatement. This is referred to in leaflet IR 160 which is an explanation of what happens at the end of an enquiry.

> '*Co-operation* – A reduction of up to 40%.
>
> If you supply information quickly, attend interviews, answer questions honestly and accurately, give all the relevant facts and pay tax

on account when it becomes possible to estimate the amount due, you will then get the maximum reduction for co-operation.'

9.14 Given the fact that your client has a right not to attend a meeting it is difficult to see how the abatement would be affected if your client did everything that could reasonably have need done except attend a meeting. It seems difficult to argue that proactively establishing the extent of any tax loss must involve a meeting with the Inspector after the records review. It should be noted that HMRC has introduced a new penalty regime, which will apply for events occurring on or after 1 April 2008 where the relevant return is filed on or after 1 April 2009. This subject is discussed in more detail in Chapter 14. However, the basic principles about penalty mitigation remain the same.

9.15 An Inspector may take the line that if the taxpayer continues to refuse to attend a meeting then it may well be the case that the client will have to be questioned under oath before the Commissioners if the case progresses that far. It will be rare for a case to progress in that way. After the initial records examination the Inspector will invariably still be looking for a lot of information to determine whether suspicions are well founded and the likely extent of the problem. You and your client are more than happy to provide information but not at a meeting because the Inspector has not provided any detail on what the issues are. There will certainly come a time in many cases where the Inspector says that progress will now be made using formal means if there is to be no meeting. Experience shows that this approach will only usually arise several months from the start of the enquiry. By then you should be clear on the merits of the HMRC case and any meeting is likely to be on relatively narrow ground because plenty of information has been provided in the meantime.

9.16 It is of course generally accepted that a co-operative and constructive approach to HMRC enquiries is adopted, but it must also be recognised that the objectives of the Inspector and those of the adviser and the client may not always coincide.

PREPARING FOR THE MEETING

9.17 The Inspector will prepare extensively for any meeting with a taxpayer and adviser. Inspectors do not have your cost constraints and invariably will be able to devote significantly more time to preparation than you. This is a primary reason for ensuring that before agreeing to a meeting you are as clear as possible on where your preparation time should be spent. The following notes are really the counsel of perfection but as a minimum.

1. the client needs to be aware of:
   - the background to the enquiry and the meeting;

- the advantages of being cooperative and making early and complete disclosures;

2 there needs to be consideration of the general areas to be covered at the meeting and the likely areas of particular interest to the Inspector;

3 the client needs to be briefed on:

- what is likely to happen at the meeting;
- how direct and open questions should be approached;
- potentially difficult areas and how to deal with these;
- the advisor's role.

Review your knowledge of the client

9.18 The adviser should generally review the case and identify strengths and weaknesses. Particular attention should be paid to those areas to which the Inspector's attention might usefully be directed if a speedy and beneficial resolution for the client is to be reached. There should be a focus on:

- the quality of the client's records;
- issues arising during the preparation of the accounts and/or tax returns and how these were dealt with;
- previous tax issues;
- the position on any previous enquiries;
- general knowledge of the advisor (and adviser's staff) of the business and private finances.

Identify any problem areas

9.19 If omissions or understatements are identified prior to a meeting with the Inspector it is critical that these are considered in some detail and disclosed at an early stage. This will signify a constructive and cooperative approach and will assist in optimising the penalty position. If disclosures are not made at an early stage of a meeting but are revealed in a piece-meal fashion this will have a damaging effect not only on the penalty loading but also on the taxpayer's (and possibly your own) credibility.

9.20 On making a disclosure it may be agreed that an early meeting with the client is dispensed with and the adviser agrees to provide an investigation report. There will be a meeting with the Inspector to agree the scope of such a report and a provisional timescale.

9.21 If the review process identifies no particular issues it will be useful at some stage to detail the research which has been done and the conclusions. Care needs to be taken on the timing of this and usually it will be appropriate once you have established that the Inspector has fired all the bullets or that there are none. There may be advantages to starting the process by saying you have looked at the papers and discussed the position in some detail with your client and you believe the return is correct. If, however, the Inspector has strong evidence to the contrary then you and your client may finish up looking less than competent and/or dishonest.

Pre-meeting client issues

9.22 At the time of receiving the opening letter the client should have been briefed on the background to HMRC enquiries and the likely course that will be taken. In particular you should outline:

- the obligations to keep proper records;
- the absolute right to enquire into tax returns;
- the power to call for relevant documents and particulars;
- the rights of appeal.

The advantages of admitting problems at an early stage should have been spelled out. There will have been a subsequent dialogue on the upsides and downsides of having a meeting at this stage and the client should be reminded of all this.

9.23 The advisor may be thoroughly familiar with HMRC meetings but most clients will experience a fair degree of stress when face to face with the investigator. The client should be briefed as far as possible on what to expect on the day. Much of the meeting, certainly the opening explanations issue of HMRC leaflets etc, will follow a fairly predictable course. Your approach and behaviour in dealing with the Inspector in a mature and professional manner will settle the client. The Inspector will expect your role to be as a facilitator. The client will be expected to answer the questions and should appreciate this.

9.24 As a general rule clients should be encouraged to keep answers to questions factual and concise. In particular clients should be made aware that if they do not know the answer to a specific question then they should not guess and only provide estimates when they are comfortable doing so. A 'review and report back procedure' is quite acceptable and may even be expected by the Inspector. Any false impressions given at the initial meeting may be difficult to correct at a later stage. This is another excellent reason for only agreeing to a meeting when you and the client are confident that you are aware of the key issues for the Inspector and it is unlikely there will be any surprises for anyone. The client should be made aware that the Inspector's usual objective in the early stages of the meeting is to put the taxpayer at ease and get them talking. The client should be encouraged to participate actively and constructively but to answer specific questions directly and more general questions with circumspection.

9.25 The client cannot be expected to remember details from many years ago. Ideally the request for a detailed agenda will have resulted in identifying these sorts of question before the meeting and appropriate answers given. Areas of weakness should be considered in detail. It is not possible to be prescriptive on what these will be but para **9.30** sets out the areas of interest for the Inspector and your judgement should throw up some likely issues. If the Inspector is looking at private finances in any detail at all then questions will invariably arise in relation to non-taxable sources. See EM 2051.

> 'Taxpayers may claim that deficiencies..or money introduced were funded from …non taxable receipts. You should at an early stage in an enquiry try to pre-empt such claims by asking the taxpayer about matters such as cash accumulation, loans and gifts received and so on. If the claim is first made at a meeting you should question the taxpayer closely about it, before he or she has had time to invent plausible circumstances to surround a false story.'

9.26 Further general guidance is then given at EM 2053 and then more specific details are given from EM 2056 through to EM 2097 although most of the text is withheld. Common explanations are:

– cash hoards;
– betting wins;
– legacies and sales of personal effects;
– illegal or immoral activities.

9.27 In these circumstances you should ask the client about these issues (although it will not usually be wise to raise a specific query on illegal or immoral income!). If there are matters of substance in the relevant period then these should be discussed in considerable detail. Are you satisfied with the explanations given and is the Inspector likely to be? In any event the client needs to understand that the Inspector will require evidence to substantiate the claims and you need to agree how best this can be obtained.

9.28 One reason for the Inspector preferring to see the client is that it helps in forming a view on their overall credibility. The adviser should do all that is possible to ensure the client comes across as honest, open, knowledgeable, and helpful. You want to come out of the meeting feeling that the client would make a very credible witness if appeals were taken to the Tax Commissioners. There is no substitute for sound preparation but over-coaching can easily give the wrong impression.

WHAT THE INSPECTOR WANTS

9.29 The Inspector will have a combination of the following objectives which should be clearer to you when considering the reasons for the meeting and the agenda:

- to obtain detailed information about the individual's personal and financial background, the nature of the business being carried on and the economics on which it operates;
- to obtain detailed information about the business records with a view to testing their reliability;
- to obtain detailed and specific information about the individual's personal finances to establish whether these stack up with the returns and accounts;
- to check facts and explanations against third party information held.

9.30 The Inspector has to be able to cast significant doubt on the accuracy of the return in order to justify continuing with the enquiry. Section 19A obliges the Inspector to establish whether the return 'is incorrect or incomplete'.

9.31 It is important for the Inspector to find problems with the records. This can then justify preparing a recalculation of the client's sales figure based on a business economics exercise which suggests that the figure in the accounts may have been understated. The preparation of a business economics exercise which casts doubt on the accuracy of the sales figure is not enough to justify displacing the accounts, if there is no reason to cast doubt on the accuracy of the records from which those accounts were prepared.

9.32 The Inspector may be able to show that the evidence about the client's lifestyle and day-to-day expenditure and his family exceeds significantly the cash available from drawings from the business and other sources for the client to live on. Similarly the funding of private assets may be unclear from the known borrowings and other established funds. If the Inspector can show that any of these 'doubtful' features are present there may well be a strong case for establishing omissions. Invariably though the Inspector will be in a much stronger position if it can be shown show that there is evidence of material inaccuracies in the records supporting the return.

Checklist for preparing for a meeting

9.33 The adviser:

1 review the case history;

2 review all knowledge of the client and business;

3 prepare and review schedules from the accounts and tax returns;

4 discuss case with accounts and tax staff;

5 identify areas of weakness;

6 discuss briefly areas of interest with the Inspector (consider a pre-meeting meeting);

7 clear up any accountancy queries and brush up on relevant technical knowledge;

8 agree with HMRC that accounts queries are to be handled before the meeting;

9 agree an agenda for the meeting;

10 agree who is to be present and a suitable place, date and time;

11 agree what information should be brought to the meeting.

9.34 To the client:

1 explain the reason for the meeting;

2 outline the history of the case to date;

3 explain what HMRC already know;

4 explain the Inspector's likely objectives;

5 summarise the expected control and format of the meeting;

6 advise on approach and demeanour;

7 identify areas of weakness and strengths;

8 identify and go through key questions and answers;

9 provide briefing note.

THE MEETING ITSELF

Format of the meeting

9.35 Most full HMRC enquiries will follow a fairly predictable format, at least in outline and will cover some combination of the following:

1 Reasons for the interview, provisions of TMA 1970, ss 8 and 9A, the rights of the IR to make enquiries into a return and the rights of the taxpayer to ask the Commissioners to determine when an enquiry should be terminated.

2 Background to the business, business history, particular expertise, types of products, types of goods sold, business performance over the years, problems encountered in running the business, expertise and experience of the proprietor, specific nature of the trade, prices, pricing policies, stock holding policies, cash control policies, economics of the business, general trends.

3 Business records: who keeps them, where, how often, what are they, what do they cover, what 'prime' records are there? What 'non-financial' records are kept? Any points form the initial review demonstrating a clear problem and profit adjustment?

4 Business economics in detail: how is the business organised in detail.

5 Personal and private expenditure, personal assets and liabilities, funding of major assets etc, other sources of income, cash windfalls and legacies, etc.

6 Technical adjustments: own use and own goods, private car adjustments, private telephone, etc, other private benefits/expenses?

7 Any omissions or additions disclosed during a meeting, proposals for further investigation.

8 Agreements for subsequent action: information to be provided, records to be reviewed, investigations to be undertaken by the accountant, etc, scope of future enquiries and also an agreed timetable for action.

Who will be present?

9.36 Always ascertain before the meeting who is to attend on behalf of HMRC. There will usually be at least two officers, one essentially conducting the meeting and the other taking notes. You need to establish whether there will be anyone there outside the norm, for example a very senior officer or a qualified accountant. Why are they attending and does this affect your approach to the meeting?

9.37 The adviser should always consider who should attend on the client's behalf and ensure HMRC are aware of the position. If the meeting is likely to be protracted, complex and generally difficult, then assistance from the office may be necessary to take notes and provide general support.

9.38 It may be appropriate from time to time to get a specialist's technical input at the opening meeting if the agenda warrants it. If personal finances are to be discussed it may be appropriate for the client's spouse to attend even though they have no business responsibilities.

9.39 If a meeting is likely to cover detailed reviews of business records or particular areas of commercial expertise it may be advisable to have an appropriate member of the client's staff at the meeting. Questions to be directed to the employee may have to be dealt with at a separate meeting or at the beginning of the discussion after which the employee can leave. They should be given clear guidelines and support in preparation for the meeting and their terms of reference and areas of expertise and knowledge about the business and the proprietor's affairs must be made clear to the inspector.

9.40 Where the business is conducted by a husband and wife in partnership or as directors in a limited company it is important to verify before the meeting the exact degree of involvement of both spouses in the business. Should any query about the level of involvement of one spouse in the business be raised by the Inspector it can then be dealt with properly. Where omissions are to be disclosed it will be of considerable importance to ascertain the extent of the involvement and knowledge of both spouses in the relevant events. HMRC's instructions tell the Inspector to offer separate interviews to both spouses initially (EM 1852 et seq). It may be necessary to insist on separate meetings where it is clear that one spouse has had no involvement in or no knowledge of what has gone on. In such cases it may be necessary for one or both spouses to seek independent advice.

9.41 For businesses run by partners or directors of a limited company the Inspector will indicate who it is believed should attend the meeting or meetings. There will usually be a clear line drawn between meetings where personal finances and business matters are to be discussed. At the former only the relevant partner or director will be present with the advisor and at the latter either all partners and directors or those with specific responsibilities for example the finance partner/director. Clearly the larger the organisation the more likely it is that not all partners/directors will attend the business side meeting.

9.42 As in the issue of whether a meeting is necessary at all so the Inspector's views on which taxpayers should attend should be fully considered with the clients. Having a number of partners/directors tied up for several hours in a meeting with the Inspector together with preparatory time may be a very significant commitment. The Inspector should be prepared to fully justify the assertion that the meetings and suggested attendees are necessary to progress the enquiry.

Where and when should the meeting be held?

9.43 HMRC's view is that 'asking for meetings at the business premises should be the norm' (EM 1830). The rationale for this is said to be that in many cases it will be easier to examine the business records there. As there is no obligation to have a meeting with HMRC in the first place the adviser and the client need to take a view on the advantages and disadvantages of holding a meeting at the business; in the tax office or at the adviser's office. It will rarely be suggested that the meeting take place at the client's home and unless there are issues such as age and infirmity any such suggestion will normally be rejected. The logistics and minimising disruption to the business will be principal factors to consider but deciding where the client is likely to feel most comfortable should usually be the key point. This is unlikely to be at the tax office.

9.44 Similarly although it will be sensible to have a degree of flexibility, the time and day best suiting the client should be 'the norm'.

9.45 Wherever and whenever the meeting is held it should be arranged that the room and set up provide for a reasonable degree of comfort and minimal opportunity for disruption. It will usually be sensible to establish approximately how long the meeting is expected to last and manage expectations if necessary.

Conduct of the meeting

9.46 Although the HMRC website says that the Personal Contact Manual was withdrawn in August 2006 para 1.2 set out how HMRC officers should:

- be helpful, courteous and considerate;
- have a polite and professional manner;
- be fair and impartial;
- give clear, honest and accurate explanations when needed;
- have regard to confidentiality;
- handle matters promptly.

9.47 All enquiries and all meetings are different and however well you and the client have prepared there may be unexpected and potentially difficult issues raised. The advisor needs to be alert and to recognise potential stress points quickly. You should always be prepared to ask for a brief adjournment of the meeting to reassure the client, to provide professional guidance and consultation, and to review the progress of the meeting so far to establish whether or not the client wishes to proceed. There may be occasions on which the adviser deems it necessary to bring the meeting to a close either because new and unwelcome information has come to light or because HMRC adopt specific procedures about which the adviser is unsure or unprepared.

9.48 A good example of the latter situation would be where it appears from the client's comments during the meeting that HMRC may regard this as a case of serious fraud. See the link for details of HMRC policy on prosecutions http://www.hmrc.gov.uk/prosecutions/crim-inv-policy.htm and Chapter 7 of this book. HMRC prosecute few cases for false accounts/returns but the case may be taken over by a Civil Investigation of Fraud team if the yield is likely to be £100,000 or more. If the yield is likely to be over £500,000 the Special Civil Investigations team may be involved.

9.49 Prolonged pauses or silence during a meeting can appear oppressive and may even be quite stressful for the client. The client should avoid unnecessary or irrelevant statements simply to keep the meeting moving and the advisor should normally fill such silences if the client is uneasy.

9.50 The adviser should be prepared to participate actively in the meeting even if at times this is clearly not to the satisfaction of the Inspector.

How should the meeting conclude?

9.51 The Inspector is told to ensure the taxpayer knows exactly where they stand. If there is likely to be additional liability then the taxpayer needs to be informed or reminded of the benefits of cooperation and what needs to be done next. If further information is needed then the Inspector should make it clear what is needed and a realistic timescale agreed. The position should be summarised by letter shortly after the meeting. See EM 1855.

Notes of meetings

9.52 The Inspector will prepare a detailed note of the meeting usually shortly after it has been held. A copy should be sent to the advisor either:

- asking for the client to signify agreement to its accuracy by signing a copy and returning it; or
- at least commenting on any amendments that are considered necessary.

9.53 There will usually be no advantage to the client in signing the notes and there is no statutory obligation to do so. If however there are points of dispute on what was said or a particular spin on what was said then these should be pointed out reasonably quickly. Similarly if what was said is properly recorded but the client or the advisor on reflection wants to give better particulars then this may be an appropriate time to do so. Clearly if points on the notes are not raised until many months after the notes were sent out then their evidential value is likely to be substantially weakened.

9.54 Inspectors should not tape or video record a meeting. If the client or agent want to tape record the meeting this should normally be allowed if it is agreed that a copy unedited tape be provided or a full typed transcript. Requests for video recordings will normally be refused on the basis that there is no obvious business advantage over an audio recording. See EM 1833/5.

Ten key areas

9.55

1 Lack of preparation and attention to detail will result in an inability to answer questions properly. Clients may be faced with questions for which they are not ready leaving them feeling exposed and vulnerable.

2 Most enquiries are settled without recourse to formal appeal proceedings and the adviser should be aware throughout any meeting that he may have to reach a compromise settlement at some stage. Identifying strengths and weaknesses and continually reinforcing the best arguments with references to points and facts in the client's favour is a key area of negotiating.

3 Having a list of priorities and certain key points to make helps the adviser gives the adviser redirect the route a meeting is taking in some cases. The adviser must be prepared to insist that the discussion is moved on if it is felt that the meeting is bogged down.

4 An ability to see the other side's viewpoint, to accept the Inspector's statutory authority and to take a constructive approach towards resolving areas of doubt and difficulty is generally to be recommended. It is likely to prove more cost-effective in the long run. Advisers must however be prepared to exercise their judgment on where co-operation ends and obsequious collaboration begins. The client is entitled to representation and to feel that he has been afforded the correct level of support.

5 Many enquiries will at some stage cover at least touch on areas where the Inspector's right to information or to take certain action is not clear cut. The adviser who is known as someone who avoids disputes on such areas may become known as a 'soft touch' and will do clients an injustice.

6 A thorough awareness of the provisions of TMA 1970 and the rights and obligations it provides is needed. Cases may involve specific areas of the Taxes Acts and careful research should always be undertaken if such technical issues are to be the subject of discussion during any meeting.

7 The adviser who lets the Inspector know that he would not take a case to appeal is sacrificing a solid negotiating tactic and, more fundamentally, is depriving his client of one of his basic rights under the enquiry process.

8 The adviser should always be prepared to call a halt during a meeting to be satisfied that the client fully understands the statutory position and what the various options are, even if this is just done to give the client breathing space.

9 The adviser should adopt a questioning and challenging approach to the Inspector's statements where appropriate.

10 Where detailed calculations are presented during an interview it will rarely be possible to test them properly. An interview is inevitably a pressure situation and even simple points or errors can easily be overlooked. Generally no comment should be made on detailed calculations presented under these circumstances and they should be reviewed later.

Employer Compliance Reviews

9.56 In general the points made in relation to the opening meetings in SA enquiries will apply to employer reviews. The essential objectives of such reviews are to ensure:

– all remuneration and benefits are being correctly dealt with;

– the extent of any irregularities are established;

– the collection of underpaid tax with interest and penalties where appropriate.

9.57 As in other areas of tackling non-compliance it is clear that the selection of cases for employer review is now based on risk assessment and that yield is the name of the game. An employer review may be undertaken if a full enquiry into a business and its principals is being considered. Full enquiries into larger businesses will often have a review of PAYE and benefits as part of the overall compliance check. In short these are not routine matters.

9.58 It is envisaged that in a full review there will be at least one visit to the employer to examine the appropriate records and 'question those responsible for the business'. The full review calls into question the employer's overall operation of PAYE, NIC, benefits etc. Aspect reviews will focus on specific issues and may well not involve a visit. See Employer Compliance Handbook (ECH)1025/1030.

9.59 The initial contact will invariably be a letter to the employer saying that a named individual will call to inspect employer's and contractor's records with a suggested date and time. It will say that there will be an initial discussion on the nature of the business and the payroll system used. A booklet (Code of Practice 3) will be enclosed which gives a detailed 17-page review of why and how the reviews are undertaken. The employer's advisor should be provided with a copy of the letter (ECH7006). It is common for advisers not to attend the meeting and this may be appropriate. However, given the risk based decision to undertake the review, the benefits and costs of the adviser attending the visit should be carefully discussed. At the very least clients need to know:

- how the review is likely to unfold;
- their risk areas;
- how to handle the visit.

9.60 The employer or contractor must produce the required records for inspection when requested. The authorised officer may inspect relevant records and documents and copy or take extracts from and remove those records and documents. PAYE and NIC records must be retained for at least three years after the end of the tax year to which they relate. (Regulation 97 of the Income Tax (PAYE) Regulations 2003 and Regulation 26 Schedule 4 Social Security (Contributions) Regulations 2001).

9.61 ECH7070 says the compliance officer should ensure the person responsible for maintaining the records is available during the initial visit which will be to where the records are usually kept. Clearly the officer has a right to inspect relevant records and it is sensible and practical to have someone senior at the meeting who can help the officer understand the systems and how they work in practice. COP 3 sets out the records they are likely to want to see and it will be sensible to try and establish the periods they want to look at.

9.62 The compliance officer will not usually highlight particular areas of interest before the meeting and in these circumstances it can be difficult to establish who should be around to answer detailed questions. For example, in terms of expenses policy that may a director with responsibilities for human resources or for the arrangements with sub-contractors a director responsible for production. Whatever the situation, there should be a conscious decision as to who will be at or available for the meeting and they should all be fully briefed.

9.63 If there is any doubt it will usually be sensible to keep the meeting at a relatively low level to allow the compliance officer to flag up areas of interest with the employer not going into any great detail on these without proper consideration. It is relatively unusual in smaller cases for the advisor to be present during the visit and their presence may put the compliance officer on notice that the employer has particular concerns. The compliance officer either at the visit or in terms of follow up may be very keen to meet a particular director or principal of the business. They may overlook the fact that their rights relate purely to inspecting records. They have no rights to meet a particular client and every request needs to be considered on its merits. In short they will meet the client when it suits you and the client not when it suits HMRC. COP 3 recognises this. 'You and your employees do not have to answer any questions and you may want to consult your professional advisor before replying …'.

9.64 The visiting compliance officer will be relatively junior and their approach is prescribed in detail in the Employer Compliance Manual. There will often be two officers from HMRC present. The driver for the visit is a lengthy printed booklet ECR2000. This comprises notes on the key issues to be considered and provides an audit trail for the review in relation to:

- why the case was selected;
- what the employer said;
- what checks were completed;
- what records were seen;
- what irregularities were identified;
- what issues needed further investigation;
- the outcomes;
- settlement details.

9.65 The visit will begin with general fact finding in terms of the nature of the business; number of directors and employees; responsibilities of key people; the payroll system used and who does what in relation to wages, PAYE returns etc. This is basic information and may be more cost effectively covered by way of a detailed note provided by the employer and advisor before or at the meeting. See ECH7042 for the areas to be covered. With the notes in front of them the compliance officer can then focus on any particular points of detail or areas of concern.

9.66 ECH7045 refers to Mandatory Assurance Checks. These are not covered in detail in the version available to the public but it does say the checks are designed:

1 to ensure all payments and benefits have been correctly treated for tax and NIC purposes and correctly reported;

2 to check all required deductions are:
   - correctly made;
   - correctly recorded;
   - fully and promptly paid over;

3 to ensure compliance under Tax Credit and CSL legislation;

4 to assist and educate the employer.

9.67 ECH7100 refers to certain records to complete these checks, specifically:

– deduction working sheets;

– records evidencing payments to employees and the department;

– evidence of employees entitlement to statutory payments.

9.68 The compliance officer needs to understand the systems being used and the idea then is to test the system by examining records to confirm what happens in practice. 'Particular attention must be applied to examination of any system with risks identified.'

9.69 Status issues will often be a significant risk area and will be covered in detail. Note that compliance officers may approach workers or ex workers to validate the client's version of the facts relating to the engagement. It is possible that such approaches may have been made before the compliance visit.

9.70 The compliance officer is told to be flexible and tailor questions to the business but experience shows the ECR2000 is often gone through in some detail with no apparent attempt to focus time and energy on areas where tax is likely to be at particular risk.

9.71 On the conclusion of the visit the compliance officer should ensure that all questions have been answered and relevant facts obtained.

9.72 The compliance officer should issue leaflet IR109 when irregularities are established. IR 109 refers to a meeting at the end of the review to discuss the findings; the amount of tax and interest arising and the position on penalties. It appears that the review will normally be extended into earlier years where there is an underpayment of £500 or more.

9.73 The process is described in very black and white terms and sets out what happens 'if you do not want to make an offer or make one we cannot accept'. That is formal determinations will be issued to recover tax, interest and penalties. Penalties would probably be sought where you are looking at tax lost of say £500 or more and they would be mitigated in relation to disclosure, cooperation and size/gravity in the normal way. Penalties for employer defaults are also currently under review, as set out in Chapter 14.

9.74 In practice the areas highlighted by the review will need to be looked at in detail to establish whether tax is likely to have been lost and a reasonable quantum. Sometimes their conclusions of the employer compliance officer are sound and often they are not. The earlier the advisor provides input the easier and less costly the visit is likely to be.

Pre-planning checklist

9.75

1 What records do they want to see?

2 What state are those records in?

3 Is all relevant information easily accessible?

4 Extract all irrelevant items?

5 Is the suggested date too early? Consider postponement?

6 Where is the meeting to be held?

7 Arrange suitable accommodation?

8 Who is to attend the meeting?

9 Appoint someone to accompany the visitors?

10 Find out exactly who is coming.

11 Get a list of what/who they will want to see.

12 Ask if there is a specific reason for the visit.

13 Check up on statutory powers.

14 Ascertain statutory obligations and rights.

15 Identify any areas of risk or vulnerability.

16 Quantify any problems, potential errors or omissions.

17 Prepare statements for early disclosure if relevant.

18 Prepare explanations in mitigation if necessary.

19 Identify likely exposure to interest and penalties and quantify.

During the visit itself

9.76 General

1 Be concise and factual.

2 Do not guess – if unsure adopt a 'report back' approach.

3 Ensure that the officers have adequate accommodation.

4 Give access only to:

- the relevant records;
- parts of the premises;
- relevant (and fully briefed) staff.

9.77 Review of records

1 Agree a timetable.

2 Delegate secretarial assistance/copying facilities if needed.

3 List all records seen and examined.

4 Resist removal of records and offer copies.

9.78 Conclusion of visit

1 Establish when the results of the review will be explained – agree a timescale.

2 Agree a timescale within which the officers will report their conclusions.

3 Agree a schedule of any matters outstanding.

4 Identify the specific areas for further research.

5 Establish who is to do what.

Checklist for areas the compliance officers are likely to review

9.79 Formal returns:

1 P11Ds.

2 VAT returns and the VAT account.

3 The wages books and records.

4 Cash records, nominal ledgers, private ledgers.

9.80 General records:

1 Clock cards, timesheets, worksheets, job cards.

2 Sickness records, absence records.

3 Holiday pay records.

4 Cash books, bank books, expense invoices, etc.

9.81 *Meetings with HMRC*

9.81 The danger areas:

1 Directors' benefits and expenses payments.

2 Accommodation and related benefits.

3 Casual labour records, overtime records.

4 Bonuses paid and weekend working records.

5 The subcontractors' scheme.

6 Students and part-time workers.

7 Status of subcontractors and consultants.

8 Travel and subsistence payments.

9 Overnight allowances and clothing allowances.

10 Class 1A insurance records and mileage records.

11 Telephone logs.

12 Tips and gratuities systems.

13 Tronc systems in operation.

14 Seasonal workers.

15 Payments to wives.

16 Cars provided for family members, entertaining and gifts, staff canteens and vending machines.

CONCLUSIONS

9.82 A meeting with HMRC is a potentially difficult experience for a client. The adviser's role is to participate actively and constructively during these meetings, to represent the client, to ensure that their rights are observed and upheld and to provide professional and positive guidance before and throughout the course of a meeting on the legal, technical and practical aspects of any case.

9.83 The adviser needs to be familiar with:

- relevant legislation;
- HMRC's statutory rights and duties;
- the client's rights and obligations;
- codes of practice on investigations and relevant parts of HMRC manuals.

9.84 This chapter is not an exhaustive review of all the aspects of HMRC meetings. It aims to provide some guidelines on how such meetings are best conducted. There can be little substitute for experience in this area of tax practice. Most practitioners can, however, perform more than adequately, even very effectively in interview situations, with the right preparation (and perhaps a little luck!).

9.85 The opening meeting is frequently the key stage of an enquiry. This is so for both the client and the Inspector. An Inspector's training includes help and guidance on interviews and a rapid realisation that the ability to conduct a well-structured and successful meeting is a major factor in conducting successful enquiries. There is little doubt that the same can be said of an adviser. The accountant or tax practitioner who performs well during interviews is likely to achieve the best settlements for his clients.

Chapter 10

The information powers of HMRC

Hartley Foster, Partner and Head of Tax Disputes, DLA Piper UK

INTRODUCTION AND THE FUTURE

10.1 The Commissioners for Revenue and Customs Act 2005 (CRCA) received Royal Assent on 7 April 2005. It provides the legal basis for the integrated department of HM Customs & Excise and the Inland Revenue – Her Majesty's Revenue & Customs (HMRC), and for the independent prosecutions office – the Revenue and Customs Prosecutions Office (RCPO). HMRC is responsible for all the functions that were previously the responsibility of the Commissioners of Inland Revenue and the Commissioners of Customs & Excise. The exception to this is prosecutions, for which, as a result of CRCA, s 35 RCPO has responsibility. This removal of the prosecution function from HMRC was, in part, following the recommendations of His Honour Judge Butterfield. In his 'Review of Criminal Investigations and Prosecutions conducted by HM Customs and Excise' (15 July 2003), which examined the reasons for the collapse of the prosecution of 15 defendants for conspiracy to cheat the revenue in *R v Gell* [2003] EWCA Crim 123 (such reasons including: (i) that it was apparent that a prosecution witness had lied in the course of a *voir dire*; and (ii) that HM Customs and Excise Officers had withheld relevant evidence from the defence), HHJ Butterfield recommended that all prosecution (as opposed to investigation) functions should be removed from HM Customs and Excise's power and instead should be conducted by an entirely separate authority.

10.2 Both HM Customs & Excise and the Inland Revenue had powers for use in criminal investigations that were set out in legislation that applied only to each department (eg the ability to apply for a search warrant under s 20C of the Taxes Management Act 1970 (TMA) applied only to the Inland Revenue). The legislation that was available to the two departments was inconsistent and it did not provide any powers of arrest to HMRC Officers in respect of offences related to ex-Inland Revenue matters. In such cases, it was necessary for HMRC to seek the assistance of the police. Although HM Customs & Excise had different functions, responsibilities and powers to those of the Inland Revenue, when HMRC was established, the powers of each body were transferred unchanged to HMRC. The powers were 'ring fenced' so that they could be used only for their original purpose. Thus, the basis on which it was determined which powers are available to HMRC was by reference to the specific tax that is being investigated. The powers of the former Inland Revenue were applicable to direct taxes; the powers of the former HM Customs & Excise were applicable to indirect taxes, customs and excise duties.

10.3 However, the government recognised, prior to the merger of the departments, that it was important to consider whether the heterogeneous powers of HMRC could be rationalised. This would make it easier for taxpayers to understand and comply with their tax obligations, and potentially could reduce the administrative burden of the tax system that falls on them. A major review of HMRC's powers, deterrents and safeguards was undertaken. (During the second reading of CRCA, the Paymaster General announced that a consultation process entitled 'Modernising Powers, Deterrents and Safeguards: A Consultation on the Developing Programme of Work' would be commenced in 2006. This consultation process included a review of the information powers available to HMRC in relation to civil tax matters, as well as where criminal activity was suspected. HMRC indicated that, in their view, the Police and Criminal Evidence Act 1984 (PACE) should become the statutory framework for the investigation of all tax related criminal activity.) Following that review and a subsequent consultation, including consultation on draft clauses, the government, in Finance Act 2007, introduced enabling legislation under which HMRC's investigatory powers in England, Wales and Northern Ireland is based on the powers contained in PACE. (A statutory code is to be introduced for Scotland, where PACE does not apply.) By Treasury Order that was introduced with effect from 1 December 2007 (see further below), these powers apply across all taxes and mean that HMRC criminal investigations are now subject to the statutory codes of practice and safeguards which attach to criminal investigations generally. A notable change is therefore that HMRC Officers now have the PACE powers of search, seizure and arrest in connection with ex-Inland Revenue matters.

10.4 In 'Criminal Investigation Powers: Publication of Draft Clauses and Explanatory Notes' (which was published on 17 January 2007), it was proposed that the use of the PACE powers would be restricted to suitably trained Officers authorised by the Commissioners of HMRC; and at paragraph 7.7 of 'The Explanatory Memorandum to The Police and Criminal Evidence Act 1984 (Application to Revenue and Customs) Order 2007 SI No 2007 3175', it was indicated that, before 1 December 2007, HMRC will publish material on its Internet site in respect of 'how criminal investigation work is organised in HMRC, which Officers are entitled to use the powers and how use of the powers is authorised'. This proposal has, to an extent, been superseded by the introduction of the enabling Treasury Order. Nonetheless, on 6 December 2007, HMRC issued a release in which it was stated, inter alia:

'Authorisation to use powers

The criminal investigation powers can be used only by officers who are authorised to use them. An authorised officer is an officer of HM Revenue and Customs, appropriately trained and engaged on operational duties in Criminal Investigation, Detection, Risk and Intelligence and Internal Governance Directorates. PACE provides that some powers can be exercised only by police constables of a particular rank. When those powers are applied to HMRC the police ranks are converted to HMRC grades of an equivalent authority—

- Sergeant — Officer
- Inspector — Higher Officer
- Chief Inspector — Higher Officer
- Superintendent — Senior Officer

HMRC has set internal authorisation levels requiring an authorised officer to get the approval of a higher graded officer before using certain powers. The authority levels for HMRC are set no lower than the authority levels in the police, the primary user of PACE powers. However in most cases HMRC has set the main authority level required at a minimum of Senior Officer grade, for example applications to a magistrate or court for a production order or search warrant. The majority of authorities in the police service are held at Inspector level, equivalent to HMRC's Higher Officer grade.'

10.5 The amendments in Finance Act 2007 increase the powers available to ex-Inland Revenue investigators; and mean that HMRC no longer needs to follow different procedures in the same investigation where both direct and indirect tax fraud are suspected. Finance Act 2007 repealed TMA 1970, s 20C and Value Added Taxes Act 1994 (VATA), para 10(3), Sch 11 with effect from a date to be appointed by Treasury Order and enabled the Treasury to make orders applying the provisions of PACE to investigations conducted by Officers of HMRC (under ss 82(2) and 83(2) of the Finance Act 2007). The Police and Criminal Evidence Act 1984 (Application to Revenue and Customs) Order 2007/SI 2007 3175, which was laid before Parliament on 9 November 2007, came into force, and applies the relevant provisions of PACE to all functions of HMRC (except where the department acts as an agent for other government departments), with effect from 1 December 2007. Thus, since 1 December 2007, HMRC Officers have had access to the appropriate powers in PACE to investigate all tax matters where criminal activity is suspected. In particular, from that date, search warrants are now obtained under PACE, s 8, Sch 1 rather than TMA 1970, s 20C (for offences concerning direct tax) or VATA 1994, para 10(3), Sch 11 (for offences concerning indirect tax).

10.6 The changes introduced by Finance Act 2007 will resolve a number of the problems that arose when HMRC Officers sought to investigate combined instances of direct and indirect tax fraud. For example, prior to the introduction of these changes, if a taxpayer was suspected of both VAT and corporation tax fraud, separate warrants for each of these offences were required to search and seize evidence from the same premises and, arguably, the taxpayer had to be arrested twice (once by the police for the suspected direct tax offence and once by HMRC Officers for the suspected indirect tax offence). There remain a number of police powers (such as the power to charge and bail suspects and the power to take fingerprints) that HMRC are unable to exercise; and it is anticipated that further rationalisation of the powers available to HMRC Officers, in accordance with the fundamental underlying principle of the proposed changes, namely that the nature of the activity, rather than the tax, should determine the ambit of the statutory power, will be introduced in due course.

10.7 Finance Act 2007 also introduced a new regime for penalties for incorrect declarations and returns. Finance Act 2007, Schedule 24 (Commencement and Transitional Provisions) Order 2008 (SI 2008/568) brings into force the provisions of Finance Act 2007, Sch 24 in relation to return periods beginning from 1 April 2008, but provides that Sch 24 shall not apply to any tax period for which a return is required to be made before 1 April 2009. This new regime is examined in more detail in Chapter 14. However, in short, under Sch 24, a single penalty regime will apply to returns (and similar documents) for income tax (including PAYE), capital gains tax, the Construction Industry Scheme, corporation tax, National Insurance Contributions and VAT. Under the new regime, an error in a 'taxpayer's document' (which is broadly a tax return or the accounts that accompany the return) gives rise to a penalty if that inaccuracy amounts to or leads to an understatement of the taxpayer's liability to tax and that inaccuracy was 'careless or deliberate'. The new approach relates the determination of penalties to the underlying behaviour that gave rise to the inaccurate return or assessment. If it was caused by a mistake or misinterpretation of fact or law and reasonable care was taken, then there is no penalty. Otherwise, to reflect the increasing seriousness of the behaviour, penalties at three different levels may be imposed: (1) failure to take reasonable care; (2) deliberate understatement; and (3) deliberate understatement with concealment. There are reductions for disclosure.

10.8 Documents in respect of which a penalty is exigible under TMA 1970, s 98 are expressly excluded from the Sch 24 penalty regime. Thus, the 'old' regime remains in force in relation to penalties for failure to comply with s 20 notices (see para **10.78**). The penalty for failure to comply with an s 19A notice remains exigible under TMA 1970, s 97AA (see para **10.100**). However, the review of penalties has yet to be completed, and amendments to the above may be proposed shortly.

SUMMARY OF THE KEY INFORMATION POWERS

Direct tax powers

10.9 HMRC has an extremely wide range of powers that it can call on to ascertain the quantum of tax due from a particular taxpayer, to confirm and collect the tax due and then to enforce payment of the tax. In this note, the focus is on the powers that HMRC can use to collect information to establish the existence of a liability to tax and to calculate its quantum. The tax information gathering powers can be divided into:

1 the issue of returns of various types; and

2 the issue of notices requiring the production of documents or information.

10.10 The first of these categories include the provisions of TMA 1970, ss 13 to 19, 21 and 23 to 28, under which notices can be served on certain persons requiring them to make returns containing information relevant to the taxable income of other persons. These include:

1 the names of employees, and details of payments to them, from an employer under s 15;

2 details of payments, such as commissions, made for services to persons other than their employees from traders (and certain others), under s 16; and

3 interest payments made by banks, under ss 17 and 18.

10.11 With regard to the second of these categories, the two main sets of provisions are:

1 the powers given to HMRC under TMA 1970, ss 20 to 20D ('the s 20 powers'); and

2 the powers that were introduced under the personal and corporate self-assessment regimes (under TMA 1970, s 19A and the Finance Act 1998, Sch 18, para 27 respectively) ('the self-assessment powers').

10.12 Wide and general information powers are bestowed on HMRC under s 20. These powers are among the most important in HMRC's arsenal of weapons to detect, quantify and prevent any loss of tax that may have arisen through either a failure to make returns or the submission of incomplete or incorrect returns (whether innocently incorrect or not). The s 20 powers are distinct from (and additional to) the self-assessment powers, which enable an Inspector to issue a notice to the taxpayer requiring 'such documents as are in the taxpayer's possession or power' and 'such accounts or particulars' as he may reasonably require in order to determine the accuracy of the return, in two important ways. First, the s 20 powers are 'free-standing' in that they can be used even if there is no open enquiry; and, secondly, third parties can be required to produce documents in their power or possession that contain information relevant to another person's tax liability. The powers that HMRC possesses in relation to direct taxes that are most relevant are ss 20(1), (3), and (8A) (which give information powers), and s 20BA (which gives a production power). Although s 20C (which gave a search and seizure power) has been repealed (and replaced with a PACE power to enter with a warrant to obtain documents), a brief analysis of this power is also provided in the final section of this chapter for comparative purposes. In this chapter, the s 20 powers are analysed first before the self-assessment powers are outlined.

Indirect tax powers

10.13 The most relevant powers in relation to VAT are in VATA 1994, Sch 11. There are two distinct powers under Schedule 11: paragraph 7 gives a power to obtain information and documents; paragraphs 10(1) and (2) bestow on authorised representatives of HMRC a right to enter premises at any reasonable time. An analysis of these powers is set out at [10.140] of this chapter.

10.14 VATA 1994, para 10(3), Sch 11 gave HMRC a right to search and seize under the authority of a warrant. Although this power was repealed by Finance Act 2007 with effect from 1 December 2007 (and replaced with a PACE power to enter with a warrant to obtain documents), a brief analysis of this power is provided in the final section of this chapter for comparative purposes.

Powers under PACE and the Serious Organised Crime and Police Act 2005

10.15 The final section of this chapter comprises:

- an analysis of the powers under PACE that were made available to HMRC Officers with effect from 1 December 2007; and
- the powers under the Serious Organised Crime and Police Act 2005 (SOCPA) which can be exercised by HMRC Officers under delegation from the RCPPO.

THE DIRECT TAX POWERS

Overview of TMA 1970, s 20

10.16 There are three main s 20 powers:

- s 20(1);
- s 20(3) (which includes s 20(8A)); and
- s 20BA.

10.17 Although, as indicated above, it has been repealed by Finance Act 2007, s 20C is also considered below.The first two are information powers, and the third is a production power. Section 20C was a search and seizure power. With regard to the information powers, notices under s 20(1) (and under s 20(2)) are served on a person in relation to his own tax liability and are known as 'first-party notices'; and notices under ss 20(3) and 20(3) as extended by s 20(8A) are served on third parties in relation to another person's tax liabilities and thus are known as 'third party notices'. A further distinction can be drawn between notices that can be issued by an Inspector and those can be issued only by the Board of HMRC; although it is rarely used in practice, s 20(2) is similar in ambit to s 20(1), but it can be used by the Board of HMRC only.

The information powers – s 20(1) and (3)

10.18 An s 20(1) or (3) notice requires the taxpayer or third party respectively to produce documents in their 'possession or power' which, in the Inspector of Taxes' reasonable opinion, contain or may contain information relevant to the tax liability of any person named in the notice. The subjective nature of the words 'reasonable opinion' gives a significant discretion to Inspectors to determine what information they consider is necessary to determine the amount of any tax liability that a person may be subject to (and there is a presumption that the Inspector is acting reasonably in this regard – see *R v Inland Revenue Commissioners and another, ex parte Mohammed and another* [1999] STC 129).

10.19 There are a number of statutory restrictions on the exercise of the s 20 information powers by HMRC. The restrictions are outlined in more detail below, but they include the following:

- The taxpayer or third party must have been given a reasonable opportunity to produce the requisite information or documents voluntarily; this is usually done by the service of a 'precursor notice' requesting the provision of the documents within a certain time limit (often 30 days) (s 20B(1)).
- Notices under s 20(1) and (3) can be issued by an Officer only after permission has been granted by a General or Special Commissioner (or in the case of a s 20(8A) by a Special Commissioner only), who must be satisfied in all the circumstances that the Officer is justified in proceeding under this section (s 20(7)).

- An Officer of HMRC may not give a s 20(1) or (3) notice to a barrister, advocate or solicitor; the decision to give such a notice must be taken by the Board (s 20B(3)).
- Notices must specify a date for compliance, which must be not less than 30 days after the date of the notice (s 20(8D)(a)).
- Privileged materials in the possession of either the taxpayer or a legal adviser are protected from disclosure.
- Neither the taxpayer nor a third party is obliged to produce documents relating to a 'pending appeal' by the taxpayer. This is a limited, but additional, form of 'litigation privilege' (s 20B(2)).
- Tax accountants are protected from disclosing audit papers or working papers that contain tax advice (s 20B(9)).
- Personal records which are excluded from police search powers and journalistic material are protected from disclosure (s 20(8C)).

Issue of a precursor notice

10.20 Before a s 20(1) or (3) notice can be issued, the Inspector must provide the taxpayer or third party with a reasonable opportunity to deliver voluntarily (or, in the case of s 20(3) only, make them available for inspection) the documents that will be specified in the notice (under s 20B(1)). This is normally done by the issue of a 'precursor' notice, requesting the voluntary provision of the specified documents within a certain time limit, often 30 days.

10.21 The issue of a precursor notice 'freezes' the documents concerned. A taxpayer or third party will be guilty of an offence (under s 20BB(1)) if it intentionally falsifies, conceals, destroys, or otherwise disposes of, a document whose production is requested by the precursor notice, or causes or permits any of the aforementioned to occur. If found guilty, a taxpayer or third party can be liable, on summary conviction, to a fine not exceeding £3,000 or, on conviction on indictment, to a maximum of two years' imprisonment, a fine or both.

10.22 In contrast with the situation under s 20BA, where a third party cannot advise the taxpayer of receipt of such a notice – under TMA 1970, Sch 1AA, para 4(1)(b), there is an obligation not to 'disclose to any other person information or any other matter likely to prejudice the investigation of the offence to which the application relates' – a third party may inform the relevant taxpayer that it has received a s 20(3) precursor notice. Informing a taxpayer would give that taxpayer the opportunity to contact HMRC directly before any s 20(3) notice is served on the third party, and therefore could negate the need for issuance of the s 20(3) notice. Under s 20B(1A) (introduced by Finance

Act 1989, s 144), a copy of the third party notice must be sent to the taxpayer whose affairs are being investigated, unless a Commissioner has directed to the contrary in the case of suspected fraud.

Consent from a Commissioner of Tax

10.23 After the period specified in the precursor notice for voluntary production of the specified documents has expired (without production of the documents), the Inspector may apply for consent to the issuing of the s 20(1) or s 20(3) notice. Consent to an s 20(3) notice may be granted by either a General or Special Commissioner; consent to an s 20(8A) notice can be granted only by a Special Commissioner.

10.24 The Commissioner must be satisfied that, in all the circumstances, the Inspector is justified in proceeding under s 20. The reasonableness of the Inspector's opinion as to the potential relevance of the information contained in the documents is a necessary, but not a sufficient, condition for the Special Commissioner to give his consent. The wording of s 20(7) clearly encompasses the possibility that, notwithstanding the fact that the Inspector has reasonable grounds for believing that the use of the power under s 20 is justified, the Special Commissioner is not satisfied that this course is justified and exercises his discretion not to give consent. The further step that the Special Commissioner must carry out is a balancing act between the reasonable requirements of HMRC to obtain information, in order to carry out the effective investigation of tax affairs, and the protection of the personal property rights of taxpayers against invasion. As this duty to give effect to this balancing act rests on the Special Commissioner alone, it is the Special Commissioner who has the role of acting as an important safeguard of the rights of citizens. Before consent is given, the Special Commissioner must be satisfied in all the circumstances that the Inspector is justified in invoking his compulsory powers. The Special Commissioner is 'the independent person entrusted by Parliament with the duty of supervising the exercise of the intrusive power conferred by section 20 …' (*per* Lord Lowry in *R v Inland Revenue Commissioner, ex parte TC Coombs* [1991] STC 97 at 108*f*).

10.25 The hearing before the Commissioner is without notice. (The Court of Appeal held in *R* (*on the application of Morgan Grenfell*) *v Special Commissioner of Income Tax*) [2001] STC 497 that Morgan Grenfell had no right to attend the hearing and that the Special Commissioner had no discretion to permit its attendance. That issue was not taken to the House of Lords (who reversed the Court of Appeal's decision on the issue of legal professional privilege). There is a potential argument that the basis on which the House of Lords overturned the Court of Appeal's decision on privilege renders that court's decision on attendance *per incuriam*. However, to succeed on such an argument it would have to be taken to at least the level of the Court of Appeal. However, the Inspector is under a duty to ensure that all relevant facts, including those unfavourable to the Inland Revenue, are put before the Commissioner and that a full record of the proceedings is kept (*R v Macdonald and CIR, ex parte Hutchinson & Co Ltd* [1998] STC 680). The Commissioners have a general power to receive evidence that would be inadmissible in a court of law (see the Special Commissioners (Jurisdiction and Procedure) Regulations 1994 (SI 1994/1811)).

Documents

10.26 Section 20D(3) defines 'documents' as 'anything in which information of any description is recorded'. Thus, included within the definition of document will be:

- correspondence, whether by letter, email or fax;
- any disk, tape or other device from which data can be reproduced;
- any film, negative, tape or other device from which a visual image can be reproduced; and
- maps, plans, graphs, drawings and photographs.

Excluded from this definition (under s 20(8C)) are personal records (eg medical records) or journalistic material, as defined by PACE, ss 12 and 13 respectively.

10.27 Following the decision of the House of Lords in *R v Special Commissioner, ex parte Morgan Grenfell & Co Ltd* [2003] 1 AC 56, documents in respect of which a claim to legal professional privilege can be asserted are excluded from the scope of s 20 notices.

10.28 It is permissible to provide copies of documents instead of the originals, but these must be photocopies or facsimile copies (under s 20B(4)(a)). Originals must be made available for inspection by a named Officer of the Board if required (under s 20B(4)(b)). Failure to comply with this requirement is regarded as a failure to comply with the notice.

10.29 A taxpayer or third party can also be required to provide a person authorised by the Board of HMRC with access to any computer or any associated apparatus or material which is or has been in use in connection with any document within the ambit of the notice (under Finance Act 1988, s 172(2)). Access must be granted at any reasonable time and suitable assistance from a computer operator or other appropriate person must be provided, if requested, to assist in accessing, inspecting or checking the computer and associated equipment. The maximum penalty for failing to allow access to a computer or provide reasonable assistance is £500.

10.30 Under s 20(1)(b), a taxpayer may be required to produce, on service of a notice under s 20, 'such particulars as the Inspector may reasonably require as being relevant to, or to the amount of, any' tax liability to which the person is or may be subject. It is considered that, by reason of this subsection, taxpayers can be required to create new documents under s 20(1) (and under s 20(2)). In *Accountant v Inspector of Taxes* [2000] STC (SCD) 522, the Special Commissioner noted that whilst s 19A(2)(a) refers to the production of documents as are in the taxpayer's 'power or possession', s 19A(2)(b), which requires that the taxpayer 'furnish such accounts or particulars as the officer may reasonably require' is not so limited expressly and thus concluded that under this subsection a taxpayer can be asked to create new documents. It is considered that this reasoning would apply equally to s 20, and therefore apply to ss 20(1) and 20(2). Section 20(3) (and (8A)) do not contain the equivalent of s 20(1)(b), and so cannot be used to require the third party to create a document (or documents).

Protection of privileged material

10.31 Material over which a claim to legal professional privilege can be sustained is protected from disclosure whether it is in the possession of the taxpayer, or his legal adviser, following the decision of the House of Lords in *R on the application of Morgan Grenfell & Co Ltd v Special Commissioners* [2002] STC 786. It is considered that the decision of the House of Lords applies also so as to protect privileged material that is in the possession of a third party from disclosure consequent on an s 20(3) notice.

10.32 Although a barrister, advocate or solicitor is not obliged to produce privileged documents in his possession without the consent of his client in response to an s 20(3) notice (s 20B(8)), the claim of privilege is not available in relation to notices issued to a legal adviser *qua* as taxpayer (see *R v Inland Revenue Commissioners, ex parte Taylor (No 2)* [1990] STC 379, and *R v Inland Revenue Commissioners, ex parte Lorimer* [2000] STC 751).

10.33 In addition to legal professional privilege, two statutorily created quasi-privileges restrict the documents that may be sought by services of notices under s 20(1) and (3):

- Under s 20B(2), documents 'relating to the conduct of any pending appeal' need not be provided.
- Section 20B(9) creates a privilege in relation to documents that are the property of 'tax advisers' or accountants.

Legal professional privilege

10.34 Legal professional privilege is a fundamental aspect of the legal system in this country. It allows a person to consult a lawyer without fear that the information that he reveals will be disclosed in court contrary to his wishes. It thus enables the client to have confidence in the confidentiality of his legal adviser and so encourages him to 'make a clean breast of it to the gentleman whom he consults' (*per* Sir George Jessell MR, *Anderson v Bank of British Columbia* [1876] 2 ChD 644 at 649). Further, legal professional privilege has been recognised as an aspect of the right to privacy under Article 8 of the European Convention on Human Rights by the European Court of Human Rights and by the European Court of Justice to be part of European Community Law. That privilege is a fundamental human right has been recognised in the UK by the House of Lords in a series of cases. (See *R (on the application of Morgan Grenfell & Co Limited) v Special Commissioner of Income Tax* [2002] STC 786, *per* Lord Hobhouse of Woodborough at 798*f* and Lord Hoffmann at 796*g-j* and 790*d*, where he said that: '[privilege] has been held by the European Court of Human Rights to be part of the right of privacy guaranteed by art 8 of the Convention for the Protection of Human Rights and Fundamental Freedoms'.) There are two heads of privilege: legal advice privilege and litigation privilege.

Legal advice privilege

10.35 There is no requirement that such documents be produced for the 'dominant purpose' of legal advice. Provided that there is a 'relevant legal context', a lawyer/client communication will be privileged. This will cover most lawyer/client communications.

10.36 Internal communications between employees of a company, even if for the purpose of seeking legal advice or preparing 'raw material' in respect of which advice may be given are not privileged, unless those employees are the 'client'. Only those employees in an organisation who are given the role of obtaining or receiving legal advice can be classified as 'the client' for the purposes of privilege.

10.37 Communications between third parties and lawyers or clients are not privileged under this head, even if they are made in connection with the seeking or giving of legal advice. The only exception to this rule is if that third party is an agent of either the lawyer or the client and is simply a medium of communication. This is strictly construed. (See *Price Waterhouse v BCCI Holdings* [1992] BCLC 583 where Millett J (as he then was) held that reports produced by accountants and sent to lawyers were not privileged, as the accountants acted as more than mere agents of communication.)

10.38 Communications with other professionals, such as accountants or chartered tax advisers, will not attract legal professional privilege under this head, even if they are giving advice on strictly legal matters, such as tax law. (See *Chantry Martin v Martin* [1953] 2 QB 286 and *Glengallen Investments Pty Ltd v Arthur Andersen* [2002] 1 Qd R 233.)

Litigation privilege

10.39 Litigation privilege covers communications that came into existence for the dominant purpose of being used in connection with or in contemplation of litigation. There is an overlap between advice and litigation privilege in that, once litigation is in prospect, then lawyer/client documents produced for that litigation will be protected under both heads.

10.40 There are two important limits on litigation privilege. First, it does not arise in respect of non-adversarial proceedings. In *Re L* [1997] AC 16, the House of Lords held (by a majority) that litigation privilege could not apply to proceedings under Part IV of the Children Act 1989 in respect of child care orders, because the proceedings were not adversarial in nature; privilege was excluded by necessary implication from the terms and overall purpose of the Act.

10.41 Secondly, the documents must be produced for the 'dominant purpose' of litigation. In *Waugh v British Railways Board* [1980] AC 521, the House of Lords adopted and applied the 'dominant purpose' test that had been put forward by Barwick CJ in his minority judgment in the High Court of Australia in *Grant v Downs* [1976] 135 CLR 674, at 677 to determine whether a report that had been prepared both for safety purposes and for the purpose of obtaining legal advice in anticipation of litigation was privileged. (Lord Edmund-Davies described the 'dominant purpose' test as the 'touchstone' of the privilege.)The dominant purpose test (which must be applied at the time of creation) acts as a filter mechanism and prevents privilege attaching to documents brought into existence for purposes other than that of legal advice. If a document has been produced partly for the purpose of litigation and partly for another purpose, that document will not be privileged if the relevant litigation purpose is a secondary or even an equal purpose. Thus, for example, communications by a tax authority with third parties in order to ascertain the value of goods for the purpose of tax legislation, even though such communications also would enable the authority to meet an inevitable challenge by taxpayers were not protected by litigation privilege. (*Alfred Crompton Amusement Machines Ltd v Customs and Excise Commissioners* (No 2) [1974] AC 405.)

10.42 There is a further important difference between the two privileges in that communications between the client or lawyer with third parties can be protected by litigation (but not advice) privilege. Although no lawyer need, in fact, have been engaged at the time of the communication, as the dominant purpose for which the communication is made must be either (i) obtaining legal advice from the client's lawyer, or (ii) use by the lawyer in aid of litigation that has commenced or is contemplated, whether litigation privilege applies to third party/client communications when no lawyer is contemplated is doubtful. This is particularly the case in the light of the recent judicial trend to seek to limit the ambit of litigation privilege. Lord Scott, for example, in *Three Rivers District*

Council and Others v Governor and Company of the Bank of England [2005] 1 AC 610 suggested that there should be a limit on third party communications being protected under the head of litigation privilege. In Lord Scott's view, even if such documents were produced for the dominant purpose of litigation, they should not be privileged unless they constitute or disclose the seeking or giving of legal advice. (See also Scott V-C in *Secretary of State v Baker (Re Barings)* [1998] Ch 356.)

10.43 The consequence of this is that if an accountant or tax adviser is instructed in relation to a tax dispute and instructing a legal adviser is not anticipated, then it is likely that communications between the adviser and the client will not be protected by litigation privilege. Such documents may, however, be protected by the statutorily created quasi-privileges under ss 20B(2) or 20B(9).

Section 20B(2)

10.44 Section 20B(2) is not coterminous with litigation privilege. It protects documents 'relating to the conduct of any pending appeal' from disclosure under service of a s 20(1) or (3) notice; it does not apply to notices served by the Board of HMRC under s 20(2). The reference to 'conduct' of appeals indicates that only documents that are brought into existence for the purposes of the preparation and presentation of the appeal are protected (see *Monarch Assurance Co Ltd v Special Commissioners and Inland Revenue Commissioners* [1986] STC 311). Section 20B(2) applies only in respect of 'pending' appeals. Until an appeal has been made by the taxpayer, s 20B(2) does not apply to documents, even if they came into existence for the purpose of contemplated litigation.

Auditors and tax advisers' documents

10.45 Section 20B(9)(a) provides that, subject to certain qualifications, which are described below, an auditor cannot be required to produce documents that are his property and that were created in the course of carrying out a statutory audit. In practice, HMRC allow equivalent protection where an accountant is appointed to carry out a non-statutory independent audit to standards similar to those required for a Companies Act audit, provided that the work on the audit is kept separate from any work on the preparation of the accounts.

10.46 Section 20B(9)(b) provides that, subject likewise to the qualifications described below, anyone appointed to give advice about the tax affairs of another person cannot be required to produce documents that are his property and which consist of 'relevant communications' with his taxpayer client or another tax adviser of the client for the purpose of giving or obtaining advice on that client's tax affairs. HMRC consider that the term 'relevant communications' can include notes of meetings and telephone calls, and internal memoranda, as well as client correspondence.

10.47 The protection for documents of tax advisers and auditors is subject to two qualifications:

1 Under s 20B(11), if the auditor or tax adviser has assisted a client in completing a return, accounts or other document or information for production to HMRC, then no protection is provided for such part of any document which contains workings or analytical information showing how a particular entry on the return, accounts etc was arrived at.

2 Under s 20B(12), where the notice requiring production of documents relates to an unidentified taxpayer (ie it is a notice under s 20(8A)), no protection is provided for such part of a document which contains information as to the identity or address of a taxpayer to whom the notice relates or in respect of any person who has acted on behalf of such a taxpayer.

10.48 Section 20B(11) and (12) are subject to s 20B(13), which provides that the s 20B(9) protection for a document in the possession of an auditor or tax adviser is not lost as a result of these qualifications if the explanatory information or the information identifying the taxpayer or adviser respectively is also contained in another document that has already been produced to HMRC.

10.49 HMRC have stated that the formal power to require access to an accountant's working papers will be used only where the information needed cannot be obtained on a voluntary basis and HMRC have no other means of satisfying themselves that a taxpayer's accounts or returns are accurate.

10.50 Section 20A applies to any tax accountant, who has been convicted by a UK court of any tax offence, or has had a penalty imposed on him for assisting in the preparation of a tax return or accounts or any information or document to be used for tax purposes that he knows to be incorrect. (For the purposes of s 20A, 'tax accountant' includes any person who assists in the preparation of a return. It may therefore include a lawyer.) *Inland Revenue Bulletin* April 2000 at pp 743–46 sets out HMRC's interpretation of the scope of this power.

10.51 An Inspector may seek consent for the issue of an s 20A notice from the appropriate judicial authority, who is to give consent only if he is satisfied in all the circumstances that the Inspector is justified in so proceeding. The appropriate judicial authority in England and Wales is a Circuit judge. A notice under these provisions against a barrister, advocate or solicitor can be issued only by the Board, with the consent of the appropriate judicial authority. It cannot require the production of any document for which a claim for professional privilege can be maintained.

10.52 Under an s 20A notice, HMRC may seek delivery of documents that are in the possession or power of the tax accountant, and which, in the Inspector's reasonable opinion, contain information relevant to the tax liability of any of his clients.

Possession or power

10.53 In contrast to s 20(1), which can require a taxpayer to create documents, s 20(3) and (8A) applies only to existing documents that are in the third party's possession or power. The terms 'power' and 'possession' are not defined in any of the taxing statutes; and there is little case law on the meaning of the phrase 'power or possession' in the context of requests for information from HMRC.

10.54 The term 'possession' applies in a variety of contexts and has a number of meanings (Palmer, *Bailment* (2nd edn, 1991) notes, at page 103 that 'Possession is a ductile and intuitive concept'; and Stroud's *Legal Dictionary* (5th edn, 1986) lists 49 different meanings). The meanings of the term 'possession' include: (i) *de facto* control or 'custody', that is, actual physical possession; (ii) the right to possession where actual physical possession is not present; (iii) ownership; and (iv) 'legal' possession in the sense of physical possession combined with a right to possession.

10.55 The most relevant to the meaning of the term in the context of s 20 is the phrase that formerly appeared in the Rules of the Supreme Court in relation to the inspection and discovery of documents for the purposes of civil litigation in the High Court. (The duty of disclosure under the Civil Procedure Rules is limited to documents which are or have been in a party's control; and so does not assist interpretatively here.) Under these Rules a party was required to list, for the purposes of disclosure, the documents that were in his 'possession, custody or power' (with the term 'custody' being added in 1964). The meaning of the threefold test was considered in a matrimonial case, *B v B* [1978] Fam 181, where Dunn J. said that:

> '… for this purpose "possession" means the right to the possession of a document. "Custody" means the actual, physical or corporeal holding of a document regardless of the right to its possession, for example, a holding of a document by a party as servant or agent of the true owner. "Power" means an enforceable right to inspect the document or to obtain possession or control of the document from the person who ordinarily has it in fact. The requirements of the rules are disjunctive in their operation, so far as possession, custody and power are concerned.'

10.56 Thus, it is clear that Dunn J was of the view that 'possession' is limited to lawful possession. *De facto* control, or physical possession without a right to possession is not sufficient. If a document has been entrusted to an individual who is acting as the owner's agent or bailee, and is physically held by that individual subject to an obligation of confidentiality to the owner, then that the document is not in the legal possession of the agent or bailee, because although he has custody (or physical possession) of the document, he does not have an unfettered right to possession of the document. Although this definition was in the context of a threefold test of 'possession, custody or power', there seems to be no reason why that definition should not apply equally in s 20, which refers to 'possession or power'.

10.57 Documents that are in the custody or physical possession of an officer or employee of a company, if held as servant or agent of the company, or by such individual in his capacity as an officer or an employee of the company, will be treated as being in the possession of the company (see *Skoye v Bailey* [1971] 1 WWR 144 and *Williams v Ingram* (1900) 16 TLR 451).

Power

10.58 Although 'power' has a number of meanings, its meaning in the context of access to information is clear. The term has been defined by the House of Lords in *Lonhro Limited v Shell Petroleum* [1980] 1 WLR 627. In *Lonhro*, the claimants sought disclosure of documents held by foreign subsidiaries of Shell. The claimants argued that, even though the subsidiary companies had refused to supply the documents further to a request from Shell, the documents were in the 'power' of Shell and were thus disclosable under Order 24, rule 2 of the Rules of the Supreme Court (which provided that 'all documents must be disclosed which the party giving discovery has or has had in his possession, custody or power'). Shell owned 100% of the shares of the subsidiary companies; and so it could remove the directors or change the articles so as to require disclosure of the documents. This argument was rejected by the Court of Appeal ([1980]) QB 358). Shaw LJ noted that, in a general philosophical sense, there was a latent power that could be used to achieve possession of the relevant documents. However, no note of futurity could be read into Order 24. As it specified documents that 'were or had been' within a party's power, that constituted the limits on what could be obtained. It could only be in the situation where company A was so subservient to the wishes of company B that compliance was guaranteed that it could be said that company B had the documents in its power.

10.59 The House of Lords upheld the decision of the Court of Appeal, Lord Diplock saying that the term 'power' means:

> 'a presently enforceable legal right to obtain from whoever actually holds the document inspection of it without the need to obtain the consent of anyone else' (at 635).

The following observation was made:

> 'The articles of association of all the subsidiaries vest the management of the company in its board of directors. It is the board that has control of the company's documents on its behalf; the shareholders as such have no right to inspect or to take copies of them. If requested to allow inspection of the company's documents, whether by a shareholder or by a third party, it is the duty of the board to consider whether to accede to this request would be in the best interests of the company' (at 634).

10.60 The rule was caveated, however: 'I say nothing about one-man companies in which a natural person and/or his nominees are the sole shareholders and directors. It may be that, depending upon their own particular facts, different considerations apply to these' (at 636–37).

10.61 The decision of the House of Lords was considered recently in the context of the information powers of HMRC in *Meditor Capital Management v Feighan* [2004] STC (SCD) 273. Meditor concerned, inter alia, documents that were held by Meditor Capital Management (Bermuda) Limited ('MCM(B)') in Bermuda and sought by HMRC by service of a notice under the Finance Act 1998, Sch 18, para 27 on Meditor Capital Management Ltd ('Meditor'), a UK resident 100% subsidiary of MCM(B). Meditor adduced evidence of correspondence between itself and MCM(B), which showed that it had asked MCM(B) twice to supply to it the documents requested by the Revenue and that MCM(B) had twice refused to do so. The Special Commissioner held that these letters were not sufficient proof that the particular documents were not in the power or possession of Meditor. He hinted that the *Lonrho* test may not be the correct test to apply for these purposes, and that simply a *de facto* ability to obtain the documents or particulars might suffice. However, this decision was in the context of Meditor having previously agreed to provide the particular documents (under the terms of agreed directions) and having provided other information that had been, both legally and factually, held on an identical basis to the particular information that it claimed was not in its power or possession.

10.62 Thus, with regard to documents held offshore by non-UK resident companies in a group of companies with a UK resident parent company, provided that the relevant company is a separate legal entity and it cannot be said that it is so subservient to the wishes of the parent company that, with regard to requests from that company, compliance will be guaranteed always, it cannot be said that all documents in the possession of a subsidiary company are in the power of the parent company. If the parent company is unable to recover the documents without taking further steps, such as amending the articles to allow the shareholders to have a right of inspection of the documents, then the parent company does not have power over the documents. This is on the assumption that the autonomy which the overseas subsidiaries enjoy is conferred on them *bona fide*, and that the local directors 'run their own show' with comparatively little interference from the parent company.

10.63 It is possible (but unlikely) that HMRC could try to obtain disclosure of documents in the power or possession of a non-UK resident company by service of a separate s 20 (either under s 20(3) or 20(8A)) notice directly on that company. There is no express statutory or judicial limitation on the territorial scope of s 20, TMA; and, indeed, HMRC has expressed the view that, for example, the reporting obligations imposed on professionals under s 218 Inheritance Taxes Act 1984 have extra-territorial effect. However, it is unlikely that HMRC would try to obtain disclosure of 'offshore information' from an offshore entity (unless that entity has a 'sufficient presence' in the United Kingdom (as that term was defined by the House of Lords in *Clark v Oceanic Contractors* [1983] STC 35)), particularly if such disclosure could expose the offshore entity to penalties or legal challenge in its own jurisdiction, as HMRC is unlikely to wish to find itself drawn into a test case as to the scope of its statutory powers in this context.

Section 20(8A)

10.64 Section 20(8A) was introduced by the Finance Act 1988, s 126. The *fons et origo* of s 126 was the *Report of the Committee on Enforcement Powers of the Revenue Departments* (Cmnd 8822) produced by Lord Keith of Kinkel ('the Keith Report'). The Keith Committee had carried out a wide-ranging review of the enforcement powers of both the Inland Revenue and HM Customs and Excise; and it recommended changes to the existing information powers of the Inland Revenue (principally s 20 as it was then enacted). At that time, the power to issue 'third party notices' under s 20(3) was limited. There were various restrictions placed upon the availability of that power in relation to the class of persons on whom it could be served; and a third party notice could be served in relation to an identified taxpayer only. The Keith Committee concluded, at 15.4.1, that:

> '… in particular it seemed to us that limitation of the third party information power in s 20(4)(b) to a person carrying on a business was unnecessary and undesirable in principle. In our view the Inspector ought to be free to serve a production notice upon any person he reasonably believes to be in possession of relevant information.'

10.65 The Keith Committee then considered the issue of identification of the taxpayer. At paragraph 15.5 it was stated:

> '15.5.1 We consider that as a matter of principle the Inspector should wherever possible be required to identify the taxpayer under investi-

gation when making a formal information production demand on a third party and we so recommend. We received a considerable body of representation against the principle of 'fishing' being associated with a general information power. Those witnesses who admitted a possible need for a fishing power, for example in relation to a specific anti-avoidance provision (Chapter 7), considered that it should be particularly enacted in each situation when it is required.

15.5.2 This seemed to us to be appropriate in relation to the kind of 'fishing' notice used in the *Clinch* case ((1973) 49 TC 52)), where a professional agent is asked for particulars of any transactions of a specified kind in which he has acted for a client. We consider, however, that it is not reasonable to attempt to exclude every information enquiry that does not relate to an identified taxpayer from those proper to the general information power. Between the ground covered by an information power associated with a specific anti-avoidance provision and the ground within a general information power where it is possible to identify the taxpayer in question, lies a middle ground which the Department represented to us is quite extensive. We consider that this middle ground lies legitimately within the scope of the general information power, because it is important that the Inspector should be able to obtain information connecting a specific transaction or situation with an, as yet, unidentified taxpayer.'

10.66 Thus, the purpose of what was to become s 20(8A) was to deal with the 'middle ground', that is, the intersection between specific anti-avoidance measures and general information powers. That the context for the introduction of this power was tax avoidance schemes was recognised by the Inland Revenue and by the Government. During the debates on the Finance Bill 1988, the Economic Secretary to the Treasury (Peter Lilley) explained that 'the clause … is intended to cover circumstances in which an Inspector may suspect abuse by a group of people and wants information' (Hansard, Standing Committee A, 28 June 1988, col 676). On 15 March 1988, when clause 118 of the Finance Bill 1988 (which was enacted as s 126 Finance Act 1988) was laid before Parliament in draft, the Inland Revenue published a press release, which commented on the draft provision. In this press release, which was entitled 'measures to improve tax compliance', it was stated, at paragraphs 10 to 12:

'Information about serious tax defaulters

10. It is proposed to allow the Revenue to call for information about taxpayers whose identity is not known to the Revenue, but who are suspected of serious tax default.

11. The Revenue can already ask for information about a particular, named taxpayer. But this authority does not cover documents giving

the names of people the Revenue cannot identify, even where it is known that something is seriously amiss. This might happen, for example, where a tax avoidance scheme is marketed, which the Revenue investigate and establish to be not legally effective. The sponsor of the scheme may have told his clients that there is no tax liability on the profits covered by the scheme and no need to include them in their tax returns. There may therefore be reason to believe that there are large amounts of income which are liable to tax, but which have not been reported to the Revenue.

12. The proposal will enable the Inspector, but only after obtaining the approval of a Special Commissioner, to require the sponsor to reveal information about those using the failed scheme. The new power will be restricted to cases of serious tax loss, and an order from the Board of Inland Revenue will be needed before the Inspector may apply to the Commissioners.'

10.67 That the power under s 20(8A) was introduced primarily for the purpose of enabling the then Inland Revenue to obtain information from sponsors of tax avoidance schemes with regard to their clients is reflected in the Enquiry Manual of HMRC, where it is stated, at EM 2406, that:

'The Revenue may be aware of the existence of serious tax irregularities but not of the identity of the person(s) involved. A tax adviser may, for example, have sold an avoidance scheme to a number of clients which is proved ineffectual in the case of one of them. This power enables the Revenue to serve a notice requiring the adviser to provide information about the others.'

10.68 Section 20(8A) enables HMRC to serve an s 20(3) notice that does not name the taxpayer to whom the notice relates (an 's 20(8A) notice'), provided that the additional tests under s 20(8A) are met. Section 20(8A) notices are a subset of s 20(3) notices (as the Court of Appeal in *R v Inland Revenue Commissioners, ex parte Ulster Bank Ltd* [1997] STC 832 indicated ('… notices given under sub-s (8A) are but a subset of notices which may be given under sub-s (3). Thus a notice under sub-s (8A) must comply with all the same conditions as apply to a notice under sub-s (3) except with regard to the naming of the taxpayer' (*per* Morritt LJ said at 838))), and so the restrictions on the powers under s 20(3) apply, *mutatis mutandis*, with the following differences:

1 Consent of the Board of HMRC is required.

2 Only a Special Commissioner may consent to issuance of an s 20(8A) notice.

3 The Special Commissioner may exercise his discretionary power to give consent to issuance of an s 20(8A) notice only if he is satisfied that each of the additional tests in s 20(8A) has been met:

(a) the notice relates to a taxpayer whose identity is not known to the Inspector or to a class of taxpayers whose individual identities are not so known (s 20(8A)(a));

(b) that there are reasonable grounds for believing that the taxpayer or any of the class of taxpayers to whom the notice relates may have failed or may fail to comply with any provision of the Taxes Acts (s 20(8A)(b));

(c) that any such failure is likely to have led or to lead to serious prejudice to the proper assessment or collection of tax (s 20(8A)(c)); and

(d) that the information which is likely to be contained in the documents to which the notice relates is not readily available from another source (s 20(8A)(d)).

10.69 By s 20(7), a Special Commissioner is to give his consent 'only on being satisfied that in all the circumstances the Inspector is *justified* in proceeding under this section'. There is thus a balancing act between the reasonable requirements of HMRC to obtain information, in order to carry out the effective investigation of tax affairs, and the protection of the personal property rights of taxpayers against invasion to be carried out by the Special Commissioner. The obligation on the Special Commissioner to carry out this balancing act is most stringent in the case of s 20(8A) notices. Here, not only does the burden fall on a third party (as is the case with all s 20(3) notices), but also there is the likelihood that the burden will be a significant one. That this is so has been recognised by the courts. It has also been recognised by Parliament. (In the Standing Committee debates on Finance (No 2) Bill 1988 with regard to the clause that was to introduce what became s 20(8A) and (8B), an amendment was tabled that a person complying with an s 20(8A) notice be entitled to claim from the Revenue his reasonable expenses of so complying (ie as per Lord Keith's recommendation). Mr Howarth MP, for example, referred, in particular, to the 'enormous obligation' that would be imposed, on, for example, banks who might be required to provide details of a class of taxpayers who might have drawn cheques over a number of years.) Further, contrary to the express recommendation of the Keith Report, there is no possibility of reimbursement from HMRC of any reasonable costs incurred by a third party in complying with the significant burden.

10.70 However, the approach taken by the Special Commissioner in the six recent cases where the power under s 20(8A) was sought to be used by HMRC to obtain from a number of banks information in relation to individuals with a UK address and a non-UK bank account or a credit card that was associated with a non-UK bank account suggests that, even in relation to s 20(8A) notices, the scales are strongly weighted in HMRC's favour. The cases are: *Re an Application by Revenue and Customs Commissioners to serve section 20 notice* [2006] STC (SCD) 71; *Re an Application by Revenue and Customs Commissioners to serve section 20 notice (No 2)* [2006] STC (SCD) 360; *Re an Application by Revenue and Customs Commissioners to serve section 20 notice* [2007] STC (SCD) 202; *Re an Application by Revenue and Customs Commissioners to serve section 20 notice* [2007] STC (SCD) 208; *Re an Application by Revenue and Customs Commissioners to serve section 20 notice* [2007] STC (SCD) 216; *Re an Application by Revenue and Customs Commissioners to serve section 20 notice* [2007] STC (SCD) 222. In these cases, the Special Commissioner considered that the statistical evidence presented by HMRC in relation to the additional tax yield that would be generated consequent on the disclosure of the information sought was sufficient to enable him to conclude that the 'class' of taxpayers was in default and that this non-compliance by the class had led to serious prejudice to the proper assessment or collection of tax. In the first two cases to be decided (which concerned the same bank), HMRC's estimate was that 20% of the cases investigated following disclosure would result in additional tax yield. The total additional tax yield from customers of that bank who fell within the 'class' was estimated at £1,855 million. The figure given in relation to the following four banks was £40m, £55m, £36m, and £150m respectively. Given that the estimated anticipated total additional tax yield in the four subsequent cases was based on a similar percentage of cases leading to additional tax yield, but the average anticipated total additional tax yield consequent on the notices served on each bank was only c.4% of the tax yield that was estimated would be generated from customers of the first bank (and all five banks were (broadly) comparable in size) it would have been incumbent on the Inspector to provide a reasonable explanation for that extremely significant difference. For the judicial control introduced by s 20(8A) to be effective, the Special Commissioner should have evaluated that explanation and accepted it as legitimate before giving his consent. There is nothing in the decisions to suggest that any explanation at all was given or requested by the Special Commissioner.

10.71 Section 20(8A) has its own appeal route: under s 20(8B).

Appeal of s 20 notices

10.72 There is no straightforward right of appeal against the issue of an s 20(1) or (3) notice. Once the notice has been issued, there are two means by which it can be contested. The first is to raise the legitimacy of the notice at penalty proceedings for non-compliance with the notice (see *R v O'Kane, ex parte Northern Bank Ltd* [1996] STC 1249 and *Taxpayer v Inspector of Taxes*

[1996] STC (SCD) 261). The second is by means of judicial review of the decision of the General or Special Commissioner.

10.73 Those cases where taxpayers or third parties, such as banks, have sought to prevent HMRC's use of its formal information powers against them by means of judicial review do not give much encouragement to potential litigants who wish to halt HMRC in this regard. Absent *R v O'Kare and Clarke ex parte Northern Bank* [1996] STC 1249, when the courts have carried out the balancing act between the effective investigation of evasion and avoidance and the protection of the rights of companies and individuals, investigation has been favoured strongly over protection of rights. For example, the Court of Appeal in *R v Commissioners of Inland Revenue, ex parte Ulster Bank* [1997] STC 636 did not comment adversely on the possibility of Ulster Bank having to incur (without possibility of recovery) costs in the region of £350,000 in order to comply with the s 20 notices that it had been served with. (For the low points in the protection of the rights of third parties see the decision of the House of Lords in *TC Coombs & Co* [1991] STC 97 and the recent decisions of the Special Commissioner in respect of applications for s 20(8A) notices against financial institutions.)

Section 20(8A) appeal

10.74 Section 20(8A) has its own appeal route – s 20(8B). Section 20(8B) gives a third party 30 days in which to appeal in writing to the Inspector against the issue of the s 20(8A) notice on the grounds that it would be 'onerous' for him to comply with it. If the matter cannot be settled by agreement between the third party and the Inspector, it is referred to the Special Commissioners who may confirm, vary or cancel the notice. The term 'onerous' is not defined in s 20, nor, as far as the author is aware, in any statute. The dictionary definition of the term is 'burdensome; oppressive'. There are no reported cases on the meaning of 'onerous' in this context. However, it is considered that the Special Commissioners would weigh the burden that compliance would impose on the third party versus the likely benefit to HMRC in terms of collection of revenue. To succeed, it would have to be shown that the burden imposed on the third party in terms of, for example, staff costs, IT time and physical constraints outweighs the potential benefit to the Exchequer that would result from compliance with the notice.

Time limits

10.75 An s 20(3) notice does not oblige a third party to provide any document, the whole of which originates more than six years before the date of the notice, unless the Inspector has obtained approval from a Commissioner to extend the time limit on the basis that he is satisfied that there are reasonable grounds for believing that tax has, or may have been, lost as a result of fraud by the taxpayer. Also an s 20(3) notice cannot be issued in respect of a deceased taxpayer if more than six years have elapsed since his death. It is considered that, s 20(8A) being a subset of s 20(3), the same time restrictions apply equally in relation to s 20(8A) notices.

Section 20 offences

Destruction of documents

10.76 A taxpayer or third party is guilty of an offence if it intentionally falsifies, conceals, destroys, or otherwise disposes of, a document whose production is requested by a precursor notice, or causes or permits any of the aforementioned to occur. If found guilty, a taxpayer or third party can be liable, on summary conviction, to a fine not exceeding £3,000 or, on conviction on indictment, to a maximum of two years' imprisonment, a fine or both.

10.77 No offence is committed if documentation is disposed of or destroyed:

1. where written permission is obtained from a Commissioner, Inspector or an Officer of the Board;
2. after a document has been delivered or inspected, or a copy has been delivered and the original has been inspected;
3. where no s 20 notice has been issued and six months have elapsed since the issue of the precursor notice; or
4. after a Commissioner has refused the application for consent to issue an s 20 notice requiring the production of the documents.

Unless an Inspector or an Officer of the Board has notified a taxpayer or third party in writing that the notice has not been complied with to HMRC's satisfaction, then it can dispose of documents after two years from the date of issue of the s 20 notice (subject to other document preservation requirements).

Failure to comply

10.78 An initial penalty of £300 can currently be levied for failure to comply with an s 20 notice, followed by a penalty of £60 per day for continuing failure. If a taxpayer or third party fails to comply with an s 20 notice, then it shall be liable to a penalty not exceeding £300 under s 98(1)(i). However, as the level of any penalty to be imposed under s 98(1)(i) cannot be determined by an authorised HMRC Officer, if an HMRC Officer wishes to impose such a penalty on a taxpayer, then he must commence proceedings by information in writing to the Commissioners (either General or Special). Following the commencement of proceedings, the Commissioners issue a summons to the taxpayer to appear before them, under s 100C(2), and hear and decide the case in a summary way. Any penalty so determined by the Commissioners to be exigible is treated as due and payable as if it was tax charged in an assessment (under s 100C(3) of TMA) and can be appealed by the taxpayer to the High Court, under s 100C(4) of TMA.

10.79 After the level of the initial penalty has been determined by the Commissioners, HMRC may impose a daily penalty for non-compliance (of up to £60) from the date of issue of the initial penalty up to the date of compliance with the notice (under s 98(1)(ii)). The daily penalty imposed by an HMRC Officer may be appealed by the taxpayer or third party to the Commissioners (under s 100B). Under s 100B(2)(a), the Commissioners may:

1 set aside the penalty determination (if they consider that no penalty is exigible);

2 confirm the penalty determination (if they consider that the amount of the penalty is correct); or

3 increase or reduce the penalty to the correct amount (if it appears to them that the amount is incorrect).

Section 20BA – the production power

10.80 HMRC's ability to obtain possession of documents in the case of suspected serious fraud has been enhanced by the introduction of s 20BA (and Schedule 1AA). Section 20BA does not require HMRC to apply for a search and seizure warrant to obtain documents from a third party, who may have evidence relating to suspected fraud; a judge may issue an order requiring the person to deliver the documents to HMRC. The appropriate judicial authority (a circuit judge in England and Wales (see s 20D(1))) may, if satisfied on information on oath given by an authorised Officer of the Board of the grounds set out below, make an order under s 20BA requiring a person who appears to have in his possession or power the documents specified in the order to deliver them to a specified HMRC Officer within ten working days (working days exclude Saturdays, Sundays and public holidays), or such other period as may be specified. Section 20BA is intended to limit the occasions on which it is necessary for HMRC to enter the premises of persons not themselves suspected of fraud; a warrant cannot be issued under s 20C if the production order procedure under s 20BA is more appropriate. Section 20BA is amended in one regard following the changes introduced by Finance Act 2007: the procedure under s 20BA can not be used to obtain 'special procedure material' (see Art 7 of the Police and Criminal Evidence Act 1984 (Application to Revenue and Customs) Order 2007 (SI 2007/3175) and further below); instead an application under Schedule 1, PACE must be made.

10.81 The grounds for issuing the order are that:

1 there is reasonable ground for suspecting that an offence involving serious fraud in connection with, or in relation to, tax is being, has been or is about to be committed; and

2 documents which may be required as evidence for the purposes of any proceedings in respect of such an offence are or may be in the power or possession of any person (under s 20BA(2)).

A person is entitled to notice of the intention to apply for an order against him under s 20BA and to appear and be heard at the hearing of the application, unless the appropriate judicial authority is satisfied that this would seriously prejudice the investigation of the offence (under paragraph 3, Schedule 1AA).

10.82 A recipient of the notice of intention to apply for an order must not do any of the following:

1 conceal, destroy, alter or dispose of any document to which the application relates; or

2 disclose to any other person information or any other matter likely to prejudice the investigation of the offence to which the application relates (under Sch 1AA, para 4) unless permission is obtained from the appropriate court, or in writing from an HMRC Officer, or after the application has been dismissed or abandoned, or after any order has been complied with.

10.83 This is an exception to the anti-tipping of provision in the case of professional legal advisers. A professional legal adviser may disclose information to his client in connection with the giving by the adviser of legal advice, or to any other person in contemplation of, or in connection with, legal proceedings and for the purposes of those proceedings. However, this exception does not apply in circumstances where disclosures are made with a view to furthering a criminal purpose.

10.84 Schedule 1AA, para 5 provides the same protection to privileged materials with regard to the exercise of a power under s 20BA as s 20C(4) did in the context of s 20C notices. In addition, Orders for the Delivery of Documents (Procedure) Regulations 2000 (SI 2000/2875), reg 7 sets out a procedure for the resolution of disputes as to legal privilege. If there is a dispute as to whether any document or parts of documents are protected by legal privilege, the person concerned may apply to the appropriate judicial authority (in England and Wales, a circuit judge) to resolve the dispute. If the application is made within the time allowed for the delivery of the documents, then they are deemed to have been delivered in accordance with the notice until the dispute is resolved. In the meantime, all the documents concerned are to be lodged with and held by the court. The Board of HMRC is entitled to at least five working days' notice of the hearing of the application, and to attend and be heard at the hearing. If the authority upholds the claim for legal privilege in whole or in part, the costs of the application are to be met by the Board of HMRC. Before the hearing of the dispute, it may be resolved by agreement between the Board and the applicant.

10.85 HMRC does not have a statutory duty to provide copies or an inventory, although there are rights to access/request copies: if an original document has been delivered and is of such a nature that a copy would be sufficient (a) for use as evidence at a trial for an offence, or (b) for forensic examination or for investigation in connection with an offence, the original shall not be retained longer than is necessary to establish that fact and to obtain the copy (s 20CC, Sch 1AA, para 8).

Section 20BA offences

10.86 Failure to comply with an order made under s 20BA is punishable as a contempt of court. Failure to comply with the obligations under Sch 1AA, para 4 is also punishable as a contempt of court.

Section 19A – power to call for documents for purposes of certain enquiries

Introduction

10.87 The 1990s saw a significant reform of the machinery of administration, particularly in the system for assessing personal tax. The essence of the reform was that those taxpayers who used to be required to make an annual tax return (mainly those self-employed persons who were assessable to tax under Cases I and II of Schedule D) are now allowed to work out their own tax bill. Assessment on a 'preceding year' basis for the self-employed has been abolished, so that all taxpayers pay tax on a current year basis. This enables taxpayers to receive one statement dealing with all their income from whatever source and one tax bill (albeit that there are separate rules for computing the amounts from each source).

10.88 The key feature of the self-assessment system is that the primary responsibility for making an assessment of the tax payable each year falls on the individual taxpayer, not on HMRC. With the introduction of self-assessment came the introduction of powers that enable HMRC to obtain information that it may 'reasonably require' for the purpose of enquiring into the accuracy of self assessment returns. These powers are the self-assessment powers (contained in TMA 1970, s 19A and Finance Act 1998, Sch 18, para 27 (personal and corporate self-assessment respectively). Although the self-assessment powers, in many aspects, resemble the powers that HMRC already possessed under s 20 (which powers were first introduced in 1970 and significantly extended in 1976), there are important differences between the two sets of powers; the self-assessment powers co-exist with, rather than replace, the s 20 powers. The powers under s 19A in respect of personal self-assessment and under Finance Act 1998, Sch 18, para 27 in respect of corporate self-assessment are to a significant extent identical in scope. For ease, references in this section are to s 19A, with differences set out only.

10.89 Once an enquiry is in progress, generally HMRC first will seek to obtain information by means of an informal request to the taxpayer. If this does not succeed, then recourse may be had to s 19A. In contrast to s 20, there is no statutory requirement to give the taxpayer a reasonable opportunity to produce documents voluntarily before an s 19A notice can be issued. In practice, it is rare for HMRC to serve an s 19A notice without having first made an informal request for the information or documents. HMRC acknowledge that its aim should be to ask for all the information they consider necessary at the outset of the enquiry; there is, however, no statutory restriction on the number of information notices that may be issued in relation to an enquiry.

10.90 Section 19A does not give HMRC a free-standing power to obtain information. An s 19A notice can be issued only 'for the purpose of an enquiry'; it is a precondition for issue that HMRC must have commenced an enquiry (under either TMA 1970, s 9A(1) (individuals), TMA 1970, s 12AC(1) (partnerships) or Finance Act 1998, Sch 18, para 24 (companies)). If there is no open enquiry, HMRC instead must rely on its s 20 powers to obtain information that it can not obtain voluntarily.

10.91 A notice issued under s 19A must be given in writing. A time limit (of not less than 30 days) must be imposed for production of the information. In *Self-assessed v Inspector of Taxes* [1999] STC (SCD) 253, a notice was quashed because it required production of documents within 30 days of the date of the notice.

What may be sought under service of an s 19A notice?

10.92 Under s 19A, an Officer of HMRC can issue a notice to the taxpayer requiring 'such documents as are in the taxpayer's possession or power' and 'such accounts or particulars' as he may reasonably require.

10.93 'Documents' are widely defined by Finance Act 1988, s 127(1) as anything in which information of any description is recorded. This includes, for example, information held on computer disk. The word 'particulars' is synonymous with information. HMRC have indicated that the word 'particulars' in s 19A is used in the ordinary sense of 'detailed account' and may include answers to specific questions or require the creation of documents that do not already exist, such as, for example, a set of accounts. In *Murat v HM Inspector of Taxes* (*aka Accountant v HM Inspector of Taxes*) [2000] STC (SCD) 522, the Special Commissioner observed that it was reasonable for an Inspector's enquiries not to be limited to existing documents and held that it was reasonable for HMRC to require the preparation of a balance sheet.

10.94 The equivalent CTSA power adopts the same wording in relation to requests for documents, but paragraph 27(1)(b) requires the production of such information (as opposed to particulars), 'in such form' as HMRC may reasonably require for the purpose of the enquiry. The use of the wording 'in such form' is thought likely to enable HMRC to request that information be provided electronically.

10.95 The taxpayer is not obliged to produce documents, accounts or particulars relating to the conduct of any appeal (s 19A(5)).

Appeals

10.96 The taxpayer may appeal within 30 days against an information notice. HMRC's view is that the taxpayer may appeal on three grounds:

1 that the information is not reasonably required for the purpose of the Officer's enquiry;

2 that the information is not within the taxpayer's possession or power; and/or

3 that insufficient time has been allowed for production of the information.

10.97 Despite the onus being on the taxpayer to show why the information is irrelevant to the question of whether or not a return is correct or complete, the Inspector will be obliged to provide his reasons for why he considers the information is reasonably required. A frequent area of disagreement is where the Inspector requests information contained in 'non-business' records, such as private bank accounts. Requests for details of personal expenditure may be intrusive and the Special Commissioners have held that they should not be sought if that can be avoided (*Taylor v Bratherton* [2005] STC (SCD) 230). However, requests for documents and information concerning the taxpayer's income are reasonable for the purposes of the enquiry into the taxpayer's affairs (*Commane v HM Revenue & Customs* [2006] STC (SCD) 81).

10.98 If the documents that have been requested do not exist, then they cannot, of course, be provided. In these circumstances, HMRC should be advised of this fact and the notice should, as a consequence, be set aside by the Inspector. Depending on the documents sought, this may lead the Inspector to consider whether a penalty should be sought for failing to comply with the self-assessment record-keeping provisions. If HMRC do not accept the validity of the taxpayer's claim that they no longer have possession of the documents in question, then, ultimately it will be for the Commissioners to determine as a fact whether this is so, either on hearing an appeal against the notice or the determination of a penalty.

10.99 Although HMRC consider that the time allowed to comply with a notice is ground for an appeal, the self-assessment legislation does not bestow on the Commissioners a power to extend the time allowed for production. The Commissioners may, however, direct that the hearing be adjourned.

Penalties for non-compliance

10.100 The penalty provisions for failure to comply are contained in TMA 1970, s 97AA and Finance Act 1998, Sch 18, para 29. An initial fixed penalty of £50 can be determined by an authorised HMRC Officer. If the failure continues after the determination of the fixed penalty, it is then open to the Officer to determine a further penalty of up to £30 for each day from the date of the initial determination up to the date when the notice is complied with. Alternatively, the Officer may commence penalty proceedings before the General or Special Commissioners under s 100C, in which case the Commissioners can impose a penalty of up to £150 per day.

10.101 The taxpayer has a right of appeal against the imposition of penalties under s 97AA or Sch 18, para 29 to the Commissioners under s 100B. In the case of a determination by the Commissioners, the appeal lies to the High Court in England and Wales and to the Court of Session in Scotland (s 100B(3)).

THE INDIRECT TAX POWERS

10.102 HMRC Officers are given wide powers in order to carry out their duties of ensuring that the correct amount of Value Added Tax (VAT) is collected. The legislation provides for a system of sanctions that aim to render a trader's lack of cooperation a self-defeating exercise. These sanctions are as follows:

1 HMRC may, as a condition of repaying any input tax to any person, require the production of such evidence relating to VAT as may have been supplied to him (Sch 11, para 4). Thus, the obvious sanction to be imposed if the person declines to produce the required evidence is to withhold repayment of VAT.

2 HMRC may issue an assessment where a person has failed to keep any documents and afford the facilities necessary to verify his return (s 73(1)).

10.103 In addition, HMRC has powers that enable it to obtain information and documents (under Sch 11, para 7), powers to inspect (under paragraph 10(1) and (2) of Schedule 11) and powers to search and seize (before 1 December 2007 under Sch 11, para 10(3) and post-1 December 2007 under PACE, s 8, Sch 1).

Paragraph 7 – powers to obtain information and documents

10.104 HMRC has a number of statutory sources of information, including suppliers and their customers. Under Sch 11, para 7, HMRC has power to demand information and documents from:

1 every person who is concerned (in whatever capacity) in the supply of goods or services in the course or furtherance of a business;

2 every person to whom such a supply is made;

3 every person who is concerned (in whatever capacity) in the acquisition of goods from another member state;

4 every person who is concerned (in whatever capacity) in the importation of goods in the course or furtherance of a business; and

5 in relation to documents only, any other person who appears to be in possession of documents which HMRC could demand from a person in categories 1 to 4 above.

10.105 A person 'concerned in' a supply includes a person who has been assigned a right to receive the whole, or part, of the consideration for a supply of goods or services.

10.106 Such a person is required to furnish such information relating to the goods, services, supply, acquisition or importation as the Commissioners may reasonably specify. The specified information must be furnished to the Commissioners within such time and in such form as they may reasonably require.

10.107 Legal professional privilege will protect documents from being provided. HMRC's view is that an Officer may demand to see copies of the tax invoice, and the corresponding bill, produced by a legal adviser, but not a copy of the advice to which the charge relates.

10.108 The documents that may be sought under para 7 are limited to those relating to the goods, services, supply, acquisition or importation concerned. A further limitation is that the documents must be produced 'for inspection' by an authorised person. This prevents HMRC Officers using this power after an investigation has commenced, as the documents would not be used for the purpose of inspection.

10.109 For the purposes of this provision a 'document' means anything in which information of any description is recorded; and a copy of a document is defined as anything onto which information recorded in the document has been copied, by whatever means and whether directly or indirectly (under s 96(1) of VATA). This will include information held or copied on paper or an electronic medium, as well as in the form of photocopies, faxes, photographs or photographic film.

10.110 An HMRC Officer may take copies of any documents produced and may make extracts from them. He may also remove any such document at a reasonable time and for a reasonable period where he considers this necessary. A person producing documents under these provisions has the following rights:

1 to be provided with a receipt on request;

2 to be provided with a copy, free of charge, of any document reasonably required for proper conduct of his business; and

3 to compensation for expenses reasonably incurred in replacing documents which have been lost or repairing documents which have been damaged.

10.111 Where an HMRC Officer has a right of access to any document, he is also entitled, at any reasonable time, to have access to any computer, associated apparatus or material (ie including software) used in connection with such a document. This power extends to inspecting a computer, apparatus or material and checking its operation. A person is required to afford such reasonable assistance as may be required for these purposes if the computer is used by him or on his behalf, or if he controls or operates the computer, apparatus or material.

10.112 Failure to comply with a demand for information may give rise to a liability to civil or criminal penalties. The prescribed civil penalty is the greater of: (i) an amount equal to the prescribed rate multiplied by the number of days on which the failure continues (up to a maximum of 100); or (ii) £50. The prescribed rate is determined by the number of previous failures (if any) taking place in the period of two years preceding the beginning of the failure in question. If there were no previous failures, the prescribed rate is £5, one £10 and two or more £15. In practice, the action taken by HMRC is often in the first instance to issue a formal warning letter and not approve any relevant VAT repayment claims.

10.113 Under CRCA 2005, s 31, it is a criminal offence to obstruct an Officer, or a person acting on behalf of, or assisting, HMRC or an Officer. A person may be liable to criminal penalties also if he either:

1 obstructs access to a computer;

2 obstructs an inspection or operational check; or

3 fails to afford assistance without reasonable excuse within a reasonable time.

Paragraph 10(1) and (2) – the power to enter

10.114 VATA 1994, Sch 11, para 10(1) enables any person acting under the authority of the Board of HMRC (an 'authorised person') to enter premises used in connection with the carrying on of a business at any reasonable time for the purpose of exercising any powers under the VAT legislation. Business premises do not have to be occupied by a taxable person; the right of entry therefore extends to business premises occupied by a trader who is not registered for the purposes of VAT, regardless of whether or not he should have been so registered.

10.115 Under paragraph 10(2), an authorised person may enter and inspect any premises, and may inspect any goods found thereon, at any reasonable time if he has reasonable cause to believe that they are used in connection with the taxable supply of goods or the taxable acquisition of goods and that goods to be so supplied or acquired are to be found there, or that the premises are used as a fiscal warehouse. The clear wording of paragraph 10(2) excludes inspection of premises concerned solely with the provision of services. The right is to 'inspect'. The distinction between 'inspection' and 'search' is not absolute. However, the general maxim is that 'inspection is by eye, search by hand'. The power to inspect encompasses walking around premises and examining goods in packing cases; it does not cover searching for hidden things or rummaging through the contents of a waste-paper basket.

10.116 Under CRCA 2005, s 31, it is an offence to obstruct a HMRC Officer or someone assisting or acting on behalf of a HMRC Officer. This is punishable with a maximum sentence of 51 weeks' imprisonment and/or fine not exceeding £1,000. Any attempt to destroy or hide any documents or mislead a HMRC Officer during a search could amount to an offence of perverting the course of justice.

PACE and SOCPA powers

PACE powers

10.117 Not all the powers that are available to the police under PACE are available to HMRC Officers. In particular, the power to take fingerprints, and the power to charge and bail suspects have not been made available to HMRC

Officers. Article 4 of the Police and Criminal Evidence Act 1984 (Application to Revenue and Customs) Order 2007 (SI 2007/3175) ensures that HMRC Officers do not have powers to charge a person, release a person on bail or to detain a person after charge. PACE has been amended so as to apply four categories of PACE powers to all taxes. These categories are:

1 search warrants;

2 production orders;

3 arrest powers; and

4 search and entry powers in order to arrest.

Search warrants

10.118 Before an analysis of the search warrant powers that are now available to HMRC Officers under PACE is provided, for comparative purposes, the powers that were available to HMRC Officers under TMA 1970, s 20C (for direct tax purposes) and under VATA 1994, Sch 11, para 10(3) (for indirect tax purposes) are summarised.

The search and seizure power under s 20C

10.119 As indicated above, s 20C has been repealed, and replaced with a power under s 8 of PACE, with effect from 1 December 2007. For comparative purposes, a brief analysis of the power under s 20C is set out below.

10.120 Section 20C enabled an Inspector (after obtaining a warrant from a circuit judge) to enter private premises (if necessary by force) to search for and remove documents that he reasonably believes to be evidence of tax fraud. No particular offence needed to be specified in the warrant other than 'serious fraud' (see *IRC v Rossminster Ltd* [1980] STC 42). The occupier of the premises had no right to be informed of the precise grounds on which the warrant was issued.

10.121 The grounds for issuing the warrant were that:

1 there is reasonable ground for suspecting that an offence involving serious fraud in connection with, or in relation to, tax is being, has been or is about to be committed and that evidence of it is to be found on premises specified in the information; and

2 in applying under this section, the Officer acts with the approval of the Board given in relation to the particular case (under s 20C(1)).

10.122 The judicial authority also had to be satisfied that the Officer concerned was acting with the specific approval of the Board (not merely with the approval of an Officer acting under the Board's authority) given in relation to the particular case (see ss 20C(1)(b), and 20C(2)). Under s 20C(3)(a) the Officer could take with him such other persons as appear to him to be necessary (this is not limited to people with a purely ancillary role eg locksmiths). In practice, as Inland Revenue Officers had no powers of arrest, normally they would be accompanied by police officers. With effect from 1 December 2007, the relevant Officers of HMRC have the power of arrest for all indictable tax offences under PACE.

10.123 Under s 20C(1B), the powers conferred by a warrant under this section could not be exercisable:

1 by more than such number of Officers of the Board as may be specified in the warrant (there is no requirement to specify the names);

2 outside such times of day as may be so specified (there is no limit when these may be);

3 if the warrant so provides, otherwise than in the presence of a constable in uniform.

10.124 Under s 20C(3)(b), an Officer of the Board who entered the premises under the authority of an s 20C warrant could seize and remove any 'things' whatsoever found there which he has reasonable cause to believe may be required as evidence for the purposes of proceedings in respect of a serious tax fraud offence (not necessarily the one that the warrant was obtained in respect of). Under s 20C(3)(c), the Officer could search or cause to be searched any person found on the premises whom he has reasonable cause to believe to be in possession of any such things, but no person could be searched except by a person of the same sex.

10.125 A single 'thing' may include irrelevant as well as relevant material. The power of seizure under s 20C(3) included a power to require information which is stored in electronic form accessible from the premises, and which the Officer has reasonable cause to believe may be required as evidence, to be produced in legible, visible form (or from which it can readily be so produced). (See s 20C(3A).)

10.126 Under Schedule 1, Part 1 of Criminal Justice and Police Act 2001 (CJPA 2001), Sch 1, pt 1 the s 50 powers of seizure under that Act were extended to s 20C. This power applied where it is not reasonably practicable to determine on the premises whether the material is, or contains, something HMRC is entitled to seize. This power is analysed further under the PACE powers section of this chapter.

10.127 Access to all the documents or items was permitted, on request and under supervision (under s 20CC(4)). Copies could be taken at the time of access or requested. If requested, the copies had to have been provided within a reasonable time (s 20CC(6) and (7)), unless the Officer had reasonable grounds for believing that to do so would prejudice the investigation (s 20CC(8)). There was no right to allow a copy to be taken at the time of search.

10.128 HMRC Officers exercising powers under s 20C followed the Codes of Practice of PACE. They are now bound by them statutorily when exercising PACE powers; see further under the PACE powers section of this chapter.

10.129 The power under s 20C was rarely used by the HMRC where the relevant documents were believed to be in the possession of non-suspect third parties. HMRC recognised that a search warrant is a very draconian tool to be used against third parties; and, in 2000, s 20BA was introduced in order to allow the Inland Revenue to gain access to original documents from unsuspected third parties without the need to have recourse to the intrusive power under s 20C. Before a warrant under s 20C could be obtained, the Board must have had reasonable grounds for believing that the use of the s 20BA procedure might seriously prejudice the investigation.

10.130 Section 20C(4) provided that HMRC are not authorised to seize items that are subject to legal privilege. Section 20C(4A) provided a definition of legally privileged documents for the purpose of s 20C. It extended the protection given to such documents to whenever they are held by 'a person who is entitled to possession of them'.

Section 20C offences

10.131 Under CRCA 2005, s 31 it is an offence to obstruct a HMRC Officer or someone assisting or acting on behalf of a HMRC Officer. This is punishable with a maximum sentence of 51 weeks' imprisonment and/or fine not exceeding £1,000. This offence is unaffected by the recent changes that have been introduced in respect of the powers of HMRC to enter premises with a warrant and so applies if an HMRC Officer is exercising a power under PACE to enter premises.

10.132 Any attempt to destroy or hide any documents or mislead an HMRC Officer during a search can also amount to the common law offence of perverting the course of justice.

The power to search under VATA 1994, Sch 11, para 10(3)

10.133 As indicated, paragraph 10(3), Schedule 11 has been repealed and replaced by PACE, s 8 (and related powers under PACE) by Finance Act 2007 and the Police and Criminal Evidence Act 1984 (Application to Revenue and Customs) Order 2007 (SI 2007/3175) with effect from 1 December 2007.

10.134 VATA 1994 Sch 11, para 10(3) enabled any person acting under the authority of the Board of HMRC (an 'authorised person') to enter premises, if necessary by force, at any time within one month from the time of the issue of the warrant and search them. Any person who entered the premises under the authority of the warrant could:

1 take with him such other persons as appear to him to be necessary;

2 seize and remove any documents or other things whatsoever found on the premises which he has reasonable cause to believe may be required as evidence for the purposes of proceedings in respect of a fraud offence which appears to him to be of a serious nature; and

3 search or cause to be searched any person found on the premises whom he has reasonable cause to believe to be in possession of any such documents or other things; but no woman or girl shall be searched except by a woman.

10.135 The warrant was given in writing. It had to specify:

1 the name of the person who applied for it;

2 the date on which it is issued;

3 the enactment under which it is issued; and

4 the premises to be searched.

10.136 A warrant had to identify the articles or persons to be sought in so far as it was practicable to do so. It could:

1 authorise persons to accompany any Officer executing it;

2 specify the maximum number of authorised persons who may execute it;

3 specify the times of day when it may be executed; and

4 provide that it may only be executed in the presence of a uniformed constable.

10.137 In addition, the authorised person could take with him such other persons as appeared to him to be necessary. This authorised the presence of, for example, police officers, locksmiths and translators, but it did not authorise them to take part in the search. The warrant had to have been executed within one month from its date of issue. A copy of the warrant had to have been given to the occupier of the premises (if he was present when the search begins) or, in his absence, the person who appeared to be in charge of the premises. In any other case (ie if the premises were empty), the copy had to have been left in a prominent place. The copy of the warrant had to have been endorsed with the name of the person searching the premises (if he was alone) or the person in charge of the search.

10.138 The person executing a warrant had to endorse it and return it to the clerk to the justices for the relevant petty sessions area. The clerk had to retain the endorsed warrant for one year and he had to allow the occupier of the premises to inspect it on request during this period.

10.139 The power to search premises was conferred by a warrant issued by a Justice of the Peace, in accordance with the provisions of VATA 1994, Sch 11, para 10(3) and PACE, ss 8 and 152. The power was used only in serious cases of suspected evasion: where the actual or potential amount of VAT involved exceeded £10,000, and other methods of investigation were either unlikely to succeed or, when tried, have failed. A Justice of the Peace could issue a warrant only where he is satisfied judicially by information given on oath that there were reasonable grounds for suspecting that an offence under VATA 1994, s 72(1) to (8) which appears to be of a serious nature, is being, has been, or is about to be committed on the premises, or that evidence of the commission of such an offence is to be found there.

The PACE power to search

10.140 With effect from 1 December 2007, applications for all HMRC search warrants will be made under PACE, s 8 or Sch 1. On an application by an HMRC Officer, a magistrate may issue a warrant for the HMRC Officer to enter and search premises if he has reasonable grounds for believing that an indictable tax offence has been committed and that there is material on the specified premises that is likely to be of substantial value (whether by itself or together with other material) to the investigation of the offence and is likely to be admissible at the trial for the offence.

10.141 The powers of seizure under PACE have been considerably extended under CJPA 2001. Its provisions aim to overcome the problems that arose either where it could not be conveniently determined in situ whether a particular item (such as a computer) was subject to seizure or where there were issues relating to whether or not material was protected by reason of legal professional privileges.

10.142 Under CJPA 2001, Sch 1, pt 1, the s 50 powers of seizure under that Act are extended to PACE, s 8. This power applies where it is not reasonably practicable to determine on the premises whether the material is, or contains, something HMRC is entitled to seize. It entitles HMRC Officers to remove material (eg computer hard drives) if they have reasonable grounds to believe that the material may contain items they are authorised to seize. In *R (on the application of H) v Inland Revenue Commissioners* [2002] STC 1354, which concerned a s 20C warrant, the High Court held that a hard disk could not be regarded as simply a container of the files visible to the computer's operating system. It was a single object: a single thing. There was no basis, therefore, for a computer not being considered a 'thing' within the meaning of s 20C(3)(b). The fact that there was also on the hard disk irrelevant material did not make the computer any less of a thing that might be required as evidence for the purposes of criminal proceedings. Accordingly, if a Revenue Officer who entered into premises under the authority of a warrant under s 20C found a computer, and he had reasonable cause to believe that the data on the computer's hard disk might be required as evidence for the purpose of relevant proceedings, he might seize and remove that computer even though it contained irrelevant material also. It is considered that the ratio of this case applies to PACE warrants.

10.143 Once the material is removed from the premises, HMRC is empowered to sift the material to determine whether it contains any relevant items that it wishes to seize. When powers of seizure under s 50 are exercised by an HMRC Officer, the taxpayer or third party must be provided with a written notice of this in accordance with CJPA 2001, s 52. The warrant must be endorsed to provide a record of those documents or items that have been removed.

10.144 Access to all the documents or items may be permitted, on request and under supervision. Copies may be taken at the time of access, or requested. If requested, the copies must be provided within a reasonable time. There is no right to allow a copy to be taken at the time of search.

10.145 An HMRC Officer exercising powers under PACE, s 8 is bound by the Codes of Practice of the Police and Criminal Evidence Act 1984. Code B provides, inter alia, that a person from whom any items are seized must, on request, be provided with a list or description of the property within a reasonable time. If an original document has been removed and is of such a nature that a copy would be sufficient (a) for use as evidence at a trial for an offence, or (b) for forensic examination or for investigation in connection with an offence, it shall not be retained longer than is necessary to establish that fact and to obtain the copy.

10.146 Items held with the intention of furthering a criminal purpose are not subject to legal privilege. In *R v Inland Revenue Commissioners and Middlesex Guildhall Crown Court, ex parte Tamosius and Partners* [1999] STC 1077, the High Court held that s 20C(4) prevented only the removal of documents with respect to which a claim to professional privilege could be 'maintained' – the seizure did not become unlawful merely because the firm of American lawyers that had been raided claimed that the documents were privileged. HMRC will often adopt the practice of applying in advance to the Attorney General to nominate a Counsel and then using that Counsel to review material to determine whether or not legal privilege applies. However, this process is undertaken only to protect HMRC; it does not preclude a taxpayer or third party challenging a decision by Counsel that material is not privileged. If there is a dispute as to whether legal privilege applies, attempts should be made to persuade HMRC to put the material in opaque, sealed envelopes and the issue of privilege resolved subsequently.

Key differences between the old 'HMRC powers' and the PACE search powers

10.147 There are a number of important differences between the procedures that were in operation pre-Finance Act 2007 and the procedures that are now in operation. Notable differences between warrants under TMA 1970, s 20C and warrants under PACE, s 8 are as follows:

1. The grounds for issuing an s 20C warrant were that: 'there is reasonable ground for *suspecting* that an offence involving serious fraud in connection with, or in relation to, tax *is being, has been or is about to be committed* and that evidence of it is to be found on premises specified in the information' (emphasis added). Under PACE, the threshold is higher. There must be reasonable grounds for 'believing' that an offence has been committed (suspicion is not sufficient). Also, the judge is only able to issue an order where he is satisfied that there are reasonable grounds for believing that an offence 'has been' committed (that it is 'being, or is about to be' committed will not suffice).
2. Applications for s 20C warrants were made to a circuit judge. An application for a PACE, s 8 warrant is made to a magistrate. (Although if special procedure material is involved, a search warrant can not be issued under s 8, and a warrant can be issued only by a circuit judge (see further below)).
3. Under s 20C(1), the judge had to be satisfied that the Officer was acting with the approval of the Board of HMRC given in relation to the particular case before consenting to issuance of a warrant. Applications for search warrants under PACE do not require such authorisation as a matter of statute (although, as a matter of practice, need internal authorisation at a senior level).
4. TMA 1970, s 20C(1AA) provided that the Board of HMRC shall not approve an application for an s 20C warrant unless 'they have reasonable grounds for believing that use of the procedure under s 20BA … might seriously prejudice the investigation'. There is no such equivalent requirement to consider s 20BA before applying for a warrant under s 8, PACE.

Production orders

10.148 'Special procedure material', items subject to legal professional privilege, and 'excluded material' are excluded from the scope of an s 8 warrant. Special procedure material consists broadly of business records that are held by a person under an obligation of confidence to a third party (see PACE, s 14).

10.149 If it is suspected that special procedure material needs to be obtained, HMRC can apply to a circuit judge (*ex parte*) for a warrant under PACE, Sch 1, para 12. If granted, this enables an Officer to enter premises and search for excluded material or other special procedure material (there are a number of conditions as to access and other criteria that must be satisfied (see Code B of the PACE Codes of Practice)).

10.150 An alternative to an order authorising such material to be seized under a search and seizure exercise is a production order (under PACE, Sch 1, paras 7–11). If a circuit judge is satisfied that there are reasonable grounds for believing that an indictable tax offence has been committed, he may consent to the issue of a PACE production order. The hearing before the judge is *inter partes* (in contrast to applications under s 20BA).

10.151 Currently, the production order powers under TMA 1970, s 20BA (direct tax) and paragraph 11 of Schedule 11 to VATA (VAT) are preserved. However, if the documents sought are believed to include special procedure material, then those documents may not be obtained under the s 20BA or para 11 production orders: a production order under PACE, Sch 1 must be used instead. Article 7 of the Police and Criminal Evidence Act 1984 (Application to Revenue and Customs) Order 2007 (SI 2007/3175) provides that PACE is to be interpreted as if s 14B was inserted after s14A, with s 14B providing that an HMRC Officer may only make an application under s 20BA of TMA or paragraph 11 of Schedule 11 to VATA if the Officer considers that an application under Schedule 1, PACE would not succeed because the material required does not consist of or include special procedure material.

Safeguards

10.152 The PACE Codes of Practice will apply when PACE powers are exercised by HMRC Officers and when HMRC Officers are investigating tax offences (see PACE, s 67) . They contain detailed regulations on the exercise of PACE powers and notes for guidance. They are admissible in evidence and any relevant provision must be taken into account by a court (under s 67(11) of PACE). PACE Code B deals with the powers to search premises and to seize and retain property found on premises and persons.

SOCPA powers

10.153 Under SOCPA, ss 60–70, Sch 1, pt 2, new investigatory powers in relation to tax crimes, inter alia, are introduced. Under SCOPA, s 60 use of these powers can be delegated by the director of RCPO to any HMRC prosecutor. The offences to which the powers relate include common law cheat of the public revenue and false accounting (Theft Act 1968, s 17), provided that, in the opinion of the investigating Officer, the potential loss to the public revenue is of an amount not less than £5,000. The powers came into effect on 1 April 2006.

10.154 An HMRC prosecutor can give, or authorise an Officer of HMRC to give, a disclosure notice to any person who has information which relates to a matter relevant to the investigation of the offence, provided that there are reasonable grounds for belief that the information in question, whether or not by itself, is likely to be of 'substantial value' to the investigation. A recipient of the notice will not only have to produce documents relevant to the investigation, but also to 'answer questions with respect to any matter relevant to the investigation' and to 'provide information with respect to any such matter as is specified in the notice' (under SOCPA, s 62(3)). There is a similar protection for privileged information or documents as is contained in TMA 1970, ss 20B(8) and 20C(4); a person may not be required to answer any privileged question, or provide any privileged information, or produce any privileged document (except that a lawyer may be required to provide the name and address of his client).

10.155 Two offences are created with regard to SOCPA disclosure notices. The first is failure to comply with the requirements set out in a disclosure notice (punishable by a maximum sentence of 51 weeks' imprisonment, with a 'reasonable excuse' for failure to comply being a defence); and, second is making a false or misleading statement in response to the requirements imposed by a disclosure notice (punishable by a maximum of two years' imprisonment).

10.156 If the recipient of a disclosure notice fails to comply with its terms, then the HMRC prosecutor will be able to obtain a search and seize warrant from a Justice of the Peace. Such a warrant will enable an HMRC prosecutor to enter and search premises, using force where necessary, and to take possession of any documents that appear to be of a description specified in the disclosure notice, or to take any other steps that appear to be necessary for preserving, or preventing interference with, any such documents. A warrant will also be able to be issued if it is not practicable to issue a disclosure notice, or where the service of a disclosure notice might seriously prejudice the investigation (under SOCPA, s 66(2)).

10.157 It is likely that these powers will be used primarily against third parties, including professional advisers. (See the comments of the Parliamentary Under-Secretary of State for the Home Department at the Committee stage of the Serious Organised Crime and Police Bill.) To date, HMRC has not made particular use of these powers.

Chapter 11

Tax appeals

Hartley Foster, Partner and Head of Tax Disputes, DLA Piper UK

INTRODUCTION

The tax appeals system

11.1 The tax appeals system in England and Wales is a complex one. Rather than have one specialist tax court that can hear all tax related appeals, different taxes carry with them different methods and routes of litigation. A document that illuminated the Byzantine intricacies of all potential tax-related litigation in England and Wales would be many times the length of this already lengthy chapter. Thus, the primary focus of this chapter is on litigation before the General Commissioners and the Special Commissioners that concerns income tax, corporation tax and capital gains tax.

11.2 This chapter is divided into four sections. The first section, by way of summary and introduction, describes briefly the various matters that may be heard by bodies that adjudicate on tax-related matters. The second section explains in detail the jurisdiction and powers of the General Commissioners and the Special Commissioners and the appeal procedures before them. The third section comprises an outline of the procedure on appeal from the General Commissioners or the Special Commissioners to the courts.

11.3 Fundamental changes to the entire tax appeals system are in the process of being introduced. On 19 July 2007, the Tribunals, Courts and Enforcement Act 2007 (TCE) received Royal Assent. TCE is an enabling Act, under which the General Commissioners, Special Commissioners, and VAT and Duties Tribunals will be abolished and replaced by a unified tribunal comprising a first tier and an upper tier. An analysis of the new system (which is currently anticipated to be introduced in April 2009) is set out in the fourth and final section of the chapter.

11.4 All statutory references in this chapter are to the Taxes Management Act 1970 (TMA), unless otherwise indicated. References to HM Revenue & Customs (HMRC) include references to its statutory predecessors.

USE OF LITIGATION AS A TACTIC

11.5 Many tax practitioners have little or no experience of taking an appeal to a tax tribunal. Indeed, there is a school of thought that regards the reaching of some form of compromise settlement with HMRC as a panacea. Although, as a general rule, reaching a negotiated settlement is preferable to resolution via litigation, that is only a general rule and the approach that should be adopted in any particular case can be arrived at only after considering fully what is best for the taxpayer, and should not be influenced by any pre-disposition against litigation. Being mindful of the adage 'if you want peace, prepare for war' and thus dealing with enquiries from the perspective that, ultimately, the underlying issues may be heard by a tribunal or court can achieve considerable improvements, both in terms of the cost of compliance and the ultimate outcome of the case. This is particularly since, under its new Litigation and Settlement Strategy (which was introduced in June 2007), HMRC also are adopting a litigation-focused approach to disagreements with taxpayers. The like approach by the taxpayer not only brings greater rigour and enables greater focus when responding to HMRC, but also allows the use of litigious tactics and the weapons that have been given to the taxpayer under self-assessment to be used. Self-assessment put the burden on taxpayers to complete returns, but, as a *quid pro quo* it introduced mechanisms of control that can be used by taxpayers. It is those taxpayers that are aware of and make full use of these mechanisms that get the best results.

SECTION ONE – THE TAX COURTS

The Special Commissioners and the General Commissioners

11.6 Litigation that concerns income tax, corporation tax and capital gains tax taxes falls within the purview of the General Commissioners and the Special Commissioners (the Commissioners). The division of jurisdiction is complicated; some is reserved to the General Commissioners, some to the Special Commissioners, and some may be heard by either body.

The Commissioners' jurisdiction also includes:

1 hearing appeals against notices of determination issued by HMRC under Inheritance Tax Act 1984, s 221;

2 determination of whether a variation of an undertaking, where HMRC and a person are bound by an undertaking relating to conditionally exempt property fail to reach agreement on the terms of a variation of the undertaking, is to have effect from a specified date, as if the proposed variation had been agreed by the person bound by the undertaking, under

Inheritance Tax Act 1984, s 35A (see *Re an application to vary the undertakings of A* [2005] STC (SCD) 103));

3 hearing applications for consent where HMRC wishes to obtain a notice to require documents to be provided by a taxpayer or a third party under s 20 (see, for example, the recent decisions consenting to the issuance of notices under s 20(8A) against four banks: *Re an Application by Revenue and Customs Commissioners to Serve a section 20 Notice* [2007] STC (SCD) 202, [2007] STC (SCD) 208, [2007] STC (SCD) 216, [2007] STC (SCD) 222);

determination of whether arrangements were effected for bona fide commercial reasons and do not form part of a scheme or arrangement of which the main purpose, or one of the main purposes, is avoidance of a liability to tax under a number of anti-avoidance provisions (such as Income and Corporation Taxes Act 1988, s 215); and

proceedings under Proceeds of Crime Act 2002, pt 6. Under Part 6, if the Director of the Assets Recovery Agency has reasonable grounds to suspect that income arising or a gain accruing to a person is chargeable to income tax, or is a chargeable gain (or, if a company, is chargeable to corporation tax) and arises as a result of criminal conduct, the Director may serve a notice on HMRC stating that he intends to carry out specified Revenue functions in relation to that person or company. The Director may thereafter issue assessments for tax, which may be appealed to the Special Commissioners. See, for example, *Khan v Director of the Assets Recovery Agency* [2006] STC (SCD) 154, and *Rose v Revenue and Customs Commissioners* [2007] STC (SCD) 129.

The section 706 tribunal

11.7 The Finance Act 1960 introduced new provisions whereby a person being in a position to obtain, or having obtained, a 'tax advantage' in consequence of a transaction in securities or of the combined effect of two or more transactions in securities could suffer the nullification of that tax advantage. The statutory provisions are now found in Income and Corporation Taxes Act 1988 (ICTA), ss 703–709 for corporation tax and Income Tax Act 2007, pt 13 for income tax. Section 704 enables a tribunal (the tribunal) to be constituted for the purposes of ICTA 1988, ss 703–709. When constituted, the tribunal comprises:

1 a chairman appointed by the Lord Chancellor; and

2 two or more persons appointed by the Lord Chancellor as having special knowledge of and experience in financial or commercial matters.

For ease, the circumstances when a tribunal may be constituted is described below in relation to ss 703 to 709 only.

11.8 Normally, the first indication that HMRC are considering the potential application of s 703 is the service of a notice under s 708 on the taxpayer to supply (within a specified time) information in his possession with respect to the transaction or transactions. If, having considered the information supplied (or alternatively following refusal of an application for clearance), the HMRC Officer decides that counteraction is appropriate, a notification under s 703(9) will be served on the taxpayer. By this, HMRC indicate that they have reason to believe that s 703 may apply to the taxpayer in respect of the transaction or transactions specified in the notification. At this stage, the HMRC Officer is not required to state which of the five circumstances he considers to apply or what are the tax advantages which he proposes to counteract. There is no right of appeal against the notification. However, the taxpayer has the right within 30 days to make a statutory declaration that the provisions do not apply to him. In the statutory declaration, the taxpayer must state the facts and circumstances on which that opinion is based. If HMRC wish to proceed with counteraction, they must send a certificate to that effect to the tribunal (under ICTA 1988, s 706(10)), along with the taxpayer's declaration and may also send a counter-statement setting out their reasons for proceeding. The taxpayer is not entitled to see the counter-statement, which will include answers to the arguments in the taxpayer's declaration.

11.9 On being sent the documents under s 706(10), the function of the tribunal is to determine whether there is a *prima facie* case for proceeding. The tribunal has no authority to seek or consider information not contained in the statutory declaration and HMRC's certificate and counter-statement, nor may the taxpayer or HMRC address further arguments to them (see the decision of the House of Lords in *Wiseman v Borneman* (1967) 45 TC 540). If they decide that there is no *prima facie* case for proceeding, then s 703 (or Part 13, Income Tax Act 2007) cannot apply to the specified transactions. HMRC has no right of appeal against the decision. However, in practice, the tribunal has seldom ruled that there is no *prima facie* case.

11.10 In the event that the tribunal decides that there is a *prima facie* case (or the taxpayer does not serve a statutory declaration), a notice of counteraction under s 703(3) may be issued to a taxpayer. He has the right to appeal this notice to the Special Commissioners by giving notice to an HMRC Officer within 30 days. The procedure as regards an appeal is in general similar to that for an appeal against an assessment.

11.11 A party that is dissatisfied with the decision of the Special Commissioners may require (as a matter of right) the appeal then to be re-heard by the tribunal. (This right to a re-hearing does not prevent an appeal on a point of law being made to the High Court (see *Marwood Homes Ltd v Inland Revenue Commissioners* [1998] STC (SCD) 53).) The matter is then entirely re-heard by the tribunal under the same procedures as apply to a hearing before the Special Commissioners.

11.12 There is no appeal from a determination by the tribunal on a question of fact, but a party may declare dissatisfaction with the determination on a point of law and then, within 30 days of the determination, require the tribunal to state and sign a case for the opinion of the High Court (the request must be accompanied by a fee of £25). The case must set out the facts and determination of the tribunal. It must be transmitted to the High Court within 30 days of receipt and sent to the other party.

The VAT and duties tribunal

11.13 The VAT tribunals were established by the Finance Act 1972 to resolve VAT disputes between taxpayers and HM Customs and Excise. In the early years, the number of cases that proceeded to the tribunals were reasonably small (in the first 12 years of their existence, the VAT Tribunals released, on average, about 160 decisions per year). There was a significant increase in the number of appeals taken by taxpayers in 1985, with the new penalty regime introduced by Finance Act 1985. With taxpayers becoming increasingly aware of, and comfortable with the concept of, taking appeals to the VAT Tribunal, the number of appeals made by taxpayers has continued to expand. At the time of publication, over 20,000 decisions have been released by the VAT Tribunal.

11.14 As new indirect taxes and levies have been introduced, so has the jurisdiction of the VAT and Duties Tribunals. On 1 January 1995, the VAT Tribunals were renamed 'the VAT and Duties Tribunals' on account of their extended jurisdiction. The jurisdiction of the VAT and Duties Tribunals now encompasses:

1 VAT;
2 customs duties;
3 excise duties;
4 insurance premium tax;
5 landfill tax;
6 aggregates levy;
7 climate change levy; and
8 airport passenger duty.

The High Court

11.15 The High Court sits as an appellate court from the Commissioners, the s 706 tribunal, and the VAT Tribunal. However, also, in very general terms, where in a tax-related matter there is no statutory route of appeal to the tax tribunals, the High Court exists as a potential jurisdiction of first instance.

11.16 The principle of 'exclusive jurisdiction' applies to delimit the jurisdiction of the High Court. In very broad terms, the principle of 'exclusive jurisdiction' has the consequence that the jurisdiction of the High Court is ousted at first instance if there is a statutory scheme containing its own system of remedies in place to deal with claims and Parliament has assigned resolution of such disputes to that scheme. Whether the correct analysis of the principle is that, where the proceedings come within the area that has been assigned to a statutory tribunal and thus concern matters over which the specialist tribunal should have exclusive jurisdiction, but jurisdiction has not been explicitly confined by statute to that tribunal (as, for example, Taxes Management Act 1964, s 5(6) and (as originally enacted) s 29(6) confined the right to challenge assessments to the tax tribunals), then the jurisdiction of the High Court is excluded (cf the House of Lords' decision in *Barraclough v Brown* [1897] AC 615) or, alternatively, retained but subject to the rule that the High Court should exercise its discretion to refuse jurisdiction (cf the House of Lords' decision in *In re Vandervell's Trusts* [1971] AC 912) remains an open question. It is my view that it is only where a taxpayer's High Court claim is an indirect way of seeking to achieve exactly the same result as it would be open to the taxpayer to achieve directly by appealing to the Special (or General) Commissioners, that the High Court's jurisdiction is excluded absolutely (as this is, or is tantamount to, abuse of process). However, if there are elements of the claim that differ, including, for example, the seeking of a remedy that the tribunal has no power to grant, the High Court jurisdiction is not ousted and it is an issue of discretion.

11.17 Matters that may be taken to the High Court include:

1. Claims to recover overpayments of tax (although if s 33 applies, this may provide an exclusive procedure. See *Woolwich Equitable Building Society v Inland Revenue Commissioners* [1992] STC 657, and *Deutsche Morgan Grenfell Group plc v Inland Revenue Commissioners and another* [2007] 1 AC 558).
2. Claims for declaratory relief (see, for example, *Buxton v Public Trustee* (1962) 41 TC 235, where a declaration was sought that trusts were charitable).
3. Claims for damages in tort (such as proceedings for negligence or misfeasance in a public office against HMRC).
4. Judicial review of decisions of HMRC or the tax tribunals.

11.18 Under Inheritance Tax Act 1984, s 222 the High Court is also an alternative first-instance venue for certain inheritance tax appeals. An appeal against a determination by HMRC may be brought before the High Court where either the appellant and the Board agree that the matters for decision on appeal 'are likely to be substantially confined to questions of law' or, in the absence of such agreement, if the appellant applies for and obtains leave from the High Court, having satisfied the court that the subject matter falls within that category. In *Bennett v Inland Revenue Commissioners*, where Lightman J gave leave for an inheritance tax appeal to go to the High Court, he held that, whilst it was a precondition for leave that the appeal be substantially confined to questions of law, it was also necessary to determine whether the issue, by reason of its novelty, importance or otherwise, was one which could and should proceed by way of appeal to the High Court. Leave was granted on the basis that a short but important issue of law was raised and it was likely that any decision of the Special Commissioners would be appealed.

The Court of Justice of the European Communities

11.19 The jurisdiction of the Court of Justice of the European Communities, or European Court of Justice (ECJ) as it is more commonly known, is defined in the EC treaties. It has jurisdiction over the following matters:

1. failure by a Member State to fulfil an obligation under the EC Treaty;
2. legality of acts of the Council and Commission;
3. failure to act by the Council or Commission; and
4. preliminary rulings.

11.20 Under Art 234, EC the ECJ has jurisdiction to give preliminary rulings concerning:

1. the interpretation of the EC Treaty;
2. the validity and interpretation of acts of institutions of the Community; and
3. the interpretation of the statutes of bodies established by an act of the Council.

The ECJ comprises fifteen judges and eight Advocates-General. The court may sit as a full court, in a Grand Chamber of thirteen judges or in Chambers of three or five judges. It is rare for the ECJ to sit as a full court. It may do so where a case of exceptional importance is concerned; and there are particular cases prescribed by the Statute of the Court (such as proceedings to dismiss the European Ombudsman or a Member of the European Commission who has failed to fulfil his or her obligations) where it must. It sits in a Grand Chamber when a Member State or an institution which is a party to the proceedings so requests, and in particularly complex or important cases. The court makes a single decision.

Decisions of the ECJ are always preceded by a detailed report ('Opinion') from an Advocate-General (A-G)) that also carries authoritative weight (but is not binding on the ECJ). When deciding a case, the ECJ often (albeit not always) follows the A-G's opinion. All cases before the ECJ are allocated a number, the last two digits of which refer to the year in which the action was started.

11.21 In matters of EC law, all domestic courts and tribunals must refer points of dispute relating to EC law to the ECJ if they consider that a decision of the ECJ is necessary to enable them to give judgment. Decisions of the ECJ will bind domestic courts on the interpretation of EC law.

11.22 The general rule is that, where a question concerning EC law arises before a national court or tribunal, the matter may be referred to the ECJ if a decision on the question is necessary to enable the national court to give judgment. However, under Art 234, the matter must be referred if there is no right of appeal from a decision of the court or tribunal. Thus, courts of last resort (typically the House of Lords in the UK) do not have a discretion as to whether to make a reference on an EC law issue which it is necessary to resolve before judgment can be given (although the court in question retains its discretion to decide whether a decision on a question of EC Law is necessary to enable it to give judgment (see *R v Henn and Darby* (Case 34/79) [1981] AC 850)). If the answer to the EC law point is '*acte claire*' (in essence so obvious that there is no scope for any reasonable doubt), then there is no obligation to refer.

11.23 The decision to make a reference is a matter for the national court or tribunal, not for the parties to the case. The court is not even bound to accept a joint submission by the parties that an issue of EC law that is not *acte claire* arises (see *Rheinmuhlen-Dusseldorf v Einfuhr-und Vorratsstelle fur Getreide und Futtermittel* (Case 166/73) [1974] ECR 33). Similarly, a reference may be made by a court against the wishes of all the parties (see, for example, *Direct Cosmetics v Commissioners* (Case LON/83/9) [1984] 1 CMLR 99). Thus, if one of the parties disagrees with the decision, he or she must appeal under national law – there is no direct right of access to the ECJ (see for example, *Marks and Spencer v Halsey* [2003] EWHC 1945. The Special Commissioners declined to refer; that decision was appealed to the High Court, where Park J referred questions to the ECJ).

11.24 In *R v International Stock Exchange, ex parte Else* [1993] QB 534 Sir Thomas Bingham set out guidelines that courts should be mindful of when deciding whether or not to refer issues of EC law to the ECJ. If the issues are almost certain to be conclusive of the outcome of these appeals, and, secondly, it cannot be said that the court can resolve the issue itself 'with complete confidence', the issues should be referred. If the delay and costs of an appeal can be avoided by the making of a reference at an early stage, then that is a relevant consideration for a court to consider (see Bingham J in *Commissioners of Customs and Excise v Samex ApS and Hanil Synthetic Fiber Industrial Company Limited* [1983] 3 CMLR 194).

11.25 It is the responsibility of the UK court, rather than the parties, to settle the terms of the reference, although, in practice, the parties are normally involved in the drafting process. The *Practice Direction (ECJ References: Procedure)* [1999] 1 WLR 260 states that the reference should 'identify as clearly, succinctly and simply as the nature of the case permits the question to which the British court seeks an answer. It is very desirable that language be used which lends itself readily to translation'. If a reference is made, the ECJ will not concern itself with the question of whether or not a reference was necessary; it will give a decision.

11.26 Article 234 of the EU Treaty provides that, where a question of interpretation or validity of EC law is raised before a court or tribunal of a member state, the court or tribunal may 'if it considers that a decision on the question is necessary to enable it to give judgment, request the Court of Justice to give a ruling thereon'. The ECJ's sole function under Art 234 is to decide what the EC law is and to assist the court on the point of law in abstract. It does not have jurisdiction to interpret national law; and it is for the referring court or tribunal to apply the relevant rule of Community law, after it has been interpreted by the Court of Justice, in the specific case pending before it (see, for example, *Marks and Spencer plc v Halsey* (Case C-446/03) [2005] ECR 10837, where the decision of the ECJ has been applied by the referring High Court ([2006] 3 CMLR 8), and further by the Court of Appeal ([2007] 2 CMLR 21)).

11.27 References can be made by the Special and General Commissioners, and VAT and Duties Tribunal, as well as by the courts; and, if it is considered that a reference is likely to be required, then it should be sought at the earliest opportunity.

SECTION TWO – APPEALS BEFORE THE SPECIAL COMMISSIONERS AND GENERAL COMMISSIONERS

The right to appeal

11.28 One of the reasons for introducing self-assessment was to reduce the number of appeals made by taxpayers. Prior to the introduction of the self-assessment regime, there were roughly five million appeals made annually in England and Wales against assessments and, of these, about four million were settled by agreement between taxpayers and the HMRC. Under the assessment regime, a taxpayer's failure to provide complete information on time often resulted in HMRC issuing an assessment in estimated figures and such assessments then would be appealed by the taxpayer to the Commissioners. A taxpayer's failure under self-assessment similarly results in the HMRC 'determining' the tax due (s 28C). However, the key difference between the regimes is that under self-assessment, the taxpayer simply has to file a self-assessed return in order to replace that determination; there is no right of appeal against a determination. Thus, self-assessment has reduced the number of appeals that arose merely because there had been a delay in the taxpayer fulfilling his statutory duties.

11.29 Following the introduction of self-assessment for both individuals and corporations, most assessments are now made either by the taxpayer or by an HMRC Officer on his behalf, based on the information in the taxpayer's tax return. There is no right of appeal against such assessments. Instead, under s 31(1), there is a right of appeal against:

1 an amendment to a self-assessment by an HMRC Officer following a formal enquiry into the return;

2 any conclusion stated or amendment made by a closure notice under ss 28A or 28B;

3 any amendment of a partnership return under s 30B(1); or

4 any assessment to tax which is not a self-assessment.

Self-assessment closure procedure

11.30 The procedure on completion of an enquiry for corporation tax self-assessment is set out in the Finance Act 1998, Sch 18. It can involve up to four stages:

1 issue of a closure notice, stating HMRC's conclusions;

2 30-day opportunity for taxpayer to amend self-assessment;

3 30-day opportunity for HMRC to amend self-assessment; and

4 taxpayer's right of appeal against HMRC amendment.

11.31 This procedure has been recognised by HMRC as being unnecessarily cumbersome; and, following a joint report by the Chartered Institute of Taxation and the Inland Revenue into income tax enquiries under self-assessment, a new 'two-stage' procedure for personal (and trustee) self-assessment was inserted into the TMA by Finance Act 2001. Under s 28A, an enquiry into a personal self-assessment is completed when, by closure notice, the HMRC Officer informs the taxpayer that he has completed his enquiries and states his conclusions. The closure notice must either state that no amendment of the return is required, or make the amendments of the return that the Officer considers are necessary to give effect to his conclusions. The taxpayer may then appeal against any amendments of the return.

11.32 An amendment to the Finance Bill 2001 was tabled to ensure that the Inland Revenue took steps to amend the corporate tax self-assessment closure procedure so as to reflect the procedure for personal self-assessment. This was rejected, the Paymaster General, Dawn Primarolo saying that: 'The Government have not turned their face against reviewing how the corporation tax self-assessment enquiry has bedded in … For many reasons, however … the time is not now'. A cynic might suggest that the reason for the reluctance to amend the legislation is the cost of making the consequential changes to HMRC's computer system that had been developed and recently introduced for corporation tax self-assessment.

Closure notice applications

11.33 HMRC not only has very wide powers during the enquiry stage, but also considerable scope for prolonging that stage. This is significant for taxpayers, as, in general, they can appeal only after the enquiry has been completed. However, valuable protection is provided to the taxpayer against HMRC by s 28A(6), which enables the taxpayer to apply to the Commissioners, during the enquiry, for a direction that the enquiry should be closed. The burden of proof is then on the Revenue to show that there are 'reasonable grounds' for not closing the enquiry. As the Special Commissioner noted in *Jade Palace v Revenue and Customs Commissioners* [2006] STC (SCD) 419:

> '… the issue on [a closure notice] application is not simply whether a closure notice should be directed, but whether it should be directed within a specified period. The reasonable grounds must cover the setting of a period.'

This procedural rule is intended to protect taxpayers against protracted and unfocused enquiries and to enable taxpayers to take control of a dispute with HMRC.

Referral of questions during enquiry

11.34 Finance Act 2001 inserted a new Part IIIA 'referral of questions during enquiry' into the TMA 1970. Section 28ZA to 28ZE sets out a procedure for personal self-assessment that enables questions relating to the subject matter of an enquiry to be referred to the Special Commissioners whilst the enquiry is still in progress. A similar procedure of referral was introduced with regard to corporation tax self-assessment (see Finance Act 1998, Sch 18, paras 31A–31D).

11.35 Referral only can be made jointly by the taxpayer and HMRC. Whilst proceedings on a referral are in progress in relation to an enquiry and until the matter referred is finally determined, no closure notice will be issued, nor can an application for a direction to give such a notice be made. The determination is binding on both parties, subject to any further appeal rights. A right of appeal was introduced under the Referrals to the Special Commissioners Regulations 2001 (SI 2001/4024), which came into force on 31 January 2002. The Regulations operate so as to apply s 56A (which provides for appeals from a decision of the Special Commissioners to the High Court) to questions referred to the Special Commissioners. Accordingly, an appeal from the Special Commissioners' determination of a referred question can be made to the High Court (and (subject to acquiring the requisite permissions) to the Court of Appeal and to the House of Lords).

11.36 This extra measure of flexibility, which enables issues to be resolved without closing down the whole enquiry, is welcomed.

Jurisdiction of the General and Special Commissioners

Introduction

11.37 The jurisdiction over direct tax appeals is shared between the General and Special Commissioners. Direct taxes are generally within the jurisdiction of both the General and Special Commissioners. However, there are some direct tax issues that are exclusive to the Special Commissioners (such as appeals concerning petroleum revenue tax or international tax issues), and some that are exclusive to the General Commissioners (such as appeals against PAYE coding notices). The division of jurisdiction between the two bodies in respect of such matters has a degree of arbitrariness to it and it is not possible to summarise succinctly to which body such appeals lie. Reference should be made to ss 46B, 46C, 46D or 47B. If an appeal is brought to the General Commissioners that raises such issues, the General Commissioners (or, if the hearing has yet to start, the Inspector) must refer those issues to the Special Commissioners for resolution.

11.38 The status of the two bodies of Commissioners is equal and there is no appeal from the General to the Special Commissioners. Each body has different qualities. The Special Commissioners are legally qualified and have technical expertise; whereas the General Commissioners are able to bring to a dispute local knowledge and commercial experience.

Cases before the Special Commissioners

11.39 Cases before the Special Commissioners range from hearings lasting less than an hour with the taxpayer appearing in person to appeals lasting a number of weeks with the parties represented by Counsel. The head of the Special Commissioners' tribunal, currently Sir Stephen Oliver QC, is known as the Presiding Special Commissioner and has the status of a Circuit Judge. Currently, there are 27 Special Commissioners. The Special Commissioners receive about 180 appeals and hear about 80 appeals each year.

Cases before the General Commissioners

11.40 There are over 3,000 General Commissioners, divided into 458 divisions loosely based upon the parish boundary system. Most tax disputes begin before the General Commissioners, who hear, on average, over 10,000 cases per year. Every General Commissioner is unpaid; and tax expertise is not a prerequisite for appointment. Hearings before the General Commissioners are informal and taxpayers normally appear in person. Decisions are not published and may be given orally.

The procedure before the Special and General Commissioners – preliminary matters

Introduction

11.41 As the Special and General Commissioners (the Commissioners) exist in a 'pre-Woolfian state', appeals before them are not governed by the Civil Procedure Rules. The procedure before the Commissioners is governed by the TMA and regulated by the Special Commissioners (Jurisdiction and Procedure) Regulations (SI 1994/1811) (the Special Regulations) and the General Commissioners (Jurisdiction and Procedure) Regulations (SI 1994/1812) (the General Regulations) respectively.

11.42 The procedures before the Special Commissioners and the General Commissioners as set out in the Special and General Regulations respectively are broadly similar. For ease, the focus of this chapter is on the Special Commissioners' procedures, with only differences in the General Commissioners' procedure set out.

Notice of appeal

11.43 An appeal must be brought by a notice of appeal in writing within 30 days after the date that the particular notice was issued. Under s 31A(5), the notice of appeal must specify the grounds of appeal. However, TMA 1970 gives no indication as to how specific the grounds should be; and it is normal for the grounds to be stated in a general way only at this stage. The detailed facts and issues of law that form the basis of the appeal can then be set out a later stage, normally in a Statement of Case and/or in a skeleton argument. Section 31A(6) provides that Commissioners may allow the appellant to put forward other grounds not specified in the notice, provided that the omission was not 'wilful or unreasonable'.

Extension of time

11.44 An appeal may be brought out of time provided that, on an application for the purpose, an Inspector is satisfied, first, that there was a reasonable excuse for not bringing the appeal within the time limit, and, secondly, that the application was made thereafter without unreasonable delay, and gives his consent in writing (see s 49). In practice, HMRC normally consents freely to 'reasonable' appeals being made out of time. In default of consent, the matter must be referred to the Commissioners; unless an election for the appeal to be before the Special Commissioners has already been made, the application must be made to the General Commissioners. The decision of the Commissioners is final, subject to judicial review.

11.45 In *R, on the application of Browallia Cal, v City of London General Commissioners* [2004] STC 296, Evans-Lombe J held that s 49 contemplates two stages. The first stage is an application to the Inspector who can, if he can discern a reasonable excuse, properly allow an appeal to be lodged out of time (thus saving the necessity of reference to General Commissioners for that permission to be granted); if the Inspector does not find that there was reasonable excuse, the second stage then arises, which is a reference of the application by the Inspector to the Commissioners for them to determine. Evans-Lombe J held that the discretion of the Commissioners:

> 'is not confined, as the Inspector's discretion is confined, to determining whether there was a reasonable excuse for the failure to lodge the appeal within time, but would also embrace such considerations as the lack of any prejudice to the Commissioners as a result of failing to lodge an appeal in time, and demonstrable injustice to the taxpayer if such an appeal is not permitted to be lodged out of time.'

11.46 The Commissioners can consider matters which an Inspector has no power to take into account and can, for example, weigh up whether there would be any prejudice to HMRC in allowing an appeal to be made out of time against whether refusing to allow a late appeal would cause injustice to the taxpayer. In *R (on the application of Cook) v General Commissioners of Income Tax and another* [2007] STC 499 Burton J said, with regard to prejudice to the taxpayer, that 'depriving of a party of the opportunity of putting forward an arguably meritorious appeal is itself an obvious prejudice'.

Right to elect for the Special Commissioners

11.47 For all matters within the jurisdiction of both the General and Special Commissioners, the 'default' rule is that an appeal shall lie to the General Commissioners. A taxpayer who wishes to have his appeal heard before the Special Commissioners must elect for this to occur within the 30-day time limit for making the appeal (under s 31D(1)). If the opportunity to elect is missed, it is still possible, under s 44(3), to transfer proceedings to the Special Commissioners, but only if HMRC, the General Commissioners and the Special Commissioners consent. There is some scope for a taxpayer to have proceedings transferred, even if HMRC do not consent; under s 44(3A), the General Commissioners may, with the agreement of the Special Commissioners, and having considered any representations made to them by the parties, arrange for the transfer of the proceedings to the Special Commissioners if they are of the view that the proceedings should be before the Special Commissioners 'because of the complexity of the appeal or the length of time likely to be required for hearing it'.

11.48 In order to prevent the Special Commissioners having to hear appeals where the taxpayer has no substantive arguments to put forward, there is a mechanism that allows HMRC to seek to have an election disregarded. Under s 31D(3), HMRC may refer the election to the General Commissioners and the General Commissioners shall give a direction disregarding the election unless they are satisfied that the appellant has arguments to present or evidence to adduce on the merits of the appeal (s 31D(5)). In practice, HMRC will only seek a direction where it is a 'delay' appeal (ie where information to settle the appeal remains outstanding), rather than a 'contentious' appeal, where there are points in dispute.

11.49 Under s 31D(2), an election for an appeal to be heard by the Special Commissioners may be disregarded also if the appellant and the inspector so agree in writing before the appeal is determined.

11.50 In practical terms, the consequence of the foregoing is that it is prudent for the taxpayer:

1 to work out exactly which body has jurisdiction; and
2 for those matters where there is concurrent jurisdiction, to decide which body should hear the appeal, having weighed up the various tactical factors that apply

before the appeal is lodged. Failure to do so could result in delay and additional expense. The factors that should be considered include:

1 the General Commissioners may have particular local knowledge that could expedite the hearing;

2 the decisions of the General Commissioners are not published (although, if privacy is an issue, the decisions of the Special Commissioners can be anonymised provided certain conditions are met (see Regulation 15 of the Special Regulations); and

3 although there is a right of appeal to the High Court from both the General and the Special Commissioners, it is an archaic procedure with regard to appeals from the General Commissioners.

Application for postponement of tax

11.51 Where the taxpayer has lodged an appeal and he considers that the tax charged is excessive, he can apply, under s 55, for postponement of the payment of part or all of the tax charged, pending the determination of the appeal. The HMRC Officer may agree with the taxpayer the amount of tax in respect of which payment may be postponed; and most cases are determined in this way. However, if agreement cannot be reached, then the taxpayer may apply to the Commissioners for a determination of the amount of tax to be postponed pending the determination of the appeal. Before the Commissioners, the taxpayer does not have to prove all the facts or succeed in the legal arguments that will have to be proved or established at the substantive appeal; instead, the taxpayer just must show 'reasonable grounds' for believing that he has been overcharged to tax. 'Reasonable' means that the grounds must be based on reason and must not be irrational, absurd or ridiculous (see *Sparrow Ltd v Inspector of Taxes* [2001] STC (SCD) 206). There is a right of appeal from the Commissioners to the High Court on a question of law (under s 56A(4)).

11.52 Only the amount of tax that depends on the outcome of the appeal is postponed until the appeal is heard. In the meantime HMRC are entitled to seek payment of the balance (which is payable within 30 days of the agreement or the Commissioners' decision under s 55(5) – see *Parikh v Back* [1985] STC 232).

11.53 In the event that the taxpayer does not apply for postponement, then the whole of the tax charged is payable as if there had been no appeal, but without prejudice to the appeal.

Withdrawal of an appeal

11.54 After a notice of appeal has been sent by the taxpayer, that appeal may be disposed of either by a Commissioners' hearing or by agreement of the parties under s 54 (see the section entitled 'Agreements settling appeals' below). A taxpayer who has given notice of appeal, but does not wish to proceed with the appeal, must notify an HMRC Officer, either orally or in writing, of this decision. The Officer may, within 30 days of such notification, notify the taxpayer in writing that the withdrawal is refused (eg if he considers that the taxpayer's profits are higher than are provided in the amendment to the self-assessment); and, if he does so, then the proceedings continue. Failing such counter-notice, or alternatively in the event that the withdrawal is accepted, the appeal is treated as if the parties had come to an agreement that the assessment should be upheld without variation.

HMRC'S litigation and settlement strategy

11.55 HMRC's Litigation and Settlement Strategy (LSS) was published in June 2007. LSS sets out the strategy that HMRC now adopts to contentious matters. In an article in the *Tax Journal* (11 June 2007), Dave Hartnett (who was, at the time. HMRC Director General) set out the aims of HMRC's LLS strategy:

> 'The LSS sets consistent standards for the way we settle disputes with our customers, whether by agreement or litigation. It ensures that where we are confident about the strength of our case and the disputed point is a significant one, we will insist on 100% of the tax or other liabilities that HMRC believes to be due. Where we accept that we do not have strong grounds for our position or the issue is less important to us, we will aim to avoid disputes altogether.'

11.56 The focus of LSS is on 'promoting positive customer behaviours' and deterring non-compliance with the tax laws. LSS covers all types of dispute about liability to pay taxes or duties, or entitlement to tax credits, absent litigation to recover debts or concerning employment matters and the term 'dispute' means any situation where HMRC are in disagreement with a taxpayer and 'the disagreement is not readily resolved'. Once this stage has been reached, LSS must be applied by the Inspector to the matter and a litigation focused approach adopted.

11.57 The two fundamental aspects of LSS are as follows:

1. Each dispute will be settled on its own merits. There will be no 'package deals' that settle a range of issues for a single undifferentiated sum of money.
2. If HMRC considers that it has a 'winnable case', it will insist on 100% of the tax or other liabilities that it believes to be due; it will not compromise on this figure. Disputes that have an 'all-or-nothing' character that will be decided one way or the other by the courts must be settled on 'all-or-nothing' basis. Thus, for example, no discount will be provided for an agreement not to litigate.

11.58 The dominant factor in determining whether or not to litigate is chance of success. If HMRC consider that the chance of success is less than 50%, then they will not pursue the case unless it can be justified by the particular circumstances, such as a very large amount of tax in question (in the case itself or from immediate precedent value), or a fundamental point of principle at stake. In all cases, the legal advice from HMRC Solicitor's Office will be a critical factor in decision making. If the amount of tax at stake is over £250 million, then the matter is referred to an Executive Committee of the Board of HMRC (known as 'Excom'), who will take the decision on whether or not to litigate.

The preparatory stages before the Special and General Commissioners

Introduction

The Special Commissioners

11.59 In contrast to litigation before the High Court, which has distinct interlocutory stages, the procedure before the Special Commissioners is comparatively flexible. However, partly because of the increasing complexity of appeals, the Special Commissioners have become increasingly aware of the need actively to case manage tax appeals. Once an appeal has been registered by the clerk to the Special Commissioners, its management will be allocated to one of the full-time Special Commissioners. This is to enable enough to be known about the appeal to ensure that it is listed before the appropriate Special Commissioners and to ensure that the factual evidence and legal arguments of each party are known to the other party before the hearing takes place. Under the Special Commissioners' Practice Statement dated September 2006, the framework that enables a case to be brought on for hearing as speedily and as effectively as possible is made up of directions. These will either be Standard Directions, comprising (i) basic or preliminary directions (which are applicable automatically in all cases and which deal with the structure of the appeal) ('the Basic Directions') and (ii) Management Directions that deal with case management matters, or bespoke directions agreed at a preliminary hearing convened for the purpose of giving more specific directions.

11.60 The aim of the directions is to prepare the appeal for hearing. The practice in all courts is now to require that all evidence and argument be committed to writing in advance of the hearing. This means that all witnesses (including the appellant) are required to prepare written statements of the evidence which they will give and both parties are required to set out their legal arguments in outline. These documents, together with any other document which is to be produced in the appeal, must be lodged with the Special Commissioners, and served on the other side, in advance of the hearing.

11.61 There are many advantages to this approach. It shortens the length of the hearing, because all the evidence and argument can be read by both sides and the Special Commissioners before the hearing begins. It means that each witness can prepare his evidence in advance and it means that each party is fully aware of the other's case. It is no longer regarded as reasonable, or in the interests of justice, for late evidence (oral or written) or argument to be sprung on the opposing party at or during the hearing of the appeal. In *Mobile Export 365 Limited, Shelford IT Limited v Commissioners for HM Revenue & Customs* [2007] EWHC 1737 (Ch), the Administrative Court criticised the approach that Counsel had adopted before the VAT tribunal. In relation to Counsel having produced 'from his papers (as a conjurer produces a rabbit out of his hat) a skeleton argument and a bundle of authorities', Lightman J said:

> 'I should conclude by saying a word about springing surprises on opponents, as were sprung on the Commissioners and the Tribunal in this case. Such tactics are not acceptable conduct today in any civil proceedings. They are clearly repugnant to the Overriding Objective laid down in CPR 1.1 (where applicable) and the duty of the parties and their legal representatives to help the court to further that objective. The objection to them is not limited to proceedings to which the CPR are applicable.'

11.62 The Special Commissioners have power to exclude any documents that are served late or, alternatively, they may admit them but allow an adjournment so that the other party has time to consider them. They also have power, under reg 24, to impose a penalty of up to £10,000 for failure to comply with Directions. For example, in *Doshi v Andrew* [2005] STC (SCD) 427, the Special Commissioner imposed a penalty of £250 on the taxpayer for failure to comply with directions. The Special Commissioner said:

> 'The point of issuing directions is to avoid any ambush. They failed completely to achieve this and the result is that I am unable to decide the appeal without giving the parties time to make further representations. I am not prepared to allow directions to be ignored in this way. Directions mean what they say and they are backed up by penalties (maximum £10,000). I issue a penalty of £250 against the appellant.'

The General Commissioners

11.63 The procedure before the General Commissioners is more flexible than before the Special Commissioners. There is no framework of standard directions; neither is there power to seek a preliminary hearing for the agreeing of directions. Regulation 15(1) of the General Regulations provides that 'at the beginning of the hearing of any proceedings the tribunal shall, except where it considers it unnecessary to do so, explain the order of proceeding which it proposes to adopt'. In practice, for any substantial matter before the General Commissioners, the taxpayer is best advised seeking to agree in advance with HMRC a timetable leading to the hearing that deals (where appropriate) with the preparatory matters, such as service of witness statements and skeleton arguments, outlined below.

Registration with the Special Commissioners

11.64 The Special Commissioners' guidance for appeals referred to them states that the following information is required before the appeal can be registered with the Special Commissioners:

1 Full name of the appellant.
2 Appellant's address for correspondence.
3 Details of representation (accountant/solicitor/Counsel).
4 Name, address and reference number of HMRC Officer dealing with the case.
5 The matter under appeal.
6 A copy of the notice of appeal.
7 Evidence of formal election of the appeal to the Special Commissioners. If formal election has not been made or the appeal is not to the Special Commissioners as a matter of statute, a copy of the letter of Transfer of Jurisdiction (s 44(3)) or confirmation that the Clerk to the General Commissioners has sent a letter to the Special Commissioners transferring jurisdiction will be required.
8 A brief statement of the point(s) at issue.
9 An estimate of the time needed for the hearing.
10 An indication whether directions have been agreed between the parties, or if standard directions are to apply.
11 Confirmation that the above information has been served on the other side.

Directions before the Special Commissioners

Basic Directions

11.65 The purpose of the Basic Directions is to provide the Special Commissioners with some of the information they need to case-manage the appeal. In particular, it is frequently at this stage that the question for determination by the Special Commissioners can be agreed.

11.66

The Basic Directions are as follows:

'1. The Party referring the appeal for registration to provide to the Clerk to Special Commissioners ("the Clerk") and the other Party to the appeal at the same time as or not later than 14 days after an acknowledgement by the Clerk of such registration a statement detailing:

(i) what that party perceives to be the issue for determination in the case;

(ii) whether or not witnesses are likely;

(iii) the anticipated duration of the hearing;

(iv) whether a hearing in private is requested.

If the information required by Direction 1 has already been provided to the other Party and to the Clerk, the Special Commissioner may initial the following Declaration and the remaining Basic Directions shall apply accordingly: "I declare that Direction No.1 has already been complied with".

2. Within 42 days after the statement in Direction 1 (or if the declaration above has been initialled, after the date of issue of these Directions) the other Party to state to the Clerk and to the first Party whether the issue for determination is agreed and, if not, to set out the areas of disagreement. Within the same time limit the other Party to provide to the Clerk and the first Party a statement detailing points ii to iv in Direction 1. This time limit may be extended either by agreement of the Parties, and such extension shall be notified to the Clerk, or by the Tribunal on the application of either party.

3. Not later than the statement in Direction 2 each Party shall inform the Clerk whether:

(a) both parties agree other directions in place of the Management Directions in the Appendix, in which case the Special Commissioners will issue the agreed directions with such modifications as they consider appropriate (provided that if either party shall object to such modifications that party may within 14 days of receipt of the Directions require a preliminary hearing to determine whether the modifications should be made); or

(b) he requires the Clerk to arrange a preliminary hearing for the purpose of determining the directions applicable to the appeal and stating the directions he proposes should be issued.

4. In any other case the Management Directions in the Appendix shall automatically apply with effect from the statement in Direction 2.

5. If the parties have not already done so, at the same time as complying with Direction 3 they shall give the Clerk dates to avoid for the hearing.'

11.67 By Direction 3, the parties are asked to indicate whether the rest of the Standard Directions are to apply, or whether they want specific agreed directions to be made, or whether they want a preliminary hearing to be held in order to give other directions. If the parties make no indication, then under Direction 4, the rest of the Standard Directions (the Management Directions) will be made.

11.68 The purpose of the rest of the Standard Directions is to ensure that all the documentary evidence, written statements of the witnesses, outlines of the arguments and the authorities to be cited are exchanged between the parties and lodged with the clerk according to a pre-arranged timetable. This should ensure that, before the date of the hearing, both parties and the Special Commissioners will have received all the documents and be familiar with the issues, the evidence and the arguments.

11.69 The time estimate of the length of the hearing is left to the parties. If there is any doubt as to the length of hearing, time should be over-estimated rather than underestimated. If a hearing has to be adjourned part-heard and further dates fixed, the gap between hearings could be weeks or even months, depending on how much further time is required and the availability of the particular Special Commissioners who heard the first part of the appeal.

The Management Directions

11.70 The Management Directions are as follows:

'Initial exchange of documents and information

5. Within 21 days from the date from which the Management Directions apply the Appellant shall provide to the Respondents:

5.1 A list of the documents on which the Appellant intends to rely in connection with the appeal together with copies of any documents that have not already been provided;

5.2 A draft statement of facts not in dispute;

5.3 The identity of any proposed witnesses of fact and an outline of the evidence of such witnesses.

6. Within 21 days from the date from which the Management Directions apply or 14 days from the Appellant complying with Direction 5, whichever is the later, the Respondents shall provide to the Appellant:

6.1 A list of the documents on which the Respondents intend to rely in connection with the appeal together with copies of any documents that have not already been provided;

6.2 Suggested amendments and additions to the draft statement of facts not in dispute;

6.3 The identity of any proposed witnesses of fact and an outline of the evidence of such witnesses.

Agreement of facts and documents

7. Within 21 days from the Respondents complying with Direction 6 the Parties shall:

7.1 Produce an agreed statement of facts not in dispute

7.2 Agree a paginated bundle of documents

8. Exceptionally, if a bundle cannot be agreed, each Party shall prepare a paginated bundle of documents taken from those sent or listed under Directions 1 and 2 upon which he would wish to rely and serve it on the other Party within 21 days of the Respondents complying with Direction 6.

Witness statements

9. Within 21 days from the Parties complying with Directions 7 or 8 they shall each serve on the other Party and on the Clerk their witness statements of fact with exhibits cross-referenced to the bundle(s) of documents.

10. Witnesses shall conclude their statement as follows: "I believe that the facts stated in this witness statement are true" and sign and date the statement.

11. The witness statements shall stand as evidence in chief of the witnesses subject to such further questions as the Tribunal shall allow.
12. In an appeal designated as a Scottish appeal, Direction 9 shall apply with the substitution of the word "may" for the word "shall" but if the parties do serve witness statements they shall do so within the same time limits: and Direction 11 shall not apply unless the party calling the witness agrees that it shall apply.

General

13. No further documentary or witness evidence shall be admitted unless the Parties agree or the Tribunal directs.
14. Following the service of all witness statements each Party shall provide the Clerk with an updated estimate of the length of hearing.
15. Core bundles to be filed with the Clerk to the Special Commissioners 14 days before the date of hearing.

Skeleton arguments

16. Not later than 14 days before the hearing the Parties shall serve a skeleton argument together with copies of the authorities cited on each other and on the Clerk.
17. Not later than 7 days before the hearing the Parties may serve a skeleton argument in reply on each other and on the Clerk.

Further Directions

18. Either Party may apply to the Tribunal for further Directions at any time before the hearing.'

Special Commissioners' preliminary hearings

11.71 Regulation 9 of the Special Regulations allows the Special Commissioners to hold a preliminary hearing if they consider that 'any proceedings would be facilitated' by so doing. In practice, the Special Commissioners normally consider preliminary hearings to be an almost essential stage in proceedings of any complexity where the Standard Directions are not sufficient.

11.72 Either party can apply for a preliminary hearing, but it is for the Special Commissioners, not for the parties, to decide whether such a hearing is appropriate. The purpose of the hearing is to identify the issues in dispute and to clarify the procedure in preparation for the substantive hearing. At the preliminary hearing, the Commissioner will give directions on those matters contained within the Standard Directions as well as in relation to those matters that are not prescribed by the Standard Directions. Thus, for example, directions can be given on the giving of expert evidence or on the seeking a reference to the ECJ. In terms of expert evidence, the directions could encompass, for example, the holding of an 'experts only meeting' and a timetable for exchanging reports (both in draft and final form).

11.73 Notwithstanding that it is not the purpose of the preliminary hearing to deal with substantive points, the Special Commissioners are empowered to determine the proceedings at a preliminary hearing, without any further hearing, if the parties agree (under reg 9(3)(b)).

Witnesses

Summoning of witnesses

11.74 A party who requires the attendance of a person either to give evidence or to produce any relevant document in his possession may apply to the relevant Commissioners for a witness summons (see Special Regulations, reg 5; and the General Regulations, reg 4). A single General or Special Commissioner may issue a witness summons requiring that person to attend the hearing or to produce the document. The summons, signed by the Commissioner issuing it, must state the name and address or otherwise identify the person to be served. The party who applied for the summons is responsible for serving it on the witness. Service is to occur:

1 in the case of an individual, by leaving a copy with him;

2 in the case of a body corporate registered in the UK, by leaving a copy with the secretary or clerk of the body corporate;

3 in the case of a foreign body corporate with a place of business in the UK, by leaving a copy with a person authorised to accept service of process on the body corporate.

11.75 The summons will not be enforceable unless:

1 the party serving the summons pays or agrees to pay the reasonable travelling costs incurred by the witness; and

2 it has been served at least seven days before the hearing (unless the witness informs the clerk that he accepts service with a shorter period).

11.76 If the witness fails to attend, then a substantial penalty may be imposed by the Commissioners (maximum £10,000 by the Special Commissioners (under the Special Regulations, reg 24(2)) or maximum £1,000 by the General Commissioners (under the General Regulations, reg 4(12))). In practice, this sanction means that if there is any doubt as to whether or not a witness may turn up, it is advisable to obtain a 'precautionary' witness summons.

11.77 Neither the General nor the Special Commissioners have power to require the attendance of a person who is not in the United Kingdom. Video conferencing facilities ('VCF') are available in the Special Commissioners; provided that the Special Commissioners consent, witnesses who are outside the United Kingdom may appear and be cross-examined via VCF.

11.78 The Special Regulations, reg 5(11) and the General Regulations, reg 4(11)) gives the Commissioners power to set aside a witness summons on an application by the person on whom it was served. In *Tilbury Consulting Ltd v Gittins (Inspector of Taxes)* [2004] STC (SCD) 1, the Special Commissioner held that, because reg 5(11) provides that a person on whom a witness summons has been served may apply to have it set aside and 'no doubt that would be done if a summons were not applied for in good faith, or if the witness was unable to give relevant evidence, or if the application were irrelevant, speculative or oppressive', the presumption is that an application for a witness summons will normally be granted.

Witness statements

11.79 In the Practice Statement that accompanies the Standard Directions in respect of proceedings before the Special Commissioners, it is stated that:

> 'a witness statement is a written statement signed by a person which contains the evidence that that person would give orally. Where a witness statement has been served, the party who wishes to rely on the evidence of the witness must call the witness to give oral evidence unless the tribunal directs otherwise. A witness statement should contain the full names, address and occupation of the witness; it should be in the witness's own words, expressed in the first person; and should be divided into numbered paragraphs and should exhibit all necessary documents. It must conclude with the words "I believe that the facts stated in this witness statement are true" and be signed and dated by the witness. The use of witness statements is optional in Scottish appeals.'

11.80 The Commissioners have power to require any witness to give evidence on oath or affirmation (under the Special Regulations, reg 17(7) and the General Regulations, reg 15(7)). In practice, the Commissioners do not always require witnesses to be sworn. A witness who has been sworn and wilfully makes a statement material to the proceedings which he knows to be false or does not believe to be true is guilty of perjury (see *R v Hood-Barrs* [1943] KB 455).

Expert witnesses

11.81 There is no right unilaterally to adduce expert evidence at the hearing of any proceeding (see the Special Regulations, reg 12 and the General Regulations, reg 9). A party who wishes to adduce expert evidence must either agree with the other party 'that the substance of the evidence shall be disclosed in the form of a written report or opinion in advance of the hearing' or make an application to the Commissioners for a direction permitting expert evidence to be adduced.

11.82 In the Practice Statement that accompanies the Standard Directions in respect of proceedings before the Special Commissioners, it is stated that:

> 'If either party intends to call expert evidence, attention is drawn to Regulation 12 (which does not apply in Scotland). Unless an agreement is made between the parties in accordance with Regulation 12(1)(a) an application should be made for a Direction relating to the calling of expert evidence.'

Documents

11.83 Under the Special Regulations, reg 6 and the General Regulations, reg 5, where a party to proceedings agrees a document, he is deemed, subject to the terms of the agreement, to admit that the document was written and signed by the person by whom, and on the date on which, it purports to have been. However, subject to any rule of law, he is not deemed to admit the truth of the contents of the document, unless he makes such an express admission.

11.84 The parties should ensure that sufficient copies of all documents should be available for the hearing, with such documents preferably contained in a paginated bundle.

Joinder

11.85 The Commissioners may join cases if some common issue arises in both or all of them or both or all of them are relevant to some common issue (under the Special Regulations, reg 7 and the General Regulations, reg 6). This power is wide, as it enables the cases to be heard either consecutively or together. For example, four cases brought by former building societies on the deductibility of the costs of conversion to banks were heard sequentially by the Special Commissioners, with the first case serving as the base case for legal argument, and variances only being addressed in the other three cases (see *Halifax plc v Davidson* [2000] STC (SCD) 251).

11.86 The Commissioners may also allow additional parties to be joined to the proceedings, either on their own motion or on the application of a party (under the Special Regulations, reg 8 and the General Regulations, reg 7). If there is a question that may affect such a person's liability to tax or in which he may otherwise have an interest, then the additional party is not entitled, unless all the other parties consent, to be present at the hearing of the proceedings, except during such part of the hearing that relates to the particular question that he has an interest in.

Information powers

11.87 In contrast to the position under the Civil Procedure Rules, there is no express duty on the taxpayer to disclose documents; and there is no formal discovery process. It is up to the taxpayer to decide what documents he will produce in order to prove his case. However, the Commissioners can require a party to:

1 deliver to them any 'particulars' that are required for the purpose of determining any of the issues in the proceedings (under the Special Regulations, reg 10(1)(a) and the General Regulations, reg 10(1)(a)); and

2 make available for inspection any 'books, accounts or other documents' that may contain information relating to the subject matter of the proceedings, provided that the material in question is already in existence and is in the possession or power of the appellant (the Special Regulations, reg 10(1)(b) and the General Regulations, reg 10(1)(b)).

11.88 This power to obtain information is that of the Commissioners; and it is distinct from HMRC's powers of information, which subsist even after an appeal has been lodged (see *R v IRC, ex parte Taylor* (*No* 2) [1990] STC 379). Until April 2003, the Commissioners could not ask HMRC to produce documents under reg 10. Now notices under reg 10 can be served on any party.

11.89 If a person fails to comply with an information notice, then the Commissioners may summarily impose a penalty on that person (the Special Commissioners, reg 24(1) and the General Regulation, reg 10(3)); there is a right of appeal to the High Court, under s 53, against the imposition of the penalty.

Human rights arguments

11.90 The Special Commissioners' Practice Statement that accompanies the Directions restates a Practice Direction issued by the Presiding Special Commissioner in October 2000. The effect of this is that any party who wishes to raise an argument about human rights must give the clerk and the other party not less than three days' notice of his intention to raise such a point and supply copies of the authorities he intends to cite at the hearing.

Listing of appeals

11.91 Any party to appeal proceedings (except in penalty proceedings that HMRC institutes under s 100C) may serve a notice on the clerk to the relevant Commissioners that he wishes a date to be fixed for a hearing (under reg 3(1)). On receipt of such a notice, the clerk must send a notice to each party at least 28 days before the date of the hearing giving details of the place, date and time of the meeting. Shorter notice may be given if the parties agree, or if the Commissioners so direct.

11.92 In practice, the listing of the appeal will normally have been agreed between the parties and fixed by the clerk to suit the convenience of the parties, their representatives and their witnesses. Also, the hearing date will usually be recorded in the directions that have been issued by the Commissioners. However, there may be circumstances when a unilateral application is merited (see, for example, *Financial Institution v Inland Revenue Commissioners* [2003] STC (SCD) 26).

Constitution of the Tribunal

General Commissioners

11.93 Section 44(5) provides that, save as expressly provided, anything that is required to be done by the General Commissioners is to be done by at least two of them. The General Regulations state that, whilst the proceedings will be valid if only two Commissioners are present, if possible, at least three Commissioners should constitute the tribunal. It is for the tribunal to decide which member will preside over the proceedings.

Special Commissioners

11.94 Section 45(1) provides that proceedings are to be heard by a single Commissioner, unless the Presiding Special Commissioner directs otherwise.

The Special Regulations, reg 13 provide that (i) a tribunal may consist of one, two or three Commissioners; and (ii) that where there are two or three members, the Presiding Special Commissioner will nominate who is to preside.

11.95 In practice, complex appeals will be heard by two Special Commissioners and less complex appeals by one. The responsibility for the choice lies with the Presiding Special Commissioner. Appeals that are 'fact-intensive', and particularly where a number of witnesses are called, are likely to be heard by two Special Commissioners. This is to enable the Special Commissioners to discuss between themselves their recollections of the witnesses' testimony (and demeanour).

Burden of proof

11.96 Under s 50(6), the onus of proof is on the taxpayer to prove that the amendment to the assessment, for example, is wrong. The standard of proof is the ordinary civil standard of 'balance of probabilities'.

11.97 Section 50(7) empowers the Commissioners to increase an assessment on appeal where it appears to them that the assessment is inadequate. The statute does not specify who has to show that the assessment is inadequate; and it is considered that the normal rule 'he who asserts must prove' applies. Thus, on the assumption that it will be HMRC who assert that an assessment is inadequate, the burden of proof, in this instance, will be on HMRC.

The hearing

General Commissioners

11.98 The procedure before the General Commissioners is informal in comparison to courts and to the Special Commissioners. All parties remain seated during the proceedings. The General Commissioners are accustomed to cases being presented by taxpayers themselves and do not presume that those advocating cases before them possess technical tax expertise. Their main objective is to ensure that they obtain sufficient information to allow themselves properly to reach a decision on the appeal before them. They will often ignore the formalities that would be imposed by the procedural framework in courts in order to achieve that end.

11.99 Guidance published by the General Commissioners in relation to hearings before them states as follows:

> '… the General Commissioners try to make appeal hearings as informal as possible. Different divisions have slightly different procedures, but they all follow the general format set out below.
>
> You or your representative will be asked to wait outside the hearing room until the Commissioners are ready to see you. The HMRC representative will also be asked to wait outside, unless they are already in the hearing room dealing with another appeal.
>
> At the beginning of the hearing, the Chair or the Clerk will tell you what is going to happen. The Chair will control what happens throughout the hearing, and he or she, and the other General Commissioners may ask you questions.
>
> The General Commissioners determine the order in which the case is presented. Normally the Chair will ask you or your representative to present your case before the HMRC Inspector speaks but sometimes the HMRC may be asked to speak first. This is called "presenting your case".
>
> The Chair will ask you to explain your appeal. Try to make sure that you tell the Commissioners information that is directly relevant to your case. You must tell the General Commissioners the facts to support your appeal not just your opinion. At the end of your presentation, try to sum up the important points that you have made. It is best to try to avoid raising new points after you have presented your case.
>
> Once you have finished, the Chair will ask the HMRC representative to present their case. The HMRC representative will be able to reply to the points that you have made, and then present their own case. You or your representative will be asked if you want to reply to the HMRC arguments.
>
> The General Commissioners will ask everyone to leave the room while they make their decision. The Clerk may stay to advise them on a legal point. Normally they will give you their decision in person on the day. Sometimes they need more time and will write to you later.'

Special Commissioners

11.100 A reasonably formal procedure is adopted before the Special Commissioners. In most cases, the appellant will start by putting his legal arguments and calling his witnesses, who may be questioned by HMRC. HMRC will then put its arguments and call its witnesses (if any), who may be questioned by the appellant. Then the appellant will have the right of reply.

Publicity

11.101 Prior to September 1994, proceedings before both bodies were held in private. Since 1994, proceedings of the Special Commissioners have been held in public; and, in December 2002, legislation was introduced to make General Commissioners' hearings open to the public.

11.102 Until 31 December 2002 an appellant had the right to have his appeal heard in private. However, since that date there is no longer an unqualified right. A hearing before either tribunal can be held in private only if the particular tribunal is satisfied that this is necessary in the interests of morals, public order, national security, juveniles or for the protection of the private life of the parties, or if they consider that publicity would prejudice the interests of justice (see the Special Regulations, reg 15 and the General Regulations, reg 13).

11.103 Agreement by the parties that the appeal should be heard in private is not sufficient. The Practice Statement that accompanies the Standard Directions in respect of proceedings before the Special Commissioners states that: 'The Special Commissioners will rule on applications for hearings in private even where these are agreed'. If such a Direction is applied for, it will be considered by the Special Commissioners on its merits having regard to the facts of the case. However, if the only argument put forward is that the appellant does not want his tax affairs discussed in public, that is unlikely to satisfy the conditions for a Direction. If there is no Direction, the appeal is heard in public.

11.104 In *Red Discretionary Trustees v Inspector of Taxes* [2004] STC (SCD) 132, the taxpayer company owned a high-profile asset that had attracted a considerable amount of press attention, and the family wealth had made the family a target for theft and violence. They had suffered a serious personal attack in which members of the family were handcuffed by four robbers at the home and a substantial amount of property was stolen. Press reports of the event were provided. HMRC indicated that they had no objection to the hearing in private. The Special Commissioners allowed the application for the hearing to be heard in private. They said:

> 'As we believe this is only the second such application under the amended rule we are setting out the chairman's reasons for granting the application in this decision for the benefit of those reading this decision when it is published in an anonymised form. The rules clearly state that consent of both parties is in itself not enough; the tribunal must be satisfied about the matters set out in (i) or (ii) of

> reg 15(2). There is a public interest in open hearings and a presumption that sittings will be in public unless sufficient reasons are shown that one of those matters is satisfied. In this case given the circumstances of the robbery and its press publicity the chairman considered that sitting in private is necessary for the protection of the private life of the appellant to a greater extent than would ordinarily be the case. Protecting the taxpayer's private life could not be achieved if part of the hearing were in private. Accordingly the chairman agreed that the hearing would be in private. If it had not been for the press publicity about the robbery the tribunal would probably have decided to sit in public and for figures to be omitted where these were not necessary to an understanding of the decision.'

(The decision of the Special Commissioners was appealed directly to the Court of Appeal (see further the section below on 'leapfrogging'), where it was heard in public: *Howell and another v Trippier* (*Inspector of Taxes*) [2004] STC 1245.)

11.105 When the Commissioners hear *ex-parte* applications by HMRC (such as for consent to issue a s 20 notice or an application under s 93(3) for a direction for daily penalties), these are heard in private (see *Re an Application by Revenue and Customs Commissioners to Serve a section 20 Notice* [2007] STC (SCD) 202). The justification for this is that these are not proceedings to which the Special or General Regulations apply.

Decisions

Special Commissioners

11.106 At the end of the hearing, the Special Commissioners may give their decision orally, but normally they will reserve their decision, which will be given in writing subsequently and which will be sent to the parties by post. The aim of the Special Commissioners is to provide a decision within two months of the hearing. Where a delay is likely, the chairman should let the clerk know so that the parties to the appeal can be kept informed. The note of meeting of the VAT & Duties Tribunals' Users Group held on 23 March 2006, records the President of the VAT tribunal, Sir Stephen Oliver QC, as inviting anyone concerned with the length of time a decision is taking to be released to write to him directly. As the President of the VAT tribunal is also the Presiding Special Commissioner, it is the view of the author that that invitation should be read across, *mutatis mutandis*, to the Special Commissioners in the event that there is an unreasonable delay in releasing a decision.

11.107 If the tribunal consists of only two Special Commissioners, then the chairman has two votes. See, for example, *Jones v Garnett* [2005] STC (SCD) 9 (which was decided by the chair's casting vote).

11.108 Under Regulation 18(8) and (10), the clerk must send to each party a copy of the documents recording either a decision in principle or a final determination, including, in the case of a final determination, a note of the provisions of TMA 1970 and the Special Commissioners Regulations and the rules of court governing appeals from the determination and of the time and manner in which such an appeal must be made.

11.109 The decisions of Special Commissioners have been published since 1994. They are published on their website and also in *Simon's Tax Cases – Special Commissioners' Decisions.*

11.110 If an appeal or any part of it is heard in private, the decision can be appropriately anonymised before publication (see the Special Regulations, reg 20(2)). However, the decision must be reported in full. In *Y Co Ltd v IRC* [1996] STC (SCD) 147, the taxpayer requested that a brief summary of the decision be released instead of an anonymised decision. The taxpayer indicated that it was extremely difficult to anonymise the decision and that by the very uniqueness of the circumstances involved in the appeal it would be possible for any reader of the decision who came from the same industry to work out who the taxpayer was. That request was denied. The Special Commissioners held that as reg 18 requires the determination to include a statement of facts as found and of the reasons, it was not permissible for only an abbreviated summary to be released.

11.111 On 27 February 1996 the Presiding Special Commissioner, formulated the policy on reporting. So far as anonymisation is concerned, it reads:

> 'In cases where anonymisation is required the Presiding Special Commissioner will seek to achieve this in co-operation with the parties. If a decision or determination cannot be anonymised to the complete satisfaction of the party requiring it, the Presiding Special Commissioner's policy is to report it in as anonymised form as he, in consultation with the Special Commissioner or Commissioners deciding the case, considers to be appropriate. To this there is one exception, which is that no report will be published where the decision cannot be effectively anonymised and to report it would defeat the ends of justice, eg where particulars of a secret process would otherwise have to be disclosed or in cases where minors were involved. The Presiding Special Commissioner will consider cases falling outside this exception on their merits.'

Whilst the policy statement predates the change in rules regarding hearings in private, it is considered that it still applies.

General Commissioners

11.112 Under reg 16, the decision may be given orally at the end of the hearing or reserved. In either event, it must be recorded in a document signed and dated by the tribunal. The clerk must send to each party a document setting out the determination, and including a note of the provisions of TMA 1970, the General Regulations and the rules of court governing appeals from the determination and of the time and manner in which such an appeal must be made. The document must contain sufficient reasons for the parties to understand why the matter was decided by the General Commissioners in the way that it was. In *R (on the application of Corr) v General Commissioners of Income Tax* [2006] STC 709, the taxpayer judicially reviewed the decision of the General Commissioners on the basis, *inter alia*, that no proper reasons were given as required by Regulation 16. Weatherup J referred to the decision of the House of Lords in *South Buckinghamshire District Council v Porter (No 2)* [2004] 1 WLR 1953, where Lord Browne of Eaton-under-Heywood said in relation to reasons based challenges:

> 'The reasons for a decision must be intelligible and they must be adequate. They must enable the reader to understand why the matter was decided as it was and what conclusions were reached on the 'principal important controversial issues', disclosing how any issue of law or fact was resolved. Reasons can be briefly stated, the degree of particularity required depending entirely on the nature of the issues falling for decision. The reasoning must not give rise to a substantial doubt as to whether the decision-maker erred in law, for example by misunderstanding some relevant policy or some other important matter or by failing to reach a rational decision on relevant grounds. But such adverse inference will not readily be drawn. The reasons need refer only to the main issues in the dispute, not to every material consideration … A reasons challenge will only succeed if the party aggrieved can satisfy the court that he has genuinely been substantially prejudiced by the failure to provide an adequately reasoned decision.'

It was then held that as the decision, although succinct, stated the essence of the reason for the conclusion and the taxpayer had not been substantially prejudiced by reason of its concise nature, the reason-based challenge did not succeed. The decisions of General Commissioners are not published.

Review of decisions

11.113 Under the Special Regulations, reg 19 and the General Regulations, reg 17, in certain limited circumstances, the Commissioners may review and set aside or vary a decision, either of its own motion or on the application of a party to the appeal. In order to do so, they must be satisfied that:

1 the decision or determination was wrongly made as a result of an administrative error by the clerk or any member of the staff of the Commissioners or a party;

2 a party failed to appear or be represented at the hearing and had good and sufficient reason for that failure; or

3 accounts or other information relevant to the case had been sent to the clerk or to the Revenue before the hearing but had not been received by the tribunal until after the hearing.

11.114 An application to reopen the appeal must be:

1 made to the tribunal within 14 days of the issue of the notice of the decision;

2 in writing; and

3 state in full the grounds for the application.

If the tribunal decides of its own motion to review the decision or determination, it must serve notice of that decision to the parties within 14 days of the issue of the determination.

11.115 In *Phillips v Burrows* [2000] STC (SCD) 112, the taxpayer sought permission for the decision to be set aside on the basis that ill-health precluded his attendance. This was rejected. There have been a number of previous adjournments made arguably on the ground of ill-health, but the medical evidence previously adduced had not been satisfactory, and previous directions of the Special Commissioners relating to the submission of detailed medical reports, have not been complied with. The Special Commissioners also said:

> '… before reaching a final view, I have also gone on to consider whether the taxpayer has satisfied me that he would have a prospect of succeeding in the appeal if the decision were to be set aside; in other words, whether his case has substance so that justice requires that there should be a rehearing. In this connection it is relevant that the failure by the taxpayer to comply with previous directions of the Special Commissioners, including directions to serve witness statements and a skeleton argument, means that it is not possible to conclude that the taxpayer would have a reasonable prospect of success if an order were made for a rehearing. It is also relevant that the taxpayer has not adduced any further evidence since the decision … to support the view that he would have a reasonable prospect of success if the appeal were reheard. Also relevant is the fact that previous directions have been deliberately ignored.'

Costs

General Commissioners

11.116 Costs cannot be awarded in the General Commissioners.

Special Commissioners

11.117 In the Special Commissioners, costs can only be awarded if a party has 'acted wholly unreasonably in connection with the hearing' (under reg 21). Regulation 21 is extremely restrictive as to the circumstances in which a cost order can be made by the Special Commissioners (see the comments by Park J in *Gamble v Rowe* [1998] STC 1247); and it is rare for such awards to be made, particularly against HMRC.

11.118 The ambit of reg 21 has been considered in a number of cases. Regulation 21 imposes a three-fold test that must be satisfied before costs can be awarded:

1 'wholly unreasonable';

2 'action'; and

3 'in connection with the hearing'.

Each of these is to be construed narrowly.

11.119 In *Salt v Young* [1999] STC (SCD) 249, the Special Commissioner, refusing HMRC's application for costs, indicated that 'wholly unreasonable conduct' is a stringent test to satisfy. The Special Commissioner said:

> 'I wish I could award [costs]. They contend the taxpayer has behaved unreasonably. Indeed he has. He has waged a war of attrition against the Revenue for years, wasting hours, days and weeks of Revenue time which could have been better employed, and making liberal use of phrases like "lying" and "malicious harassment". … The Revenue who, in order to survive, have to develop a pachydermatous resistance to this sort of thing, have behaved with admirable restraint. Only two things prevent me from acceding to their request. The first is that, although on an objective test I suspect that the vast majority of reasonable men would say that the taxpayer has behaved unreasonably, on a subjective test the taxpayer believes that he is justified in acting as he does. He is not visibly deranged. He is not, he says, suffering from paranoia; I am not qualified to be a judge of that. More to the point, however, the 1994 regulations require that, before making an award of costs, I should be of the opinion that the taxpayer has acted wholly unreasonably in connection with the hearing. The taxpayer has been unreasonable, but he has not been wholly unreasonable, and his unreasonableness is only connected with the hearing to a very minor extent.'

11.120 In *Carter v Hunt (Inspector of Taxes)* [2000] STC (SCD), the Special Commissioner held that the word 'acted' indicates the taking of a positive course of action. Simply adhering to an untenable legal argument does not satisfy the 'acted' test, unless the party knew that the argument was untenable ('None the less I would be prepared to accept that a party had acted wholly unreasonably in connection with a hearing where he had flogged a dead horse of a legal argument knowing it to be one.'). Further, if there is a policy justification for HMRC's taking a case where they consider that a successful outcome is unlikely, then this may be sufficient to prevent an award of costs against them. In *Homeowners Friendly Society Ltd v Barrett* (*Inspector of Taxes*) [1995] STC (SCD) 90, the Special Commissioner said:

> '… we do not believe that it is wholly unreasonable for an appeal to be pursued on a technical point of law where there is no authority even where the Revenue have little faith in a successful outcome. Questions of public policy sometimes dictate that the Revenue should take a case to appeal in order to establish with certainty exactly what the law is.'

However, it is considered that if such an approach is adopted in a future case by HMRC, the question whether LSS has been followed will be pertinent.

11.121 Regarding 'in connection with the hearing', the behaviour by HMRC during an enquiry that precedes legal proceedings is irrelevant (see *Conlon v Hewitt* (*Inspector of Taxes*) [2005] STC (SCD) 46, where the Special Commissioner held that 'the provision is primarily aimed at conduct which has caused the awardable hearing costs to be greater than they should have been'). However, where the entire course of conduct by HMRC and reason for an investigation is motivated solely by bad faith, then that may be a relevant consideration in considering whether there has been 'wholly unreasonable conduct'. In *Scott and another* (*trading as Farthings Steak House*) *v McDonald* (*Inspector of Taxes*) [1996] STC (SCD) 381, the Special Commissioners accepted the evidence of the taxpayers that the Inspector was not willing to settle the appeals as he wished to 'get his own back' on the taxpayers' accountant, who had complained to Head Office regarding the Inspector's conduct. The Special Commissioner held that HMRC had 'acted wholly unreasonably in connection with this hearing, having shown bad faith' and made an award of costs in respect of the costs of preparation for the hearing against HMRC.

11.122 If an award of costs is made, it can be made on the indemnity basis. In *Carvill v Frost* (*No 2*) [2005] STC (SCD) 208, the Special Commissioners decided that they had the power to specify the basis for an assessment of costs, and that HMRC's conduct was unreasonable to a sufficiently high degree for costs to be awarded on the indemnity basis. In particular, HMRC's decision not to resist the taxpayer's appeals could, and should, have been taken nearly four years earlier.

Legal assistance

11.123 Legal assistance is available in certain limited circumstances: when the proceedings concern a tax penalty that may be 'criminal' under the European Convention on Human Rights and it is 'in the interests of justice' (see *Customs and Excise Commissioners* v *Han and Yau* [2001] STC 1188 and the Lord Chancellor's Direction of 2 April 2001).

Changes to the costs system?

11.124 The limited ability of a successful party to obtain costs in direct tax litigation before the General and the Special Commissioners stands in contrast to the position in indirect tax cases, where costs can be awarded against either party, but HMRC will only seek costs against unsuccessful appellants in very narrowly defined circumstances (normally where either it is a 'substantial and complex' case or the taxpayer has misused the system by, for example, making a 'vexatious or frivolous appeal'. This policy was set out in a written answer by the Treasury Minister of State to an arranged parliamentary question in July 1978. The answer is known as the 'Sheldon Statement'). The system of three different costs regimes has been criticised widely, not merely by tax practitioners, but also by the Special Commissioners. For example, in *Carter v Hunt* [2000] STC (SCD) 17 the Presiding Special Commissioner said at 24:

> 'In the present situation the protection given to the Revenue by Regulation 21 of the 1994 Regulations, in an appeal like this where large costs are involved and the amount of tax at stake is relatively small, has imposed a real injustice on the taxpayer. The costs rules are in urgent need of overhaul and I hope this case will be seen as a starting point.'

In *Carvill v Frost* (*Inspector of Taxes*) [2005] STC (SCD) 208, the Special Commissioners again indicated that, in their view, they should have a proper costs jurisdiction.

11.125 TCE, s 29 provides that costs shall be in the discretion of the tribunal in which the proceedings take place, subject to Tribunal Procedure Rules (which will be introduced subsequently). In the Explanatory Notes to the Tribunals, Courts and Enforcement Bill it is stated in relation to the clause that became s 29:

> 'Many tribunals' powers to award costs are currently limited, either because they have no powers to award costs, or because the scope of any power they have is limited. This clause grants the tribunals the discretion to order costs and expenses in the same way as courts. It is

not intended that these provisions will apply in all jurisdictions, rather that there will be flexibility as part of the creation of the new system to determine where a costs regime would be appropriate and whether there should be any limits to such a regime (for example, that costs should be awarded only against a party who has acted vexatiously or unreasonably). This is why subsection (1) is subject to provision made under the Tribunal Procedure Rules.'

11.126 In the *Leggatt Report*, which is one of the *fons et origo* of the current recommended changes to the tax appeals system, it was recommended expressly that no change to the existing costs system should be made). Sir Andrew Leggatt's recommendation was that there be no changes to the current costs system in *any* tribunals (the consequence of this in relation to the tax tribunals would be that the current tri-partite system would be maintained). In the Consultation Paper *Transforming Tribunals* (which was published on 28 November 2007), it is proposed that no costs will be the default position.

11.127 It is considered that neither of these approaches is optimal for taxpayers. In my view, a full costs jurisdiction should apply in tax matters, with the Sheldon statement that seems to be slipping into desuetude given a statutory footing. It is considered that only such a flexible costs regime, first, will ensure that taxpayers are not inhibited from bringing strong cases where the amounts of tax are comparatively small and, secondly, will act as a bar on HMRC, particularly post its introduction of LSS using the perceived costs of litigation as a weapon to dissuade taxpayers from advancing cases that should succeed. To the extent that there is concern that a full costs regime would encourage hopeless appeals being brought by taxpayers, introducing a wasted costs regime and a strike-out regime into the rules of procedure of the new combined tax tribunal system should deter both 'wholly unreasonable' conduct and appeals.

Agreements settling appeals

11.128 Litigation which has been commenced before the Commissioners by notice of appeal can be validly settled by agreement only if the agreement complies with the relevant statutory provision, namely s 54. In short, an s 54 agreement has the same consequences as a determination to the same effect by the Commissioners; and the agreement binds the parties to it in the same way as a determination binds the parties to an appeal (see *Tod v South Essex Motors (Basildon) Ltd* [1988] STC 392). It cannot be determinative of tax liabilities for years after that to which the assessment in question relates (see *MacNiven v Westmoreland Investments Ltd* [2001] STC 237 in which, although the Inspector's reasoning in the agreement referred to the amount of excess management expenses that were intended to be carried forward, the Court held that this did not bind HMRC to take those into account in future years). Save as otherwise provided in the Taxes Act, the determination of the Commissioners is final and conclusive (under s 46(2)). Thus, an s 54 agreement is similarly final and conclusive and the issues that are resolved by it cannot be re-litigated by the parties.

11.129 A s 54 agreement is capable of rectification (*R v Inspector of Taxes, ex parte Bass Holdings Ltd* [1993] STC 122) and it may be vitiated by mutual mistake (see *Fox v Rothwell* [1995] STC (SCD) 336). Moreover, as a consequence of the agreement being final and conclusive, the taxpayer has a statutory 'cooling-off' period of 30 days. During this period, he can resile from the agreement by giving notice in writing to the HMRC Officer; and he is not required to show cause in order to resile.

11.130 An agreement between HMRC and a taxpayer made outside s 54 will be binding only in limited circumstances. Whilst HMRC, under its care and management powers, may enter into 'back duty' agreements (whereby it agrees to settle for less than the tax that may be due), HMRC does not have power to enter into 'forward tax agreements' (where it is agreed, in advance, that specified amounts will be paid annually in lieu of tax that otherwise would be due (see *Al Fayed v Advocate General for Scotland* [2002] STC 910)). HMRC does not have power to agree not to perform its duty to collect tax in accordance with the statutory procedure. If a taxpayer enters into such an agreement, it will be enforceable only by way of judicial review proceedings, and HMRC will be bound only if their failure or refusal to abide by the agreement amounts to an abuse of power.

SECTION THREE – APPEALS FROM THE SPECIAL COMMISSIONERS AND THE GENERAL COMMISSIONERS

Appealing from the Special Commissioners

11.131 Either party can appeal to the High Court from a decision of the Special Commissioners if he is 'dissatisfied in a point of law' (under s 56A). The Special Commissioners are the final arbiters on questions of fact; and a decision of the Commissioners on a pure question of fact cannot be interfered with (absent a finding of fact that no person acting judicially and properly instructed as to the relevant law could have come to: see *Edwards v Bairstow* [1956] AC 14). As the finding of facts by the Special Commissioners cannot be disturbed, it is extremely important that the taxpayer takes the opportunity to establish a factual matrix that supports his appeal at the hearing before the Special Commissioners.

11.132 Either party can appeal on a point of principle, even if no final determination in terms of figures has been made.

High Court

11.133 There is a time limit of 56 days after the issue of the Special Commissioners' decision for appealing to the High Court. Leave to appeal is not required; and the notice of appeal is made by way of an Appellant's Notice to the High Court stating the grounds of the appeal. The Civil Procedure Rules apply to appeals from the Special Commissioners to the High Court. One of the main changes to the rules of procedure and evidence that have been introduced under Civil Procedure Rules is in respect of skeleton arguments. Under the old procedure, the skeleton argument was produced shortly before the hearing; whereas now, under the Civil Procedure Rules, it must be served within 14 days from the date of service of the Appellant's notice. This is a major change in emphasis and requires considerable thought to be given to the appeal at a much earlier stage.

Court of Appeal

11.134 Although s 56(5) provides that an appeal from the High Court 'shall lie to the Court of Appeal', the scope for appealing from the High Court to the Court of Appeal in appeals that commenced before the Special Commissioners has been curtailed by the Access to Justice Act 1999. The Act introduced a general requirement to obtain permission to appeal to the Court of Appeal and, under s 55(1) of this Act 'second appeals' are to be granted only in exceptional circumstances. No appeal may be made unless the Court of Appeal considers that (a) the appeal would raise an important point of principle or practice, or (b) there is some other compelling reason for the Court of Appeal to hear it. This test applies even if the taxpayer succeeded before the Special Commissioners, but lost on appeal to the High Court. Although the change was introduced to ensure that 'second appeals would … become a rarity' (per Brooke LJ in *Tanfern Ltd v Cameron-McDonald* [2000] 1 WLR 1311 at 1320C), it is often not too difficult to demonstrate an 'important point of principle' in tax matters.

11.135 The Access to Justice Act 1999, s 54(4) provides that there is no appeal from a decision of the Court of Appeal to refuse permission to appeal to that court. It is only the Court of Appeal itself that can grant permission to appeal to the Court of Appeal. Absent an express order from the High Court, permission must be sought within 14 days from the date of the High Court decision.

House of Lords

11.136 An appeal from the Court of Appeal to the House of Lords requires either permission of the Court of Appeal or leave of the House of Lords. If permission is refused by the Court of Appeal, a petition for leave to appeal may be made to the House of Lords within one month from the refusal to grant permission by the Court of Appeal. The petition for leave will be referred to an Appeal Committee. It does not give reasons for its decision and in the event that it declines leave, there is no right of appeal. Leave to appeal will be given only to cases 'which raise an arguable point of law of general public importance which ought to be considered by the House at that time'.

Leapfrogging

11.137 It is possible to leapfrog either the High Court or the Court of Appeal, but, in practice, these options are rarely exercised. An unsuccessful attempt to leapfrog the Court of Appeal was made by HMRC in *Deutsche Morgan Grenfell Group plc v Inland Revenue Commissioners* (The Court of Appeal heard the case: [2005] STC 329).

11.138 Section 56A(2) provides that in order to appeal from the Special Commissioners directly to the Court of Appeal requires three criteria to be fulfilled. The first is that the Special Commissioners must certify that 'their decision involves a point of law relating wholly or mainly to the construction of an enactment which was fully argued before them and fully considered by them'. Secondly, both parties must consent and, thirdly, leave to appeal must be granted by the Court of Appeal. The application for leave will be determined by a single judge. He may make his determination without a hearing; and his decision is final.

11.139 The Administration of Justice Act 1969, pt 2 provides that, in certain civil proceedings, appeals from the High Court can be made directly to the House of Lords. A direct appeal to the House of Lords is available either where the appeal relates mainly to the construction of an enactment or statutory instrument and the point at issue has been fully argued in the House of Lords or where the High Court judge is bound by a previous decision of the Court of Appeal or House of Lords and the point at issue was fully considered by the Court of Appeal or House of Lords in those previous proceedings. The High Court judge must issue a certificate enabling that party to apply to the House of Lords for leave to appeal directly to it. The application to the judge for such a certificate must be made immediately after his decision is given; and there is no appeal against a refusal to issue a certificate. Provided that a certificate has been issued, the petition for leave will be considered by an appeal committee of the House of Lords without a hearing; and, as with the application for leave to appeal directly to the Court of Appeal, this decision is not appealable.

Appealing from the General Commissioners

11.140 In order to appeal from the General Commissioners to the High Court, a 'statement of case' for the opinion of the High Court is required (see the

General Regulations, s 56 and regs 20–22). Any party may, within 30 days of the decision, give notice requiring the General Commissioners to sign and state a case for the opinion of the High Court on a point of law. This notice must be accompanied by payment of £25 made out to the clerk to the General Commissioners who heard the appeal (this is a statutory fee). The General Commissioners may give notice to the party requiring him to identify the point of law; and if the party fails to identify the point of law or the General Commissioners are not satisfied that the question identified is a point of law, then the General Commissioners may refuse to state a case. A case stated must set out the facts and the final determination of the tribunal. Within 56 days of the notice of requirement to state a case or the identification of the question of law involved, a draft of the case must be sent to all parties. The parties are allowed 56 days after the draft case has been sent to them to make written representations on the written case. This gives the taxpayer an opportunity to ensure that the facts are accurately set out. The importance of this opportunity cannot be overstated.

11.141 A further 28 days is then allowed to enable any party to make further representations in response to the representations of the other party. When the time limit for making representations has expired, and after taking those representations into account, the General Commissioners are to state and sign the substantive case.

11.142 To appeal, the party must then submit the case stated to the High Court within 30 days of receiving it. This time limit is a mandatory one; and the Revenue and the taxpayer have no power to extend the time limit by mutual agreement (see *Petch v Gurney* [1994] STC 689 and, more recently, *Significant Ltd v Farrel (Inspector of Taxes)* [2006] STC 1626).

11.143 Section 56(8) provides that either party may appeal from the High Court to Court of Appeal and thence to the House of Lords provided that permission is obtained in each case; and from the High Court stage onwards, the procedure is the same as appeals that originated before the Special Commissioners.

Costs beyond the Commissioners

11.144 Costs are in the discretion of the court, but the general rule of litigation is, in short, that the successful party will have its costs paid by the unsuccessful litigant. This rule applies at all stages after the Commissioners. However, success at a later stage does not enable the costs of the hearing before the Commissioners to be recovered from the unsuccessful party.

SECTION FOUR – THE TAX APPEALS SYSTEM IN THE FUTURE

The origin for change

11.145 The existing tax appeals system is a complex one. Rather than (as is the case in many other European countries) having one specialist tax court that can hear all tax related appeals, in the United Kingdom different taxes carry with them different methods and routes of litigation, and, moreover, not all tax related matters may be litigated before the specialist tax tribunals (for example, only the High Court may judicially review the action of HMRC).

Reform of this labyrinthine system has been mooted for many years. It was over 12 years ago that the Institute of Fiscal Studies' Tax Law Review Committee started its work on the subject. In 2001, a Consultation Document ('the LCD paper') that was based, to a large extent, on recommendations in the Institute of Fiscal Studies' Tax Law Review Committee's Report of October 1999 was issued by the Lord Chancellor's Department. It was released as part of the consultation exercise that was undertaken to ensure that all government departments operated in a way that was 'compatible with individuals' rights under the European Convention of Human Rights. In essence, the Lord Chancellor's Department proposed refinements to the existing system. The LCD paper proposed (in accordance with a recommendation of the Tax Law Review Committee) a move to a unified tax tribunal that would hear all tax appeals. Under the proposal, the unified tax tribunal would be centrally administered, but would comprise special and general lists, which would be heard centrally and locally respectively. The other significant issue that was addressed in the LCD paper was that of costs, and, in particular, the divergence of regimes between the Special Commissioners, the General Commissioners and the VAT and Duties Tribunal. The Tax Law Review Committee recommended that the Special Tax Tribunal should adopt the rule in indirect tax appeals; and, in its reply to the LCD Paper, the Special Commissioners endorsed this recommendation.

The Leggatt Inquiry

11.146 Many tax practitioners (including the author) were of the view that the timing of the release of the LCD paper by the Government was an indication that the Leggatt Inquiry, which was, almost simultaneously, considering the tribunal system in general, would not lead to fundamental changes to the operation of the tax appeals system being proposed. In contrast to the reforms suggested in the LCD paper, which were, in essence, refinements, rather than changes, to the existing system, in his Report, Sir Andrew Leggatt proposed a revolutionary change: a single homogeneous system for all tribunals. It was proposed by Sir Andrew Leggatt that the existing 'system' of tribunals, where each tribunal had evolved its own rules and procedure as a solution to the particular requirements in its particular area of law, be replaced by a single consistent procedure and structure for all tribunals. Thus, regardless of which area of law within which the particular tribunal operates, the same procedure would apply. The proposed outline structure was as follows:

1 there will be a general tax tribunal (the general tax tribunal), with jurisdiction to hear the cases presently heard by the General Commissioners and straightforward VAT cases, such as those dealing with reasonable excuse;

2 the second-tier tribunal (which largely will be a successor of the existing Special Commissioners and the VAT and Duties Tribunal) will hear appeals from the general tax tribunal and will be able to set precedent binding on the general tax tribunal;

3 the second-tier tribunal will also hear, at first instance, the most complex appeals arising from decisions made by the Inland Revenue or by HM Customs & Excise;

4 appeals from the second-tier tribunals will go direct to the Court of Appeal;

5 permission will be needed for an appeal from the general tax tribunal to the second-tier tribunal; and

6 permission will be needed for an appeal from the second-tier tribunal to the Court of Appeal.

The tax tribunals were expressly included within the proposed new system.

11.147 In July 2004, the Government published its response to the Leggatt Report in a White Paper entitled 'Transforming Public Service: Complaints, Redress and Tribunals'. The key proposal that was set out in the White Paper is a unified tribunal service organisation. Most of the proposals of Sir Andrew Leggatt were accepted. Under the White Paper, it was proposed that the current jurisdictions of the VAT and Duties Tribunal, the Special and the General Commissioners would be combined. The High Court's role in tax appeals will be eliminated; and, instead, there will be a two-tier tax tribunal system, with a right of appeal from the second tier tribunal to the Court of Appeal. The first-tier will be responsible for hearing most direct and indirect tax appeals at first instance; the second-tier tax tribunal (the Upper Tribunal) will be an appellate tier to which an appeal will lie with permission from the first tier on a point of law (it will also have a first-instance jurisdiction for cases that are of sufficient size and complexity to justify starting at that level). Decisions of the Upper Tribunal (almost certainly) will be binding on the first-tier.

11.148 Prior to the 2005 election, the unified tribunal service organisation was intended to come into being in April 2006; and a draft Courts and Tribunals Bill, with the aim of implementing these reforms, was published. After some delay, TCE received Royal Assent on 19 July 2007.

The Tribunals, Courts and Enforcement Act 2007

11.149 Most of the proposals of Sir Andrew Leggatt have been accepted by the Government and TCE reflects the approach set out in his Report (as set out at para **11.146**). TCE is an enabling Act, under which most of the existing tribunals (including the General Commissioners, Special Commissioners, s 706 tribunal, and VAT and Duties Tribunals) will be abolished and their functions transferred to a unified tribunal that comprises a first-tier and an upper tier. The first-tier will be organised into specialist divisions or 'chambers', such as tax, health and welfare and social benefits. Each chamber will be headed by a Chamber President and the tribunals' judiciary will be headed by a Senior President of Tribunals. Lord Justice Carnwath has been designated to fill this role. Details of the new appeals structure have been set out in the *Transforming Tribunals* Consultation Paper. Implementation of the new appeals structure (which will require Statutory Instruments prescribing commencement dates, rules, and transitional provisions) will occur by stages.

Transforming tribunals

11.150 This Consultation Paper sets out the Government's proposals for the first-tier and Upper Tribunals created by TCE. The consultation (which ended on 22 February 2008) sought views on areas such as how the chambers in the tribunals should be structured, the assignment of judges within and across the chambers and the role of non-legal members in the new tribunals. As at the date of publication, it is not known whether or not the proposals set out in *Transforming Tribunals* will be introduced in such form. Set out below are some of the most important proposals (with commentary).

Chambers

11.151 The chambers are intended to be flexible groupings, able to maintain and expand expertise and to incorporate new jurisdictions where most suitable. There will be five chambers: (i) Social Entitlement; (ii) General Regulatory; (iii) Health Education and Social Care; (iv) Taxation; and (v) Land Property and Housing. The provisional view of the Governments is that the Upper Tribunal should be divided into three chambers: (i) Administrative Appeals; (ii) Finance and Tax; and (iii) Land.

11.152 Each chamber will have its own Chamber President ('the President'), who will report to the Senior President. As the aim of the Government is that the President will preside over both the first-tier and Upper Tribunal, the President will need to be a judge of the Upper Tribunal. It is anticipated that all the current Special Commissioners and VAT Tribunal Chairmen will transfer into the new tribunal, with the majority transferring to the first-tier (where they will be known as 'Judge of the First-tier Tribunal'). It is anticipated that some will be transferred to the Upper Tribunal (with the title 'Judge of the Upper Tribunal') and will be joined by Judges from the High Court. A system of 'ticketing' will be introduced within each chamber. The President will issue tickets to judges and members that identify their suitability to sit in a particular jurisdiction. Thus, for example, a Special Commissioner who is also a VAT Tribunal Chairman is likely to be issued with an indirect and direct tax ticket that enables him (or her) to hear both such appeals. A procedure known as 'Assignment' is also proposed to be introduced. This would enable cross-chamber transfer (with the consent of the relevant President). Judges of the Upper Tribunal may sit in the first-tier tribunal where the weight of the case justifies it.

Judicial review

11.153 The extent to which the Upper Tribunal can exercise its judicial review jurisdiction will 'be determined by decisions of the High Court … or by an order made by the Lord Chief Justice with the agreement of the Lord Chancellor'. Absent an order delimiting jurisdiction, this introduces a degree of uncertainty. For example, may the first-tier tribunal be reviewed by the Upper Tribunal? Given, first, the effective abolition of the High Court stage for tax cases, and, secondly, the fact that only High Court judges (or other judges approved by the Lord Chief Justice and the Senior President) will be able to exercise the transferred judicial review jurisdiction, it is considered that the judicial review jurisdiction of the Upper Tribunal should be identical to the Administrative Court's. Moreover, it is considered that when the Upper Tribunal sits *qua* a judicial review tribunal, the rules that apply in the Administrative Court in relation to all matters, such as procedures, available remedies (including declaratory relief), publicity and costs, should apply (*mutatis mutandis*).

Appeals

11.154 The taxpayer's choice as to first-tier or Upper Tribunal will be extremely limited. A holder of an office specified in an order made by the Lord Chancellor (which will probably be the Chamber President) 'may specify criteria relating to classes of case (for example, group litigation proceedings and lead cases) which will always be heard in the Upper Tribunal'. In addition, parties will be able to make 'special applications' in respect of other types of case that it should be heard before the Upper Tribunal first. Onward appeals from the first-tier to the Upper Tribunal will lie only with permission; and 'it is the Lord Chancellor's intention to use his powers under s 13(6) of the 2007 Act to prescribe that appeals from the Upper Tribunal to the Court of Appeal will only be permitted in cases of general importance or for other compelling reason (as for second appeals from the courts)'.

11.155 Under the current procedure in direct tax cases, a taxpayer has a number of appeal stages open to him. Absent those matters where jurisdiction is reserved to either the Special Commissioners or to the General Commissioners, the taxpayer may choose as to which of those two bodies will hear his appeal at first instance. The taxpayer then has: (1) a right of appeal from the decision of either body to the High Court as of right; (2) a right of appeal from the decision of the High Court to the Court of Appeal with permission; and (3) a right of appeal from the decision of the Court of Appeal to the House of Lords with permission. In addition, notwithstanding that these options are rarely exercised, the taxpayer may (on meeting the appropriate criteria) leapfrog either the High Court or the Court of Appeal.

11.156 Thus, the new system is significantly more restrictive in terms of options. It is considered that the proposed test for appeals is too stringent. It is not clear whether the intention is that the test for all appeals from the Upper Tribunal is 'general importance or for other compelling reason' or if this to apply only in relation to second appeals, ie where the case has been appealed from the first-tier. It is considered that it is too restrictive in any event, but particularly if it applies to all Upper Tribunal appeals. This could lead to a taxpayer, whose case is assigned to the Upper Tribunal, potentially against his will and consequent on a request by HMRC, having only one stage of appeal.

CONCLUSION

11.157 In the very near future, the General Commissioners, the Special Commissioners, the s 706 tribunal, and the VAT and Duties Tribunal, each with their own intricate rules, will disappear and all tax appeals will go to the one tribunal.

11.158 On a general level, the Government is to be applauded for seeking to rationalise the old tribunal system and to make the administration of tribunals more consistent and coherent. (It is noticeable that the term 'tribunal system' is not used in the Leggatt Report, on the basis that the tribunals so lacked any form of organisation that it would be a misnomer). Sir Andrew Leggatt noted that, whilst overall the 70 different administrative tribunals in England and Wales dealt with nearly one million cases a year, only 20 of those tribunals heard more than an average of 500 cases a year and many were defunct. In his Report, it was concluded that the quality of the tribunals 'varies from excellent to inadequate'.

11.159 Particularly post the merger of the Inland Revenue and HM Customs and Excise, rationalisation in the sense of having a specialist Tax Chamber that can hear disputes relating to all taxes is to be welcomed; and simplifying the Byzantine intricacies of the different procedures applying to the different tax tribunals is also a commendable step (to take one small example from many, the archaic 'case stated' procedure before the General Commissioners has been overdue for abolition for many years). However, it is essential that, with these changes, the tribunals' rules do not cease to be appropriate and proportionate to the specific jurisdiction and the specific matters that are being litigated. The UK's tax system is extremely complex; in my view, in many instances, it is only by having had the matter litigated through a number of stages that the correct decision is reached ultimately. In 2006, the House of Lords delivered judgment in four direct tax cases (*Pirelli Cable Holding NV v Commissioners of Inland Revenue* [2006] STC 548; *Mellham v Burton* [2006] STC 908; *Agassi v Robinson* [2006] STC 1056; and *Deutsche Morgan Grenfell plc v Commissioners of Inland Revenue* [2007] STC 1); in all four cases, it reversed the decision of the Court of Appeal. Curtailing the stages of appeal potentially to one hearing in the revolutionised system cannot be justified and should be resisted.

Chapter 12

Settlement negotiations

Phil Berwick, CTA, ATT, Director of National Tax Investigations, Tenon

INTRODUCTION

12.1 Dictionary definitions of 'negotiate' include 'to reach an agreement or compromise by discussion' and 'to get over an obstacle'. In the context of HM Revenue and Customs (HMRC) investigations, both meanings are equally valid: there are a multitude of potential obstacles to be overcome. These include an intransigent Inspector, the client, and the practitioner himself. This chapter will explore ways of navigating the various obstacles that the practitioner may face.

12.2 The practitioner will often be instructed by his client to get the best settlement possible. What is the Inspector's authority to negotiate? This can be found in Taxes Management Act (TMA) 1970 and common law. TMA 1970, s 1(1) as amended by the Commissioners for Revenue and Customs Act 2005, states the Commissioners for HMRC shall be responsible for the 'collection and management' of income tax, corporation tax and capital gains tax. The 'care and management' authority is an important part of HMRC's powers. Without it, HMRC would not be able to issue extra-statutory concessions (departures from the strict interpretation of the law where such an interpretation could give an unfair result).

12.3 In the context of an investigation settlement, the authority enables an Inspector to reach an informal agreement with a taxpayer where complex matters of statutory interpretation are concerned, where precedents derived from case law appear to be in conflict with the particular matter in hand, or even where the facts themselves are open to dispute and different interpretations.

12.4 The 'care and management' power permits negotiations so that an agreement can be reached which is acceptable to both parties, ie HMRC and the client. The authority permits the agreement to be reached without recourse to the legal process, which would be time-consuming, expensive and may result in a decision that was unacceptable to both parties. The Court of Appeal held, in *CIR v Nuttall* [1990] STC 194, that the power to enter into settlement negotiations and make agreements was not overridden by the specific provisions of TMA 1970, s 54.

START THE NEGOTIATING GROUNDWORK EARLY

12.5 For the purpose of this chapter, it is assumed that there have been omitted profits from the client's tax return. Where, in practice, this is established, the practitioner should direct his attention to minimising the level of the additions sought by the Inspector.

12.6 It is important for the practitioner to appreciate that the groundwork for settlement negotiations should start at the beginning of an investigation. Cooperation of the advisor, as well as the client, is taken into account by the Inspector when considering the level of penalty at the end of an investigation. The practitioner should ensure that, from the time of the Inspector's opening letter, he is not responsible for any unreasonable delays in providing information requested by the Inspector, or in respect of the general progress of the enquiry.

12.7 Where there are going to be delays in, for example, the provision of information, the Inspector should be kept informed. The practitioner should instil a sense of urgency into his client so that he appreciates the seriousness of the situation, and will qualify for the maximum penalty abatement for cooperation.

ARE INTEREST AND PENALTIES DUE?

12.8 Except for the smallest of investigation cases, the Inspector will seek interest and a penalty. Where the amount of omitted profits exceeds £2,000, the Inspector will not only seek additions for earlier years, but also interest and a penalty.

CALCULATION OF INTEREST

12.9 When the additional liabilities have been agreed, the resulting tax will be calculated together with any interest. This is automatic and there may not be scope for reducing the interest charged. Interest is charged under the provisions of TMA 1970, s 86.

PENALTY NEGOTIATION

12.10 Where HMRC has suffered a loss of tax, the Inspector will seek, in addition to the tax due, interest and a penalty, subject to his internal guidelines (see above). The maximum penalty is 100% of the tax, mitigated at present by reference to disclosure, cooperation and seriousness (which incorporates size and gravity). A new penalty regime has been introduced as from 6 April 2008, consisting of a series of 'stepped' penalties based on taxpayer behaviour. Consideration of these areas, including a review of the new penalty regime and the additional criteria that HMRC will consider from 6 April 2008, is discussed in Chapter 14. The likelihood is that, under the new regime, HMRC will recover a greater percentage penalty in many cases.

12.11 The Inspector will consider what he thinks is the appropriate level of mitigation, and, consequently, penalty. It should be noted that the Inspector's figure is not cast in stone. It is important to remember that it is the client who is making the offer to HMRC: the Inspector should only be giving an indication of the level of penalty that is likely to be accepted by the Board.

12.12 Practitioners should bear in mind that some Inspectors do not give detailed consideration to each of the mitigating factors mentioned above. They review a case, and regard it to be, for example, 'a 40% case', taking a global consideration of the facts, without breaking the mitigation down under the three headings. Practitioners are advised to contact the Inspector to discuss penalty mitigation. When they do so, they should request a breakdown of the penalty loading under the three mitigation areas. If the Inspector has not fully thought out the penalty mitigation in this way, he may have no choice but to agree to a lower figure.

12.13 The penalty mitigation does not depend solely on the actions of the client. An error by the agent, or delay by him, will count against the client as if it was him that was directly responsible for the error or delay. The taxpayer may be able to argue that this should not be the case where complex issues are involved and he can claim that he was incorrectly advised. Where the taxpayer does suffer an adverse penalty loading because of error or delay by his advisor he may decide to seek compensation from the agent.

12.14 When considering the relevant penalty mitigation, the Inspector will consider any delays, etc from the time that the investigation started. That is why it is important for practitioners to prepare for their settlement negotiations at the start of an enquiry, by ensuring that the Inspector's reasonable requests are complied with without unnecessary delay. That does not mean that you agree to unreasonable demands, either in timescale or nature of information requested, by the investigator. Your client should not be penalised because you challenge an overzealous Inspector.

12.15 The practitioner needs to be particularly careful where he has taken over a case from another advisor. This situation can be fraught with difficulties for the new advisor, who should ensure that the client is fully aware of the seriousness of the position.

PAYMENTS ON ACCOUNT

12.16 Inspectors are instructed to ask for a payment on account in investigation cases. Making such a payment has two advantages for the client. It shows the Inspector that the client is treating the investigation seriously, and should assist when negotiating the penalty mitigation at the end of the enquiry. Secondly, it helps to mitigate the interest, accruing on a daily basis, where there has been an underpayment of tax. When a practitioner is aware that there are additional liabilities, he should recommend to his client that a payment on account is made.

12.17 During the course of an investigation further liabilities may become apparent, and the practitioner should recommend the making of such additional payments on account as are deemed necessary. If the client is not able to make a lump-sum payment, he should be advised to make monthly payments of such amount as he can afford. It should be noted that the client will not always make payments on account when recommended to do so by the practitioner. Some may prefer to wait until the settlement figure is known, and then arrange finance to meet the liability in full. It is imperative that the practitioner makes the recommendations regarding payments on account, and, preferably, puts them in writing, even where the client has stated that he will settle in full, so that he is protected against any claims from his client regarding the imposition of interest or an adverse penalty loading.

12.18 The Inspector's interest computation should be checked carefully. This is particularly important where payments on account have been made, or there are tax repayments due to the client, to ensure that the correct interest credit has been included.

12.19 For a sole trader or partnership, it is important to remember that an increase in the tax payable for years under enquiry will automatically increase the payments on account which should have been made for the following year(s) under TMA 1970, s 59A. Surcharges on late-paid tax for self assessment years under TMA 1970, s 59C may also be included within contract settlements, but not where a tax-geared penalty has been charged on the same tax (TMA 1970, s 59C(4)).

VAT DISCLOSURE

12.20 Where there has been a disclosure made to the tax Inspector, it is extremely likely that there are VAT implications. The practitioner should consider the possibility of VAT irregularities, and make sure that appropriate action is taken. Although the Inland Revenue and HM Customs and Excise merged in April 2005, there are very few HMRC Officers who are trained in both disciplines.

12.21 Until that time, it is advisable to put the VAT office on notice at an early stage in the investigation that there is a disclosure to be made. This should assist in minimising the penalty position in relation to the VAT offences. Final details of the irregularities can be provided when the settlement has been agreed with the Inspector. The VAT officer will usually accept adjustments based on the settlement figures with the Inspector. It should be borne in mind, that, where there are VAT implications, the figures agreed with the Inspector take this into account.

PROFESSIONAL COSTS

12.22 HMRC has set out its position regarding accountancy expenses arising out of self-assessment enquiries (EM 3981). Where the enquiry does not result in an addition to profits, or there is an adjustment to the profits for the year of enquiry only and that alteration does not arise as a result of negligent or fraudulent conduct, the additional accountancy expenses will be allowable.

12.23 In all other cases, ie where there has been fraudulent or negligent conduct, or there are adjustments for more than one year, the professional costs of dealing with an HMRC investigation are not allowable deductions for income tax or corporation tax purposes. Where the fees include work done in connection with ongoing compliance obligations, eg the preparation of accounts, or P35 completion, that element will be allowable in the normal way.

12.24 Where such costs may be allowable, they should be agreed with the Inspector during the settlement negotiations, rather than waiting until the next tax computation is submitted, when the practitioner's position is weaker.

12.25 When the client is VAT-registered the VAT element can be reclaimed to the extent that it relates to the business. If the client is not billed separately for the work done on the business affairs and the personal tax affairs of its proprietor or directors, the VAT reclaimed must be restricted. Also, the appropriate entry must be made in the owner's drawings account. When dealing with a company, the relevant amount should be debited to the director's current account, or a benefit returned on form P11D, as appropriate.

WHY NEGOTIATE?

12.26 Some practitioners may query why they should negotiate with the Inspector. They should remember that the Inspector's role is to establish the amount of tax etc, to be paid by the client. The Inspector has various statutory powers to enable him to do his job. The practitioner's role is to obtain the best settlement for his client. This can usually be best achieved by negotiating the level of additional liabilities etc with the Inspector, rather than proceeding down a formal route.

12.27 There are several practical reasons why it is advantageous for the advisor to reach a negotiated settlement, and these are considered below.

Reduce the length of the investigation period

12.28 If additional profits can be agreed between the Inspector and the practitioner, this should be quicker than the Inspector going down the formal route. Under this process, the Inspector issues a closure notice for self-assessment years, and estimated assessments for pre-self-assessment years. The closure notice and, if issued, estimated assessments must be appealed against, with a subsequent hearing of the appeals before the Commissioners, Special or General. This process takes time, and can add several months, if not longer, to the investigation period.

Finality for the client

12.29 A negotiated settlement gives the client finality, without the uncertainty of taking the case before the Commissioners.

Financial (professional fees)

12.30 Although there may be meetings or telephone conversations with the Inspector to reach a negotiated settlement, the time costs for the client should be cheaper than becoming embroiled in the time-consuming, and costly, process of assessments, appeals and Commissioners' hearings.

Financial (tax, etc savings for the client)

12.31 The outcome of a negotiated settlement should be that both sides benefit. When reaching an agreement with the Inspector, without recourse to the formal route, the additions should be lower. This has the consequential effect that the tax, interest and penalty will be reduced, resulting in a lower overall settlement. The negotiated settlement will also be reflected in the penalty loading, the client enjoying higher mitigation because the Inspector has not had to use his formal powers to bring the investigation to a conclusion.

Finality for the practitioner

12.32 It should be remembered that handling an HMRC investigation is time-consuming for the advisor. This is particularly an issue for smaller firms of advisors. The practitioner has a duty to all his clients, not just those under enquiry, and the strain of dealing with only a handful of HMRC investigations, or one large one, can severely stretch the resources of the smaller practice. A practitioner in such a position should consider engaging the services of an investigation specialist.

What is negotiable?

12.33 As in any negotiating situation, when settling an investigation case, anything is potentially negotiable. The Inspector may say that he cannot give ground on a particular area because of, for example, case law, but the practitioner may be able to obtain a concession in another area.

12.34 The interest and penalty figures follow from the amount of tax due. It makes sense to start by considering how the level of tax can be mitigated. Where the additional tax arises from income, the practitioner should concentrate on minimising the figure for the year under enquiry, as this will determine whether the Inspector also seeks additions for earlier years, and, if so, for how many.

12.35 It may be possible to restrict the number of earlier years that the Inspector seeks additions for. Was there, for example, a change in the nature of the business that gave rise to the omissions starting? By reducing the level of additional income etc, the practitioner keeps the tax down, which will lead to lower interest and penalty. Where the enquiry has been ongoing for a number of years, the Inspector may also seek additions for later years. The comments above also apply to restricting any such additions sought by the Inspector.

12.36 The practitioner should explore all options when negotiating, including alternative treatments of particular items. Conceding that an item should be taxed under a different provision may result in more tax payable, but may lead to a lower settlement because of favourable penalty mitigation.

CONSIDERATION OF GREY AREAS

12.37 In most investigation cases, there will be three broad areas into which potentially taxable items fall. There will be those items that are agreed by both parties as being taxable; there will be certain items that are accepted as being non-taxable; and there will be those items that fall in between the first two categories.

12.38 Before accepting that an item is taxable, the practitioner should consider all available options. Although the client's case may not be absolute, the Inspector may be prepared to offer concessions. The practitioner should also be prepared to do the same, although he will be seeking to ensure that he gains more than he concedes!

12.39 There are various examples of grey areas: the distinction between income (liable to income tax) and capital (liable to CGT, or possibly not taxable at all) is a common area of difficulty. Protracted negotiations may be required to agree on the treatment of such items. The practitioner should be aware that different allowances, exemptions and reliefs may apply which reduce or eliminate the tax bill, or transfer liability from the client to someone else. A compromise solution can often be the best conclusion for both parties.

12.40 Tax avoidance schemes can be another area of complexity. The client may have implemented a strategy that is at the very edge of current tax understanding. Where HMRC has a contrary view it will challenge any such arrangements. HMRC is taking an increasingly aggressive view of avoidance, and has established specialist units within Special Civil Investigations to deal with the more serious or complex cases.

12.41 It is often in the interest of both parties to reach a compromise settlement where there are complex technical issues. This avoids the need for lengthy, and costly, recourse to the legal process to obtain a definitive answer. Once the courts have given their decision, it is too late to negotiate a better settlement if that decision did not go in the client's favour.

LITIGATION AND SETTLEMENTS STRATEGY

12.42 HMRC introduced its Litigation and Settlements Strategy (LSS) on 11 June 1007. The guidance sets out HMRC's principles for bringing tax disputes to a conclusion. A central theme of the LSS is seeking non-confrontational solutions 'where possible'. The LSS sets out the principles determining whether HMRC will litigate to resolve a case. HMRC anticipates that most of its discussions with taxpayers will not fall within the term 'dispute'. Where there is a substantial and material difference of opinion about tax liabilities in a case, particularly where that difference will not be easily resolved, a practitioner should refer to the detail of the LSS (available on HMRC's website) for consideration as to how HMRC may proceed.

THE ART OF NEGOTIATION

12.43 An investigation settlement is no different in many respects to negotiating in other areas of life. Each side wants to win more than they lose. There are numerous publications available which detail negotiating skills, and here it is intended to give a few pointers relevant to tax investigations.

Negotiate

12.44 The first point to remember is that it is perfectly acceptable to negotiate. Tax investigations are contentious and adversarial arenas into which the practitioner is standing on behalf of his client. Some practitioners are wary of negotiating, especially where the Inspector's case seems cut and dried. It is the practitioner's duty to do whatever he legitimately can, within the law and the ethics of his profession, to seek to minimise the amount of tax, etc that his client has to pay.

12.45 If the practitioner is not comfortable with negotiating, he should seek specialist help for this part of the enquiry process – even if only for a second opinion as to the reasonableness of the Inspector's proposals.

Pitch at the right level

12.46 When starting discussions, the practitioner must ensure that his figures are not too high (from the client's point of view). It is inevitable that the opening figures will not be the final ones, so the practitioner should allow room for movement, and be prepared to make concessions from his starting position. The Inspector will always be looking for an increase on the opening figures, as he will be looking to maximise the position for HMRC.

12.47 With this in mind, the practitioner should work backwards from what he thinks will be the finishing position. It is important not to concede too much before negotiations begin as this will inevitably result in an unsatisfactory settlement figure. As well as dealing with the demands of the client, and managing his expectations, the practitioner must also take into account the Inspector's position in the negotiations.

How strong is the client's case?

12.48 When deciding where to pitch the client's offer, the practitioner must take into account the relative strengths and weaknesses of the client's case. Serious irregularities cannot be brushed aside, and must be taken into account in the negotiations. Where the issues concern highly technical matters, ambiguity over the taxability of transactions, etc, this should be brought to the Inspector's attention.

12.49 It should be remembered that the Inspector does not have the final say on the level of a settlement. The client can appear before the Commissioners to present his case, although the risks in taking the dispute there should be stressed. As the practitioner reviews the case, he should consider what view the Commissioners would make of the evidence available. This can help the practitioner to plan his dealings with the Inspector.

Consider the outcome

12.50 When negotiating with the Inspector, it is important that the practitioner has a clear idea of the best possible outcome, what he thinks will be the result, and the worst position that will be acceptable to the client. These positions may change, during the course of the meeting, or several meetings, if the situation cannot be finalised in one session.

12.51 Discussions with the Inspector to finalise the additional liabilities may take place over the telephone or at a meeting. It is preferable for the client not to be present, so that you can concentrate on the issues. Thorough preparation is important, so that you know the strengths and weaknesses of your client's case.

The Inspector is not the enemy

12.52 You should regard the Inspector as a partner, rather than as an enemy to be defeated. You may have to deal with the same Inspector in the future, and you do not want him to be seeking revenge for a previous 'defeat'. For the same reason, it makes sense not to say or do anything rash.

12.53 There are some practitioners who take great delight in 'bashing' HMRC. Others relish lengthy delays in dealing with correspondence from the Inspector and attach little priority to progressing enquiries. These types of attitude are not conducive to effective negotiation.

Agree on minor issues

12.54 If agreement cannot be reached on the level of additional profits, try to see if there are any areas that can be agreed, for example, treatment of a particular receipt, or even the level of a private usage adjustment, and then return to the main area.

12.55 The best result is one when both sides are satisfied that the outcome is in their best interests and the best they could have achieved.

No two cases are the same

12.56 The practitioner should approach each settlement for what it is – a unique situation. You cannot treat each case the same because the facts will be different and you are dealing with an individual, the Inspector. There is no tried and tested formula that can be used in every case. Inspectors will react differently depending on the approach.

Avoid premature concessions

12.57 After thorough preparation, and having assessed the relative strength of the client's case, the practitioner should not give too many concessions too soon. He should be prepared to stick by his arguments. Investigations are adversarial by nature, and the practitioner must be prepared to argue his side with the Inspector.

12.58 The practitioner should not be rushed into making concessions by the Inspector. The investigator is also under pressure to settle for the reasons mentioned earlier. If the practitioner gives in too easily, the Inspector may regard him as an 'easy touch' and may seek more concessions than he would otherwise do so.

12.59 The practitioner should ensure that concessions are not given away; they should, if possible, be given in exchange for a concession by the Inspector.

Previous experience

12.60 Your settlement discussions should be planned, taking into account what you have learnt about the Inspector in your previous meetings and conversations with him. If you have been brought in at a late stage, and are meeting the Inspector for the first time, you will need to assess the Inspector at the meeting, and from whatever discussions you have had with him.

CLAIMS, ALLOWANCES AND RELIEFS

12.61 The re-opening of accounts and tax returns for earlier years provides an opportunity to make any claims that have been overlooked, or make claims to relief earlier than has been the case. Before starting negotiations with the Inspector, the practitioner should conduct a thorough review of the case to establish whether there are any potential claims, allowances or reliefs that should be made. This includes the ability to make claims that would otherwise be out of time.

12.62 The Inspector can be expected to challenge claims for expenses that are not supported by vouchers. Often, the Inspector can be persuaded to concede an allowance for some additional expenditure, depending on the circumstances of the case. The Inspector cannot resist a claim for additional expenditure where he is seeking additional profits that required, for example, additional materials, labour or fuel.

REMITTANCES BY NON-DOMICILED INDIVIDUALS

12.63 Wealthy non-domiciled individuals have long been a favourite target for Inspectors. Often, there is considerable difficulty in identifying the source of funds remitted by non-domiciled individuals resident in the UK. The amounts involved can be substantial, and Inspectors are aware of this. The practitioner is advised to undertake a thorough review of funds remitted, and the bank accounts from which the amounts were made, if appropriate, and establish the arguments that can be made. The Inspector will expect to see an audit trail, demonstrating the origin of the funds. Time spent by the practitioner will usually be worthwhile, because of the substantial sums often involved. New legislation applying from 2008/09 will reduce the risk represented by non-domiciled individuals to HMRC.

INNOCENT ERROR AND REASONABLE EXCUSE

12.64 Penalties will be due under TMA 1970, s 95 where HMRC can establish fraudulent or negligent conduct. These phrases are not statutorily defined, but negligent conduct is characterised as the failure to do what a reasonable person should recognise as his duty. This is a simple test for HMRC to demonstrate: late paid or additional tax will be sufficient in most cases. HMRC will usually resist claims for penalty mitigation on the grounds of an innocent error or reasonable excuse; although it does recognise that there are situations when mitigation is appropriate.

12.65 Where a person has a serious illness this would qualify as a reasonable excuse, and the Inspector will often be sympathetic. What the taxpayer would have to ensure is that he gets his tax affairs in order following recuperation. Few illnesses are so serious that a person is unable to instruct someone else to deal with matters on his behalf, or advise HMRC of the reason for the delay. The wording of TMA 1970, s 118(2) indicates that a 'reasonable excuse' defence will not protect a taxpayer who fails to take the necessary action once the 'excuse' has ceased to apply.

12.66 Ignorance of the law is not a defence, and would not qualify as a reasonable excuse. HMRC will not automatically accept that a person did not know that a receipt or transaction gave rise to a tax charge. The credibility of the excuse will depend on the complexity of the transaction, and the client's background and technical knowledge. It is always worth contending, where adjustments are of a detailed technical nature, that penalties based on negligence should not be due.

12.67 Where the amounts involved are anything other than minimal, it will be difficult to claim innocent error. If, however, the client was not aware of, for example, accumulated income from a trust where he was unaware that he was a beneficiary, he cannot be expected to include the details on his tax return.

12.68 Where the Inspector cannot establish fraudulent or negligent conduct, TMA 1970, s 97 treats an error in a tax return as negligent unless it is corrected without unreasonable delay.

ADVANTAGES FOR THE INSPECTOR

12.69 As with any negotiation situation, it is worthwhile considering the position from the other side – what's in it for the Inspector?

Time

12.70 The Inspector does not have the cost issues that the practitioner and his client need to consider. He can spend weeks, or even months, pursuing minor issues. What the investigator does have to consider is his portfolio of investigation cases. The process of issuing assessments or closure notices is a relatively straightforward task for the Inspector, with instructions usually passed to a clerical officer, although this can be onerous, particularly where numerous years are involved.

12.71 Although some Inspectors relish the prospect of taking a case to the Commissioners, many more seek to avoid this route, unless absolutely necessary. Preparing a case for the Commissioners is a labour-intensive and time-consuming process for the Inspector, even where responsibility for conducting the hearing is passed to one of HMRC's specialist Appeals Units.. Most Inspectors do not like the thought of, perhaps, weeks of intensive preparation, and will prefer to reach agreement by negotiation.

12.72 Remember that any 'without prejudice' offers will be withdrawn once formal proceedings have been commenced. Often, though, Inspectors will be prepared to reach a negotiated settlement up to, and on, the date of the Commissioner's hearing.

WORKLOAD

12.73 Although the practitioner may handle only a few investigations at any one time, the Inspector will often have a large portfolio of such cases. He is under pressure to settle cases, and register new ones. When your client's case is finished, he can move on to another taxpayer. A negotiated settlement gives him that opportunity far sooner than finalisation via the formal route.

WHEN AGREEMENT CANNOT BE REACHED

12.74 It is recognised that not every case can be settled by negotiation. There may be particular issues on which agreement cannot be reached, or there may be an intransigent Inspector who will not move from his unreasonable opening proposals. In these cases, there may be no alternative other than to go to the Commissioners, particularly if the officer in charge does not encourage his Inspector to adopt a conciliatory position.

12.75 The practitioner faced with this situation should still seek to agree as much as possible with the Inspector, so that it is only the contentious issues that have to be considered by the Commissioners. Details on presenting a case at the Commissioners are contained in Chapter 11.

12.76 Where there is an assessment under appeal, it should be noted that the Inspector can issue a further assessment even though the main assessment could be increased under the provisions of TMA 1970, s 50(7). The Inspector is likely to take this course of action where there is a substantially inadequate assessment under appeal and the client has not made a suitable payment on account. Case law has confirmed that the Inspector can raise a further assessment under TMA 1970, s 29(3) in these circumstances, see *Duchy Maternity Limited v Hodgson* [1985] STC 764.

THE SETTLEMENT PACKAGE

12.77 When considering what is the best possible settlement for the client, the answer will not usually rest only on the amount of tax to pay. The practitioner needs to consider the overall position and aim to get the most advantageous result for the client in the circumstances of the case. This will include a review of the following:

1 the level of tax, interest and penalty;

2 what amounts are included in the settlement (eg the Inspector may be persuaded to include non-investigation liabilities, effectively giving your client more time to pay);

3 the funding of the settlement;

4 the period of time to repay the liabilities;

5 the level of forward interest charged by the Inspector in an instalment arrangement; and

6 agreement from the Inspector on the future treatment of a contentious issue.

12.78 Often, the client is looking at the overall settlement package – what is it going to cost, and over what period does he have to repay the HMRC – rather than a detailed consideration of the individual component parts (tax, interest, penalty, etc). Before embarking on negotiations with the Inspector, it is important that the practitioner discusses the situation with the client. The practitioner can ensure that he is aware of his client's expectations, and that they are reasonable.

12.79 The client must be made aware of the different outcomes to the negotiations. It will usually be helpful to give the client the 'best-case' and 'worst-case' scenarios. This can help to stabilise the client's level of expectation about the settlement. The client should have been kept informed throughout the investigation process, and this practice should continue until the formalities have been finalised. The client needs to able to make an informed decision about the level of offer to be made to HMRC.

12.80 During the negotiating process, there will be various proposals and counter-proposals. The practitioner should recognise when he has gained as many concessions as possible from the Inspector, taking into account materiality. There is no point continuing to negotiate where the saving to the client may only be a few hundred pounds in tax, etc when it costs him more than that in the advisor's time.

FUNDING THE SETTLEMENT AND TIME TO PAY

12.81 The advisor should discuss the client's means, and how he intends to repay HMRC. A person who has deliberately understated income for tax purposes does not usually make provision for the eventual settlement with HMRC. Banks and building societies are not always agreeable to lending funds to meet an investigation settlement. HMRC prefers to reach agreement about the level of settlement, rather than make a person bankrupt. Taking that course of action would result in them only obtaining a proportion of the money due, and they will, usually, reluctantly provide time to pay.

12.82 Practitioners should be aware that HMRC are taking a much tougher stance with regards to settlement of liabilities. Bankruptcy is being pursued by HMRC more vigorously than two or three years ago. This course of action is a possible outcome if the client is unable to pay a significant proportion of the agreed liabilities.

12.83 If the client is not in a position to make a standard offer, the Inspector will seek a certified written statement of means. This will include details of all assets and liabilities (including those of his spouse and children or anyone to whom he has transferred assets), full details of current income and outgoings, and details of any likely changes in the following three to five years, for example, the maturing of an endowment policy, or impending retirement.

12.84 The Inspector will always want any liabilities settled as soon as possible, usually within 30 days of the acceptance letter (see below). During the course of an enquiry, the investigator will regularly request further payments on account, and ask the practitioner to ensure that any payments made reflect the additional liabilities established. At the end of the investigation, the Inspector will want HMRC to be repaid in full in the shortest possible time.

12.85 If the client is unable to make immediate payment, details of his current and future income will need to be established. The client's assets, and liabilities, will already have been identified, from the statement that the Inspector will have requested as part of the settlement process. The Inspector will not agree to a lengthy instalment arrangement if the client has substantial funds in a bank account, or, for example, several properties unencumbered by loans.

12.86 In cases where the client does not have sufficient funds to make immediate repayment of the settlement in full, an instalment arrangement must be considered. Repayments can be made over several months, or even years.

12.87 Inspectors are reluctant to accept instalment offers, particularly those extending beyond two years. An offer where there is a repayment period not exceeding three years can be agreed locally. A longer instalment period requires approval from HMRC's compliance division. Where an instalment arrangement is accepted, the Inspector will seek to apply forward interest for the duration of the repayment period. This should be included in the negotiations with the Inspector. He may agree not to charge forward interest for a period of time, perhaps three or six months.

12.88 The 'time to pay' aspect should not be overlooked when negotiating with the Inspector. The Inspector may agree to a period longer than 30 days for repayment to be made, and for this to be interest-free. That will depend on the amounts involved, and the negotiating skills of the practitioner. Readers should be aware that Inspectors are, generally, taking a tougher stance in all matters relating to settlement, and that includes their position on any interest-free period.

12.89 HMRC's Enquiry Manual does not comment on the length of interest-free period that is acceptable. Practitioners should seek as long a period as possible, although the extent of any interest-free period granted will depend on the circumstances. A period of 60 to 90 days would not be unreasonable, or longer where the amount involved is substantial. The Inspector will need to be satisfied that the client needs further time to obtain funding for the settlement, and the client will be making a cash offer, rather than paying by instalments.

THE LETTER OF OFFER

12.90 Where settlement of an HMRC investigation is by negotiation, the agreement is set out in a written contract, called a 'letter of offer', submitted by the client, detailing the amount to be paid. Where the offer is agreed, HMRC sends the Board's formal acceptance letter, which creates a legally-binding contract with the client. In practice it would be unusual for an offer not to be accepted where agreement had been reached with the Inspector about the level of offer to be made. An acceptance letter may not be sent when the client has made a sub-standard offer (see below).

12.91 The payment terms are contained in the offer letter. The usual terms are that payment will be made within 30 days from the date of the acceptance letter. Where payment is to be made over a period of time, the offer letter sets out the date of the first and subsequent instalments. As mentioned above, the time granted will depend on several factors, including the practitioner's negotiating skills.

12.92 As with any contract, action can be taken where the terms are broken. The client must be made aware of the implications of, for example, failing to make an instalment payment, before he signs the offer letter. The Inspector will be reluctant to renegotiate the terms of a contract at a later date if, for example, future income does not meet the projected figure and the client is unable to meet both his obligations under the contract and his ongoing self-assessment liabilities. The practitioner should ensure that the settlement terms are reasonable, and that the client will be able to adhere to them.

12.93 Contract settlements will continue to be the normal way in which investigations are concluded. The process does not sit comfortably with the provisions of TMA 1970, s 28A(5) which requires the issue of a formal notice at the completion of an enquiry into a self-assessment return. The Inspector will not normally issue a completion notice where there is a contract settlement including 1996/97 and later years. The contract settlement provides finality in the investigation proceedings. The practitioner can seek a completion notice, if desired, although this may not give the client any additional protection.

MAKING SUB-STANDARD OFFERS

12.94 There may be a temptation to submit a sub-standard offer. This should be resisted. Once the level of a settlement has been agreed with the Inspector it would be unwise to submit an offer in a lower figure. If there are genuine reasons why the client cannot make a 'full' offer, this should be taken into account when negotiating with the Inspector, before submitting a formal offer. If a sub-standard offer is submitted it may be accepted, providing it is reasonably close to the expected offer, but the Inspector is likely to exercise extreme caution when negotiating with the practitioner on subsequent cases.

12.95 There may be exceptional circumstances where the submission of a sub-standard offer may be justified, for example, where the Inspector is intransigent, but it is not recommended that this is done as a matter of course.

SETTLEMENT MEETINGS

12.96 Most Inspectors requested settlement meetings in the past. The purpose of the meeting was for the client to sign the letter of offer, and, usually, for the Inspector to deliver a moral lecture on tax evasion. Now, most settlements, particularly in smaller cases, are dealt with by correspondence. The Inspector accepts an assurance that the significance of the various documents signed by the client (offer letter, statement of assets, certificate of bank accounts operated and certificate of full disclosure) has been explained by the practitioner. It is important that the advisor does this in unequivocal terms to the client, in writing, to ensure that he fully appreciates the seriousness of the situation.

12.97 The dangers of signing an incomplete statement of assets or certificate of full disclosure, ie the possibility of criminal proceedings by HMRC, should be stressed to the client. Often, at this late stage in the investigation, the client may disclose additional assets. Although the Inspector will not be impressed by late disclosure of further assets or sources of income, and this can impact on the penalty mitigation, it is preferable to the client signing an incomplete statement or certificate and being prosecuted.

12.98 Although a settlement interview may be requested, particularly in larger cases, there is no statutory obligation on your client to attend such a meeting. If a formal meeting is held, it is important that the client is fully briefed beforehand. The client should be advised merely to listen to the Inspector, and sign the documentation when requested.

12.99 The practitioner should be aware that the meeting is not for the benefit of the client, but provides the Inspector with an opportunity to give the client a rap on the knuckles and warn him about his future conduct. The practitioner should ensure that any debate about, for example, the level of penalty, is agreed before the settlement meeting. At the meeting the client only has to listen, and sign the relevant documentation (which should have been checked in advance by the practitioner).

RELATIONSHIP WITH THE INSPECTOR

12.100 It is important for the practitioner to establish a good rapport with the Inspector conducting the investigation. A frosty relationship with the Inspector will not be helpful when it comes to negotiating a settlement. It is equally important that the relationship does not become 'cosy'. What is desired is a healthy professional respect between the Inspector and the practitioner.

12.101 If the advisor does not know the Inspector from previous dealings with HMRC, he should endeavour to establish a rapport at an early stage of the investigation. The following steps can help to achieve this:

1 agree the work to be done by the practitioner at the beginning of the investigation;

2 carry out the work agreed, within an approved realistic timescale, or keep the Inspector informed of any unforeseen delays;

3 using the telephone or meetings to make progress, rather than lengthy letters, particularly those of a legalistic nature, which tend to prompt replies of similar length and style;

4 comply with reasonable requests for information or documentation by the Inspector, or be prepared to say why certain items are not considered reasonable or relevant to the investigation; and

5 adopting an appropriate tone in correspondence – some practitioners adopt an unnecessarily aggressive stance, which is not conducive to establishing a good rapport with the Inspector.

RELATIONSHIP WITH THE CLIENT

12.102 The relationship with the client can be fraught with difficulty during a HMRC investigation. If the practitioner has acted for the client for many years, there can be a sense of betrayal when it emerges that the client has been guilty of irregularities. The advisor can also feel disappointed that he did not identify the misdemeanours when preparing the accounts. These thoughts must be banished from the practitioner's mind if he is to best represent his client at this difficult time. Often, particularly in large or complex cases, investigation specialists are engaged to deal with HMRC; the client is then handed back to the practitioner 'clean'.

12.103 Clients will want different things from their advisors during the investigation. They will all want, initially, to be spared from criminal proceedings. Their priority then shifts to a desire for the settlement cost to be as low as possible. Some clients will let the practitioner get on with his job without much contact other than to supply information or records. Others want to know all the detail of the discussions with the Inspector. Whatever level of detail the client wants, it is imperative that the practitioner makes the client aware of the seriousness of the situation, and the implications where irregularities have been discovered.

12.104 Some clients may try to bury their head in the sand and ignore the consequences of their actions. The practitioner should ensure that his client is not in the dark about the final outcome. The advisor is not doing the client, or himself, any favours in withholding details of the case until presenting the Inspector's settlement proposal – particularly where the amounts sought are substantial. This can only create difficulties for the practitioner, both in settling the case with the Inspector and tarnishing the relationship with the client.

12.105 The client should be kept informed at all stages during the progress of the investigation, and made aware of his options, if any, at a particular stage of the case. Some clients will want to fight all the way, and may seek their 'day in court'; others will take a commercial view and want the investigation concluded as soon as possible, almost regardless of cost. The practitioner needs to deal with both extremes, and every position in between, but must act in accordance with his client's instructions.

12.106 Much of the advice on handling clients is common sense, and good case management. Dealing with the client should extend to billing arrangements. Although the client may normally receive one bill a year, following preparation of the accounts, it is recommended that practitioners bill monthly during an investigation. Time spent in dealing with the Inspector's enquiries can be substantial. There is a better prospect of recovery where monthly bills are issued, rather than one large bill issued at the end of a lengthy investigation.

12.107 The effect of an investigation on a client should not be underestimated. Even with the practitioner acting as a buffer between the client and the Inspector, the strain can be immense. There will be a tremendous pressure on the client's business and personal affairs. The practitioner should watch for signs that the stress is taking its toll on the client.

12.108 The penalty mitigation process should be explained to the client. The practitioner should highlight the arguments that can be used to mitigate the penalty. He should also mention any areas of weakness that the Inspector will use to argue for a higher penalty. The client may come up with further arguments, and should be encouraged to do so.

12.109 Handling the client during an investigation can be as demanding as the negotiations with the Inspector. With thorough preparation, a good understanding of the relative strengths and weaknesses of the client's case, and an appreciation of the Inspector's position, the practitioner will be best placed to negotiate the obstacles in his way during the investigation and achieve a successful conclusion.

Chapter 13

Employees and directors

Alastair Kendrick, Tax Partner, Bourne Business Consulting LLP

SCOPE OF CHAPTER

13.1 The review of employees and directors used to be carried out by a number of different Revenue agencies. These have now been re-focused to form Employer Compliance Units, who can be expected to cover both the tax and the NIC implications of both salary and benefits paid to employees and directors. The main exception to this single focus is Special Civil Investigation Office, which may become involved in serious cases.

Over recent months we have seen a move to significantly change the way in which reviews of employees and directors are organised. It is likely the result of this change will see a substantial reduction in the volume of the reviews and that these will be more focused in the case of larger concerns on a 'risk assessment' basis. It is possible that the more routine review of the larger concern will cease. It is also likely that, in a significant number of occasions, any reviews will be specific to areas of potential risk (aspect reviews) rather than general reviews looking at all areas of compliance. There is a specialist group recently formed to support caseworker Inspectors involved in dealing with the larger corporation (Large Business Office Inspectors).

13.2 The purpose of this chapter is to look specifically at the points which an audit or investigation team may raise in respect of employee/director tax issues. It aims to identify those points which are most vulnerable to challenge and, where possible, it suggests how such challenges can be best dealt with. It cannot cover all areas and in particular does not attempt to deal with the tax rules applicable only to certain occupations, such as those of footballers, divers and farm-workers. In general, directors are swept up in the category of 'higher paid employees' although when a particular point is relevant to directors only, this is identified.

13.3 Another chapter of this work covers the penalties and interest which HMRC may charge following a review of employee tax issues. The way negotiations should in general be conducted is also separately dealt with, and this chapter will thus only identify those negotiation points which are specific to employees and directors. Self-assessment is also dealt with elsewhere although where this has a significant impact on PAYE/ Schedule E tax compliance, it is referred to briefly in this chapter. The review requirements relating to certain National Insurance contributions, (NICs) are covered elsewhere in this book , but the NIC treatment of payments and benefits is also mentioned here, where appropriate.

INTRODUCTION

13.4 As is well known, an employee is taxable on all 'emoluments' from his or her employment (ITEPA 2003, s 6 and 7). Emoluments are defined to include 'all salaries, fees, wages, perquisites and profits whatsoever' (ITEPA 2003, ss 10(2), 62(2)). Emoluments may include payments from third parties.

13.5 National Insurance contributions (NICs) are payable on 'earnings'. This is similar to the HMRC definition of emoluments, and now includes most benefits in kind).

13.6 In order to review compliance with the tax legislation, HMRC have broad authority to examine records held by the employer. These include:

1 copies of P9Ds and P11Ds;

2 P46s;

3 petty cash records;

4 expense claim vouchers;

5 cash book/purchase ledger vouchers;

6 timesheets and clock cards;

7 tachographs;

8 cheque book stubs; and

9 bank statements.

13.7 In addition such powers extend to enable HMRC to ensure the following aspects have been correctly dealt with:

1 minimum wage;

2 student loan repayment;

3 tax credits.

13.8 They will in addition wish to carry out what is called a 'payroll cleanse' which is to ensure that the employer is using the correct National Insurance number for the employee. Whilst this review is voluntary it is sensible to permit it to be undertaken, given there is the threat in that the rules may at some point be changed which would enable penalties to be imposed for the use of an incorrect NI number.

13.9 It is the inspection of these records which allows HMRC to check both compliance with the PAYE regulations and the more general rules for the taxation of benefits. The appropriate application of National Insurance (NI) is likely also to be reviewed.

13.10 This chapter analyses the review/investigation approach into four main areas:

1 compliance with the PAYE regulations;

2 directors;

3 Schedule E benefits; and

4 liability for tax arising.

PAYE COMPLIANCE ISSUES

13.11 The overall reason for reviewing PAYE records is to ensure that the correct amount of PAYE and NICs has been deducted from the earnings of the employees and directors of the business. This requires that the company has:

1 deducted PAYE and NICs from all relevant payments;

2 calculated the correct amount of PAYE and NICs;

3 included all employees and directors on the payroll.

13.12 It is in the employer's interest that these areas are regularly reviewed, either by in-house specialists or an external adviser, so as to ensure that an HMRC visit will not produce unwelcome and expensive surprises. It is recommended that the employer apply for appropriate dispensations and make himself aware of any working rule agreements (WRAs) applicable to his industry.

13.13 If the company is conducting any pre-review or check, it is worth noting that HMRC standard procedures require them to question those responsible for completing wages and similar records. Similar discussions should be conducted by the internal review team. It is common to find, in the course of such a review, that the procedures actually being carried out in practice are not exactly as management imagine.

13.14 The employer should also not forget that HMRC officials carrying out a PAYE or Schedule E review are under instructions to keep their eyes open for any indications that the employer has been deliberately evading tax. This includes VAT for example; the HMRC team will then introduce colleagues responsible for those areas.

13.15 The following are some review points relevant to employee/director issues:

1. Does the workforce on the books look like the workforce on the premises?
2. Are there indications of shiftwork (and possibly an additional workforce paid through a second set of books)?
3. Does the business look prosperous?
4. Have there been any recent improvements or alterations to the premises?
5. Is the apparent lifestyle of directors in keeping with the level of remuneration?
6. Are any directors paid less than employees?
7. Do the directors control the wages records and payments?
8. Is the wages clerk related to the directors?
9. Are cash wages paid?
10. Are significant round sum payments made? (Even if it seems reasonable that these represent genuine business expenditure, large amounts paid without supporting documentation point to a lack of control.)
11. Is there a large casual wages charge (ie large relative to the size of the business)?
12. Are wages paid to domestic staff or gardeners?
13. Do spouses or other relatives receive excessive wages?
14. Is there the opportunity to earn extra income?
15. If the main income is by cheque, is there a subsidiary business generating cash?
16. Are the directors personally in control of cash/petty cash/chequebooks?
17. Is there a poor system of cash control?
18. Are there cash takings where you would not expect them?
19. If there is a high level of cash takings, is it all banked?
20. Is cash in hand kept at a steady level or does it fluctuate?
21. What was the cash in hand figure at the beginning and end of the year?

22 Are the records inaccurate, not up to date, written up after a period from memory and not from vouchers and receipts?

23 How often is the cash book balanced?

24 Is personal expenditure paid by the business?

25 Is the expenditure not supported by receipts or vouchers?

26 Is there evidence of altered or false invoices, that is where Special Civil Investigation Office (previously Special Compliance Office (SCO)) have not taken up the case?

27 Are unusual benefits provided (for example yachts, caravans, holiday homes, trips abroad, fines paid, school fees, upkeep of animals, prizes awarded by third parties)?

28 Are round sum entertaining expenses paid?

29 Are any company vehicles rarely used for business (including those used by relatives)?

13.16 If the employer is using a computerised payroll system (or if this is outsourced to a third party payroll provider) the Revenue team will be interested to know the particular system and what security is in place over the overrides to the system. One area looked at would be payroll parameter reports which show ayments made throughthe system are dealt with for income tax and National Insurance. They will also be interested to ascertain who is authorised to override electronic systems and what exception reports are then generated.

13.17 As well as a review of employment taxes being the trigger for an investigation of other areas, the reverse can also be true. When HMRC review business accounts they are instructed to consider whether costs in the profit and loss account may point to PAYE irregularities. Such costs may include:

1 payments to casuals;

2 commissions, fees, or consultancy payments;

3 wages payments where there is no evidence of a PAYE scheme; and

4 suspiciously large items which may conceal additional payments to employees or uncertified subcontractors.

13.18 In particular, whenever a close company is investigated for whatever reason, the official is required to review the company's compliance with its PAYE obligations.

Subjecting earnings to PAYE/NICs

13.19 As has been stated above, not all emoluments are within the scope of PAYE and/or NICs Even a cursory overview shows up significant differences in tax and NIC treatment, despite recent attempts at greater alignment of the two systems. Some particular points to note are set out below.

Round sum allowances

13.20 These are allowances paid to an employee whether or not he spends them in a particular way. As such they are taxable and subject to NICs (*Fergusson v Noble* (1919) 7 TC 176). However, where an allowance is set at a level which is simply intended to reimburse the employee's actual expenditure for 'a specific and distinct business expense', it will not be regarded as a 'round sum allowance'. Ideally such flat rate payments, eg for travel or subsistence, should be discussed with the local Inspector in advance and a dispensation agreed.

13.21 Where there is no dispensation, and *an audit review* identifies the payments, the employer should see how far he can establish that his allowances were a reasonable estimate of actual necessary expenditure incurred by employees in performing their duties and seek to exclude this from the settlement. It will be the practice of HMRC to ensure that the specific arrangements in place for payment of round sums, which had been disclosed when the dispensation was agreed, is being followed.

Sick pay

13.22 Sick pay paid to employees is generally within the scope of PAYE. Exceptions do occur, eg where sick pay is provided by a third party after an employment has ceased, or when an employee has contributed to a sickness insurance scheme. In the latter case only the part of the sick pay attributable to the employer's contribution, if any, attracts PAYE and NICs (SE 1340).

Tips and service charges

13.23 This is an area in which we have seen significant interest over recent years and the approach of HMRC change. The position is now set out in booklet E24 which clarifies that there is little change from the historical position save that the employer is using tips to form part of the minimum wage of the employee then National Insurance arises on these irrespective of how the tips are paid.

13.24 Tips paid in cash to the employee or into a communal pool are taxable as earnings from the employment, and may be subject to PAYE and NICs, depending on the role of the employer. The table below summarises the position (ECM 13203; CWG2 (1998) 29).

Employer decides basis of distribution	*Employer distributes tips*	*Employer to deduct/account for:*
Yes	Yes	PAYE/NICs
Yes	No	NICs
No	Yes	PAYE

13.25 Service charges are more complex. Where employees receive a share of the service charge made by the employer to customers, the employer must *always* account for NICs (CWG2 (1998) 28).

13.26 However, PAYE has to be deducted by the person responsible for distributing the service charge to employees. This may not be the employer, but may, for example, be the bar steward or head waiter (Income Tax (Employments) Regulations 1993, reg 5). Such an arrangement is generally known as a tronc. Where the troncmaster has been found not to operate PAYE satisfactorily, the principal employer can be made responsible, but only for future amounts (reg 3). The troncmaster is still responsible for amounts underpaid in the past. However, it is true to say that in such cases an auditor will look very carefully at the arrangements to see if the troncmaster was genuinely independent of the employer. It is in my experience rare for anyone to be willing to take on the responsibility of running the tronc and when they fully understand the implications of this role they resign.

Remuneration in non-cash form

13.27 Over recent years a number of schemes have sought to avoid NICs and PAYE by paying remuneration other than in cash, eg by using gold bullion, coffee beans or fine wines. However, successive anti-avoidance legislation has sought to prevent the use of such devices. HMRC have also had some success when challenging schemes before the courts, see *DTE Financial Services Ltd v Wilson* [1999] STC 1061 and *NMB Holdings v Secretary of State* which was heard on 14 July 2000. Whether a particular method or asset is caught may thus depend on the years for which it was in force and the case law position. See Revenue Press Release 18 May 1999 for treatment of interest on NICs found to be overdue as a result. The remaining areas will be covered within the disclosure rules.

13.28 There have been a number of methods used to provide bonuses to employees without the requirement to apply PAYE or National Insurance at the time of the award. These have largely been the subject of HMRC scrutiny and in many cases it is not possible for the payer of the bonus to receive any tax relief for the payments made until the PAYE and National Insurance is settled. The most popular route adopted in this area was the payment of the bonus via an employee benefit trust. It is generally the case that HMRC in discovering such an arrangement in place will refer the matter to a specialised team to consider

Terminations

13.29 A pre-audit review should also check that any termination payments have been correctly included for PAYE purposes. While it is widely known that there is an exemption for the first £30,000 of a termination payment (ITEPA 2003, s 403) this does not apply to every payment made on cessation of an employment, and a single lump sum may be composed of a number of different amounts. Points to note are set out below.

Contractual payments

13.30 HMRC will seek to tax any termination payment, which is contractual. They have sought to tax termination payments both where the contract provided explicitly for such a payment, and where there was an expectation that such a payment would be made. In the latter situation HMRC argue that the payment is an implied contract term. This situation was the subject of the case of *SCA Packaging Ltd v HMRC* and also the subject of a Tax Bulletin 63. It seems though at the time of writing that HMRC have decided to soften their approach to this matter. It is though important for an employer to ensure that PILON'S cannot be considered contractual on grounds of custom.

13.31 NICs are also sought on contractual amounts, and the same comments apply. However, with NICs there is an extra point: the employer should also resist any attempt to charge NICs on any redundancy payment, as such payments are specifically excluded from NIC liability.

Payments in lieu of notice (PILONs)

13.32 The HMRC view of contractual payments extends to PILONs (*Tax Bulletin* 24 August 1996). If a PILON is contractual, HMRC will seek to exclude it from ITEPA 2003, s 403. HMRC's view was supported in *EMI Group Electronics Ltd v Coldicott* [1999] STC 803. However, in this case, the Revenue accepted that payments in lieu of notice to junior employees were not taxable emoluments, since the employees had no contractual right to them.

Restrictive covenants

13.33 HMRC have also sometimes sought to argue that part or all of the termination payment is in respect of a restrictive covenant and therefore taxable

(ITEPA 2003, s 225). However, HMRC significantly reduced the scope and believe these to only be of relevance if the payment being made is a restriction on the employee, which is not specified in their employment contract. Where a restrictive covenant would apply, the employer should seek to apportion the payment being made to apportion the covenant and the balance.

Dismissals

13.34 There have also been attempts to argue that s 403 is only applicable to redundancies, and not, for example, where someone is dismissed. There are no grounds for this restrictive interpretation within the very broad wording of the section:

> 'This section applies to any payment (not otherwise chargeable to tax) which is made, whether in pursuance of any legal obligation or not, either directly or indirectly in consideration or in consequence of, or otherwise in connection with, the termination of the holding of the office or employment or any change in its functions or emoluments.'

Retirement

13.35 A further line of HMRC attack has been on payments made to individuals nearing retirement. They have sought to argue that the termination payment is in effect a non-approved retirement benefits scheme, which would make it taxable (ITEPA 2003, s 394). This should be resisted as it is difficult to believe that a court would agree with the Revenue, and it is doubtful whether HMRC would be prepared to take such a case to court.

13.36 If this point is raised by HMRC it should be noted that in particular the termination of employment because of redundancy or inefficiency is frequently referred to as 'early retirement' even though the employee has been deprived of his employment prematurely, often against his wishes. In both these situations, any ex-gratia lump sum paid by the employer should not be regarded as chargeable. This is so even if the employee also becomes entitled, at the time of termination, to immediate pension benefits from the employer's approved superannuation scheme.

Continuing benefits

13.37 On termination some employees are provided with continuing benefits, such as the use of a company car or a beneficial loan. New rules were introduced by s 58 of FA 1998 which rewrote TA 1988, s 148 (ITEPA 2003, s 403) and they were further explained in a *Tax Bulletin* article (September 1998). These rules apply to payments received after 5 April 1998, unless the sums were already taxed in earlier years.

Employment Termination Settlements

13.38 The HMRC view of continuing benefits pre-FA 1998 is explained in the HMRC press release dated 17 March 1997: Taxation of Benefits received after the Year of Termination. This press release also describes special arrangements available for employment termination agreements entered into from 6 April 1996. These special arrangements offer taxpayers a simpler approach to taxing such continuing benefits. A *Tax Bulletin* article (June 1997) further expands on the issues involved.

13.39 Employers who are attacked under the continuing benefits rules for these years are advised to read the Press Release and *Tax Bulletin*. However, despite the detailed arguments set out therein by the Revenue, it is arguable that continuing benefits which cannot be transferred have no market value and thus were not assessable. The only reported case on the point is *George v Ward,* [1995] STC (SCD) 230 (Sp C 30), when the taxpayer lost the argument that there was no tax to pay on a continuing benefit. It was, however, held that tax should be charged by reference to the period for which the benefit was actually made available rather than for the longer period set out in the termination agreement. If *George v Ward* is raised by HMRC in support of their taxation of continuing benefits, they should be reminded that it is merely a Special Commissioners Case, and thus does not create a binding precedent. It is also the view of many tax advisers that it was wrongly decided.

13.40 Since ITEPA 2003, s 403 only applies where an item is 'not otherwise chargeable to tax', the Revenue official may argue that certain continuing benefits cannot form part of the £30,000. Targets include gifts of assets, taxable under ITEPA 2003, s 203, and loan write offs, taxable under ITEPA 2003, s 188. Such problems could be avoided if the employee was given the cash which was then used to buy the asset at its market value, or to repay the loan. If this route was not taken, and the official seeks to argue that the amounts are taxable, reference should be made in the HMRC press release of 17 March 1997 which clearly suggests that both cars and loans can fall within the £30,000.

13.41 Where the 'continuing benefit' is a small regular gift, such as a Christmas box to pensioners, the employer could argue that, if it is taxable under Schedule E at all, it should be exempted.

Other issues

13.42 Terminations are complex and are occurring with increasing frequency. Their cumulative cost and the value of the tax-free amounts are significant, and thus can be expected to draw an Inspector's attention. In addition to the points raised above, other relevant issues arise where:

1 The employee has been made redundant and then subsequently re-employed. The Inspector will review such cases to ensure that the redundancy was genuine at the time it was made.

2 The employee has 'retired', received a lump sum from his pension tax free, and then been re-employed. In these cases the Pension Schemes Office may challenge the tax-free status of the lump sum and may even threaten the qualifying status of the pension scheme itself. For a discussion of this issue, see Adrian Waddingham's article in *Taxation,* 18 May 2000. Therefore, it is important to demonstrate that there has been a genuine cessation of employment, with a re-employment on wholly different terms. It may be worth consulting an employment lawyer.

3 The employee is given 'garden leave', ie continues to receive his salary but is not required to report to the office. This is taxable under Schedule E in the normal way.

4 The employee has spent some time abroad. In this case a higher amount can be paid tax free; if he or she is retiring through ill-health, there is no £30,000 limit ITEPA 2003, s 413.

Salary sacrifice arrangements

13.43 A salary sacrifice is an arrangement under which the employee agrees to take a cut in future remuneration in exchange for some other benefit, such as an increased employer contribution to the employee's pension fund.

13.44 An HMRC official may check a sample of such salary sacrifices to ensure that they:

1 are in writing, signed and dated;

2 stating clearly that the employee is varying his or her right to remuneration; and

3 are not retrospective.

13.45 Failure in any respect will mean that HMRC will view the sacrifice as ineffective, so that the employee remains entitled under his contract to the originally sacrificed amount and should thus have been taxed on it. The NIC implications will follow, plus a possible over-funding of the pension scheme if the re-categorised amount takes the employee above his contribution limit.

13.46 There are special rules relating to life changing circumstances. HMRC have given guidance of what constitute these significant life style changes to warrant an early exit from a salary sacrifice arrangement. HMRC at the time of any review will want to be satisfied that those who have existed early from a salary sacrifice had circumstances, which they would consider to fall within their guidance.

Calculation of the correct amounts of PAYE/NICs

13.47 In these days of computerised PAYE, it is often thought that calculation errors are unlikely to occur. This is not the case, although some of the errors occur not because of the system itself but through faulty inputs – the 'garbage in, garbage out' principle. Particularly vulnerable are PAYE systems which are supplied with information from more than one source, such as two or more departments or subsidiaries. As part of any *pre-audit* review some mechanical checks on the operation of the system are therefore useful. HMRC's review will make similar checks. Some areas where the wrong amounts may be erroneously brought into the calculation are set out below.

Timing of taxing the earnings

13.48 Specific rules exist to establish when earnings are taxable, and these are different for employees and directors. Employees are taxable on the earlier of receipt and entitlement ITEPA 2003, s 10. Particular care needs to be taken with bonus payments and commission.

13.49 The special rules for the taxing of directors' remuneration are likely to be checked by HMRC. The remuneration is taxable on the earliest of:

1 receipt of the emoluments;

2 entitlement to the emoluments;

3 determination of the emoluments; or

4 crediting the emoluments to an account with the company.

13.50 It is the fourth of these which most commonly gives problems, because companies do not always realise that the account in question does not have to be the director's own account. A credit in the company's salaries account is enough, or a written note in a minute book. Neither does a restriction (a 'fetter') on drawing out the money prevent the credit from being regarded as remuneration (TA 1988, s 203A(1)(c)), although in such cases there are no NICs until payment is made. Companies should also be aware that 'director' includes a shadow director (TA 1988, s 202B(6)). However, the company should note that to be taxable:

1 the entry must identify the director, and

2 it must be for an emolument. In particular, an accounts provision which has not been agreed, or remuneration which is contingent on the happening of some future event, is not an emolument.

(SE 5351)

13.51 Inspectors will review this area by:

1 asking if any directors' remuneration has been deferred;

2 paying particular attention, when examining records, to any annual fees, bonuses, etc and establishing the date on which they should have been subject to PAYE.

13.52 There are also special NIC rules for directors, under which the earnings period is a year rather than a month or a week (their regular earnings period). This has the effect of accelerating the payment of NICs. These rules were softened by s 49 of the Social Security Act 1998. Directors may now pay primary contributions for eleven months as if they were employees, with a recalculation and 'catch-up' payment in month 12 if necessary. Failures in earlier periods are often treated leniently by auditors as long as the correct amount of NICs has been paid in the tax year. However, problems can arise with directors who leave in the year.

13.53 This is an area often overlooked by payroll departments especially when using electronic payrolls. This special rule does however, only applies to statutory directors and not those who simply carry the title of 'director'.

New employees

13.54 Sometimes the first month's salary is paid by cheque whilst the administrative arrangements to include the employee on the payroll are in process. Ensure that any such payments are included in PAYE pay.

NICs, SSP, SMP issues

13.55 The cost of errors in these areas, and particularly in employer's NICs, can be substantial. HMRC will check that these amounts have been correctly calculated for a sample of employees. The accuracy of the following may be reviewed:

1 any non-standard calculations, such as reduced rate NICs and small employer's relief for SSP;

2 contracted-out amounts;

3 National Insurance Contributions;

4 SMP amounts paid and the amounts offset against NICs due – the SMP rules are complex and in general less well supported by either computer systems or trained staff than PAYE. For employers with relatively low numbers of women on maternity leave, the cost of errors in this area may be small, but for organisations with large female workforces it may be worth checking that the rules are understood and being operated correctly;

5 correct application of the NIC aggregation rules.

13.56 One important point for employers is the limited scope they have to collect under-deductions of NICs from employees. Such sums can only be recovered if they occur in the current tax year; if later, the cost is purely one for the employer.

Payroll giving schemes

13.57 If the company is operating a payroll giving scheme, the Inspector will ask to see:

1 the employer's contract with the approved agency;

2 form CHY 140(1) if for a period prior to 2000 (form abolished by FA 2000, s 38);

3 the employer's written authority to make deductions from the employees' pay.

13.58 He will also check that:

1 PAYE is being operated on a 'net pay' basis but that NICs are calculated on the true gross pay;

2 for years before 2000/1, that the deductions are within the maximum annual limit (the annual limit was abolished by FA 2000, s 38); and

3 the company has paid the donations to the agency within 14 days of the end of the income tax month in which they were deducted.

Third parties

13.59 Where a cash payment, such as a round sum allowance, is paid as a reward in connection with an individual's employment, the paying company has to deduct PAYE. This is because of ITEPA 2003, s 684.

13.60 An 'employer' is defined as 'any person paying emoluments'. This means that PAYE obligations may stretch more widely than is sometimes presumed. It should, however, be noted that the client is not liable for the NICs on these payments. For the position of benefits paid to third parties.

Including all employees and directors on the payroll

13.61 Ensuring that all employees are correctly included on the payroll is a key audit task. HMRC will look particularly closely at any individuals paid by the company who have not been included in PAYE, such as casuals, agency workers, students those regarded as self-employed, and one-man companies. Recently they have paid particular attention to subcontractors.

13.62 There will also be particular attention paid to directors. HMRC review instructions say that that all directors should be identified at the time of interview, and that the records should be checked to see if there is any director whose remuneration has been concealed.

Self-employment v employment: basic principles

13.63 There is no definition of either 'employment' or 'self-employment' in the legislation, and the HMRC/CA will thus rely on the principles established in a series of tax cases. These have sought to distinguish between the individual who works under a contract of service (and is thus employed) and one who works under a contract for services. The distinction was summarised in the case of *Market Investigations Ltd v Minister of Social Security* [1969] 2 QB 173:

> 'Is the person who has engaged himself to perform these services performing them as a person in business on his own account? If the answer to that question is "yes" then the contract is a contract for services. If the answer is "no" then the contract is a contract of service.'

13.64 This is a developing area and regard should always be had to recent case law in establishing the latest position. There is increasing interest in this area caused by the introduction of the personal services legislation.

Currently the basic principles which a court would adopt in deciding whether an individual is an employee or not are:

1 Is the person in business on his own account? This was discussed in the case of *Hall v Lorimer* [1994] STC 23, in which the judge said:

> 'In order to decide whether a person carries on business on his

> own account it is necessary to consider many different aspects of that person's work activity. This is not a mechanical exercise of running through items on a check list to see whether they are present in, or absent from, a given situation. The object of the exercise is to paint a picture from the accumulation of detail. The overall effect can only be appreciated by standing back from the detailed picture which has been painted, by viewing it from a distance and by making an informed, considered, qualitative appreciation of the whole.'

Some of the details that will be considered (*Market Investigations Ltd v Minister of Social Security* [1969] 2 QB 173) include:

(a) How much control is exercised over the individual? Control includes control over *where* the individual does his work, *when* he does it, *what* he does and *how* he does it. The relative importance of each will vary, eg a surgeon is not told how to perform an operation (*Morren v Swinton and Pendlebury Borough Council* [1965] 1 WLR 576).

(b) Does he provide his own equipment? There is a presumption that employers will generally provide major items of equipment which are necessary for employees to do their job. Similarly many self-employed people own their own equipment. However, there are many exceptions to this. 'Little significance can be attached to the provision of small tools (or even major items) where it is customary for them to be provided' (SE 604). Cases on this point include *Ready Mixed Concrete (South East) Ltd v Minister of Pensions and National Insurance* [1968] 2 QB 497.

(c) Can he hire his own helpers? If he can, he is more likely to be self-employed.

(d) Does he take financial risk, so that he can make a loss as well as a profit? If he can, he is likely to be self-employed. If there is no financial risk, it is still possible, albeit unusual, that the individual will be self-employed. (*Addison v London Philharmonic Orchestra Society Ltd* [1981] ICR 261).

(e) Can he 'profit from sound management'? A self-employed person is often in this position: the efficiency with which he carries out his job will affect his income. The same may, however, apply to some employees, such as those paid on piece work.

2 Can the individual send a substitute to do the job? If he can, this is almost conclusive evidence in favour of self-employment, as the requirement for personal service is a normal ingredient of most service contracts.

3 What were the intentions of the parties? Although not conclusive, what the parties intended should be taken into account.

4 How is the individual paid? Again, this is not conclusive, but generally only employees have paid holidays, sick pay, maternity pay and pensions.

5 Is the individual effectively selling his skills to a succession of different companies? This is a very difficult test to apply, and the tax case of *Hall v Lorimer* [1994] STC 23 is the best illustration of its application. Mr Lorimer was a vision mixer who customarily worked for 20 or more production companies. Most of his engagements lasted for only a single day. The HMRC have said that they believe that *Lorimer* will have particular relevance to engagements where:

(a) the worker provides similar services to many engagers; and

(b) there is a mutual intention not to create employment; and

(c) the worker has a business-like approach to obtaining and organising his engagements and incurs expenditure in this area of a type not normally associated with employment.

In addition the following pointers may be present although their absence would not inevitably mean employment:

(d) the worker has many short-term engagements;

(e) the worker is providing professional services or services requiring the exercise of rare skill and judgment;

(f) the worker is engaged for a specific task;

(g) as a result of the number of different engagers the worker incurs expenditure travelling to various workplaces similar in nature to 'home to work' travel but considerable in amount when compared to the level of expenditure that is likely to be incurred by an employee who resides close to his/her work place;

(h) the worker bears a greater financial risk than an employee because payment is made after the payer has been invoiced, exposing the worker to the risk of delayed payment and bad debt; and

(i) the extent to which the worker is able to influence the rate of pay is greater than is normally the case in employment situations, for example evidence of tendering.

6 It is, however, possible for a person to be neither an employee, nor in business on their own account, see the comments of Nolan J in *Wickens v Champion Employment* [1984] ICR 365.

Self-employment v employment: the audit approach

13.65 As stated above, in seeking to establish whether individuals are employees, HMRC will apply the above case law principles to the facts of each case. To establish these they will:

1 Interview some or all of the individuals. This may well occur without the engager being aware.

2 Ask to see any documentation concerning the terms under which the individual was engaged. This may include the original job advertisement, any oral instructions given when he started work, the written contract (if any) and written company procedures.

3 Seek to confirm actual practice which may be other than described in the written agreements. (Remember that this works both ways: the written documentation may not be helpful, but if the company can establish that the actual procedures are otherwise, this should also be taken into account).

4 Seek to discover whether there are other workers doing similar duties and if so, whether they are employed or self-employed.

5 Ask whether the worker was previously an employee of the 'employer' – if so they will ask when the change occurred and what differences exist in the terms of engagement.

13.66 HMRC have developed a employment status tool indicator on their website in to which the detailed terms of a contract can be populated and from which it will give an indication of whether that person engaged should be treated on a self-employed or employed basis. Clearly in any Revenue review in this area they will want to see if the status tool was used and also whether the information fed in to this was correct and therefore its conclusion can be relied upon. This may result in a formal ruling that the individuals the company has been treating as self-employed are in fact employees. If the company disagrees with the ruling it may be necessary to take a test case to the courts. Whether the ruling is to be applied for past years or only for the future is a matter for negotiation, often as part of an overall audit settlement.

13.67 Where an individual is retrospectively re-categorised as an employee, there will be a recalculation of the outstanding tax and NICs. In such cases the Schedule D tax and Class 4 NICs should be allocated against the Schedule E tax, and the Class 2 against the Class 1 NICs (*Hansard* (*1984*) *vol, 55 No 108 cols 62–3*). The shortfall (plus possibly interest and penalties) is to be paid by the employer, with the limited recovery rights. The position is now changed following the principles outlined in the case of *Demibourne.*

13.68 Even before their merger, HMRC and the CA used the same case law in arriving at their status decisions, and agreed that they would accept each other's rulings. However, the CA, and now HMRC, had the power to *determine* that particular groups of workers should be treated as Class I (employed) or Class II (self-employed). They made use of these powers for the following groups of workers:

1 electoral workers (generally exempt from NICs);

2 examiners, moderators, etc of certain examining bodies (generally treated as self-employed);

3 domestic employment by close relatives (generally exempt from NICs);

4 ministers of religion (generally treated as employees);

5 office and telephone cleaners (generally treated as employees);

6 part-time or visiting lecturers, teachers or instructors (generally treated as employees);

7 engaging of a person by his or her spouse (generally treated as an employee).

13.69 The practice of HMRC in this area is currently changing following the case of *Demibourne Ltd v Revenue & Customs Commissioners* SpC 486. This case outlined the position of how income tax paid under Schedule D by the worker could be used against the tax liability of the engager. Whilst the future approach is still not final HMRC are now only prepared to offset tax paid by the worker if that person consents and this will be given in the form of a credit against the engager which is still likely to leave a balance of liability payable.

Casual workers

13.70 A 'casual' in common parlance is someone who is not permanently employed by an organisation. There is no special legislation covering such people, and the normal rules for employment status, described in the preceding section, therefore apply.

13.71 However, it is in the case of casuals that the concept of mutuality of obligation comes into its own. For an individual to be an employee there must be an ongoing obligation on the part of the person who employs him to supply him with work and an ongoing obligation on the part of the worker to take work which is offered. There is a long line of cases on this point, of which *O'Kelly v Trusthouse Forte plc* [1984] QB 90 is perhaps the most significant.

13.72 From the employer's point of view, casuals represent a review vulnerability. The company may genuinely believe the casual worker to be self-employed, eg because the worker has no sick pay or holiday pay and is known to undertake a succession of similar contracts. However, the individual may nevertheless be a employee, see the comments of Lord Griffiths in *Lee Ting Sang v Chung Chi-Keung* [1990] 2 AC 374:

> '… the picture emerges of a skilled artisan earning his living by working for more than one employer as an employee and not as a

> small businessman venturing into business on his own account as an independent contractor with all its attendant risks. The applicant ran no risk whatever save that of being unable to find employment which is, of course, a risk faced by casual employees who move from one job to another …'

13.73 Organisations with a large number of branches are particularly vulnerable if the branch manager has authority to cover short-term staff shortages. The amounts paid to each casual may be small, but if multiplied across a branch network and carried back for six years, the total cost can be substantial.

13.74 Another risk area is casual payments made to existing employees for extra duties such as unscheduled overtime. This may also not have been correctly dealt with under the NIC aggregation rules. A classic case is the teacher who does occasional evening classes for the same local authority which employs him during the day.

13.75 In dealing with an audit attack on casuals, the company should:

1. check whether there is any scope for arguing that some of the individuals are genuinely self-employed, applying the principles set out above, and in particular *O'Kelly v Trusthouse Forte* and the *Hall v Lorimer* case;
2. review whether any of the workers were supplied by *bona fide* employment agencies, in which case the agency rules may apply;
3. perform a detailed sample check to establish whether and how many workers are below the threshold for taxation and NICs – this may be possible where the casuals are known to other workers in the organisation, eg family members or friends;
4. consider writing to the individuals asking them to complete forms P46 on a retrospective basis;
5. if the payment should have been taxable, seek to have it reduced by the personal allowance which would have been available, on the basis that such individuals are unlikely to have used it elsewhere. Likewise full use should be made of the lower rate band in assessing tax underpaid (this argument may be resisted by HMRC but may be useful when negotiating an overall settlement).

Agency workers

13.76 People supplied by a third party agency who are not employed either by the agency or the company can be *deemed* employees (ITEPA 2003, s 44). In this case PAYE is operated by whoever pays them. The deeming provision operates where: 'an individual ('the worker') renders or is under an obligation to render personal services to another person ('the client') and is subject to, or to the right of, supervision, direction or control as to the manner in which he renders those services' (ITEPA 2003, s 44). Exceptions to this deeming provision include musicians, entertainers, models and (until 6 April 1998) subcontractors (ITEPA 2003, s 44).

13.77 Where an organisation engages a worker through a foreign agency without a branch or agent in the UK, the UK organisation is deemed to be the employer for PAYE and NIC purposes

13.78 The Inspector will seek to establish whether the deeming provisions should be applied, and in so doing will:

1 Review the contractual relationships. If the agency has only introduced the worker to the company then the deeming provisions will not apply (*Brady v Hart (t/a Jaclyn Model Agency)* (1985) 58 TC 518). However where this is the case the auditor will then review whether the worker is an employee of the organisation for which he is working.

2 Check whether any travelling expenses or associated subsistence have been paid to cover the workers' travel costs in getting to the job. Such expenses are regarded as home to work travel and as such are taxable. PAYE is deductible by the person making the payments, which may be the company for whom the individual is working. Before settling on this point with the auditors, the company should check whether in fact some of the expenses cover detached duty away from the normal place of work, in which case they will be allowable. There is also a concessional relief available for travel between clients.

One-man companies

13.79 One-man companies are common in some industries, such as computer consultancy. There should be no problem with using the services of such companies, an attempt to make the client liable for the PAYE and NICs on payments to such personal service companies was defeated (IR Press Release 23 September 1999). The company is registered and will receive its own tax return; the salary paid to the director will be subject to PAYE by the one-man company. There will only be a liability on the payer if the amount represents non-business costs, such as a round sum allowance (see Frequently Asked Question on IR35 Number 17). The personal service company's client may also have a reporting obligation if benefits are provided and should also:

1 ensure that the individual *has* such a company and not be misled by business names on headed paper, such as 'Jim Brown Computing' which may simply be a trading name with no corporate identity;

2 be sure that a formal contract has been entered into with the company to make it clear that the individual is not being employed directly.

HMRC is likely to ask to see copies of the contracts between the service companies and the organisation using the company's services.

Students

13.80 Students are likely to be outside PAYE, but to establish this they need to have completed a form P38(S). Where this has not been completed HMRC will seek back tax. The employer should try to obtain the forms retrospectively, as with casuals or put forward the arguments at para **13.75** points 3, 5. Other points to watch are that:

1. there is no exemption from NICs, so that the normal rules apply – thus NICs should be operated where the student's earnings exceed the lower earnings limit;
2. where a student's period of vacation work is at Easter, two tax years may be straddled. In such cases a form P38(S) is required for each year.

Special arrangements may apply to foreign or agricultural students.

Cleaners

13.81 Certain cleaners are deemed to be employees for NIC purposes. These deeming provisions apply to cleaners who work in an office or other non-domestic premises and are accepted as self-employed for tax purposes. However, the deeming rules will not be applied if the cleaners are operating in partnership or have their own employees. The rules also do not apply to window cleaners, but do apply to cleaners of telephone kiosks.

13.82 The employer in the office which they clean must operate Class 1 NICs on what he pays them. An official will seek back payment of Class 1 NICs on payments to a 'self-employed' cleaner if non-deduction is discovered during a review.

DIRECTORS

13.83 In many respects the investigation of directors is the same as that for higher paid employees, but there are a number of special points:

1 The Revenue take a special interest in anyone who may be able to override an organisation's normal accounting controls. Apart from deliberate fraud, the HMRC official will also look for expense claim forms from directors where the expenses are not fully vouched, or are self-certificated. It will be for the company to prove that the payments were for genuine business expenses, rather than a benefit to the director.

2 For the same reason the interface between the individual's own returns and the company's may also be checked. In the case of a more complex investigation each director may be asked whether his own returns are correct and complete to the best of his knowledge and belief. The personal files of the directors may also be called for.

3 Directors of close companies are subject to particularly close examination, eg to ensure that personal expenditure has not been put through as a business expense.

SCHEDULE E BENEFITS AND REIMBURSED EXPENSES

Dispensations

13.84 A dispensation releases an employer from the obligation to include expenses payments and benefits on employees' P11Ds. It also releases the employee from including the items on his tax return. Without a dispensation HMRC may argue that *all* reimbursed expenses and all benefits must be reported on the P11D and the individual's tax return, even where the reimbursed expenses were incurred solely for business purposes.

13.85 However the legal position is that only 'benefits provided for the employee such as give rise to any charge to tax' need to be reported Thus if the business reason is quite clear, the employer should resist any penalty for not having included an amount on the P11D. It is of course simpler if employers pre-empt such problems by applying for dispensations where appropriate (IR Leaflet IR 69 explains how to do this).

13.86 To obtain a dispensation the employer will need to show that:

1 the expenses are necessarily incurred in the performance of the employees' duties;

2 claims to expenses are independently checked and authorised;

3 where possible expense claims are accompanied by receipts or other evidence;

4 the employer has procedures to ensure that advances of expenses are fully accounted for, and any excess advancc has been repaid by the employee.

13.87 HMRC will check current dispensations at the beginning of their review. Problems can arise where:

1 an examination of the company's records shows that the terms of the dispensation have not been complied with, eg if amounts in excess of agreed subsistence allowances have been paid;

2 the dispensation was for a limited period and has not been renewed;

3 the dispensation only covered some companies or individuals in the group but has been applied to others.

If either 2 or 3 are found to apply, the employer should seek to prove that, had a dispensation been applied for, the company would have satisfied the requirements.

Working rule agreements

13.88 Working rule agreements (WRAs) are collective agreements drawn up between representatives of employers and trade unions to govern rates of pay and conditions of work in a number of industries. HMRC is not a party to these agreements but have agreed that certain WRA allowances paid for daily travel and lodging should not be taxed or liable for NICs.

13.89 This is broadly on the basis that the employees would otherwise be able to claim a deduction for the expenses under ITEPA 2003, s 336, although HMRC have indicated that 'it now seems likely that many such expenses payments might not be deductible under the general expenses rule, with the result that the tax treatment of WRAs is, at least in part, concessionary'.

13.90 The WRA allowances generally cover travel, accommodation and subsistence and are normally payable only to specific groups of employees within the construction and allied industries. The modified tax procedures are negotiated nationally and apply only where the employer adopts the terms and conditions of the relevant WRA. However, the employer does not have to be a member of the relevant employers' federation, nor do employees have to belong to the union negotiating the allowances, for these procedures to operate (IR Press Release of 13 February 1981).

13.91 It is possible that some payments made by an employer could fall within a WRA, but the employer is ignorant of its existence. HMRC may point out the WRA and apply its provisions to past payments; if the employer wishes to check for himself, a complete listing of current WRAs and their tax consequences are given in and this should be available at every tax office and on the Revenue website.

13.92 If the employer is aware of the WRA but has not been operating it correctly, he will be invited to make a settlement to cover the difference between the WRA amounts and the amounts actually paid. Should such a settlement be resisted, HMRC can make a determination under the legislation, which would of course be on the stricter provisions of ITEPA 2003, s 336 without the concessional WRA elements

Scope of benefits

Benefits assessable on all employees

13.93 Although the benefits legislation is commonly thought of as applying to 'higher paid' employees, some benefits are assessable on *all* employees. These are:

1 All vouchers other than those for meals worth less than 15p per day). Note that:

   (a) vouchers exchangeable for cash are taxable as earnings ITEPA 2003, s 7; and

   (b) a travel voucher includes a season ticket.

2 Gifts of assets. The second-hand value is assessable. It may be possible to argue that the gift was not 'by reason of the employment' but was made to the employee in a personal capacity, see *Reed v Seymour* (1927) 11 TC 625, HL, although HMRC can be expected to challenge this.

3 Living accommodation, where the rules in ITEPA 2003, s 7 apply to determine the value.

4 Payments made by the employer to meet the employee's pecuniary liability, such as telephone bills or school fees (*Hartland v Diggines* (1926) 10 TC 247; *Nicoll v Austin* (1935) 19 TC 531).

National Insurance

13.94 From 6 April 2000, Class 1A NICs are due on all benefits unless *either* Class 1 already applies, *or* the benefit is:

- covered by a dispensation;
- included in a PAYE Settlement Agreement;
- provided to employees (other than directors) earning less than £8,500;
- a reimbursed expense which is wholly for business; or

- shares or options. In some cases these will already be subject to a Class 1 NIC charge.

13.95 In years before 2000/1, benefits in kind were not generally subject to NICs. However, Class 1A NICs have been due on cars and fuel since 1991, and NICs were also payable where the company settled the employee's liability rather than providing the asset or benefit directly. Thus if a company provided clothing for its employees, there were no NICs; if it reimbursed the employees for the cost of the clothing, NICs were payable. It was generally possible to replace contracts between the employee and a supplier with a contract between the company and the supplier, and thus avoid the NICs. However, the Inspector may resist this where the benefit being provided is clearly an individual's personal liability, such as a child's school fees, although a properly structured contractual agreement may withstand attack.

13.96 The reimbursement of expenses is strictly subject to NICs ie there is no deduction equivalent to the tax rules. However, reimbursements could be excluded if 'they are specific and distinct payments of, or a contribution towards, expenses actually incurred by the employee in carrying out his work'.

13.97 It is important to bear in mind that Class 1A National Insurance only arises on benefits provided to employees who are themselves liable to Class 1 National Insurance on their earnings. If therefore benefits are provided to inpat employees who are continuing to have Social Security deductions collected in some overseas territory then Class 1A National Insurance will not arise on any benefits they may receive.

Benefits assessable on higher paid employees and all directors

13.98 A 'higher paid' employee is one who is remunerated at the rate of £8,500 per year (ITEPA 2003, s 66(4)). There two potential traps for the unwary:

1. benefits and reimbursed expenses must be included in calculating the £8,500, even if these are covered by a dispensation or would be allowable under the normal expenses rules;
2. the £8,500 is a *rate* of pay. Thus an employee paid £2,000 a month for three months of the year is 'higher paid' within the definition.

13.99 However, employee pension contributions on a 'net pay' basis and payroll giving amounts are both deductible in this calculation.

13.100 At the time of writing this update there are proposals to overhaul of these rules and to take out the current concessions to 'lower paid' workers.

13.101 A director is within the scope of the benefits legislation irrespective of his earnings level unless he has no material interest in the company and either is a full-time working director or the company is a charity or non-profit-making concern (TA 1988, ss 167–168).

13.102 Benefits and reimbursed expenses are taxable if they are made or provided 'by reason of the employment'. Although the HMRC Manual says that 'the legislation deems this to be the case if it is the employer who is making or providing them' (ITEPA 2003, s 71), there remain cases where something can be provided by the employer to the employee which is not a benefit, if it is not given in return for 'acting as or being an employee' (*Hochstrasser v Mayes* (1959) 38 TC 673; *Mairs v Haughey* [1993] STC 569). Nevertheless it must be accepted that the deeming provision is wide ranging in scope.

13.103 Points which may be picked up on a Revenue review include the following:

1. Any amounts paid to the employee's family or household must also be included on the P11D (or P9D, where applicable). Note, however, that 'family or household' does not include an unmarried partner who is not a dependant or a member of the employee's household (ITEPA 2003, s 721(5)).
2. The amount included on the P11D or P9D must be the full VAT-inclusive cost. The fact that some or all of the VAT may be recovered by the employer from Customs and Excise is irrelevant.

Self-assessment

13.104 Under self-assessment the employer is required to show the cash equivalent value of the items included on P11Ds and P9Ds. Suffice it to say that under self-assessment the need to understand the benefits legislation and the penalties for non-compliance are both greater than before 1996/97(when self-assessment came in to force).

Value of benefits

13.105 The general rule on valuing a benefit is that the employee is taxable on the money's worth of the benefit, ie its cash equivalent. ITEPA 2003, s 203(2) and ITEPA 2003, s 204 states that the cash equivalent of the benefit is its cost, less any part made good by the employee to those providing the benefit. VAT is included whether or not it is recoverable by the employer.

13.106 The case of *Pepper v Hart* (1992) 65 TC 421 established that by 'cost' the statute did not mean full cost but marginal cost. Thus an airline employee who has the use of a spare seat on the airline which would otherwise be unused is only taxed on the extra cost to the airline of carrying one more passenger, not on the total cost of the flight divided by the number of passengers.

13.107 HMRC have agreed that the marginal cost principle should apply to in-house benefits and to the use of assets employed in the business. Thus where a telephone is provided for business use it is accepted that the employee does not have to pay a proportion of the line rental or any other standing charges. However, there are cases other than in-house benefits and assets used in the business where marginal cost can be applied. Where appropriate the Revenue can be successfully challenged on this restrictive interpretation of *Pepper v Hart*.

13.108 A further point to note is that where an employee is charged for part of the cost of the benefit, there may be VAT on the amount so charged, depending on the normal VAT rules. The area in practice most affected by this used to be payments for the private use of company cars but this has now changed. However, the same point continues to apply to other supplies, such as the use of holiday accommodation.

Areas likely to be investigated

13.109 In investigating the taxation of benefits, the Revenue official will concentrate on areas where the employer is most likely to have made mistakes. Some of the main ones are covered below. It should, however, be emphasised that this is a review of vulnerabilities and not a complete summary of the benefits legislation. In particular, for years 2000/01 and subsequently, the National Insurance costs should be taken into account.

Accommodation (ITEPA 2003, s 97 – ITEPA 2003, s 113)

13.110 Where living accommodation is provided by the employer for employees, HMRC may check the following:

1. That any job-related accommodation (ITEPA 2003, s 99(1)) is so in fact. Accommodation is job-related and thus exempt from tax if it is either:
   - (a) *necessary* for the proper performance of the duties, or
   - (b) provided for the *better* performance of the duties in an employment where the provision of accommodation is *customary*, or
   - (c) required to protect the employee's *security*.

   The difficult area here is (b), which is subject to erosion by HMRC. For example, they are currently challenging the customary right of cemetery attendants to live on site, although most people would not consider this to be a perk. In job-related accommodation cases it may be worth considering an appeal to the Commissioners if the facts are strong and HMRC continue to challenge the position.

The job-related exemption does not, however, apply to the payment by the employer for household furniture, which is subject to the 20% rule for assets. Nor does it apply to the payment by the employer of household bills or ancillary costs such as cleaning. However, it should be noted that:

(a) P9D employees escape tax if the liability is met directly by the employer, but not if the employer reimburses the employee's costs;

(b) structural alterations, or alterations which would be the landlord's responsibility under the Landlord and Tenant Act 1985, s 11 are also not taxable;

(c) where the accommodation is provided in an institution, such as a hospital or school, the benefit of such ancillary costs as cleaning can be reduced using *Pepper v Hart* principles;

(d) where there is a liability, it is capped at 10% of the employee's net emoluments, ie his emoluments after deducting pension contributions, capital allowances and allowable expenses and before including the benefit of the household costs (ITEPA 2003, s 315).

2 That the calculation has been carried out correctly. This is based on the rateable value; for new properties with no rateable value an estimate is used (IR Press Release of 19 April 1990).

3 That 'expensive' accommodation (broadly that which cost more than £75,000 (ITEPA 2003, s 105)) has been correctly identified and that the benefit has been accurately calculated. Note here that properties which originally cost less than £75,000 do not fall within the 'expensive' category even if the current market value is more than that, unless improvements subsequent to the purchase and before the year of assessment, together with the purchase price, have taken the cost above £75,000.

4 That any 'perk' accommodation, such as London flats or holiday homes, have been correctly ssessed.

5 That any accommodation provided to a shadow director has been taxed.

13.111 Many employers who provide expensive accommodation set up lease premium arrangements to minimise the benefit in kind charge. These arrangements work with the employer paying a premium to the landlord which then means that the monthly rent is reduced. On this basis given the rent is reduced then the benefit in kind is reduced.

If such arrangements have been organised HMRC at the time of any review would want to be satisfied that there is a valid arrangement in place and it is worth checking whether the arrangement was cleared with HMRC at the outset. It is the opinion of HMRC that these arrangements are only applicable when the lease premium covers a period in excess of 12 months.

Assets used by employees (ITEPA 2003, s 203(3))

13.112 Where an asset remains the property of the employer but the employee can use it privately, the taxable benefit is on the 'annual value of the use of the asset, unless specific provisions exist to tax it separately, such as company cars. The 'annual value' is 20% of the market value of the asset when first used privately. Points to note in an audit context are that:

1. the 20% charge is replaced by the actual cost of hiring the asset if this is greater;
2. if the original cost is enhanced by further expenditure, this must be added when calculating the annual value;
3. if ownership of an asset is transferred to an employee, the normal rule is that there is only a benefit if the asset is transferred at less than market value at the date of transfer. However, these rules are amended where there has been private use, see ITEPA 2003, s 203(3);
4. the cost of the asset includes VAT, whether or not this can be recovered by the employer;
5. if the asset is provided part way through the fiscal year, there is no pro-rating of the benefit charge;
6. if the private use of an asset has been prohibited, the company can argue that there was no benefit (*Gilbert v Hemsley* (1981) 55 TC 419);
7. from 2000/1 there is a specific exemption for any assets where the private use is 'not significant'. This covers the use of telephones, photocopiers and fax machines, as well as computers provided for work which do not fall within the ITEPA 2003, s 320 exemption. Unsurprisingly, this relief does not extend to the private use of aeroplanes, boats or cars, even if private use is not significant.

Cars

13.113 The provision of cars for employees is a fruitful area for a compliance review. Under self-assessment employers are required to calculate the cash equivalent of the benefits. This will increase the employer's exposure to interest and penalties.

13.114 The cost of incorrect handling of company cars is compounded when one looks at Class 1A contributions. If an error is made in calculating the value of the car, or the business miles, this will affect the value of the car and the fuel for both tax and Class 1A purposes. Thus an error in this area can prove extremely expensive.

13.115 Particular points to note are that:

1 All cars with private use have been included on the P11Ds. A fleet listing may be used for this purpose. Check especially:

- (a) new cars;
- (b) second cars;
- (c) cars provided other than by the company's fleet department, eg by a branch for use by a salesman;
- (d) hire cars provided before the employee's company car could be made available.

2 Since 1994/95 cars have been included on the P11D at original market value, not cost.

- (a) The original market value is broadly the manufacturer's list price, and is defined as the price which was 'published by the car's manufacturer, importer or distributor (as the case may be) as the inclusive price appropriate for a car of that kind if sold in the United Kingdom singly in a retail sale in the open market on the relevant day (ITEPA 2003, s 216(3)). The inclusive price means the price including delivery, VAT, customs duty and car tax.
- (b) Particular care is needed when the car is acquired second-hand, as the original market value must still be used, not the second-hand cost.
- (c) As the definition in s 216(3) quoted at (a) above makes clear, cars obtained by the employer at a volume discount must be included at the price that would have been charged if only a single car had been bought by a retail customer.

3 Any accessories also need to be treated correctly (ITEPA 2003, s 125). Standard accessories will be included in the car's list price. If optional accessories are provided with the car, then their price must be added to the list price when calculating the total price of the car. Note that:

- (a) carphones provided by the employer are exempt;
- (b) only those optional accessories attached to the car are added to the price (this includes accessories such as a roof-rack which is attached although it can be removed, but does not include emer-

gency triangles, first aid kits, car rugs, etc – in practice the value of such excluded items can be regarded as *de minimis*, although strictly there is an annual value charge of 20% on their cost;

(c) optional accessories paid for by the employee such as car stereo equipment are not added to the car price;

(d) optional accessories necessarily required for the employee's job, such as a towbar, are also not added to the price;

(e) the removal of an item from the car which would have been provided as standard does not reduce the list price;

(f) the price to be used for accessories, as for the car, is the open market list price and not the actual cost (ITEPA 2003, s 126). Personalised number plates on a company car are not generally assessable (SE 3439);

(h) complex rules apply to replacement accessories.

4 Where the individual 'in the year concerned … is required, as a condition of the car being available for his private use, to pay any amount of money for that use' the scale charge can be reduced. The strict wording here means that if the payment is not *required*, or the requirement was not *in the year concerned*, the Inspector may argue that the payment was ineffective. He may also question whether the payment was for private use, or merely, for example, to obtain a better model than that otherwise available at his grade. The company should have made clear the purpose of the contribution in its documentation (IR *Tax Bulletin* November 1991).

From 1 August 1995 there is no need to charge VAT on the private use payment, provided the input tax is also excluded (VAT Information Sheet 12/95 of 1 June 1995). Different rules applied before 1 August, see Customs and Excise News Release 9/92 of 19 June 1992.

5 Capital contributions to the cost of the car by the employee reduce the price of the car for assessment purposes, as long as the contribution does not exceed £5,000 (ITEPA 2003, s 132). Note that this only applies to reduce the value of the car when used by that employee and not when it is transferred to another employee.

6 Where a car is classified as a pool car, the Inspector will check that the strict conditions in ITEPA 2003, s 167(1) are being complied with. These are that:

(a) the car is available to, and actually used by, more than one employee and is not ordinarily used by any one of them to the exclusion of the others;

(b) any private use of the car by any of the employees is merely incidental to its business use;

(c) it is not normally kept overnight at or in the vicinity of the residence of any of the employees except while it is being kept on premises occupied by the person providing the car.

Note that *all* the conditions must be met. Pool cars are a frequent target of Inspectors and can cost employers significant sums in settlement where cars do not in practice meet the requirements.

Particularly difficult is the second requirement and the interpretation of 'merely incidental', which is a qualitative test. If the private use follows from the business use then the incidental test is passed, but not if the private use of the car is independent of its business use (HMRC have a rule of thumb that a car is not regarded as 'normally kept overnight' at employees' homes if the total number of nights on which it is taken home by employees, for whatever reason, is less than 60% of the total number of nights in the period under review (IR Booklet 480)). However they also warn, at SE 3492, that:

> 'If a car is taken home often enough to approach the 60 per cent limit – though without breaking it – it is unlikely that all the home to work journeys will satisfy the "merely incidental" test.'

Note that where a chauffeur employed to drive pool cars is obliged to take the car home overnight this will not disqualify the car from being a pool car.

7 The Inspector will also check that there has been correct calculation of the total taxable car benefit. In addition to items 1 to 6 above this will include adjustments to the list price for:

(a) business mileage;

(b) cars more than four year old at the end of the tax year (TA 1988 Sch 6, para 5 and TA 1988, s 168(5)(b) and (d) respectively) – note that this applies even if the car is not kept to the end of the fourth year; in respect of periods prior to 2002/03;

(c) periods when the car was unavailable – the period of unavailability must be for at least 30 consecutive days and it is not enough that the driver cannot drive for the period, eg because of illness or a driving ban (TA 1988, Sch 6, paras 6 and 9);

(d) the 50% uplift on second cars (TA 1988 Sch 6, para 10(5)).

8 Where a company car is sold to an employee at less than the open market value the difference will be assessable as a benefit on the employee. If the price at which the car was transferred is significantly different from that given for a car of that age and type in, say, *Glass's Guide*, then the

employer may need to prove that the market value of this particular car was less than would be expected, eg because the car was in poor condition.

9 Although car parking is exempt from tax under ITEPA 2003, s 237(2) there is an NIC cost if the car parking charge at an employee's permanent place of work is reimbursed to the employee (CWG2 (2000) page 75).

10 Where a chauffeur is used by an employee for private journeys, his costs are taxable on the employee. SP 2/96 discusses HMRC's view on the use of a chauffeur to collect senior personnel from home so they can work in the car. While discouraging, the statement of practice does not preclude a claim that such a car is a pool car and that the private use is incidental, but it does increase the difficulty of having such a claim accepted. If it is not, then the Inspector will seek the cost of both car and fuel benefit, as well as the chauffeur costs.

The latter is based on the relevant proportion of his wages, including waiting time, overtime, pension contributions, and NIC costs. The amount of exposure can be reduced if the chauffeur does other jobs.

11 Parking fines are taxable on an employee if the penalty notice was actually handed to him at the time of the offence, or if the employee owns the car. But if the notice was fixed to a car owned by the employer, and the employer pays the fine as the registered owner, there is no Schedule E liability on the employee. The Revenue Manual says that:

> 'If the employee voluntarily pays a fine in these circumstances, and the employer reimburses it, the employee will be chargeable on the emolument arising. A deduction for the expense may then be allowed to the employer.'
>
> (IM 699)

Where the fine is not taxed on the individual, HMRC will, however, seek to disallow it in the company's tax computations. This is on the basis that it was not 'wholly and exclusively' in the course of the company's trade (*CIR v Alexander von Glehn & Co Ltd*, (1920) 12 TC 232).

13.116 A number of employers have offered employee car ownership schemes which uses their purchasing power to obtain discounts for employees to permit the employee to purchase a car from a third party provider. This provider offers an arrangement to manage the vehicle to ensure the vehicle is maintained and with a guaranteed buy back price on the vehicle at the end of the loan period. In addition employers involved in this area will often provide insurance on the vehicle to ensure this is adequately insured for any business travel.

13.117 It is the case that the employer will often support the employee car ownership scheme with some financial support which is either paid directly to the employee or to a third party eg the provider. It is the case at the time of any employer compliance review that HMRC will wish to ensure that any financial support met by the employer is identified and tax/NIC on this correctly dealt with.

13.118 To make employer car ownership schemes financially viable many employers will use the approved mileage allowance payments (AMAP) to cushion the tax impact on any payment made to the employee. This is an area which will be of particular interest to HMRC who will want to be certain the payment fits in to the category of approved mileage allowances and, in regard to National Insurance, falls within the appropriate earnings period. The rules at reg 22A are complex but need to be followed to ensure that the NIC relief can be obtained. This is a very topical issue for HMRC.

13.119 The rules on vans changed over recent years and the level of the benefit is now significantly increased to £3,000. However, the benefit only arises if the van is made available for private use. The change in the rules however take of private use normal commuting journey. Therefore if the vans use is available to the employee for business travel but is taken home each day then no benefit will arise subject to the employee not being permitted to use the van for additional private use. At the time of any HMRC they will want to ensure that the policy and practice of employers do not permit unlimited private use.

Credit cards

13.120 These are taxed under the vouchers legislation, ITEPA 2003, s 7. Employers should ensure that any corporate credit cards are properly controlled, so that expenditure is analysed between private and business. There is no tax liability if all private expenditure is reimbursed to the employer, and there is also no tax on credit card interest or annual/joining fees for the card (SE 2011).

Commissions and discounts

13.121 Until the publication of HMRC Statement of Practice SP4/97, the taxation of commissions, rebates and discounts was in disarray. SP4/97 states that where an employee receives commission by reason of his employment, this is taxable. If in cash, the amounts should be subjected to PAYE. If invested, for instance in a financial product, then the value of the uplift should be reported on the employee's P11D. Particular areas of interest or difficulty include:

- If the employee receives a discount rather than a commission, there will be no tax if either the discount is also available to the public or the amount paid by the employee is above cost to the employer (*Pepper v Hart* (1992), 65 TC 421);
- The taxable commission can be reduced by any rebate which passes the 'wholly exclusively and necessarily' test. This is likely to be the case where the product is sold to a third party at arm's length, but employers should beware of rebates passed on to friends and relatives.
- The previous Statement, SP 5/95 contained many errors, and its predecessor, SP 3/79 was much narrower in scope. The confusion over taxability could be used as a defence against too robust an attack by the Revenue's officials on past years.

Conferences

13.122 The official is likely to ask if the employees attend conferences, and be particularly interested in any which are overseas and/or where a partner is invited. He will ask to see itineraries and programmes for the conference, as well as other relevant documentation, such as invitations. Because of the cost of such meetings, especially those overseas, and the number of attendees, the expense of a settlement in this area can be substantial. The official is likely to ask a number of questions.

13.123 *What is the business content?* The Revenue official may argue that any business purpose was *de minimis*, indeed a mere front for the overseas trip. The Schedule E Manual (SE 4261) instructs him as follows:

> 'Overseas trips variously described as conferences, conventions or seminars are often no more than incentives intended either to reward past performance or to motivate employees for the future. Although a minimal "business" element such as an address by a company executive may have been included in the programme do not give a deduction if it otherwise consists of social occasions, excursions and leisure activities.'

13.124 Where the conference does have some business content, the best the company can achieve is a reasonable apportionment of costs between business and private, but the Revenue now discourage this. Their Manual says:

> 'Avoid accepting an apportionment of travel expenditure on a percentage basis calculated by looking at the relative time spent on business and non-business activities. Such an apportionment cannot

be readily justified in law. In any potentially contentious case an "all or nothing" approach should be taken with regard to travel costs.'
(SE 4260).

13.125 *Was the trip necessarily incurred?* Here HMRC may not accept that a conference was necessary if the employee himself decided to go (*Owen v Burden* (1971) 47 TC 476). Senior employees should therefore ensure that they are 'instructed' to attend, and do not simply authorise their own attendance. Similarly HMRC may argue that a seminar to improve an employee's qualifications to do his job or to keep his knowledge up to date is not allowable (*Humbles v Brooks* (1962) 40 TC 500; *Parikh v Sleeman* (1990) 63 TC 75), unless the education forms an integral part of the performance of the duties of the employment.

13.126 *Did partners attend?* Attendance of partners at a conference is likely to increase the Revenue's doubts about the business purpose of the conference. In addition they will check whether the cost of the spouse's attendance has been included on the P11D for the employee. The following should be noted:

1 There is no benefit where the person attending is not a member of the employee's family or household (ITEPA 2003, s 721(5)). The employee must show that the expense of taking his spouse with him is necessarily incurred in the performance of his duties. In assessing whether the 'necessarily' test is satisfied, the Revenue will ask whether his duties would have required someone else to go with him, such as a secretary or interpreter. The company will need to prove that either:

   (a) the spouse has some special skill or qualification associated with her partner's job which is needed on the trip (although not necessarily full-time). An example might be where the wife is a competent linguist and acts as an interpreter at business meetings; or

   (b) the wife's presence is essential to act as hostess at a series of business entertaining occasions which the employee is required to organise as part of his duties. It is insufficient that the employee and his wife merely attend functions where other guests are accompanied by their spouses; or

   (c) the employee's health is so poor that it would be unreasonable for him to travel alone.

Entertaining clients

13.127 This has long been a favourite of HMRC, who have a dual weapon:

- ICTA 1988, s 577(1)(a) prohibits a deduction for entertaining costs from *trading profits*.

- Subsection 1(b) states that no deduction for such expenses shall be made from emoluments chargeable to tax under Schedule E.

- However, subsection (3) prohibits a double disallowance where the employer pays for, or reimburses, the cost of the entertaining, and the cost is disallowed in the trading computation. Where this is the case, the employee still has to satisfy the test in ITEPA 2003, s 328(1).

13.128 HMRC may thus wish to check that there was a genuine business reason for the entertainment, and that the company is not simply being used as a tax-efficient vehicle for private entertaining by senior management or directors.

13.129 It is true that genuine entertainment of third-party business contacts, such as customers or suppliers, would qualify for relief under s 198. However, in such cases HMRC may check that the amounts have been correctly identified as disallowable in the company's corporation tax return (TA 1988, s 577(3)). Indeed, under self-assessment the P11D requires the employer to state whether any entertaining expenses included on the P11D (ie those not covered by a dispensation) have been or will be disallowed.

13.130 The position is different where the employer is a non-trading entity, such as a local council or charity (SE 4151).These organisations, and their employees, are not affected by s 577 because any entertainment which they may provide is not 'in connection with a trade' and therefore is not 'business entertainment' as defined in s 577(5). The employees of such organisations are therefore entitled to a deduction for any entertainment expenses they may incur which satisfy the conditions of ITEPA 2003, s 328(1) provided only that the expense is incurred out of their taxable emoluments.

13.131 The position is different again where the employer is a representative office of an overseas company. In that case the company's profits, whilst chargeable to tax overseas, are not subject to UK tax. As a result there can be no disallowance on the company under s 577(1)(a), and s 577(3) thus cannot operate to protect the employee, while s 577(1)(b) denies the employee a deduction for business entertainment expenses irrespective of whether the expenses are, or are not, reimbursed by the employer. This often results in the employees being taxed under Schedule E in respect of their reimbursed entertainment expenses with no possibility of an off-setting deduction under s 198. This harsh position is set out in *Tax Bulletin* 42, August 1999. However, it may be possible to change the Revenue's mind if the overseas company is in a treaty country, on the grounds that the tax exemption derives from the treaty. There is always the possibility of arguing that the position is unfair and not within the Revenue's commitment to human rights which requires that all taxpayers should be treated equally.

Entertaining – staff

13.132 For many years, HMRC adopted a tolerant attitude where staff entertaining was concerned. As long as the cost was either included as a benefit on their P11D (the technically correct position) or disallowed in the company's tax computation, they accepted the position. However, a stricter approach was set out in *Tax Bulletin* 42, August 1999, which said that the disallowing of staff entertaining 'is inconsistent with the concept of self assessment, and should no longer be adopted'. The old approach will continue to apply for accounting periods ending not later than 30 April 2000 (*Tax Bulletin* 45, February 2000); thus for these earlier periods it should be possible to agree a disallowance in the company computations in preference to the more onerous (and usually more expensive) adjustment to an individual's emoluments.

13.133 There remain many areas of difficulty, eg where the employer entertains an employee or two employees have lunch 'on the firm' this is taxable on the employees as a benefit. This includes a meal out as a reward for doing a good job, or having lunch in a restaurant to provide a relaxed ambience for a team meeting. In general the Revenue take the view that 'meetings over a meal with other members of the same organisation are normally social, with work matters being insufficient to make the meeting a necessary business occasion' (ECM 13029). You can therefore expect that such costs will be challenged.

13.134 However, the Revenue are prepared to accept that there is no benefit where the nature of some meetings would qualify for ITEPA 2003, s 328(1) relief, eg:

1 meetings for the negotiation of the renewal or alteration of a service contract; or

2 a briefing visit where local staff are detained beyond normal hours to fit in with a visit from head office.

13.135 However, the employer is on weaker ground when the person being entertained is from a branch rather than a connected company, as a branch has no separate existence. Here some use may be made of HMRC's agreement that 'where the colleague being entertained would be entitled to tax free subsistence, (his) costs can be discounted' (NAG 5.130).

13.136 The company has no grounds for a defence where the individuals are from the same site, unless the costs involved are no more than they would have been had they eaten in the company's subsidised or free restaurant.

13.137 A problem may arise where one employee has paid for the mutual staff entertaining, in that the full bill should have been entered on his P11D. However, HMRC will normally agree that the bill should be shared among all attendees. Where a higher rate taxpayer paid the bill, this apportionment will have the effect of reducing the overall tax charge. In practice, the company may wish to include such items in a PAYE settlement agreement.

Gifts

13.138 Gifts provided by the employer are generally taxable under the deeming provisions of ITEPA 2003, s 71. However, HMRC will accept that there is no benefit if the gift is either provided on personal grounds (eg a wedding present) or as a mark of personal esteem (SE 1182). See also long service awards and third party benefits.

Loans

13.139 Cheap or interest free loans supplied by or by arrangement with the employer are taxable if they fall within the detailed rules of ITEPA 2003, s 7(5). Particular points to note are as follows:

1. Certain loans are classed as 'qualifying' and are exempt from these provisions (ITEPA 2003, s 180). These include loans to buy into a partnership, to buy shares in, or lend money to, a close company, and to buy machinery or plant for use by the partnership or employment. From 6 April 2000, loans to acquire a main residence are no longer qualifying, and from the same date qualifying loans do not have to be included on a P11D (ITEPA 2003, s 180(50)). For earlier years the loan should have been reported by the employer, leaving it for the individual to claim ITEPA 2003, s 328(1) relief. However, it would be unusual for HMRC to take this point.
2. Allowable relocation loans are also not a benefit, but see para **13.146** for details of the rules which must be satisfied here.
3. Loans on the same terms as those provided to members of the public are excluded (ITEPA 2003, s 180(5))), if the lending of money is part of the business of the employer. A deregulatory amendment introduced by FA 2000, Sch 10(5)(1) improved the position for such loans, and the rules were backdated to cover the previous six years. Previously the 'same terms' requirement was strictly interpreted, so that a relaxation of lending criteria or a waiver of fees for staff loans, as compared to those for the public, caused the loan to fall outside this exemption (IR Interpretation, August 1994).
4. There is a *de minimis* exemption for cheap or interest-free loans below £5,000. Where the total amount loaned has exceeded £5,000, the full amount, and not just the excess, will come within the rules. The total

value of loans to each individual must therefore be checked. In practice loans can be granted from different sources within the company, eg one department may provide season ticket loans, and another loans for car purchase. Because all season ticket loans are below the *de minimis* amount, they may have been ignored when looking at whether there is a benefit.

5 The *de minimis* exemption is only valid if the loan does not exceed the £5,000 limit at *any time* in the tax year.

6 The loan interest must not simply be *payable* in a tax year, it must actually be paid (ITEPA 2003, s 7(5))). Where the loan is interest bearing but the interest has not been paid, the loan must be reported on the P11D. The employee can recover the tax charged once he has paid the interest (s 174(1)). In an audit situation the employer should check whether the employee has now paid the interest, and if so should seek to limit the cost of settlement to sufficient interest to cover the period during which HMRC would have had the tax if the P11D had been correct originally.

7 Loan guarantees are also included within the loan benefits legislation.

8 In some cases the company may argue that the loan has not been granted 'by reason of' the employment, but because of the private circumstances of the employees. They may find support for this in *Hochstrasser v Mayes* (1959) 38 TC 673.

9 Loans written off are taxable, even when the write-off happens after the individual has left (ITEPA 2003, s 188(2)).

10 For years before 2000/01 a benefit could arise if the loan interest rate fell below the Revenue approved rate for any part of the tax year. This could happen where the company follows a market rate and HMRC rate falls more slowly. For 2000/1 and subsequent years, the official rate is set at the beginning of the tax year, making it easier to monitor whether a benefit has arisen (IR Press Release, 25 January 2000).

11 Under self-assessment the actual benefit of the loan must be calculated. HMRC will check a sample of such calculations to ensure that they have been carried out correctly.

Long service awards

13.140 The tax rules exempt certain long service awards from tax. However, the requirements of the concession have to be met; it is not enough that, for example, the total sum spent is less than that allowed by the Concession but the gifts are made more frequently. A small gift made every 5 years can cause expensive gifts made after 20 years to be taxed.

Mobile phones

13.141 Finance Act 1999 changed the rules for mobile phones, to the enormous relief of all those involved in PAYE reviews with the possible exception of the HMRC official (ITEPA 2003, s 316(1)). For years from 1999/2000 onwards, the following points are relevant:

1. mobile phones provided by the employer are exempted from tax from 6 April 1999 (however, limited to one phone per employee);
2. however this does not cover the reimbursement of private calls made on the employee's own phone, which remain taxable;
3. neither does it cover the cost of vouchers used by employees to make calls, unless covered by ITEPA 2003, s 328(1).

13.142 For years before 1999/2000, mobile phones were a notoriously difficult area for employers to police, as many departments of an organisation may have had authority to buy such phones, and their existence may not have been notified to the tax department. Apart from this general control issue, the following points should also be considered:

1. There was no tax charge on a mobile phone used privately if the employee was both *required* to pay, and did pay, the cost of any private use. If the employee was not required to pay, eg by written instructions before the beginning of a tax year, even if the costs were reimbursed, HMRC had argued that this would not allow the employee to escape a tax charge. However, the wording of the section was that the payment must be made *for* a tax year and thus retrospection should be permitted.
2. The reimbursement must have been of the full cost, not just the call charges. Full cost required that the employee paid a proper proportion of the equipment rental or, if the employer owned the equipment, the 20% annual value charge. In practice this was generally covered by requiring the employee to reimburse private calls plus a certain mark-up.
3. The tax was chargeable in full even if only one private call had been made and not reimbursed. There were no *de minimis* rules. However, if the telephone was first made available part way through the year, or ceased being available at a date during the year, or was unavailable for at least 30 days at some point, the charge could be reduced.

Personal incidental expenses (ITEPA 2003, s 240)

13.143 Employees often incur incidental expenses when staying away from home, such as laundry, personal phone calls and newspapers. Until FA 1995 these items tended to be covered by dispensations, although under strict law they do not meet the requirements of ITEPA 2003, s 328.

13.144 From 6 April 1995 a specific relief was introduced. Now, an employee is not taxable on personal incidental expenses up to £5 per night (£10 outside the UK) if he is away on business for at least one night. The new relief was heralded as deregulatory, in practice it is more likely to cause problems for employers when audited.

13.145 Particular note should be taken of the following:

1. If the payment is more than £5, the whole amount is taxable and subject to NICs.
2. If an employee stays away for several nights consecutively, the total allowance is the £5 times the number of nights away. For example, where an employee stays away for four nights and claimed £5 on the first night, £5 on the second, £6 on the third and £4 on the fourth he would be within the exemption because the total does not exceed £5 × 4. Where the number of nights is not consecutive, no averaging is allowed.
3. Where the limit is exceeded the employer should check that the employee was not bearing some costs of other employees. If he was, HMRC will accept an apportionment (HMRC Booklet 480 App 8).

Prizes

13.146 A prize won in a competition only open to employees is within the scope of Schedule E. See also gifts (para **13.138**), suggestion schemes (para **13.152**), and third party benefits (para **13.154**).

Relocations

13.147 The rules for relocations were made infinitely more complex by the introduction in 1993 of TA 1988, Sch 11A. This lays down detailed rules as to which relocation costs are allowable, or, as the legislation puts it, eligible. Eligible expenses of up to £8,000 per relocation will not be taxed.

13.148 Note that there is no requirement for overpayments of such eligible expenses to go through PAYE, even where the excess is a cash sum. However, payments of ineligible amounts must be taxed under the normal rules, which include the application of PAYE where appropriate.

13.149 In particular a reviewer will check that:

1 The employer has clearly separated eligible and ineligible relocation costs, and that the latter have been either taxed under PAYE or included on the employee's P11D as appropriate. Ineligible costs include:

(a) abortive relocation costs (ie where the employee doesn't actually relocate after all);

(b) council tax;

(c) duplicate costs of any items which are not 'domestic', such as school fees or season ticket costs;

(d) higher cost housing payments for moving to a more expensive area – these were allowed, within limits, until the new legislation was introduced;

(e) transport and installation costs of non-domestic items, such as boats or horses;

(f) travel allowances paid to employees who choose not to relocate.

2 The £8,000 limit on eligible expenses has not been exceeded in the tax year, and if it has, whether the excess has been included on the employee's P11D.

3 Where a relocation crosses a tax year, the amount spent in the previous tax year has been carried forward in calculating whether the £8,000 limit has been exceeded.

4 The time limits on paying or providing eligible relocation expenses/benefits have been adhered to. If expenses have been paid after the time limit, has permission been sought from the local Inspector to extend the limit? In practice, where permission has not been sought but it is reasonable to believe that an extension would have been granted had a request been made, the Inspector will generally accept this.

5 The payment of any flat rate allowances as part of the £8,000 limit has been agreed in advance with the local Inspector of Taxes (IR Press Release 14 April 1993). If not, the employer can argue that the allowance should be accepted if it is:

(a) required to be spent on eligible costs; and

(b) broadly within the limits allowed to the civil service. Unfortunately these are no longer published, as each government department has been given authority to set its own limits. The most recent allowances were set in 1993 as follows:

Married householder	£2,705
Single householder	£1,645
Single non-householder	£635

Reasonable increases on these amounts to allow for inflation should be accepted by HMRC.

6 The complex rules for beneficial bridging loans have been complied with. Interest on bridging loans can be included as an eligible cost but only insofar as the £8,000 limit has not been used to cover other eligible relocation expenses. Interest therefore forms the top slice of eligible costs. This unused slice of relocation relief is then used to determine how long the beneficial loan can be outstanding before it becomes taxable. The formula for calculating this is given in ITEPA 2003, s 288(4).

7 Any guaranteed price scheme is being correctly operated. Again, this is complex, and failure may mean that significant sums fall into tax. HMRC explained the legal position in the *Tax Bulletin* of April 1995.

13.150 Note that until 6 April 1998 the Contributions Agency rules on relocation were not affected by the Schedule 11A rules and thus some elements of a relocation package were taxable but not subject to NICs (CWG2 (1998) 78). However for relocations after 6 April 1998 the NI rules broadly follow the tax legislation, although a number of important differences remain. In particular, there is no £8,000 cap for NI purposes, so if an expense qualifies as allowable, no NI was charged, irrespective of the amount. A further year of grace was allowed for relocation payments made via a PSA agreement, with no contributions being due until 1999 (SI 1988/680). Employers should thus analyse the position of their relocated employees with care before agreeing to any audit settlement.

Staff social functions

13.151 The Inspector will check whether staff social functions fall within ITEPA 2003, s 264. It is important to ensure that:

1 the allowable limit (currently £150 per attendee) has not been exceeded;

2 in calculating the £150 the employer has:

(a) included VAT, and

(b) where relevant, travel to the function and accommodation, and

(c) that the cost is on a per head basis of those who actually attended, not those who could have attended;

3 the function was open to employees generally. In practice a number of departmental functions which are of a similar nature will be accepted as falling within this condition;

4 if the allowable limit for a single function has been exceeded, the full amount is taxable and not just the excess;

5 if there have been a number of functions and the total cost is more than £150, HMRC will disregard those functions which total £150 or less but will tax the others in full.

Note that the concession currently in place is more generous than the previous version, and that more restricted rules apply to tax years before 1995/96.

Subsistence

13.152 Along with travel, this is perhaps the most fruitful area of review for an HMRC official. Particular points which will be checked are whether:

1 The payments of subsistence allowances or the reimbursement of actual costs are reasonable in amount. In establishing what is reasonable HMRC generally use the civil service limits as a guide. The employer should resist too rigid an adherence to the civil service limits, which have no statutory basis. What is reasonable depends on the circumstances.

2 Allowances are paid or amounts reimbursed only when the employee is away from his normal place of work or holding a travelling appointment.

3 Meals for late working have been taxed. However, the Revenue concession can be argued to apply if the meals are available to all who work late.

4 Where a working rule agreement applies, the terms have been followed.

5 Complex new rules on travel and subsistence were introduced with effect from 6 April 1998 (ITEPA 2003, s 328). However, it should be noted that subsistence is treated as part of travel, and thus any food or accommodation provided in conjunction with travel which does not fall within the new rules, will itself be taxed and subject to NIC.

Suggestion schemes

13.153 These are exempt from tax if they fall within ITEPA 2003, s 321. Note that the NIC rules are more generous (CWG2 (2000) 70). See also Incentive Valuation Unit.

Telephones

13.154 The official will check whether the employer has reimbursed any part of home telephone costs. See also mobile phones at para **13.142**.

1 All home telephone calls paid should have been included on the P11D (other than necessary business calls). Evidence will be required to support the business calls unless they are covered by a dispensation.

2 Line rental is regarded as taxable (*Lucas v Cattell* (1972) 48 TC 353) unless:

   (a) employees can show that it is genuinely part of their duties to deal with emergencies; or

   (b) the employee's home is the place of employment; or

   (c) the contract for the telephone is in the employer's name; or

   (d) the telephone is used exclusively for business.

In (a) and (b) a proportion of the rental charge is allowable. HMRC generally seeks to allow only the same proportion as the business use of the telephone is of the overall use. In (c) there is no charge to either tax or NICs (*Pepper v Hart*; CWG 2: 79 and (d)).

Third party benefits

13.155 To date this has not been a significant review area but the position is changing with self-assessment. Many gifts are covered by the concession, which exempts from tax gifts received by employees from a third party by reason of their employment and totalling £150 or less from the same source in a single tax year. Until 1995/96 the limit was £100. This concession does not cover gifts provided by, or by arrangement with, the employer. The only review risk here is that if the limit is exceeded the full amount, not just the excess, is taxable.

13.156 The reporting rules for third parties under self-assessment have increased the risks to employers. These cover expenses payments or benefits provided to employees by a third party other than those covered by the concession. They took effect for 1996/97 onwards and require that where a third party benefit is provided, the third party must provide the employee with details of the cash equivalent of the benefit in writing by 6 July after the end of the tax year. The employer of the employee who has received these third party benefits is also required to tell HMRC the name and address of the provider (FA 1995, s 106(9)(c); SAT2 and SAT3). Where the benefit has been provided by arrangement with the employer, the latter must provide details of both the amounts and the name and business address of the other person (FA 1995, s 106(9)(b)).

13.157 These are extensive requirements and, combined with the self-assessment enquiry powers will have a significant effect on companies' audit settlements.

Travel

13.158 Reimbursing employees' travel expenses, or paying an allowance to cover travel costs, is invariably the subject of Revenue review. New legislation on travel and subsistence was finally introduced with effect from 6 April 1998 (ITEPA 2003, s 337). This was supplemented by the publication, in January 1998, of the Revenue's 'Employee Travel: a Tax and NIC Guide for Employers'. This booklet is destined to become the reviewers' bible, and any employer who wishes to ensure compliance with the new rules would be advised to study its numerous examples. The Guide has been further extended by Tax Bulletin articles (*Revenue Tax Bulletin* December 1997; February 1998 and April 1998).

13.159 Problems are likely to arise when considering the operation of:

- the two year rule for site-based employees;
- the interpretation of 'substantially ordinary commuting';
- whether an employee has more than one permanent workplace;
- the difference between employees with an 'area' and those with 'travelling appointments'.

It should be remembered that the Guide is only a guide, not dogma. In cases of dispute, reference should be made both to the legislation and to its purpose: see IRPR 24 September 1997 and 9 January 1998.

13.160 For earlier years, the Revenue will look in particular for:

1. Payment of travel costs other than those necessarily for business. Note that the 'wholly and exclusively' test does not apply to travel, see ITEPA 2003, s 337. This will include any reimbursement of home to work travel other than those included in a WRA, eligible relocation costs, emergency call outs (see point (4) below) and amounts payable on a secondment which is expected to last less than a year (see point (5) below). Note that where an employer reimburses home to work costs HMRC may seek to recover the fuel scale charge which applies when petrol costs for private use are paid by the employer.
2. Cases where employers reimburse business miles. Here the HMRC applied the 'triangular travel' principle. This only allowed the employer to reimburse on a tax-free basis the lower of the actual miles travelled on business and the miles which would have been travelled to reach that location if the employee had set off from his normal place of work rather than from home. Failure to tax any payments in excess of this can be very expensive for the company. However, it should be noted that this principle is a derivation by HMRC from the law, and has never been established as such in either statute or case law. It is unclear whether HMRC would be prepared to take a contested case to court, and an employer faced with a large retrospective liability may want to obtain a counsel's opinion on the law as it stands.

3 Proper controls over mileage reimbursements to ensure that only allowable business miles, according to HMRC's definition, are being reimbursed. The rates of reimbursement will also be reviewed: are they in line with the fixed profit car scheme rules? Have they been agreed with the local Inspector? Excess payments for mileage can be an expensive part of a review settlement, as what appear to be relatively small amounts are spread over a large number of miles and employees. Note that under self-assessment the employer must report details of the mileage paid, including any profit, on P11Ds, unless this has been covered by a dispensation.

4 Transport vouchers (including season tickets and travel passes) provided for any employees by reason of their employment, including those in the form P9D category. These are taxable unless the travel is genuine business and does not include home to work. Employees who worked at a succession of different places (site-based employees) were regarded as having a 'normal place of work' at each site, and thus any reimbursement of travel costs or a travel allowance was taxable as was subsistence. Since the employee was likely to have counted this travelling as business rather than private, the reclassification was also likely to affect his car benefit calculation and the employer's NICs. This has in practice resulted in some very large settlements following HMRC reviews. Contrast this with secondments at point (5) below. Both areas are significantly affected by the new rules.

13.161 In addition, the following general points on the review of travel should be noted:

(1) Cases where an employer pays for or reimburses the cost of late night travel home. This is taxable unless it falls within the concession, which requires that:

   (a) public transport has ceased or could not reasonably be used; and

   (b) the employee travels from home to work by public transport; and

   (c) normally works fairly regular hours; but

   (d) is occasionally required to work late (HMRC in practice accepts that 60 occasions a year or fewer is occasional);

   (e) the pattern of late working must not be regular, eg every Friday.

   The same rules apply to NICs.

(2) Where an employee holds a travelling appointment, the reimbursements or allowances are more flexible and are likely to include travel from home. It may be necessary for the employer to establish that an employee or a group of employees hold a travelling appointment, for which there is no definition in law. HMRC's view is that 'for an employee to hold a

travelling appointment … travel must be a fundamental part of the job and not just to put the employee in a position to do the job' (ECM 13099).

(3) Employees who are based at home and travel from there. These are regarded by HMRC as working from home usually as a matter of personal choice. To have the costs of home to office travel allowed, the employer must demonstrate that it is an objective requirement of the employment that the employee must work at home. Often the Inspector will ask whether the employee has a desk and other facilities on the employer's premises, and if they do will reject the premise that the employee is home-based. Such a finding is expensive for the employer with a number of employees who work in this fashion. It is advisable to obtain clearance in advance of any review that the employees are 'home-based'. The current HMRC position is described at para 2.13.1 of the Consultative Document on Employee Travel of 13 May 1996. For a defence, see *Horton v Young* (1971) 47 TC 60 and HMRC's view of this in SE 4402.

(4) Where an employer pays emergency call-out expenses, these will be taxable unless the employee has given instructions before leaving home and had continuing responsibility for the emergency whilst travelling to the normal place of employment (*Pook v Owen* (1969) 45 TC 571). Health service employees have for some time generally been required to certificate any such travel expenses to say that they met these criteria. If this is not done, the Inspector is likely to attack any such reimbursement.

(5) Under the pre-FA 1998 rules, home to work travel (and subsistence) was not taxable if the employee had a normal place of work and was temporarily seconded to another. For periods before 6 April 1998 the payment was tax free if:

  (a) the absence did not exceed 12 months; and

  (b) the employee returned to his normal place of work at the end of the secondment.

If it became obvious at some point in the period that the employee would not return within 12 months, payments were taxable from that date (P7 (1996) T5). The same rules applied to NIC (NI 269 164:83).

LIABILITY FOR TAX ARISING

13.162 Where an employer does not tax an item which should have been included in PAYE, the primary liability for any back tax, interest and penalties is with the employer). The employee cannot currently be made to pay the tax unless it was reasonable to assume that he knew the item should have been taxed and that it had not been onwards.

13.163 There is a statutory exception for directors, on the basis that 'in practice the failure to deduct tax from remuneration nearly always occurs in respect of certain directors'. So special legislation was introduced to treat the amount of any tax paid by someone other than the director as a benefit chargeable on the director (ITEPA 2003, s 223(7)). Note that this only applies to directors as defined at para **13.101**.

13.164 The position is different for benefits. Here the primary liability for paying the tax rests with the employee, and the employer can therefore refuse to settle the unpaid tax on benefits which is uncovered during a review, and require that HMRC assess the individuals. However, HMRC can penalise the company for filing an incorrect P11D, and this can result in fines of up to £3,000 for each incorrect form.

13.165 The refusal to settle the tax under-deducted on P11Ds can be used judiciously to reduce the costs of a settlement, as HMRC will often be reluctant to go to the trouble and expense of assessing hundreds of employees on what is, individually, often a fairly small amount.

Chapter 14

The new penalty regime

John T Newth FCA FTII FIIT ATT, Independent Tax Journalist

14.1 Tax advisers and accountants have become familiar with the former tax penalty regime under TMA 1970, s 95 and the corresponding legislation for corporation tax defaults, PAYE defaults and VAT offences, as well as the penalties for failure to notify chargeability to tax. However HMRC and the government have taken the view that the imposition of tax penalties was being imposed unevenly, and in the view of HMRC, some penalties were far too lenient for the type of tax offence committed. Another issue was the desire for the standardisation of penalties following the merger of the Inland Revenue and Customs & Excise.

CONSULTATION DOCUMENTS

14.2 Accordingly in March 2005 a consultation paper was published entitled 'HM Revenue & Customs and the Taxpayer: Modernising powers, deterrents and safeguards'. A consultation committee was established and the views of business representatives, the professions and the general public were canvassed.

14.3 A further consultation paper was published one year later in March 2006 entitled 'HM Revenue & Customs and the Taxpayer: Modernising powers, deterrents and safeguards: a consultation on the developing programme of work'. This was followed by the publication of a further consultation document in December 2006 entitled 'A new approach to penalties for incorrect returns'.

14.4 Even more recent was the publication of two further Consultation Documents issued by HMRC on 10 January 2008 in the 'Modernising Powers, Deterrents and Safeguards 'series. One was entitled 'Penalties Reform: The Next Stage', and it broadly confirms the views of HMRC made in the December 2006 Consultation Document.

14.5 The other new Consultation Document was entitled 'A New Approach to Compliance Checks: Responses to Consultation and Proposals'.

14.6 The new measures set out in these latest Consultation Documents will be considered in more detail later in this chapter.

New legislation

14.7 The results of the earlier consultations formed the basis of new legislation that was included in the 2007 Finance Act. The Finance Act 2007, s 97, Sch 24 sets out the new HMRC approach to penalties for incorrect, negligent and fraudulent returns. Legislation regarding penalties for failure to notify and late notification and for deliberate failure to respond to formal HMRC information requests is included in the 2008 Finance Bill at Clause 117, Schedule 40 and Clause 118, Schedule 41. Some of the 2007 Finance Act legislation will be amended accordingly. It is intended that a single penalty regime embracing direct and indirect taxes will be ratified by the 2008 Finance Act.

14.8 Budget included two relevant Budget Notices. BN96 deals with Penalties for Incorrect Returns & Failure to Notify a Taxable Activity. BN97 covers Compliance Checks, and as far as penalties are concerned refers to penalties for failure by the taxpayer to comply with information notices etc.

14.9 The new legislation covers inaccuracies in returns and claims, together with related accounts, documents, statements and declarations. It should also be noted that the new penalty regime does not alter the existing penalty legislation for late filing of self-assessment and CTSA returns, or failure to notify chargeability. However, this aspect, as well as deterrents for obstructing information notices issued by HMRC, has been dealt with by provisions included in the 2008 Finance Bill. Proposals are also made for penalties regarding failure to notify and late filing or returns embracing direct taxation, National Insurance and VAT.

14.10 The new and proposed legislation embrace both direct and indirect taxes, notably income tax, corporation tax, construction industry deductions, PAYE returns and VAT returns. Proposals included in the 2008 Finance Bill are intended to bring other taxes within the new penalty regime. The new penalty provisions do not apply to Tax Credits.

14.11 In effect, the new and proposed legislation replaces the existing s 95 penalty for incorrect returns for income tax purposes, the corresponding CT legislation, penalties imposed in respect of PAYE returns and some sections of the VAT legislation. The 2008 Finance Bill extends the proposed legislation to other taxes and introduces proposals to amend penalties for failure to notify and late filing, and deliberate failure to respond to information notices issued by HMRC.

14.12 Accordingly, the following legislation is or will be repealed:

1 Income tax –Taxes Management Act 1970, ss 93 and 95.

2 Corporation tax – the Finance Act 1998, Sch 18, paras 20(1) and 89(1).

3 PAYE and NIC –Taxes Management Act 1970, s 98A(4).

4 Value added tax –Value Added Tax Act 1994, ss 60, 61 and 62.

5 Corporation tax – the Finance Act 1998, Sch 18, paras 17 and18.

6 The Social Security (Contributions) Regulations 2001, reg 87.

14.13 It must be stressed that this book will be published before the Finance Act 2008 receives Royal Assent, so that the 2008 Finance Bill proposals as originally drafted and referred to are provisional only and are subject to amendment before they become statutory law.

Date of implementation

14.14 The new legislation contained in the Finance Act 2007 commences for income tax return periods commencing after 31 March 2008, where the return is filed after 31 March 2009. Correspondingly, the legislation commences for corporation tax periods for the year ending 31 March 2009 and later where the company has a 12-month accounting period. See also the HMRC Compliance Handbook at CH81001 and subsequent paragraphs.

14.15 Two Statutory Instruments confirm these dates, namely the Finance Act 2007, Sch 24 (Commencement and Transitional Provisions) Order 2008 SI 2008/568 and the Social Security (Contributions) (Amendment No 3) Regulations 2008 (SI 2008/636).

14.16 Two Notices were included in the 2008 Budget and these are expanded on in the 2008 Finance Bill. BN96 refers, in connection with incorrect returns involving 'other taxes' such as inheritance tax and environmental taxes, to return periods commencing on a date on or after 1 April 2009 where the return is due to be filed on or after 1 April 2010. However, the new penalties for failure to notify are expected to have effect for failure to meet notification obligations that arise on or after 1 April 2009.

14.17 BN97 states that information powers and penalties for failure to comply with these obligations will have effect on or after 1 April 2010. Time limits for making assessments and claims will need a transitional period and so will become fully operative on or after 1 April 2010.

14.18 The apparent consequences of the primary legislation, secondary legislation and 2008 Budget Notices and Finance Bill are that, although the penalty legislation is being standardised as regards different taxes, the dates of commencement for different taxes and failure to notify do not coincide.

THE CURRENT PENALTY REGIME

14.19 Those practitioners who undertake investigation and enquiry work on behalf of clients will be familiar with the current penalty regime under TMA 1970, s 95.

14.20 HMRC could impose a mitigable penalty of up to 100% of the tax deemed to have been lost due to fraudulent or negligent conduct of an individual, partnership or company.

14.21 No penalty was imposed where the taxpayer (or his or her adviser) made an error innocently and the error was remedied without delay. Where a penalty was imposed, the 100% maximum was mitigated on the following bases:

1 up to 20% for disclosure or up to 30% for unprompted disclosure;

2 up to 40% for cooperation;

3 up to 40% based on the seriousness of the case (this used to be termed size and gravity).

The total mitigation could not exceed 100%.

14.22 Generally speaking, HMRC have not previously penalised taxpayers for the defaults of agents, as set out in the HMRC Enquiry Manual at EM5140.

14.23 It appears that tax penalties of over 25% were rarely imposed except in serious cases, and this is one of the reasons that led to the consultations and new legislation. The views of HMRC also stated that:

- the average rates of penalties actually charged fell within a narrow band which provided insufficient room to differentiate between different types of behaviour;
- some of the terminology, such as 'negligence' is opaque to most taxpayers;
- there is not one regime but three, which adds to the lack of clarity for taxpayers about the rules and the potential outcomes; and
- the VAT misdeclaration penalty is not explicitly behaviour-rated and the high objective tests means that for many there is no sanction where a return is incorrect due to a failure to take reasonable care.

Whether one agrees with HMRC views or not, it is clear, as will be illustrated later, that the new regime is likely to yield higher penalties in the future in enquiry and investigation cases.

14.24 For failure to notify chargeability under TMA 1970, s 7 within six months of the end of a tax year a mitigable penalty of up to 100% of the tax unpaid at 31 January after the year of assessment could be imposed. The penalty for late submission of a self-assessment return was £100, a further £100 if the return was six months late and a continuing penalty of up to £60 a day in serious cases and where the Commissioners imposed the penalty.

14.25 For failure by an employer to submit returns such as Forms P11D timeously, the penalty was up to £300 plus £60 a day for the continued failure to file after the initial penalty had been imposed.

14.26 For an individual who failed to inform HMRC of the commencement of self-employment within three months of starting, a penalty of £100 could be imposed by the NI Contributions section of HMRC.

14.27 For companies a flat rate penalty of £100 was imposed if the CT return was submitted late within three months of filing date, or £200 in other cases. The amounts were increased to £500 and £1,000 respectively for a third successive failure. For serious delays in filing where the return was not filed within 18 months, an additional tax-related penalty could be imposed of up to 10% of the unpaid tax where the return was filed within two years of the due date or 20% of the unpaid tax in other cases.

TRANSITIONAL RULES

14.28 It is not entirely clear whether the new legislation will be retrospective, but leading commentators have suggested that it will not be. This means that the two penalty regimes will run side by side for the next 20 years or so. The new regime will apply to defaults occurring after 31 March 2008 for defaults in connection with the main taxes and to defaults occurring after 31 March 2009 for other taxes, failure to notify chargeability and obstruction of HMRC information powers. The previous legislation under what were TMA 1970, ss 7, 93 and 95, the Finance Act 1998, Sch 18, paras 17–18 and other existing legislation will apply to tax defaults occurring before either 1 April 2008 or 1 April 2009.

14.29 However, this matter is still open to discussion and consultation, so that taxpayers cannot count on this view at this stage.

THE NEW REGIME

14.30 Finance Act 2007 sets out a new penalty regime for errors and defaults that previously came within the ambit of TMA 1970, s 95 and other legislation that has been repealed. The legislation introduced by Schedule 24 to the Finance Act 2007 applies to income tax, corporation tax, capital gains tax and VAT. HMRC have dealt with the new legislation in detail in the Compliance Handbook in the Manual series at CH81001–CH84950.

Application of penalties

14.31 Tax penalties are applied to 'potential lost revenue' of HMRC. The new regime is intended to focus on taxpayer behaviour. As will be seen in the following paragraphs, penalties are 'stepped' so that they will increase depending on the seriousness of the taxpayer's failure, although 'size and gravity' is not mentioned in the legislation or associated literature. Accordingly the idea is to move from a 'nil' penalty for an innocent mistake to much higher penalties for deliberate understatements of tax, particularly when compounded by concealment. Guidance as to how HMRC will interpret taxpayer behaviour has been published.

Documents subject to the new regime

14.32 These are listed in Sch 24, para 1 and apply to documents which contain an inaccuracy which amounts to or leads to:

1. an understatement of an individual's liability to tax,
2. a false or inflated statement of a loss by an individual, or
3. a false or inflated claim to repayment of tax.

Income tax or capital gains tax

14.33

- Personal tax returns under TMA 1970, s 8.
- Trustee returns under TMA 1970, s 8A.
- Return, statement or declaration in connection with a claim for an allowance, deduction or relief.
- Partnership returns under TMA 1970, s 12AA.
- Statements or declarations in connection with a partnership return under TMA 1970, s 12AB.
- Accounts in connection with a partnership return.

Income tax

14.34 Return for the purposes of PAYE regulations.

Construction industry deductions

14.35 Returns under the CIS Scheme.

Corporation tax

14.36

- Company returns under the FA 1998 , Sch 18, para 3.
- Return, statement or declaration in connection with a claim for an allowance, deduction or relief.
- Accounts in connection with ascertaining liability to tax.

VAT

14.37

- VAT returns.
- Returns, statements or declarations in connection with a claim.

Income tax, capital gains tax, corporation tax and VAT

14.38 Any document which is likely to be relied upon by HMRC to determine without further enquiry a question about:

1 The taxpayer's liability to tax.
2 Payments made by the taxpayer by way of or in connection with tax.
3 Any other payment by the taxpayer including penalties.
4 Repayments or any other kind of payment or credit to the taxpayer.

14.39 Communicating information to HMRC by any form or method is included, notably by post, fax, e-mail or telephone.

DEGREES OF CULPABILITY

14.40 Schedule 24, para 3 states that inaccuracy in a document provided to HMRC is:

1 'careless' if the inaccuracy is due to failure by the taxpayer to take reasonable care,

2 'deliberate but not concealed' if the inaccuracy is deliberate but the taxpayer does not make arrangements to conceal it, and

3 'deliberate and concealed' if the inaccuracy is deliberate and the taxpayer also makes arrangements to conceal it, for example by submitting false evidence in support of an inaccurate figure.

14.41 An inaccuracy in a document given by a taxpayer to HMRC, which was neither careless nor deliberate when the document was given, is to be treated as careless if the taxpayer:

– discovered the inaccuracy at some later date, and

– did not take reasonable steps to inform HMRC.

Mistake/innocent error

14.42 The position has not changed in this respect. No penalty is imposed when the taxpayer has taken reasonable care to prepare and submit his or her self-assessment tax return. This default is only treated as 'careless' (see definition above and explanation below) where the taxpayer discovers the default and does not inform HMRC within a reasonable time.

14.43 The term 'reasonable' is considered in the draft consultation documents. It is interpreted according to the situation of the individual taxpayer. It reflects materiality in the sense of the size of the default compared with the size of the taxpayer's business. In effect the previous 'size and gravity' or 'seriousness' concepts are retained, but in another form.

14.44 Comments in the Consultation Document of December 2006 suggest that HMRC might regard the following as innocent errors:

– An innocent error after taking reasonable care.

– A reasonable view of the law that proves to be wrong or is not pursued.

– An act or omission that does not form part of a pattern of behaviour and is untypical of the taxpayer concerned.

– The adoption of a treatment for tax purposes that is clearly disclosed to HMRC in a return or accounts, even if it is subsequently changed by agreement or tribunal decision.

Examples given include:

1 An arithmetical error but not as big so as to produce an error which should have been noticed.

2 Misclassifying an unusual item which is not big enough to prompt the need for professional advice.

3 A mistake made by an assistant or employee.

4 Omitting a small (relative to overall liability) item from the return.

5 A reasonable judgment is made eg on a valuation.

A reasonable view of the law is adopted even if this differs from HMRC guidance.

Carelessness

14.45 The penalty for 'carelessness' is 30% of the potential tax lost. This is subject to mitigation down to nil where there is an 'unprompted disclosure' and to 15% where there is a 'prompted disclosure'.

14.46 An additional ingredient of this penalty is that it may be imposed in respect of a document submitted to HMRC on the taxpayer's behalf. This clearly applies, *inter alia*, to the accountant or tax adviser.

14.47 It can be seen that mitigation of the penalty is only granted for 'disclosure' although, as will be seen later in this chapter, account is also taken in effect for cooperation by the taxpayer and the seriousness of the case. The December 2006 Consultation Document gives examples of behaviour that would be construed as not taking reasonable care, including:

– A breach of duty existing at a time when the duty should have been performed.

– Not doing something that the person knew or should have known ought to have been done and which the person concerned had the power to do.

– The absence of such skill, care and diligence as it was the duty and capacity of the person to bring to the work.

– Omitting to do something that a reasonable person would do and the person concerned could do, or doing something that a reasonable person would not do.

– Negligence. Importing some duty of neglect of duty in relation to facts or the interpretation of the law, provided the capacity to perform the duty is present.

Specific examples of carelessness are:

1 Making large arithmetical mistakes.

2 Mis-classifying items of income and expenditure without giving the matter adequate consideration or taking professional advice.

3 Keeping incomplete books and records.

4 Omitting occasional items of income and gains.

5 Having insufficient quality control over the work of others.

6 Applying PAYE wrongly occasionally or to an unusual item without checking on the correct treatment.

Failure to notify HMRC of under-assessment

14.48 A completely new penalty is announced for failure to notify HMRC of an under-assessment of income tax, corporation tax, capital gains tax or VAT. This penalty is imposed when the taxpayer fails to take 'reasonable steps' to notify the under-assessment of tax to HMRC within 30 days. This penalty is also a mitigable amount up to 30% of the potential tax lost, but can be reduced to 0% for an unprompted disclosure or 15% in the case of a prompted disclosure.

14.49 As in the case of taxpayer carelessness, this penalty is extended to acts by a third party acting for the taxpayer, notably the accountant or other tax adviser.

14.50 In assessing whether the penalty should be imposed, account is taken of the competence of the taxpayer to recognise that tax has been under-assessed, and what steps should have been taken by him or her if the under-assessment was recognised. This initial review is quite apart from the consideration of mitigation for disclosure.

Deliberate understatement of tax

14.51 Where the taxpayer deliberately understates the tax liability, but such understatement is not concealed, the maximum mitigable penalty is 70%. This is mitigable by 50% in the case of an 'unprompted disclosure' and 35% in the case of a 'prompted disclosure', so that the penalty under these circumstances may be mitigated to either 20% or 35%.

14.52 Deliberate understatement of tax without concealment is defined as:

- deliberately not doing something which ought to be done; or
- deliberately getting something wrong.

14.53 Examples of this behaviour include:

1 Not recording all sales, especially where a pattern of under-recording appears to rule out a genuine misunderstanding.

2 Including personal expenditure in business expenditure in circumstances that rule out a genuine misunderstanding.

3 Making inadequate private use adjustments where the amounts are significant.

4 Omitting significant amounts of income.

5 Adopting inappropriate accounting treatment.

6 Describing transactions in a misleading way.

7 Deliberately misinterpreting the law with a view to understatement.

Deliberate understatement with concealment

14.54 Where the taxpayer understates tax deliberately, and this default is also concealed, the maximum penalty is 100% of the potential loss of tax, but once again can be mitigated.

14.55 Mitigation of up to 70% can be gained in the case of an 'unprompted disclosure', making the penalty 30%. In the case of an 'unprompted disclosure' mitigation of up to 50% is available, which would produce a penalty of 50%. The 'quality of the disclosure' is all important.

14.56 There is no statutory definition of concealment. However an example is the making of a deliberate error for tax purposes, covering it up, perhaps by producing a false document, and then destroying incriminating documentary evidence. Basically, it is submitting false evidence in support of figures known to be incorrect. This type of default is one step down from a situation where HMRC and the Revenue and Customs Prosecution Office (RCPO) would consider a criminal prosecution.

14.57 Examples of deliberate understatement with concealment are:

- Creating false invoices or altering invoices.
- Backdating or post-dating contracts or invoices.

- Creating false minutes of meetings or minutes of fictitious meetings.
- Destroying books and records.
- Deliberately misleading accountants or HMRC.
- Systematic diversion of income into undisclosed bank accounts and covering up the traces of this action.
- Invoice routing, for example the purported sale or purchase of goods through a tax haven company (with no activity undertaken by that company even though contracts exist showing the contrary) leaving profits untaxed in that company.
- Creating sales records that deliberately understate the value of the goods sold, the balance of the full price being paid separately to the person.
- Describing expenditure in the business records in such a way as to make it appear to be business related when it is in fact private (possibly with the supplier agreeing to change the description on the relevant invoices).
- Alteration of genuine purchase invoices to inflate their value.

Potential lost revenue

14.58 The penalties described above are applied to 'potential lost revenue', which Sch 24, para 5(1) describes as the additional amount due or payable in tax and national insurance as a result of correcting the inaccuracy or assessment.

14.59 Potential lost revenue includes over-repayments made by HMRC. Calculations of group relief and close company relief for loans under TA 1988, s 419(4) are ignored for the purposes of assessing potential lost revenue, but this does not prevent a penalty being imposed for an inaccurate claim for relief.

14.60 The HMRC Compliance Handbook at CH8230–CH82370 makes it clear that losses over-claimed will contribute to potential lost revenue.

Special reduction

14.61 Another new concept is the 'Special reduction' that HMRC may apply in special cases. This penalty reduction will be applied rarely, and the taxpayer and his or her advisers will have to make a strong case for special circumstances to apply. It is not yet clear in what circumstances this reduction will apply, but inability to pay the tax or penalty will not be valid, and neither will the proposition that tax underpaid has been covered by an overpayment by another taxpayer.

14.62 HMRC have used the acronym SMART in the Compliance Handbook to illustrate the conditions that must be fulfilled, as follows:

- Specific – directly related to the business or individual being penalised.
- Measurable – in order to have a penalty cancelled the person needs to be able to demonstrate that conditions have been met.
- Achievable – the person must be able to met the conditions.
- Realistic – unrealistic conditions cannot be imposed (for instance a condition that a business employ a full time resource may be unreasonable for a small business with few business transactions).
- Time bound – the conditions must be met by a certain date.

Timing differences

14.63 In cases that do not involve unrelieved losses, where timing differences are involved, a non-mitigable penalty of 5% may be imposed. The penalty is 5% for each year of the delay or part thereof.

Suspended penalty

14.64 Another new concept is the suspended penalty. At the lower end of the penalty scale, where HMRC allege carelessness, involving a penalty of between 0% and 30% of the potential tax loss, HMRC may agree to suspend the penalty for up to two years. In order for this to happen the taxpayer must agree steps to remedy the situation. HMRC will impose conditions during the suspension period. If the taxpayer complies with the conditions and satisfies HMRC, then the suspended penalty will be cancelled. HMRC must state:

- what part of the penalty is being suspended;
- the period of the suspension, which must not exceed two years; and
- the conditions which must be complied with by the taxpayer. These can include specific actions and time limits.

Quality of disclosure

14.65 It should be noted that mitigation of penalties is now only given for disclosure. Disclosure is defined in Sch 24, para 9(1) as:

- informing HMRC about the rcturn inaccuracy or under-assessment of tax;

- providing reasonable help to HMRC in quantifying the potential tax loss; and
- allowing HMRC access to books, records and information for the purpose of ensuring that the inaccuracy or understatement has been completely corrected.

14.66 A disclosure is 'unprompted' if it is made at a time when the taxpayer has no reason to expect that HMRC has discovered the default or is about to discover it or an under-assessment. In any other circumstances the disclosure is 'prompted'.

14.67 The quality of a disclosure is judged principally in times of timing, nature and extent, although other factors may be considered.

14.68 In comparing this aspect of the new regime to the current penalty regime, it is noticeable that no mitigation is given specifically for cooperation by the taxpayer (and his or her agent). However, cooperation is taken into account in effect because disclosure includes providing help to HMRC and allowing access to books, records and information.

14.69 Similarly, seriousness will be reflected in the category of the penalty imposition in respect of the tax deemed to be potentially lost by the taxpayer's default.

14.70 The HMRC Compliance Handbook at CH82430 sets out three elements of disclosure. These are telling HMRC about the facts, giving HMRC reasonable help and allowing HMRC access to records. The elements of disclosure may be weighted as follows:

1 Telling 30%.

2 Helping 40%.

3 Giving access 30%.

New penalty concepts

14.71 The new legislation has spawned a number of new concepts applicable to the imposition of penalties for the type of income tax, corporation tax and VAT defaults already described. These are as follows:

- As already discussed there is a potential penalty for failing to notify HMRC of an under-assessment of tax.

- The penalties are applied to the 'potential lost tax revenue'. Broadly speaking, this is the additional tax found to be due as a result of the inaccuracy, default or failure to report under-assessment. Note that it is equally applicable to VAT.
- Group relief is ignored in estimating the potential tax lost relating to a given accounting period.
- The 5% penalty for timing differences, as described above.
- Extension of the penalties for carelessness and failure to report under-assessment of tax to actions or failures by a third party acting for the taxpayer. This is aimed principally at the accountant or other tax adviser. This is in sharp contrast to the current regime, where the HMRC Enquiry Manual at EM 5140 exempts the taxpayer generally for the defaults of the agent.
- Where there has been a deliberate understatement of tax, HMRC will have the power to attribute CTSA penalties to directors. This applies to cases where the potential maximum penalty is 100% or 70%. Where the taxpayer is a company and the default is due to the actions of an officer of the company, the penalty may be imposed on both the company and the officer. However, to avoid double counting, HMRC is not permitted to recover a penalty of more than 100% in total.
- The scope of corporation tax extends to other bodies such as unincorporated associations and in these situations the definition of an officer means:
  1. A director.
  2. A manager.
  3. A secretary.
  4. Any other person managing or purporting to manage any of the company's affairs.

* The overstatement of losses may attract a tax penalty.

AMOUNT OF THE PENALTY

14.72 In assessing the penalty HMRC will proceed by:

- Fixing a penalty for the nature of the action.
- Basing the penalty on the 'potential lost revenue'.
- Taking into account whether any disclosure was prompted or unprompted.

– Considering the 'quality' of the disclosure.

14.73 The legislation defines disclosure as the following:

1 The taxpayer tells HMRC about the inaccuracy.

2 They give HMRC reasonable help in quantifying the inaccuracy.

3 The quality of the disclosure is assessed, which includes timing, nature and extent.

Time limit

14.74 The time limit for making a penalty assessment is being reduced. The current provision for direct tax allows a penalty determination to be made up to three years after the final determination of the tax lost. This is reduced to 12 months from either:

- the end of the appeal period for the decision correcting the inaccuracy; or
- if there is no assessment, the date on which the inaccuracy is corrected; or
- where the taxpayer has failed to tell HMRC of an under-assessment, the end of the appeal period in respect of the assessment relating to the tax understated.

APPEALS

14.75 Taxpayers will be able to appeal to an independent body against the imposition or amount of any penalty, as is possible under the current regime. Where the appeal relates to whether a penalty should be suspended or whether HMRC should reduce the penalty due to special circumstances, the appeal body may consider whether HMRC's decision is reasonable.

CONSEQUENCES AND ACTION

14.76 Taxpayers and their advisers will have to decide on their reaction to the new legislation. Accountants and tax advisers may well consider that this subject should be highlighted in a client newsletter, or as part of a client seminar. Whether they will wish to advertise the fact that penalties are extended to errors by the adviser of which the client was unaware is something that each firm will need to consider.

14.77 The new regime certainly underlines the need for good professional indemnity insurance, as clients are unlikely to be too pleased to have to pay a tax penalty for the default of their agent.

14.78 Other actions that could be considered are:

- A review of the risk management programme relating to the tax affairs of the particular client. This may bring the opportunity for some added value services by the accountant.
- The marketing of professional expenses insurance by the professional practice. This will not cover any additional tax, interest or penalties imposed on the client, but would help towards the professional fees incurred, which are likely to be substantial in the case of any investigation or enquiry.

14.79 It should also be remembered that the new penalty regime still leaves room for negotiation of penalties by the professional adviser, and this aspect of investigation work remains extremely important. Current investigation practitioners will have to review their tactics in the light of the new legislation.

VAT PENALTY CHANGE

14.80 On 1 September 2007, HMRC issued Public Notice 160 entitled 'Enquiries into indirect tax matters'. This notice relates to the procedure for civil evasion penalties for indirect tax defaults, where the alleged default is outside HMRC Code of Practice 9. Code of Practice 9 relates to serious fraud cases, so that PN160 will apply to lower value cases where there is evidence of dishonest conduct, in accordance with VATA 1994, s 60.

Key features

14.81 Key features of the new procedure are:

- The taxpayer will be notified that they are suspected of conduct involving dishonesty.
- HMRC will disclose the matters that are subject to enquiry, for example, sales and purchases in a particular VAT return period, but will not disclose the specific evidence that leads the department to suspect dishonest conduct.
- The taxpayer will be invited to co-operate with HMRC enquiries, to disclose any irregularities. Cooperation and disclosure will lead to mitigation of the maximum penalty of 100% of the VAT deemed to have been lost.

- The taxpayer and his or her adviser will be invited to attend a meeting with the HMRC investigator. The taxpayer will be invited to make disclosure of any irregularities, and also, in relevant cases, to make payments on account of any additional VAT due, which would reduce interest charged on late VAT payments. Notes of the meeting will be made by the HMRC investigator, so that in many ways the procedure mirrors that for direct tax.
- The maximum penalty is 100% of the VAT underdeclared. This will be reduced by:
  - up to 40% for early and truthful explanation as to why the VAT arrears arose and the true extent of them;
  - up to 40% where the taxpayer fully embraces and meets responsibilities under the procedure, for example, by supplying information promptly, disclosing and quantifying irregularities, attending meetings and answering questions.
- In most case the maximum penalty mitigation will therefore be 80%, making the actual penalty 20% of the VAT underdeclared. In exceptional circumstances, however, consideration will be given to a further reduction, for example where the taxpayer has made a full and unprompted voluntary disclosure.
- Appeals may continue to be made to the VAT & Duties Tribunal, both against the amount of the additional VAT and any civil evasion penalty imposed.
- The taxpayer is obliged to pay the professional costs incurred in dealing with any VAT Enquiry.

It can be seen that this is another example of the merger between the Inland Revenue and Customs & Excise bringing direct and indirect tax legislation and procedure closer together. Unfortunately, this particular Notice was not widely advertised at the time of issue.

PENALTIES REFORM: THE NEXT STAGE

14.82 This was the title of the latest HMRC Consultation Document issued on 10 January 2008.

Extension of penalty regime

14.83 The Consultation Document proposed that the new penalty regime outlined earlier in this chapter should be extended to include the following:

- Environmental taxes, such as aggregates levy, climate change levy and landfill tax.
- Excise duties such as alcohols, tobacco, oils, gambling and air passenger duty.
- Inheritance tax.
- Insurance premium tax.
- Pension schemes, in particular the 'accounting for tax' form.
- Petroleum revenue tax.
- Stamp Duty Land Tax and Stamp Duty Reserve Tax.
- Accounting to HMRC for repayments of student loans.
- Recovery of statutory payments from HMRC such as sick, maternity and adoption pay.

14.84 The current penalties for inheritance tax, stamp duties, petroleum revenue tax and pension schemes are similar to the previous penalty regime referred to earlier in this chapter, with a mitigable penalty of up to 100% of the understated tax.

14.85 The Consultation has considered penalties under the following categories:

- Incorrect returns.
- Failure to notify a new taxable activity.
- Late filing and late payment.
- Record keeping and information powers failures.
- Other regulatory failures.

14.86 HMRC considers that the relationship between sanctions needs to be considered. For example, in tackling serious non-compliance, it seems likely that the penalty response to three different ways of deliberately evading tax should be the same, ie:

- not notifying HMRC of a taxable activity;
- understating tax due; and
- not submitting returns at all.

Employers' responsibilities

14.87 The Consultation Document also asked whether it would be sensible to align the same penalty response to all types of errors on employers' P35 end of year returns. This would include errors relating to PAYE, national insurance contributions, statutory payments and student loans. This would be promoted as a simplification measure.

Third party penalties

14.88 Another change under consideration is a regime of imposing penalties on third parties who deliberately withhold information or provide false information. An example of this is inheritance tax, where penalties are currently imposed on the personal representatives where an incorrect inheritance tax return has been submitted.

14.89 However evidence suggests that sometimes those who benefit from an understatement of inheritance tax are the beneficiaries of the estate who have deliberately withheld information about the deceased's assets from the personal representatives.

Deterrents regarding information requests failures

14.90 Where taxpayers fail to cooperate when requests by HMRC to examine documents and information and obstruction to a planned visit to premises is involved, a penalty may be considered. The particular circumstances include failing to:

- keep adequate records;
- produce records for HMRC to see;
- allow access to assets or premises;
- produce supplementary information under the first party information power; and
- produce information under the third party information power.

14.91 The circumstances outlined above would not necessarily lead to a loss of tax, so that a tax-geared penalty would not be appropriate.

14.92 It should be remembered that, under current legislation, a penalty of up to £3,000 may be imposed under TMA 1970, s 12B for failure to keep adequate records.

Failure to notify

14.93 Currently the obligation to notify taxability, particularly for a new business, varies between the various taxes, as follows:

- For income tax and corporation tax notification of chargeability must be made within six months or twelve months respectively of the end of the tax period. There is a separate requirement for a company to notify within three months of coming within a charge to corporation tax.
- For Class 2 national insurance, notification must be made within three months of the trader becoming self-employed.
- For VAT a trader is required to register when turnover exceeds or is about to exceed the VAT exempt threshold.
- For excise duties and environmental taxes, the obligation is normally when the trader commences operation or signifies an intention to do so.
- For other taxes, there is no notification process, only a requirement to file a return.

Current penalties

14.94 Current penalties for failure to notify are also diverse, as follows:

- For income tax the penalty is a mitigable amount of up to 100% of the tax due but unpaid 10 months after the tax period in the case of income tax and 12 months for corporation tax. The £300 penalty for failure by a company to notify when it comes into charge is rarely imposed.
- For Class 2 NICs the penalty is £100 for failure to notify chargeability within three months of commencing business. Two-thirds of such penalties are cancelled for a variety of reasons.
- Current VAT penalties are complex. Failure to notify where the intention is to evade tax and the actions involve dishonesty may produce a penalty of up to 100% of the tax evaded (mitigable).

14.95 In other VAT cases involving late notification the penalty depends on the degree of lateness, as follows:

1. 5% of the tax due for a failure of up to 9 months;
2. 10% where the late notification is between 9 and 18 months; and
3. 15% for over 18 months.

14.96 There is minimum penalty of £50 where no VAT is due, but all the current VAT penalties are mitigable on the grounds of reasonable excuse. For excise duties there is a fixed penalty of £250 for failure to notify and in some instances criminal sanctions can be imposed. HMRC may also be able to seize goods and equipment. Environmental taxes and insurance premium tax have penalties for failing to notify of 5% of the tax due.

14.97 The report suggests that the £100 penalty for late notification of a liability to Class 2 National insurance contributions should be removed, and be replaced by a new penalty geared to the amount of both NICs and income tax unpaid when late notification occurs.

14.98 In addition, where late notification for income tax purposes is deliberate, the report suggests that consideration should be given to imposing a penalty at the same level for a deliberately incorrect return. Deliberate concealment should make the penalty even higher, again matching the incorrect return penalties. Reductions for taxpayer disclosure should also apply, with an increase of mitigation for unprompted disclosure.

14.99 A moderate penalty should be imposed where there has been a failure to notify, but there has been no evidence of deliberate intent. Where there is disclosure by the taxpayer, penalties might be no lower than 10% for unprompted disclosure and 20% for a prompted disclosure. In many ways the suggestion is that the penalties for late notification should mirror the new penalty regime for incorrect returns. However, this would include a 'reasonable excuse' element.

14.100 Similarly there will be penalties for failure to comply with an information power. These would be brought into line across the taxes to which information powers apply. It is likely that an initial penalty would be sufficient in the vast majority of cases and apparently a figure of £300 is under consideration. However, there are those taxpayers who may try to seek an advantage in unreasonably delaying the provision of information. Where there are further delays, a daily penalty, possibly of up to £60 a day, could be brought into play although it is not envisaged that the daily penalty should continue to be charged beyond the point at which it become disproportionate to the tax at risk. In exceptional cases, following an appeal by HMRC, the new upper tier tribunals will be able to impose a tax-geared penalty where HMRC believe that the taxpayer has perpetuated continued failure or obstruction resulting in the taxpayer paying significantly less tax than would otherwise be the case.

14.101 HMRC state that full disclosure in regard to notification means:

- telling HMRC when the new activity started;
- taking active steps to quantify the tax under-declared as a result; and
- giving access to HMRC to allow them to check matters.

Appeals

14.102 There will be a right of appeal to an independent tax tribunal against the penalty and its amount. For penalties for deliberate failure to notify the onus would be on HMRC to demonstrate the behaviours to a high degree of probability. For other failure to notify penalties the onus would be on the taxpayer to displace the penalty, as under current legislation. The suggestion is that the grounds to displace a failure to notify penalty should be through the reasonable excuse provision, specified in law, and which would also form the grounds for appeal to a tribunal.

Reasonable excuse

14.103 The consultative document also makes a case for a single 'reasonable excuse' provision to be introduced within HMRC, to apply to both direct taxes and also VAT. At present reasonable excuse is treated slightly differently for the two taxes. This definition would have legislative backing and would apply across the tax regime, including cases of failure to notify, and defaults regarding HMRC information powers.

Commencement date

14.104 The commencement date for the provisions included in the two Consultation Documents issued on 10 January 2008 and referred to in the 2008 Budget Notices BN96 and BN97 is on or after 1 April 2009 for failure to notify and failure to comply with information notices, and return periods commencing on 1 April 2009 where the return is filed on or after 1 April 2010.

THE 2008 FINANCE BILL

14.105 The matters considered in the Consultation Documents issued, and in particular those of 10 January 2008, formed part of the draft legislation included in the Finance Bill 2008, as originally enacted. The Clauses and Schedules relevant to the subject of penalties are:

- Clause 108 and Schedule 36. Information and Inspection Powers.
- Clause 109. Computer Records.
- Clause 110 and Schedule 37. Record-keeping.
- Clause 117 and Schedule 40. Penalties for Errors.
- Clause 118 and Schedule 41. Penalties for Failure to Notify etc.

It should be stressed that this draft legislation may be amended by the time that the Finance Act 2008 becomes statutory law.

Computer records

14.106 Clause 109(6) provides that a penalty of £300 may be imposed for obstruction in or failure to provide computer records required by HMRC.

Record-keeping

14.107 Various amendments are made to TMA 1970, s 12B but the maximum penalty of £3,000 remains.

Penalties for errors etc

14.108 Numerous small amendments are made to the Finance Act 2007, Sch 24 by the Finance Bill, Sch 40.

14.109 The main provision is that the penalties for tax errors are extended to Insurance Premium Tax, Inheritance Tax, the two Stamp Duty Taxes, Petroleum Revenue Tax, Excise Duties and a whole list of other taxes and duties.

14.110 Another amendment is that where an error in a taxpayer's document is attributable to another person, penalties of up to 100% of potential lost revenue may be imposed, but subject to reductions and the special reduction based on taxpayer behaviour.

14.111 Clause 117(3) provides that the provisions set out in the bill shall become effective for return periods commencing on or after 1 April 2009, where the return for that period is filed on or after 1 April 2010.

Information and inspection powers

14.112 Clause 108 and Schedule 36 deal with HMRC Information and Inspection Powers. In part 7 of the Bill para 37 imposes a penalty of £300 for obstruction and failure to comply with HMRC. This includes concealment, destruction or disposal of documents and is subject to the reasonable excuse provisions.

14.113 Paragraph 38 states that a daily penalty of up to £60 may be imposed where the offence continues. Penalties under both paras 37 and 38 must be imposed within 12 months of the 'relevant date'. There is an appeal procedure explained in paras 45 and 46.

14.114 Where the offence continues HMRC may apply to the Upper Tax Tribunal for a tax related penalty, which is additional to the initial and daily penalties. The draft legislation states that all penalties must be paid within 30 days.

14.115 Concealment, destruction and disposal of relevant documents are treated very seriously. The penalty is a fine or imprisonment for up to two years as well as a fine.

14.116 It is assumed that these provisions will apply for obligations on or after 1 April 2009.

Failure to notify

14.117 Clause 118 and Schedule 41 deal with Penalties for Failure to Notify etc. Clause 118(3) provides that the new legislation will apply to obligations on or after 1 April 2009.

Legislation affected

14.118 The draft legislation affects or replaces:

1 TMA 1970, s 7 for income tax and capital gains tax.

2 FA 1988, Sch 18, para 2 for corporation tax.

3 Various VAT obligations including obligation to notify and liability to register.

4 Various obligations for IPT, Aggregates Levy, Climate Change Levy, Landfill Tax, Excise Duty and numerous other taxes and levies.

VAT

14.119 Schedule 41, para 2 imposes a penalty on the unauthorised issue of a VAT invoice.

Penalty imposition

14.120 Paragraph 5 explains that penalties will be imposed, inter alia, on the basis of acts that are 'deliberate and concealed' or 'deliberate but not concealed'.

14.121 The penalty to be imposed is:

1 100% for acts that are deliberate and concealed.

2 70% where the default was deliberate but no concealed.

3 30% in other cases.

14.122 The penalty is applied to potential lost revenue, and for income tax and capital gains tax relates to tax unpaid on 31 January after the end of the tax year. For corporation tax purposes the date is 12 months after the end of the accounting period.

Reductions for disclosure

14.123 Schedule 41, paras 12 and 13 deal with reductions for disclosure by the taxpayer. The actions that will trigger this are:

1 Letting HMRC know about the default.

2 Giving HMRC reasonable help in quantifying the tax unpaid by reason of the default.

3 Allowing HMRC access to business or other records for the purpose of checking how much tax is unpaid.

14.124 Disclosure is quantified by HMRC on the basis of the following:

1 Whether the act or failure by the taxpayer is unprompted and the taxpayer has no reason to think that HMRC has discovered or is about to discover the relevant act or failure.

2 Whether the act is prompted.

14.125 HMRC consider the quality and completeness of the disclosure and its timing (how promptly). The nature of the disclosure is also considered, in the sense of the level of evidence provided and degree and extent of access provided to test the disclosure.

14.126 In many ways this legislation mirrors that included in the Finance Act 2007, Sch 24 regarding penalties for errors to returns.

14.127 The potential reductions in penalties are as follows:

(a) The unprompted disclosure penalty of 100% can be reduced to not less than 30%.

(b) The prompted disclosure penalty of 100% can be reduced to not less than 50%.

(c) The 70% unprompted disclosure penalty of 70% can be reduced to not less than 20%.

(d) The 70% prompted disclosure penalty can be reduced to not less than 35%.

(e) In the case of an unprompted disclosure where the 30% penalty could be imposed, HMRC may reduce the penalty to nil or 10% where HMRC become aware less than 12 months after tax becomes unpaid by reason of failure to notify the relevant items. This reduction will depend on the quality of the disclosure.

(f) In the case of a prompted disclosure where a 30% penalty could be imposed, this may be reduced to not less than 10%, or in any other case 20%, depending on the quality of the disclosure, where HMRC becomes aware of the failure within 12 months.

In some instances HMRC will consider a special reduction (para 14).

Other issues

14.128 There can be no 'doubling up' of penalties, so that the total penalty cannot exceed 100%. This is of particular significance where both a company and one or more of its officers both attract a penalty (paras 15 and 22). In this connection, as well as a director, a company officer includes:

- A manager.
- A secretary.
- Any other person managing or purporting to manage the company's affairs.

An assessment of a penalty must be paid within 30 days (para 16).

14.129 Paragraphs 17–19 set out the appeals procedure and the concept of reasonable excuse is explained in para 20. Paragraph 21 describes provisions in respect of agents.

Appendix 1:

The Chartered Institute of Taxation and The Association of Taxation Technicians – Interim Guidance Issued In March 2004 – Anti Money Laundering (Proceeds of Crime and Terrorism) – Guidance For Taxation Practioners

These notes are for guidance only and have not been approved by the Treasury (see paragraph 3.5.5). They are not a substitute for being aware of the law relating to money laundering and any developments affecting this or obtaining specific legal advice. Neither The Chartered Institute of Taxation nor The Association of Taxation Technicians accept any responsibility for any loss or damage suffered by any person in consequence of them acting or refraining from acting as a result of anything contained in or omitted from this publication in printed or electronic format. Any person who is also a member of another professional body which has issued guidance on money laundering should pay due attention to that guidance. Although NCIS may in limited circumstances be willing to provide advice, this advice will not necessarily constitute a defence in law.

GLOSSARY AND INTERPRETATION

1.

ATT	**The Association of Taxation Technicians**
CCAB	**The Consultative Committee of Accountancy Bodies**
CEMA	**Customs and Excise Management Act 1979**
CIOT	**The Chartered Institute of Taxation**
Customs	**HM Customs and Excise**
DPA	**Data Protection Act 1998**
ICTA	**Income and Corporation Taxes Act 1988**
JMLSG	**Joint Money Laundering Steering Group**
MLR 2003	**Money Laundering Regulations 2003**
MLRO	**Money Laundering Reporting Officer or Nominated Officer**
NCIS	**National Criminal Intelligence Service**
NIS	**National Investigation Service**
POCA	**Proceeds of Crime Act 2002**
Revenue	**The Inland Revenue**
TMA	**Taxes Management Act 1970**
UK	**United Kingdom**
VATA	**Value Added Tax Act 1994**

2. The guidance refers to reports being made to a firm's MLRO. In the absence of a MLRO (for example for members working as sole practitioners) the report should be made directly to NCIS.

3. Words importing the masculine gender include the feminine, words in the singular include the plural and words in the plural include the singular.

1. INTRODUCTION

1.1 Content and other available guidance

1.1.1 Members should read this guidance in conjunction with the CCAB[1] Anti Money Laundering (Proceeds of Crime and Terrorism) second interim guidance published in February 2004 (www.ccab.org.uk under Documents) and guidance issued by the TAX Faculty of the ICAEW in September 2003[2]. The CCAB guidance, to which the CIOT and ATT contributed, provides very useful general information on the requirements of the new regime introduced by POCA and the MLR 2003. This document looks at how to deal with tax offences under the new rules. It also includes Revenue approved guidance on the interaction with the Hansard procedure and some additional guidance in procedural areas such as identification checks for clients.

---

[1] CCAB members are ICAEW (www.icaew.co.uk), ACCA (www.acca.org.uk), CIMA (www.cimaglobal.com), ICAS (www.icas.org.uk), CIPFA (www.cipfa.org.uk) and ICAI (www.icai.ei)

[2] 'TaxLine:Tax Practice. Money Laundering: A Tax Supplement from the Tax Faculty' No.4 September 2003 Interim anti money laundering guidance issued by the Chartered Institute of Taxation and the Association of Taxation Technicians in March 2004

1.2.1 Effective dates for the legislation

1.2.1 POCA has been in force since 24 February 2003. This created the principal money laundering offences described in 2.2 below. In addition, with effect from 1 March 2004 the tax profession was brought into the regulated sector, so that the obligation to make suspicious activity reports, as set out in section 3, applies to tax practitioners. MLR 2003 impose additional requirements on firms. The key obligations applying from 1 March 2004 are set out in paragraph 1.3 below.

1.3 Key obligations under the new regulated regime

1.3.1 The new regime is effective from 1 March 2004. From that date members in practice have to:

- Appoint a Money Laundering Reporting Officer (MLRO). Sole practitioners without any employees will effectively be the MLRO for their own practice. See CCAB guidance chapter 15.
- Establish appropriate internal procedures to prevent money laundering. See CCAB guidance chapter 17.
- Train staff so that they know how to identify money laundering, how to identify clients and how to report suspicions to the MLRO (suspicious activity reports).
- Verify the identity of new clients and maintain evidence of identification. See Appendix 1 for further information.
- Report, via the MLRO if applicable, suspicions and knowledge of money laundering to the National Criminal Intelligence Service (NCIS). Members should note that there is no de minimis limit and they will have to

report all suspicions and knowledge of criminal activity irrespective of the level of proceeds or the gravity of the crime.

2. OFFENCES UNDER POCA

2.1 Definition of money laundering

2.1.1 Historically money laundering has been the term used for a number of offences involving the laundering of the proceeds of serious and drugs crime, as well as the laundering of terrorist funds. Under the new legislation, it now includes possessing, or in any way dealing with, or concealing, the proceeds of any crime. Tax evasion is a crime. The proceeds or monetary advantage arising from tax related offences are treated no differently from the proceeds of theft, drug trafficking or other criminal conduct. Further details can be found in chapter 4 of the CCAB interim guidance.

2.2 The principal money laundering offences

2.2.1 A person commits one of the principal money laundering offences under POCA if he:

- conceals, disguises, converts, transfer or removes (from the United Kingdom) criminal property;
- enters into or becomes concerned in any arrangement which they know or suspect facilitates (by any means) the acquisition, retention, use or control of criminal property by or on behalf of another person; or
- acquires, uses or has possession of criminal property (see paragraph 3.3).

There are similar offences under the Terrorism Act 2000 concerning property that is intended to be used for the purposes of terrorism.

The principal POCA money laundering offences apply to everyone. No conviction for the underlying criminal conduct is necessary for a person to be prosecuted for a money laundering offence.

When providing tax advice, inter alia for example on property transactions, setting up trusts, inter-family gifts, creating offshore structures etc, a member should be aware of the need to consider whether the transaction on which he is advising 'facilitates (by any means) the acquisition, retention, use or control of criminal property'. This point was highlighted in the High Court (Family Division) case *P v P* [2003] (EWHC 2260 (Fam)) where there was concern that the funds forming part of the divorce settlement were derived from tax evasion.

If a member has suspicions that his actions are so facilitating, he should report to his MLRO. The following steps will then occur:

- The MLRO will decide on whether a report should go to NCIS under the reporting obligations in section 3 below.
- It will be determined whether the firm wishes to continue acting.
- If the firm wishes to cease acting, the MLRO will consider how the firm can cease to act without tipping off (see paragraph 4.1 below).
- If the firm wishes to continue acting, the MLRO will use the statutory option of seeking consent from NCIS to continue to act. POCA provides a defence to any allegation of facilitating or assisting if NCIS consent or deemed consent is given. See also paragraph 13.1.4.

3. MAKING A REPORT

3.1 General

3.1.1 A member is required to make a report to his firm's MLRO where in the course of his work as a tax adviser he knows or suspects or has reasonable grounds for knowing or suspecting that another person is engaged in money laundering. A person is engaged in money laundering if they are committing any of the principal money laundering offences set out in paragraph 2.2 above or are attempting, conspiring, inciting, aiding, abetting, counselling or procuring any of those offences.

It should be noted that there are equivalent requirements for certain other professionals including lawyers, insolvency practitioners and accountants. Since 1993 these provisions have applied to banks and financial service businesses.

3.1.2 The requirement to make a report is not restricted to the activities of clients. It may arise in relation to the activities of any person whom the member comes across in the course of his work. See also paragraph 3.4.4.

3.1.3 In practice suspicions that a person acquires or possesses criminal property are likely to be the most common, for example, a client who lies on his tax return and underpays tax, possesses criminal proceeds.

3.1.5 POCA provides that disclosure to the MLRO will not be taken to breach any restriction on the disclosure of information, including client confidentiality, and constitutes compliance for the reporting party under the regulations.

3.1.6 Once a report has been made to the MLRO, the MLRO must consider whether a report should be made to NCIS. A failure by the MLRO to report the knowledge or suspicion of money laundering will itself be an offence (see sections 13 and 14).

3.1.7 Suspicions of crimes that are not specifically tax related (e.g. theft, false accounting, the making of corrupt payments like bribes and backhanders, and more technical crimes such as financial assistance for the purchase of own shares or Banking Act breaches) may also arise during the course of tax work. The detail of these offences is outside the scope of this guidance but a member should be mindful of them, especially if they are relevant to his area of practice. These must also be reported to the MLRO if there may be proceeds.

3.1.8 A report is required irrespective of the fact that the relevant authorities (such as HMRC or even the Police or SOCA) are already fully aware of the matter.

3.1.9 The obligation to report for members only arises from 1 March 2004. Knowledge or suspicion arising before then will be dealt with under the law then prevailing, when the regulated sector was more narrowly drawn. Under that law it would have been possible for a tax practitioner to make a report to secure the protection of a defence against any allegation of facilitating money laundering.

3.1.10 Significant additional information concerning a report made previously should be reported to the MLRO.

3.2 Knowledge or suspicion

3.2.1 Suspicion has been defined as requiring a degree of satisfaction, not necessarily amounting to belief, but at least extending beyond speculation as to whether an event has occurred or not. It is not necessary to have actual knowledge of the exact nature of the underlying criminal activity. If a member is in doubt whether there are sufficient grounds for suspicion, he should make a report to the MLRO. There is no requirement to perform additional work on an assignment in order to investigate the suspicion, although it may be appropriate to investigate a cause for suspicion if that is required for the assignment.

3.2.2 The second leg of the test for knowledge or suspicion is that the member had reasonable grounds for knowing or suspecting. This is an objective test and involves asking whether a reasonable person would have known or suspected, even if the member in fact did not. It reinforces the message that members should not shut their eyes to obvious facts or refuse to draw obvious and reasonable conclusions from those facts.

3.3 Proceeds of crime (criminal property)

3.3.1 Before making a report a member must also consider:

- whether there are proceeds which constitute a person's benefit from criminal conduct; and
- whether the alleged offender (the money launderer) knows or suspects that the proceeds are a benefit from criminal conduct.

3.3.2 Proceeds is a broad concept and covers indirect benefits. In tax matters, where there is an underpayment of tax, prima facie there are proceeds, although these may or may not arise from a crime.

3.3.3 If the client is enjoying any benefit, including cash flow advantage, for example, by the deliberate concealment of accounting profits from HMRC, then there will be proceeds from the crime.

3.3.4 There can still be proceeds even where a person has spent the results of the crime unless they have made full restitution including interest and penalties as appropriate.

3.3.5 When considering whether a person knew or suspected that the proceeds arose from a crime this can be assumed to be the case where you suspect that the person has committed an offence involving dishonesty, including deliberate tax evasion.

3.4 Identifying a crime

3.4.1 Members are not required to be experts on criminal law. Under the regulations they are required to be trained in and have knowledge of the main money laundering offences. A member is not required to have a detailed knowledge of what constitutes a criminal offence beyond what could reasonably be expected of a person of that individual's position and seniority. A member practising in tax would be expected to have a knowledge of tax offences commensurate with his professional qualifications and sphere of practice.

3.4.2 The activities which a member is required to report are outlined in paragraphs 2.2 and 3.1.1 above.

3.4.3 A member is required to report money laundering crimes wherever they take place. Actions which would be a criminal offence in the UK must be reported. There is no requirement to report matters which are a criminal offence in another country but arc not criminal in the UK. There is a requirement to report matters which would be criminal if they occurred in the UK but are not criminal in the jurisdiction where they occurred.

3.4.4 Members should note that they must report offences discovered during the course of their business irrespective of who committed the crime. The requirement to report applies not only to crimes committed by the client but also to such offences which have been committed by any other party, for example:

- Prospective clients (including those who perhaps approach a member about a possible Hansard disclosure – see also paragraph 8.2).
- Members of a client's staff (e.g. the petty cash clerk sacked for theft, the executive who does not appear to be reporting his own tax properly).
- Agents of or advisers to the client.
- The counter party to a deal or the target of a deal (e.g. where a due diligence exercise reveals tax evasion).
- Promoters/brokers of schemes (e.g. where the scheme is suspected to amount to tax evasion).
- Business associates.

3.5 Failing to report

3.5.1 A member will commit a criminal offence if he fails to make a money laundering report when he should have done so. There are three statutory exceptions of which members ought to be aware.

3.5.2 The first is that a member may have a reasonable excuse for not disclosing the information or matter. Reasonable excuse is not yet defined and whether a member has followed these (and possibly also other relevant) professional guidelines may be taken into account in determining whether an excuse is reasonable in particular circumstances.

3.5.3 The second is that the member is a professional legal adviser and the information or matter came to him in privileged circumstances. This second defence is available where the member is also a practising solicitor or barrister and where the information came to him in privileged circumstances. Where a member is acting in support of a legal professional adviser, for example reporting in respect of forensic work, it remains uncertain whether the second defence is available. Members who are practising lawyers are advised to consult the Law Society or Bar Council guidance on privilege. Other members are advised to consult the CCAB guidance.

3.5.4 The third is that the member does not know or suspect that another person is engaged in money laundering and he has not been provided with training in accordance with MLR 2003 by his employer.

3.5.5 In deciding whether a person has committed an offence the court must consider whether he followed any relevant guidance issued by a supervisory authority or any other appropriate body which has been approved by the Treasury. The CIOT and ATT currently have not applied for Treasury approval of these guidelines and are not a supervisory body as defined by MLR 2003.

4. TIPPING OFF

4.1 General

4.1.1 It is a criminal offence if a person knows or suspects that an internal or NCIS report has been made or that a money laundering investigation is being or is about to be conducted and makes a disclosure which is likely to prejudice any investigation which might be conducted as a result. A member should avoid discussing proceeds of crime and/or money laundering reporting with clients upon whom he has made a report. If a client asks a member whether he has made a report to NCIS the member should decline to answer. Knowledge of the report and the reportable circumstances should be kept on a need to know basis within the member's practice and the focus for reporting should be the MLRO. Normal enquiries as part of the assignment, including enquiries to clarify the matter giving rise to the suspicion, and discussions with other members of the client service team, would not normally amount to tipping off, although additional care must be taken after a report is made.

4.1.2 There may in some cases be a conflict between the obligation to avoid tipping off and other legal or professional obligations, for example, when a member is asked to give professional clearance to an incoming or successor adviser. This could create some difficulty if a member had suspicions that the former client was involved in, say, organised crime or money laundering and the client was not aware of the member's suspicions. In such cases the MLRO should seek guidance from NCIS and if necessary take legal advice.

4.1.3 Situations may arise where the tension is so great between not tipping off the client, and the need for the client (and possibly also other parties) to know that there is a consent issue in regard to proceeding with a transaction where there is a money laundering risk, that NCIS or the Courts will have to be approached to decide how to proceed. In the case of P v P (2003) the court discussed whether a solicitor could tell his client whether he intends to make a report to NCIS. The court suggested guidelines for good practice on when to tell a client or opponent that a report has been made. The Law Society has published guidance on P v P which is available as an annex to the Law Society's money laundering guidance (see http://www.lawsociety.org.uk/dcs/pdf/mlguidance2.pdf). NCIS has also issued guidance on P v P (see www.ncis.co.uk/legaldisclosures.asp).

4.1.4 However, in a tax evasion case, where a member has resigned because of the client's refusal to make a full disclosure to the tax authorities, the client will usually be aware of the reason for the member's resignation. Giving the same information in response to a request for professional clearance should not amount to tipping off. However the fact that a money laundering report has been made, or indeed not made, should not be mentioned in the response to the professional clearance request.

4.2 Data protection

4.2.1 Under s7 DPA a person is entitled to make a request to an organisation as to enquire whether personal data is being held about them. The data controller must respond to such requests detailing whether data is being processed, and if so what the data is, the source of the data, the purpose of the processing, and to whom the data is or may be disclosed. These provisions would require a data controller to provide information on whether reports have been made to a MLRO or NCIS.

4.2.2 However, s29 DPA provides that s7 does not apply if its provisions would 'be likely to prejudice':

(a) the prevention or detection of crime,

(b) the apprehension or prosecution of offenders, or

(c) the assessment or collection of any tax or duty or of any imposition of a similar nature.

A member who had made a report of their suspicions would still have to respond to such a request but could omit any information relating to a report made to a MLRO or NCIS by claiming the exemption provided by s29 DPA. It would be appropriate to keep a record of any such decision and the reasons for it.

4.2.3 Guidance issued by HM Treasury in conjunction with the Information Commissioner in April 2002 makes it clear that the MLRO is entitled to claim the s29 DPA exemption even if a report of suspicions has not been forwarded to NCIS, and has remained an internal matter, since such reports may be the basis for 'establishing a pattern of future transactions that arouse suspicion', and as such disclosure would be likely to prejudice future detection.

5. TAX OFFENCES

5.1 Introduction

5.1.1 As mentioned in paragraph 3.4.1 above a member is not required to be an expert on criminal law. A tax practitioner would be expected to be aware of the boundaries between tax avoidance, which is legal, and tax evasion, which is criminal, and be able to identify conduct in relation to direct and indirect tax which is punishable by the criminal law. There will be no question of criminality where the client has adopted in good faith and honestly and without mis-statement a technical position with which HMRC disagrees.

5.1.2 The main areas where offences may arise in direct tax are:

- tax evasion, including making false returns or accounts or deliberate failure to submit returns;
- deliberate refusal to correct known errors; and less commonly;
- failure to obtain consent under s765 ICTA.

5.1.3 Innocent or negligent errors may be criminal offences in indirect tax (see section 10 below).

5.2 TMA tax 'offences'

5.2.1 The TMA provides a civil penalty regime covering both fraudulent and negligent conduct. It is only fraudulent or dishonest conduct which is reportable under POCA. The money laundering legislation is only concerned with the proceeds of criminal conduct. Therefore, it is only that conduct which the law treats as criminal offences which can lead to money laundering issues.

5.2.2 Where conduct may attract a civil penalty under the TMA but may also, on the particular facts, amount to criminal conduct then the conduct is criminal. By way of example, only, knowingly assisting in the preparation of an incorrect return etc could give rise to a civil penalty under s99 TMA 1970, but the conduct concerned would typically amount to a criminal offence (such as false accounting or cheating the Revenue) as well. Any case where fraudulent conduct is suspected should be reported.

5.3 Prosecution policy – the need to report

5.3.1 In the tax environment, there are many circumstances in which the tax authorities have a long and established practice of dealing with matters on a civil basis. A policy view is taken that this is a more cost effective approach and that the interest and penalties that can be charged on a civil basis constitute sufficient restitution and deterrent.

5.3.2 This is the case across direct tax and VAT where criminal prosecutions are very much the exception.

5.3.3 However, the practices or anticipated practices of HMRC are irrelevant to the reporting obligations under POCA. If a member suspects that a criminal offence may have been committed, and that there may be or may have been proceeds, he is obliged to report, irrespective of the fact that a criminal prosecution may in the member's view be highly unlikely in practice.

6. RELUCTANCE TO CORRECT PAST ERRORS

6.1 Innocent or negligent error – direct tax

6.1.1 It is not uncommon for members to become aware of errors in or omissions from clients' tax returns. If the member has no cause to doubt that these came about as a result of innocent mistake or negligence then he will not have formed a suspicion. However, a real doubt in the member's mind would be sufficient to put the member on enquiry. See paragraph 6.3.

6.2 Innocent or negligent error – indirect tax

6.2.1 In the case of indirect tax, the original innocent or negligent error may in itself amount to a reportable matter and this needs to be considered in addition to the client's subsequent conduct – see section 10 below on handling the original error.

6.3 Unwillingness or refusal to disclose to the tax authorities

6.3.1 Where a client indicates that he is unwilling or refuses to disclose the matter to HMRC in order to avoid paying the tax due, the client appears to have formed criminal intent and hence the reporting obligation arises. A member should also consider whether he can continue to act and consult the CIOT and ATT handbook Professional Conduct in Relation to Taxation for further guidance. This paragraph applies equally to potential clients for whom the member has declined to act.

6.4 Adjusting subsequent returns

6.4.1 Where the law permits the correction of small errors by subsequent tax adjustments, and the original error was not attributable to any criminal conduct, then the adjustment itself will not give rise to the need to report, since no crime will have been committed. However, it should be noted that the legislation does apply to any conduct which constitutes the laundering of the proceeds of any criminal offence however trivial.

7. INTENTION TO UNDERPAY TAX

7.1.1 A client may suggest that he will in the future underpay tax, typically then submitting an incorrect return, which would be tax evasion when it occurs.

7.1.2 A member can and should apply the normal ethical guidance to persuade the client to comply with the law. Should the client's intention in this regard still remain in doubt, the member should consider carefully whether he can commence or continue to act and if in doubt should seek specialist legal advice.

7.1.3 A member should not discuss with the client the possibility of a future money laundering report.

7.1.4 A suspicious activity report may well be required in such cases, depending upon the facts and circumstances.

8. TAX EVASION

8.1 General

8.1.1 Where a member knows or suspects, or has reasonable grounds for knowing or suspecting, that a client or other party is engaged in tax evasion in the UK, this will clearly amount to one or more of a number of possible criminal offences, such as theft, obtaining pecuniary advantage by deception, false accounting, cheating the Revenue, the offence of fraudulent evasion of income tax under s 144 Finance Act 2000 or a range of specific indirect tax offences (see section 10 below). A member should therefore report the matter to his MLRO immediately.

8.1.2 If the suspected evasion is of taxes outside the UK, in circumstances which would be a criminal offence if the conduct occurred in the UK, this should also be reported immediately.

8.1.3 Although a member cannot discuss with the client the money laundering report that he is required to make (he must avoid 'tipping off' or prejudicing a money laundering investigation which are criminal offences), he can and should apply the normal ethical guidance in the CIOT and ATT handbooks Professional Conduct in Relation to Taxation and Professional Rules and Practice Guidelines to persuade the client to act properly. A member will need to consider carefully whether he can continue to act if the client refuses to make a full disclosure to HMRC.

8.2 Hansard cases

8.2.1 In circumstances where a potential or current client asks a member to act in the making of a Hansard disclosure to HMRC, a suspicion of tax evasion will usually arise.

8.2.2 HMRC and the Government (in Parliament through an assurance given by Bob Ainsworth, the Home Office Minister responsible for the Proceeds of Crime Act) have gone on record that the Hansard process should not be affected by the new reporting requirements. If the client is a suitable case for Hansard and actively pursues a voluntary disclosure, Hansard will continue to be available. See Appendices 2, 3 and 4 for further information on this subject. A member should be aware that notification to the Revenue is not a substitute for a report to SOCA. Where appropriate a report must also be made to SOCA as soon as the member has knowledge or suspicion or reasonable grounds for knowledge or suspicion of tax evasion.

8.2.3 A member should advise a client to seek legal advice where this is considered to be in the client's best interests. However it cannot be proper for a member to advise a client or potential client to seek legal advice for the sole purpose of avoiding the making of a money laundering report either by the potential client or the member.

8.3 Civil settlements with Customs

8.3.1 Customs have indicated that they will take a similar approach to the civil settlements process that is their equivalent to Hansard, and that their prosecution policy will not be affected by the POCA changes.

9. FAILURE TO OBTAIN TREASURY CONSENT – S765 ICTA

9.1.1 This section is relevant to members who deal with transactions by companies with international aspects – those transactions that may require consent relate to the creation or issuing or transferring of shares or debentures.

9.1.2 Under s766 ICTA 1988 companies, their officers and advisers may be guilty of criminal offences if a transaction requiring special consent under s765(1) takes place without such consent. The person needs to know that the actions were unlawful under s765(1) in order to be guilty of a criminal offence (s766(1)). In practice this is of limited assistance in cases of innocent oversight because s766(2) puts the burden of proof as to the person's state of knowledge on to the individual in the case of directors.

9.1.3 The next question is whether there are proceeds. If a client has undertaken a tax planning transaction for which Treasury consent was needed and would have been unlikely to have been granted, the tax not paid as a result of the planning would constitute proceeds from the crime. In other circumstances there may be no proceeds, but this will need to be considered on the facts. Where there are proceeds, the member should finally consider whether the alleged offender knew or suspected that the proceeds arose from criminal conduct. The member would usually advise the client that a criminal offence may have occurred, so that the client would then have the requisite knowledge.

9.1.4 When a member realises that there has or may have been a breach of s765 ICTA, he will need to consider making a suspicious activity report based on the factors discussed above. A member should err on the side of caution and contact his MLRO if he has any concerns. The member should also consider what other action is appropriate, for example, advising the client to notify the Revenue.

10. INDIRECT TAX

10.1 Overview

10.1.1 Where indirect tax is concerned, innocent or negligent errors may be criminal offences.

The most pervasive offence in indirect tax legislation is s167(3) CEMA which provides: 'If any person –

(a) makes or signs, or causes to be made or signed, or delivers or causes to be delivered to the Commissioners or any officer, any declaration, notice, certificate or other document whatsoever; or

(b) makes any statement in answer to any question put to him by an officer which he is required by or under any enactment to answer,

being a document or statement produced or made for any purpose of any assigned matter, which is untrue in any material particular then without prejudice to subsection (4) below he shall be liable on summary conviction to a penalty of level 4 on the standard scale'.

'Assigned matter' is defined in section 1 of CEMA as meaning 'any matter in relation to which the Commissioners are for the time being required in pursuance of any enactment to perform any duties'.

10.1.2 This broadly makes most errors, however innocent, criminal offences in VAT and all other indirect taxes managed by Customs. The fact that VAT matters are in practice handled under the civil penalties regime in most circumstances is irrelevant (see paragraph 5.3 above) to the fact that there is an offence under s167(3) CEMA.

10.1.3 There are three reasons that innocent or negligent indirect tax errors may not need to be reported in some cases:

- In some cases an innocent or negligent error will have resulted in the overpayment of tax, in which cases there are no proceeds, direct or indirect, and hence no money laundering offence.
- For a suspicious activity report to be required an alleged offender must be engaged in money laundering. This requires there to be proceeds from criminal activity which the alleged offender knows or suspects arise from criminal activity. If the member is sure that the client or other alleged offender has no awareness whatsoever that innocent or negligent indirect tax errors amount to criminal offences, then no report is required. Members are advised to err on the side of caution in considering this.
- As a result of prolonged lobbying by the CIOT and ATT, Customs and Excise and NCIS have now recognised that the potential requirement to report s167(3) crimes presents practical difficulties, for both practitioners and themselves. The latest draft of the guidance which NCIS will issue to accompany the form on which suspicious activity reports should be made states in relation to s167(3) offences that 'It is the position of NCIS and HMCE that disclosure is not required in these circumstances'. It is not clear what the legal basis for this position is. However, if the guidance is issued in this form, it should give a reasonable excuse for not reporting s167(3) crimes.

Members are advised to make a suspicious activity report in any case where they consider that the information could be of value to the authorities, irrespective of the second and third points above.

10.1.3 Where a member is not required to make a report arising from a criminal offence under s167(3) CEMA, he needs to consider whether there are any other criminal offences which might trigger a report. There are large numbers of specific criminal offences in the indirect taxes legislation and these are outlined in paragraphs 10.2 and 10.3 below. However, in essence they all amount to variations on tax evasion and involve some intention to avoid paying the correct tax.

10.2 Other offences applicable across indirect tax

10.2.1 There is a range of crimes in the Customs and Excise legislation, covering such areas as:

- the bribing of a Commissioner, officer or appointed or authorised person;
- the obstructing of an officer performing any duty, or similar conduct;
- production, signing etc of untrue documents and statements;
- the counterfeiting or falsifying of documents;
- obstructing, or failing to assist in, the inspection of a computer;
- the breaching of conditions applied in respect of relief from VAT conferred on specified classes of persons, such as members of visiting forces; and
- the failure to furnish a supplementary declaration under the Intrastat procedure.

10.2.2 There are a number of other offences relating to particular indirect taxes, such as tobacco products duty, betting and gaming duty, aggregates levy etc. The legislation in respect of these duties, taxes and levies provides the offences specific to them.

10.3 Other offences applicable in VAT

10.3.1 Fraudulent evasion of VAT (s 72(1) VATA)

A person who is knowingly concerned in, or is taking steps with a view to, the fraudulent evasion of VAT by him or any other person is liable under this offence. A person's conduct may amount to fraudulent evasion under this provision if he understates payments due to the Commissioners for a prescribed accounting period. In certain circumstances the overclaiming of VAT (eg a refund in respect of bad debts) may also result in fraudulent evasion.

10.3.2 Production, furnishing or sending of false documents and statements (s72(3) VATA)

This involves the production, furnishing or sending of a false document with the intent to deceive. In addition, it includes knowingly or recklessly making a false statement.

10.3.3 Conduct which must have involved an offence (s72(8) VATA)

Where a person's conduct during any specified period must have involved the commission by him of one or more of the offences listed above, then, regardless of whether the specifics of the offence(s) are known, he is guilty of an offence.

The purpose of this provision is to cover cases where it can be proved that an offence has been committed during a period spanning a number of prescribed accounting periods, but it is not clear to what extent it was committed in any particular prescribed accounting period within the total period concerned. It is only one offence, even if it covers more than one period.

10.3.4 The possession and dealing in goods on which VAT has been evaded (s72(10) VATA)

A person commits an offence, and is liable to penalties, if, having reason to believe that tax has been or will be evaded on them, he either acquires possession of any goods; deals with any goods; or accepts the supply of any services.

10.3.5 Supplying of goods or service without providing security (s72(11) VATA)

A person who is required, under VAT Act 1994 Schedule 11 para 4(2), to give security for the further payment of VAT as a prerequisite for making taxable supplies and who makes those supplies without the provision of security, has committed an offence.

11. CIVIL LIABILITY

11.1.1 There can be a conflict between the money laundering legislation and civil law. The money laundering legislation does not seek to recompense the victim of criminal activity but to take away the proceeds. By contrast, under civil law in England & Wales a victim of crime may have a claim against those who became involved in, or provided assistance in, the process of laundering money. For example, a member could become involved in a civil liability claim as follows. A member suspects that monies held in his firm's client account are the proceeds of a crime and a report is submitted to NCIS. The victim of the crime, who is the true owner of the assets, may have a civil claim to recover that money. In certain circumstance the member's firm may be considered to be a constructive trustee for the true owner.

Whilst civil liabilities may arise in contexts other than the holding of client monies, this is one of the most likely scenarios for them to arise. Members are therefore advised only to handle client monies where they are wholly comfortable as to the source, destination and all the parties involved.

The Law Society money laundering guidance provides a good overview of civil liability issues.

12. MLR 2003

12.1 The regulated sector

12.1.1 The MLR 2003 come into force on 1 March 2004 and implement the provisions of the second European Union directive on money laundering. They apply to persons undertaking 'relevant business'. Under Regulation 2, the definition of 'relevant business' includes:

'The provision by way of business of advice about the tax affairs of another person by a body corporate or unincorporate or, in the case of a sole practitioner, by an individual' and

'the provision by way of business of accountancy services by a body corporate or unincorporate or, in the case of a sole practitioner, by an individual'.

12.2 The obligations

12.2.1 Members must comply with the requirements of the MLR 2003. Accordingly, members must have procedures in place for the purposes of identifying clients, for record keeping and internal reporting (see section 13 below).

12.3 Training

12.3.1 Appropriate measures must be taken to make relevant employees aware of the money laundering legislation and training must be given in how to recognise and deal with transactions which may be related to money laundering.

12.4 Identification

12.4.1 Members must implement identification procedures to require the production of satisfactory evidence of identity as soon as is reasonably practicable after first contact is made with the client. For evidence of identity to be satisfactory it must be:

- 'reasonably capable' of establishing that the client is the person he claims to be; and
- the person obtaining the evidence must be satisfied that it does in fact establish that the client is the person he claims to be.

For further guidance see Appendix 1.

12.4.2 There are a number of exceptions to this requirement, which are in Regulation 5. It will not always be clear cut as to whether or not a client will fall into one of the exceptions. Members should obtain legal advice if they are concerned about this. Members may decide that it is advisable as a matter of best practice to require verification of identity for all clients.

12.4.3 Where a member provides consultancy services to another firm the member must ascertain who his client is (ie is it the firm or the firm's client?) and undertake the appropriate identification checks. Where the services are provided to the firm's client, then in addition to obtaining evidence of identity of the firm, under Regulation 4(3)(d) the member must also take reasonable measures to establish the identity of the firm's client and maintain a record of the evidence obtained. The obligation to take reasonable measures is rather less than the obligation to obtain satisfactory evidence but it must still be complied with.

12.5 Record keeping

12.5.1 The MLR 2003 require records to be kept of all identification evidence obtained. A copy of that evidence must be kept, or information as to where a copy of that evidence may be obtained. If this is not possible, information must be kept enabling the evidence of identity to be re-obtained. The records must be kept for a period of five years from the date the relationship with the client comes to an end.

12.5.2 Records must also be kept of all the transactions that have taken place for a particular client. These must be kept for five years from when the transaction is completed.

12.5.3 Firms would also be well advised to keep records of money laundering training, so that they can demonstrate that they have complied with the obligation to train relevant principals and staff.

12.5.4 Firms, and indeed every individual within the firm, should for their own protection keep records of money laundering reports made and matters considered in deciding whether to make a report. In particular, either the individual client handler or the MLRO might be called upon at a later date to justify why a report was not made in a particular case (for example where another advisor involved did make a report). Hence any consideration of possible reports should be documented. It is preferable for these records to be kept confidentially and not on client files to minimise any risk of the alleged offender inadvertently being tipped off – the less people who know the better.

13. REPORT TO THE MLRO AND CONSENT TO PROCEED

13.1.1 A report to the MLRO should set out the type of offence, the grounds for suspicion and why it is believed there may be proceeds. If the MLRO is to make a report to NCIS he will also need identity details of the client or other party about whom there is suspicion – ie full name, address, business/occupation, date of birth/company and VAT number, and any other identity information, to the extent that it is available. A member making a report to the MLRO is not obliged to seek out information which is not already held; this contrasts with the obligation on the part of the MLRO to consider all information held by his firm. A report is also required even where the identity of the subject of the report is unknown.

13.1.2 It would be in the client's interest for the NCIS report to contain any relevant fact such as 'Our client has instructed us to make a voluntary disclosure to the Revenue/Customs' or 'We anticipate that our client will instruct us to make a voluntary disclosure to the Revenue/Customs'.

13.1.3 Reports to NCIS must be made by the MLRO.

13.1.4 Where, before a specific transaction takes place, a member is suspicious that a money laundering offence may be committed, consent from NCIS (or a Customs Officer) is required before proceeding with that transaction. This is called 'authorised disclosure' and is the option to report described at paragraph 2.2.1. An example might be where a member is involved in advising on an arrangement for transferring funds overseas which the adviser suspects resulted from a crime such as tax evasion. The MLRO should consider whether it is appropriate for the firm to continue to act in these circumstances and if so he should apply to NCIS for consent. In these circumstances NCIS have 7 working days (the 'notice period') from submission of the money laundering report to give or refuse consent, so early notification to NCIS is vital. If NCIS do not respond within the notice period, the transaction can proceed and the disclosure defence will be available. If NCIS refuse consent, the law enforcement agency has up to a further 31 days in which to decide what action to take, for example to apply for a restraint order.

13.1.5 A fast track system has been put into place for urgent requests for consent. Application for the fast track should be by filing the usual form by fax, with a covering letter requiring the fast track. A defence may still arise after a 'prohibited act' has taken place if a person has a good reason for his failure to make the disclosure before the act took place, and the disclosure is made as soon as practicable after the transaction.

14. THE MONEY LAUNDERING REPORTING OFFICER

14.1.1 As noted in paragraph 1.3.1, under the MLR 2003, members in practice will have to appoint a MLRO. The MLRO should be at a sufficiently senior level within the practice to be able to act independently and not to be influenced by others when considering whether or not to submit a report to NCIS. The MLRO will often, but not necessarily, be a principal.

14.1.2 A sole practitioner need not appoint a MLRO if he does not employ any staff nor acts in association with any other person. He will in effect carry out the role of MLRO for his business.

14.1.3 The MLRO is responsible for ensuring that the practice has satisfactory systems in place so that the practice can meet its requirements under the MLR 2003. He is also responsible for ensuring that the principals and staff are adequately trained in their obligations under the MLR 2003.

14.1.4 The MLRO may wish to undertake training additional to that provided for other staff within the practice.

14.1.5 The MLRO needs to be aware of the form in which reports must be submitted to NCIS. He also needs to understand when it is necessary to ask NCIS for consent to continue to act and the associated time limits.

14.1.6 Thc MLRO should consider identifying a lawyer who could advise the practice regarding the MLR2003 should the need arise.

14.1.7 Further guidance can be found in chapter 15 of the CCAB interim guidance.

14.1.8 POCA creates two separate offences applying to MLROs working within or outside the regulated sector. If a MLRO working within the regulated sector improperly fails to report to NCIS, and he knows or suspects or has reasonable grounds for knowing or suspecting that another person is engaged in money laundering, he will commit an offence and be liable to a term of imprisonment of five years. MLROs working outside the regulated sector must have knowledge or suspicion that a person is engaged in money laundering to commit the offence.

15. HOW INTELLIGENCE WILL BE USED BY THE AUTHORITIES

15.1.1 Subject to the requirement to make, where appropriate, a suspicious activity report to the MLRO, the member must at all times take care not to breach client confidentiality and make disclosures beyond the basic reporting obligations. Where the MLRO is involved, the member should have no need to deal directly with NCIS and where enforcement agencies act based upon intelligence received from NCIS, they may only do so using the usual statutory powers available to them.

15.1.2 There are some specific information powers in POCA. Under s 345 of POCA production orders may be issued which apply to the investigations concerning the proceeds of criminal conduct. A production order will require a person to produce material to the appropriate officer for him to take away; or require that a person give an appropriate officer access to the material. The order must be for a period no longer than 7 days, unless it appears to the judge that a shorter or longer period is more appropriate. For an order to be granted the judge must be satisfied that there are reasonable grounds for believing that the specified person is in possession or control of the material, and the material is likely to be of substantial value to the investigation. Legally privileged documents will be protected.

15.1.3 Reports relating to pure tax matters are likely to be passed on by NCIS to the Inland Revenue or Customs and Excise as appropriate.

15.1.4 The approach for direct tax offences is set out in question 6, Appendix 2.

15.1.5 Customs have seconded staff to NCIS from the National Investigation Service (NIS). The NIS cell will either allocate suitable cases to NIS operational teams or pass smaller cases to local fraud units. Cases not adopted will be referred back to NCIS.

15.1.6 There are no clear protocols as to how reports that are relevant to both the Revenue and Customs will be handled and it may be that there will be uncoordinated enquiries by both bodies in this event.

16. ENGAGEMENT LETTERS

16.1.1 A practitioner is under no obligation to advise clients in the engagement letter that he may be required to submit a report to NCIS should he have knowledge or suspicion of money laundering. The legislation makes it clear that the duty to report suspicion overrides client confidentiality.

16.1.2 If a practitioner wishes to make general reference to his money laundering reporting obligations before agreeing to act for a client, he may do so provided that no suspicion of money laundering has been aroused. If a member wishes to give a warning, wording on the following lines could be used:

> '[This firm/practice is]/[I am required] under the Proceeds of Crime Act 2002 to make a report to the National Criminal Intelligence Service if [we]/[I] become aware during the course of [our]/[my] professional work, of any circumstances which give rise to knowledge or suspicion or reasonable grounds for suspicion of a money laundering offence. The offence of money laundering may be committed by concealing, arranging or acquiring the proceeds of any criminal conduct including the proceeds of tax evasion, even if the conduct occurs outside the UK.'

However, members should take extreme care to avoid the offences of tipping off (see paragraph 4.1) or facilitating the acquisition, retention etc of criminal proceeds (see paragraph 2.2), both in any warning given and in any follow up discussion. No warning should be given if any concerns have already been raised (eg if the client or potential client has made an appointment to see an investigations/back duty specialist). No advice should be given to clients on how to avoid NCIS reports since to do this might constitute a criminal offence (eg 'Don't tell me anything I shouldn't know about your French tax position' or 'I recommend that you consult a lawyer rather than any other type of professional in relation to …'). It is recommended that any member wishing to enter into discussions and briefing of clients and potential clients in relation to their money laundering obligations should obtain legal advice on their proposed script, including responses to common questions.

16.1.3 There are other situations in which members may be obliged to make disclosures of normally confidential information to various parties, in some cases without informing their clients, for example where a s20BA TMA notice is issued. Members might therefore prefer to use a more all embracing form of words in their engagement terms rather than expressly referring to proceeds of crime obligations eg

> 'Neither we nor you will be prevented from disclosing confidential information which is required to be disclosed by law or any professional or regulatory obligation.'

APPENDIX 1 IDENTIFICATION OF CLIENTS – VERIFICATION PROCEDURES

The Joint Money Laundering Steering Group (JMLSG) Guidance notes (Chapter 4 – Know your customer and identification evidence) provide comprehensive guidance on this area. These are available on the JMLSG website at a cost of £50 www.jmlsg.org.uk. The following notes suggest some of the identification checks which could be carried out. The nature and extent of checks to be carried out in any particular case is a matter for professional judgement. The procedures followed should be recorded.

Individuals

The purpose of this is to confirm that the individual is who he says he is. A person's identity is his name (or names where more than one is used) and address where he may be found.

Identity can be checked by an official document ideally bearing a photograph – for example a current signed passport or current UK photo card driving licence. It is helpful to record the date of birth if that is available.

The client's address should also be verified using different documentation to that used to confirm identity, for example

- face to face home visit
- checking the electoral register
- making a credit reference agency search
- asking to see a recent utility bill, bank or building society statement or local authority tax bill (original documents only)
- checking a local telephone directory.

Non UK residents

For prospective clients who are not normally resident in the UK but who make face to face contact with a member, a passport or identity card will normally be available as evidence of identity. The identity and address should be confirmed with a reputable financial institution or professional adviser in the client's home country or country of residence.

Where non UK resident prospective clients are not seen face to face the following procedures should be followed, for example

- a branch office, associated firm or reliable professional adviser in the prospective client's home country may be used to confirm identity or as an agent to check personal verification details
- where a member has no such relationship in the prospective client's country of residence, a copy of the passport authenticated by an attorney, a notary or an embassy consular authority may be obtained
- a reputable credit or financial institution in the prospective client's home country may confirm the client's true name and permanent address.

Companies and other organisations

General

Because of the potential difficulties in identifying beneficial ownership and the complexity of their organisations and structures, legal entities and trusts are among the most likely vehicles for money laundering, particularly when fronted by a legitimate trading company. Particular care should be taken to verify the legal existence of the prospective client, to identify the ultimate beneficial owner(s) and/or controller(s) of the entity and to ensure that any person purporting to act on its behalf is authorised to do so.

Companies, partnerships and sole traders (business)

The principal requirement is to identify those who have ultimate control or significant influence over the business and its assets. Particular attention should be paid to any shareholders or others who inject a significant proportion of the capital or provide financial support or who will benefit from it. Enquiries should be made to confirm that the entity exits for a legitimate trading or economic purpose and that it is not merely a 'shell' company where the controlling principals cannot be identified.

Before a business relationship is established a company search and/or some other commercial enquiries should be made to verify the business history and ensure that the business has not been, or is not in the process of being dissolved, struck off or wound up.

If a member becomes aware of changes to the client's structure or ownership, or if suspicions are aroused by a change in the nature of the business transacted, further checks should be made to ascertain the reason for the changes. However the member would need to investigate with caution to ensure that the client is not 'tipped off'.

Where the prospective client is a company

- quoted on a recognised, designated or approved investment exchange, or
- is known to be a wholly owned subsidiary or a subsidiary under the control of such a company

no further steps to verify over and above the usual commercial checks and due diligence will normally be required. The evidence for accepting that the prospective client comes within one of these categories should be recorded as should evidence that any individual representing the company has the necessary authority to do so.

Where the prospective client is an unquoted company, an incorporated business or a partnership, the member should identify the principal directors/partners and/or shareholders in line with the requirements for individual clients. In addition the following documents should normally be obtained:

- for established businesses, a copy of the latest report and accounts (audited where applicable)

- for new businesses, a copy of the business plan, cash flow projections and any other records enabling monitoring of the development of the new business
- a copy of the certificate of incorporation/certificate of trade or equivalent.

The member may also undertake a credit reference agency search or take a reference from a bank or from another professional adviser.

Trusts (including occupational pension schemes) and nominees

Where a member is asked to act for trustees or nominees, the identities of all controlling parties should be verified. These include all trustees, the settlor and at least the principal beneficiaries.

Trusts and nominee accounts are a popular vehicle for criminals wishing to avoid identification procedures and mask the origin of the money they wish to launder. Particular care needs to be exercised when the accounts are set up in offshore locations with strict bank secrecy or confidentiality rules. Trusts created in jurisdictions without equivalent money laundering procedures in place will warrant additional enquiries.

Where sufficient information cannot be obtained about the underlying nature of the trust the nominee company or the source of funds a commercial decision will need to be taken whether to act for the prospective client or not. Unless an acceptable explanation for the absence of this information is available from a reliable and respectable source it would be prudent to decline to act.

In the of occupational pension schemes, verification can best be accomplished by obtaining proof of Inland Revenue approval for the scheme. Otherwise, the identity of the principal employer has to be verified, and also (by inspecting the scheme's trust documents) that of the trustees. There is no need to verify the identity of those who are to receive scheme benefits, unless either they are making their own contributions into the scheme (independently of payroll deduction means) or the member is to give them advice individually.

Registered Charities in England and Wales

The Charity Commission for England and Wales holds a central register of charities and allocates a registered number to each. Where the business is a registered charity, the Charity Commission should be asked to confirm the registered number of the charity and the name and address of the Commission's correspondent for the charity concerned. A similar system is operated in

Scotland by the Scottish Charities Office. There is no comparable facility in respect of charities in Northern Ireland; a full verification must be undertaken instead.

Local authorities and other public bodies

Where the client is a local authority or other public body, the member should obtain a copy of the resolution authorising the undertaking of the relevant transaction or business activity. Evidence that the individual dealing with the member has the relevant authority to act should also be sought and retained.

APPENDIX 2 MONEY LAUNDERING AND DISCLOSURES TO THE INLAND REVENUE: A QUESTIONS AND ANSWERS GUIDANCE NOTE

The content of this note has been agreed between the Inland Revenue, the ATT and CIOT.

Object of note

To provide guidance about the practical effect of the money laundering legislation on disclosures of tax evasion by tax practitioners.

Questions and answers

1. Will the new money laundering requirements make any difference to the Revenue's willingness to use Hansard or in local offices their willingness to come to a settlement without prosecution?

The Revenue have confirmed that the money laundering requirements will not affect the Hansard or local office procedures.

2. Which government departments should I as a tax practitioner inform when I am approached by an individual who tells me that he wants to make a full disclosure of undeclared taxable income and/or gains?

Traditionally, you as a tax practitioner, having taken instructions and collected all necessary information from your client, have informed the Revenue and/or Customs, depending on the circumstances.

But if you have reasonable grounds for knowing or suspecting that your client has intentionally evaded tax then the new money laundering laws will also apply. You or your Money Laundering Reporting Officer (MLRO) if you have one, will be obliged also to make an immediate report to NCIS ('National Criminal Intelligence Service') in a (yet-to-be-determined) specified form. Where you have a MLRO, you must notify him or her and they will in turn consider whether a report should be made to NCIS. See chapter 15 of the CCAB interim anti money laundering guidance regarding the need to appoint a MLRO where you do not have one.

3. Should I make a report to NCIS when I receive a COP 9 letter from the Revenue?

It is your knowledge or suspicion that counts rather than the Revenue's suspicion. You should make up your own mind whether such a letter gives you grounds for making a report applying the criteria in Section 330 POCA 2002 ie do you know or suspect, or have reasonable grounds for knowing or suspecting, that the client is engaged in money laundering as defined at Chapter 10 of the CCAB interim anti money laundering guidance.

4. When should I make a report to NCIS?

The money laundering legislation says that NCIS must be told 'as soon as is practicable'. NCIS has told us that this means, in essence, immediately. So if, for example, someone comes in to your office and says he wants to 'come clean' or uses other words which indicate an intention to disclose past tax irregularities, then NCIS must be told without delay. Even if the person has not given their name and address (or may not have given their proper name) a report must still be made to NCIS. Obviously this can only cover the information you have been given.

5. It is possible that the potential client may not instruct me at all. Will the Revenue monitor me as the tax practitioner named in the NCIS report to see if a disclosure emerges, and if so for how long?

The Revenue recognise that the potential client may go elsewhere (or nowhere) for advice. They have said they have no intention of monitoring reputable practitioners after NCIS reports have been submitted.

6. Once I have told NCIS, what happens next assuming no other agency is involved?

NCIS will pass reports to a special intelligence unit within the Inland Revenue Special Compliance Office ('SCO') in the first instance. The unit will consider whether it is suitable for investigation towards criminal prosecution. If it is not, the case will either be considered for enquiry under a SCO Code of Practice or referred to a special intelligence unit at TIDO, Llanishen, Cardiff. Where it is considered appropriate to pass intelligence on to relevant staff in local offices neither the fact that the intelligence has come from NCIS, nor the identity of the original source of the intelligence, is disclosed.

NCIS will acknowledge receipt of your report. They will subsequently advise you when details are passed to the relevant law enforcement agency, for example, the Revenue.

7. Does the need to report to NCIS before I am ready to tell the Revenue affect the timing of my providing information to the Revenue about my client's undeclared income and or gains? Although I have made a report to NCIS when approached by a potential client with a tax disclosure to make, I may not immediately be able to approach the Revenue because I will have to be formally instructed and the approach to the Revenue approved by the client. Collecting and collating the information will inevitably take time especially where several individuals or entities are involved. How long will the Revenue regard as a reasonable period before the approach is made while leaving Hansard open?

The Revenue have confirmed that a delay would not jeopardise the Hansard approach where it would otherwise be available provided that the taxpayer is taking active steps to regularise their affairs. Doing nothing involves the risk that Hansard may not be available and that prosecution may follow; or at least that penalty abatements are at risk.

One option, having obtained the client's permission, is to put down a marker by writing to the Revenue, saying you have been instructed by a named client to act for them in coming to a settlement about undeclared income or gains. You would also provide a date by which you expect to be able to let the Revenue have details.

8. To which Revenue office should I send the marker letter?

That is for you to decide. The same considerations apply as apply when you are deciding which Revenue office to approach initially with a client who wishes to 'come clean'.

9. How long a time period for providing the information would the Revenue consider reasonable in my 'marker' notification?

It will depend on the circumstances of each case but the Revenue have indicated that they will take a reasonable approach.

Your estimated timetable will obviously depend on your assessment of the likely complexity of your client's affairs.

10. What happens if I miss my self-imposed deadline set out in my marker letter?

The Revenue appreciate that the information may be difficult to obtain. You should obviously inform the Revenue if you wish to extend your self-imposed deadline. You will need to reassure the Revenue that the client is taking active steps to help you move matters forward.

11. What is the position where the Revenue already had concerns about a taxpayer and the money laundering notification is the trigger for the raid or the launch of an investigation? The Revenue may not be prepared to wait, possibly due to concerns that documents might be destroyed. Would Hansard still be a possibility for my client if the normal conditions are met (for example if the raid does not indicate that my client is unsuitable for Hansard)?

The Revenue have informed us that receipt of a report from NCIS or your 'marker' notification will not necessarily make them deviate from their proposed course of action. The Revenue will look at the NCIS report in context of all other information available to them regarding a case when prioritizing the cases for investigation.

12. Will the Revenue wait for a reasonable period of time before launching an investigation on receipt of a report from NCIS?

In the majority of cases, given the time it would take for NCIS to pass information to the Revenue SCO and for the Revenue to consider what action to take, the time lag between the report to NCIS and the making of a voluntary disclosure to the Revenue may not be an issue in practice. You should monitor the receipt of acknowledgements to track progress. If you are concerned you could consider the use of a marker letter as discussed above.

APPENDIX 3 EXTRACT FROM INLAND REVENUE WORKING TOGETHER ISSUE 13 – PUBLISHED JUNE 2003

Proceeds of Crime Act 2002 and the Money Laundering Regulations 2003

Summary

Home Office legislation, the Proceeds of Crime Act 2002, has been brought into force in stages. This article concerns Part 7 of this Act, which reformed the law on money laundering and is expected to have a significant effect on professional advisers. This article is intended to:

- raise awareness of this new legislation
- cover its interaction with the Inland Revenue in the area of tax evasion.

Other parts of the Act, for example those concerning the establishment and operation of the Asset Recovery Agency, are not dealt with in this article.

Introduction

The Proceeds of Crime Act 2002 requires those in what the legislation terms the 'regulated sector' to report where they know or suspect, or have reasonable grounds for knowing or suspecting, that another person is engaged in laundering the proceeds of crime.

The existing regulated sector, which includes for example banks and investment businesses, is due to be expanded by the Money Laundering Regulations 2003 to include:

- Estate agents
- Casinos
- Insolvency practitioners
- Tax advisers (a person appointed to give tax advice about the tax affairs of another person)
- Accountants and auditors (those providing by way of business accountancy or audit services)
- Legal advisers (those providing by way of business legal services which involves participation in a financial or real property transaction)
- Company formation agents
- Dealers in high value goods, including auctioneers, whenever payment is made in cash, and in an amount of 15,000 euro or more.

These Regulations that expand the regulated sector are expected to be laid around mid June[3]. The Government is however intending to allow a further 3 month period from when they are laid until the Regulations actually come into force. This will allow those affected by the Regulations time to implement training programmes and anti-money laundering procedures.

Previous money laundering legislation has principally concerned the laundering of drug or terrorist funds. The new legislation concerns the proceeds of all crime and this includes all acts of tax evasion and fraud.

For professional advisers (tax advisers, accountants, auditors and legal advisers) this means, as with others in the regulated sector, that if in the course of their business they know or suspect that their clients or others have committed a money laundering offence, including tax evasion, they are required to report their suspicions to the National Criminal Intelligence Service (NCIS).

This is without *de minimis* limit and thus covers all suspicions irrespective of the amounts involved. The wording in the legislation also captures not just actual knowledge or suspicion, but a more stringent test of whether there were 'reasonable grounds' for such knowledge or suspicion.

Although this is not mandatory upon them yet, some professional advisers have already submitted reports in anticipation of the legislation taking effect.

[3] The regulations will become effective three months after they have been laid before the House of Commons. There have been many delays and as at the date of publishing the effective date is still not known.

Requirement for Professional Advisers to Report Knowledge or Suspicion of Tax Evasion

Professional advisers will be required to report their knowledge or suspicion of money laundering (including acts of tax evasion) on a Suspicious Activity Report (SAR) form as soon as is practicable after the information came to them.

The legislation states that a disclosure must be made 'in the prescribed form and manner as set out by the Secretary of State'. The form or forms for this are currently under review. For the time being the existing SAR form should be used which is available from NCIS and can be downloaded from their website at www.ncis.co.uk.

All SAR forms must be submitted direct to NCIS. This is the case whether the report concerns the proceeds of tax evasion or any other form of criminal activity. NCIS is the government body to receive these reports as only they have the information to check whether there are links to wider criminality.

The Inland Revenue is not a receiving body for these reports. Where a voluntary disclosure about unpaid liabilities due to tax evasion is intended to be made to the Revenue the professional adviser is still required to make a SAR to NCIS at the earliest opportunity.

Reports that Concern Tax Evasion

Reports that relate to tax evasion will be referred within NCIS to an Inland Revenue team who will analyse and evaluate them. Where the only criminality identified from this analysis is tax evasion, the reports will be forwarded by

NCIS to the Inland Revenue or HM Customs & Excise as appropriate. For offences of evading direct taxes or NICs the Inland Revenue will be the investigating body and, in England and Wales, the prosecuting body for these offences. In Scotland the Procurator Fiscal and in Northern Ireland the Director of Public Prosecutions are the prosecuting bodies. Reports forwarded by NCIS to the Revenue will be received by Special Compliance Office (SCO).

Effect on Inland Revenue Enquiries and Hansard

Any Inland Revenue enquiries that result from or are informed by disclosures forwarded from NCIS will be carried out in the same manner as any other Inland Revenue enquiry.

In particular reporting a case to NCIS ahead of notifying the Revenue will have no bearing on how the Revenue may treat a case, if the taxpayer is actively seeking to set their affairs straight. This also applies to cases dealt with under the Inland Revenue approach to civil settlements known as 'Hansard'.

Confidentiality of information received by the Inland Revenue will of course remain of uppermost importance. In cases other than criminal investigations by SCO, procedures are in place such that investigators receive only the factual information from a SAR with no knowledge of who made the original disclosure.

Tipping Off

The Proceeds of Crime Act also contains an offence referred to in the legislation as 'ipping off'. This makes it an offence for a person who knows or suspects that a SAR has been submitted to NCIS then to make a disclosure likely to prejudice any resulting investigation or to disclose that they suspect that an investigation may be taking place. The most obvious example of this would be where a professional adviser made their client aware that they had sent a SAR to NCIS. This offence, as with others under this legislation, is a criminal offence.

Approaching the Inland Revenue to make a disclosure on behalf of a client about unpaid tax liabilities after the SAR has been sent to NCIS does not constitute tipping off.

Other Aspects of the Legislation

The Act defines the principal money laundering offences of concealing, making arrangements, acquisition, use and possession of what is described as 'criminal property', Criminal property is anything situated anywhere in the world and is defined as money; all forms of property, real or personal, heritable or moveable; other intangible property; property obtained by a person who has an interest in it; things in action.

Where criminal conduct occurs outside the UK it is still within the scope of the Act if it would constitute an offence if it occurred in the UK.

The legislation also contains provisions whereby consent may be necessary from NCIS to proceed with a transaction. Where before a specific transaction takes place it arouses suspicion that it would result in a money laundering offence being committed, consent from NCIS is required before proceeding with that transaction. An example might be where a professional adviser was involved in advising on an arrangement for transferring funds overseas, which the adviser suspected resulted from crime (ie from tax evasion).

In such circumstances NCIS have 7 working days from submission of the SAR to give or refuse consent, so early notification to NCIS is vital. If NCIS refuse consent, law enforcement has up to a further 31 days in which to decide what action to take, eg to apply for a restraint order.

The legislation also acknowledges professional privilege in certain circumstances where legal advice is given by a professional legal adviser.

Further Information and Help

Further information can be obtained from the Home Office website at www.homeoffice.gov.uk/crimpol/oic/proceeds/index.html and the Treasury website at www.hmtreasury.gov.uk/Documents/Financial_Services/money/fin_money_index.cfm

The legislation itself can be found at http://www.legislation.hmso.gov.uk/acts/acts2002/20020029.htm

In addition the accountancy and taxation bodies are in the process of preparing authoritative guidance in this area for approval by the Treasury. The Revenue is also planning to tell you more on the website.

APPENDIX 4 EXTRACT FROM PARLIAMENTARY DEBATE ON 24 JANUARY 2002 ON TAX EVASION AND THE HANSARD PROCEDURE

Mr Ainsworth was Parliamentary Under Secretary of State for the Home Department

Mr Ainsworth: I take the point that one of the consequences of extending the possession offence under clause 323 that covers any criminal proceeds, whether or not they are one's own or another's, is that a tax adviser or an accountant will be duty bound to make a report. The hon. Member for Beaconsfield has taken soundings, and we have consulted fully on the matter. We have talked to the Revenue, the police and NCIS. Before we think about how we want the provision to work, it needs to be said that tax evasion is a serious, criminal offence. The hon. Gentleman did not suggest that it should be treated as anything other than that.

While the sums involved in tax evasion could, in some cases, be small, the offences with which we are concerned are serious. The main argument that has been advanced is that, when accountants and tax advisers are brought within the regulated sector, many clients who have a genuine desire to put their tax affairs straight through the Hansard process will be less inclined to seek the views of tax advisers, knowing that the matter will have to be reported to NCIS. They will be far more likely to seek advice from the solicitor next door who will not have to report the matter to NCIS, because of the legal privilege exemption. It is also argued that clients will no longer be so keen to regularise their tax affairs and that there will be a substantial loss of revenue as a result.

The facts do not bear that out. The Inland Revenue's analysis is that, against a background of a rough figure of £100 million of revenue recovered in total through the Hansard procedure, only about £15 million is recovered through Hansard disclosures, which are made spontaneously to the Revenue without there being any prior knowledge on the Revenue's part. The Hansard procedure is used, and the view of the tax authorities is that it is used more often than not when they are already on to the case, and in some circumstances they are more than happy to accept that they can regularise the position in that way. The sum is not huge and the Revenue advises that it would not expect to lose all of it anyway. It sees a counterbalancing effect of improving compliance through the more robust reporting regime. In short, the Revenue does not see an overall loss to it as a result of the clause. Indeed, it believes that there may be an increase.

It is important to point out that in the majority of cases a tax adviser will not know whether the criminal proceeds in the hands of his client were derived from tax evasion rather than another crime. The hon. Gentleman said that if the Revenue became aware that there was other criminality, obviously it would report that to NCIS, but the Revenue will not necessarily know whether other criminality is involved. NCIS, rather than the Revenue or the tax adviser, will be best able to decide whether the case is purely one of tax evasion, rather than other criminality.

Much has been said about the idea that NCIS will be swamped with minor reports of tax evasion. We accept that there will be an increase in the number of reports that will be made to NCIS, but we consulted NCIS, and it is satisfied that it can cope with the additional work load. It takes the view that it would be better to allow it to dismiss a report as relating only to minor tax evasion than to risk losing an important money laundering lead. The sums involved do not necessarily determine whether money laundering is involved.

[24 January columns 1141–2

He went on:

When there is no evidence of wider criminality beyond tax evasion, NCIS will in any event pass cases back to the Inland Revenue to be dealt with, as happens at present. It is already public knowledge that the Revenue has a presence in NCIS. There is nothing new about a close liaison between the Revenue and NCIS on matters of this kind.

Concerns have been raised because reports must be made to NCIS as soon as practicable after the information gives rise to knowledge or suspicion. NCIS may pass on reports to the Revenue long before they would have been received under the Hansard procedure, which can take many months to sort out. However, I reassure the Committee and those who made representations that when that happens, the Revenue will not withhold the offer of a Hansard arrangement to settle the matter purely on the basis that it learned about the evasion from a report sent from NCIS, rather than being notified by the taxpayer or his adviser. That is important, because we have been asked for that assurance. The Revenue will not deal with cases differently because they were received via NCIS rather than directly.

[24 January columns 1142–3

Mr Ainsworth was then asked by Dominic Grieve:

Mr. Grieve: I am glad to hear that, although the problem is a little more twisted than that. A person will no longer be able to get advice from their tax adviser about making a Hansard agreement. The adviser might say, "I'm sorry, but there's no such thing as a Hansard agreement – goodbye," and then, without the client's knowledge, pick up the telephone and say to NCIS, "My client was seeking a Hansard agreement. I sent him away, but I think that you should know about it." Legal professional privilege would prevent that. The irony is that NCIS will have to get information through another channel; the voluntary declaration via the tax accountant will come to an end. Surely that would be the consequence of the measure. The accountant or adviser will not be able to tell the Revenue because of legal professional privilege.

Mr. Ainsworth: He will. The hon. Gentleman says that if the adviser tells the Revenue, he will be guilty of tipping off, but clause 325 states that the tipping-off offence applies where the disclosure may "prejudice any investigation". I do not see how telling the Revenue could ever be prejudicial to an investigation. Of course, the Hansard procedure supports my assurance.

Yes, there is a fear that the measure could discourage people from coming forward, knowing that a report will be made to NCIS – rightly so, if serious criminality is involved. We must assure people that we do not intend to alter the Hansard process, and that the intervention of NCIS in the information stream will not alter the way in which the case is dealt with when it eventually reaches the Revenue. The Revenue is not in a position to know whether criminality, other than tax evasion, is involved, nor is the accountant or tax adviser. NCIS knows that; it collects such information. However, if the tax evasion is purely minor, it will be passed on to the Revenue, which will deal with it. We are trying to ensure that that will not change.

[24 January column 1143

APPENDIX 5 OTHER SOURCES OF INFORMATION AND GUIDANCE

The following websites may be helpful when seeking additional guidance/ information regarding Money Laundering

- Consultative Committee of Accountancy Bodies – www.ccab.org.uk (and member sites – see 1.1.1)
- The Law Society – www.lawsociety.org.uk
- National Criminal Intelligence Service – www.ncis.gov.uk. Note – this guidance does not have any statutory authority but it is persuasive.
- Joint Money Laundering Steering Group – www.jmlsg.org.uk

Appendix 2:

An Anti-Money Laundering Strategy for the Inland Revenue

1. BACKGROUND

1.1 What is money laundering?

Traditionally, money laundering has been viewed as the 'processing' of all illegal or 'dirty' money derived from the proceeds of any illegal activity (e.g. the proceeds of drug-dealing, smuggling, fraud, theft, tax evasion or handling of stolen goods). This takes place through a succession of transfers and deals until the source of illegally acquired funds is obscured and the money takes on the appearance of legitimate or 'clean' funds or assets.

Money laundering can be used as a means to disguise the nature of profits generated from many types of criminality. This criminality can be tax evasion and thereby of direct interest to the Inland Revenue. Or it can be other serious forms of criminality, such as dealings in drugs, alcohol, tobacco or people trafficking. These crimes are of interest to others such as Customs and the police, and the Inland Revenue will work with these bodies to ensure that effective and co-ordinated action is taken against those engaged in such activities. In some cases money laundering is used to disguise both tax evasion and other criminality, in which case the Revenue will work with others to investigate and prosecute, sharing information as necessary.

However, the Proceeds of Crime Act 2002 updates, expands and unifies the money laundering offences. The predicate offences, which trigger other money laundering offences, include all criminal acts, irrespective of where in the world they occur.

It is also a money laundering offence to make arrangements to facilitate the use, acquisition or retention of criminal property on behalf of another person. And the definition is extended so that in certain circumstances no process is needed at all to trigger a money laundering offence. All that is needed is the acquisition, use or even possession of criminal property for money laundering offences to apply. So the mere possession of the proceeds of tax evasion in someone's wallet is sufficient for money laundering to have taken place. The definition has clearly been extended some way beyond traditional views of what money laundering is like.

A recent government estimate suggested that annually around £25 billion of criminal money might be available for money laundering in the UK.

1.2 The Inland Revenue's role within the Government's Anti-Money Laundering Strategy:

The Inland Revenue has agreed its core role within the Government's wider anti-money laundering strategy to be:

an investigatory and prosecuting body in the laundering of the proceeds of tax, national insurance contributions or tax credit fraud

further, we have agreed within the detail of that strategy that:

Inland Revenue has a role in the detection and investigation of money laundering. Investigation and prosecution by the Revenue is directed at combating the laundering of the proceeds of tax, national insurance contributions or tax credit fraud, with particular emphasis on professionals who facilitate tax evasion.

Where money laundering offences relate to wider criminality beyond tax evasion, the Revenue discloses this information to the appropriate law enforcing authority.

So our agreed role is partly one of investigation and prosecution and partly one of enabling others in law enforcement to achieve their objectives in countering money laundering. We will disclose information to them if it is legally possible to do so and we seek to find ways to disclose rather than reasons not to.

The legislative gateway to allow for this is in the Anti-Terrorism (Crime and Security) Act 2001, section 19. It is Revenue policy to make such disclosures. It will do so in accordance with the Memoranda of Understanding agreed with other law enforcing organisations and with its published Code of Practice governing such disclosures.

Further, we will take a positive approach to sharing our particular expertise in financial investigation, which is a valuable resource, potentially of significant use to others countering money laundering. As a part of this commitment to sharing our expertise, we will consider the scope for seconding our staff to other organisations.

2. ROLES AND RESPONSIBILITIES WITHIN GOVERNMENT

The lead organisations within Government and their core responsibilities are:

a) HM Treasury leads for the UK in international bodies (e.g. FATF), issues the Money Laundering Regulations, and is responsible under the Proceeds of Crime Act for approving guidance notes produced by industry.

b) Home Office is responsible for the UK primary legislation setting out the criminal law on money laundering and terrorist financing.

c) The Financial Services Authority devises and enforces the Rules. It also has powers to bring criminal prosecutions for breaches of the Money Laundering Regulations (but not the primary money laundering law).

d) The Financial Intelligence Division of the National Criminal Intelligence Services (NCIS) is the Financial Intelligence Unit (FIU) for the United Kingdom. It is the central, national unit responsible for receiving, analysing and disseminating Suspicious Activity Reports (SARs) in the UK.

e) Police forces are responsible for investigating money laundering and terrorist financing cases. HM Customs and Excise is both an investigatory and prosecuting body for money laundering, drug trafficking, indirect tax fraud and a number of other assigned matters. Customs operates the supervision of MSBs and will supervise dealers in high value goods under the Money Laundering Regulations 2003.

f) CPS, SFO and Customs are all prosecuting authorities. SFO prosecute money laundering cases where the underlying predicate offence involves serious or complex fraud. Customs have prosecution powers in relation to drug trafficking and indirect tax fraud with the CPS dealing with other cases (and fraud/drug cases investigated by the police).

g) The Foreign and Commonwealth Office is responsible for providing technical assistance to priority countries, and helping to implement international anti-money laundering standards through FATF-style regional bodies.

h) The Money Laundering Advisory Committee (MLAC) provides a forum for key stakeholders to co-ordinate the AML regime and review its efficiency and effectiveness. It examines industry produced guidance notes and makes recommendations prior to submission for government approval.

i) Joint Money Laundering Steering Group (JMLSG) prepares, publishes and promotes industry guidance on the prevention of money laundering for the financial services industry. It provides a forum for the sharing of information and represents the financial services industry in discussion with government and regulatory bodies.

3. THE INLAND REVENUE'S PROSECUTION POLICY

As described above, the Inland Revenue's involvement in tackling money laundering is limited to those cases in which tax evasion is a feature. The Proceeds of Crime Act 2002 creates a new mirror offence of money laundering when someone commits tax evasion, even in the absence of any transfer of movement of these funds.

So the Inland Revenue is interested in money laundering because of the underlying tax evasion which may exist. There are also instances whereby funds are moved or transferred and complex financial structures are created. The intention may be to disguise the true nature and source of money, which is in reality the proceeds of tax evasion. The Revenue has an important role to play in detecting and investigating any such arrangements.

The new offences of money laundering create further options under which to charge a tax evader. The commonly used charges for tax evasion are False Accounting or the common law offence of cheat. A new offence of being knowingly concerned in the fraudulent evasion of income tax was created in the Finance Act 2000.

Where these cases fit the Board's prosecutions policy, a criminal investigation may be carried out by the Special Compliance Office (SCO). Prosecutions are carried out in serious cases across the range of offences and in all the areas of law for which the Board are responsible. The Board operate a policy of selective prosecution intended to bolster their overall enforcement strategy. The focus is on cases where prosecution will do most to promote compliance with the law by deterring tax, contribution and tax credit fraud. So criminal sanctions are used in those cases which counter identified risks to the compliance base. This is an important theme of the emerging departmental compliance strategy.

An exemplary approach is adopted, with publicity given to successful cases, providing a message that no tax evader should feel immune from criminal prosecution. The exception is only in those cases in which taxpayers come forward, voluntarily and unprompted, and make a full disclose of their evasion.

The Board's criminal prosecution policy for money laundering offences will follow these same principles.

3.1 The Revenue's role as a prosecutor

Where there are mixed cases of tax evasion and other money laundering offences, the Revenue will investigate the matter to the extent that there is tax evasion and it will disclose the other matters to other organisation to investigate further.

The Revenue will support other parts of U.K. Government in their efforts to tackle crime. The Revenue is a law enforcing organisation and a prosecuting body in its own right in England and Wales. It will investigate and prosecute in cases of money laundering which involve tax evasion and will offer co-operation and assistance to others investigating and prosecuting other money laundering offences where the law, its Memoranda of Understanding and Codes of Practice enable it to do so.

The Revenue is a signatory to the Convention between prosecuting authorities agreed on 11th February 1998 and published through a response by the Attorney General to a Parliamentary Question on 8th April 1998. Within this Convention are principles agreed between prosecuting authorities about co-ordination and co-operation in the circumstances of two or more prosecuting authorities considering action against the same individual for related offences.

The Attorney General confirmed in his response that proceedings brought by the Crown Prosecution Service will ordinarily encompass charges relating to tax evasion only in circumstances where that is incidental to allegations of non-fiscal criminal conduct.

We have agreed with other prosecuting bodies about how we will treat cases of serious tax evasion and associated money laundering. In particular, we have reached agreement, in principle, with the Crown Prosecution Service, the Serious Fraud Office and the Financial Services Authority that in cases in which the only predicate offence is tax evasion, then the Inland Revenue and its Special Compliance Office will be the investigating body. The Board of Inland Revenue will be the prosecuting body and its published prosecution policy will remain unaffected.

But for those cases in which there is both tax evasion and some other criminality, these other prosecuting authorities can give no undertaking that they will not prosecute for the money laundering offences, irrespective of the approach taken by the Inland Revenue to the predicate tax evasion offences.

3.2 Roles and responsibilities within the Inland Revenue

CCP will be responsible for overall co-ordination of the Revenue policy and strategy on countering money laundering. It will work with others on the departmental Working Group to monitor developments, the management of risks and progress made.

SCO is the only part of the Inland Revenue which conducts criminal investigations and its staff are trained in the conduct of such investigations accordingly. So criminal investigations into acts of money laundering which are predicated by tax evasion are to be carried out by SCO. SCO's Anti-Money Laundering Unit is the focal point for such investigations and the delivery of other aspects of the Inland Revenue's anti-money laundering strategy, including the sharing of information and expertise.

SCO will work with the Inland Revenue Solicitor's Office, who prosecute offenders on behalf of the Board of Inland Revenue, which is a prosecuting body in its own right in England and Wales. Cases in Scotland and Northern Ireland are prepared for criminal prosecution and referred to the Procurator Fiscal and the Director of Public Prosecutions respectively, so that these bodies may consider whether they wish to proceed with a criminal prosecution.

SCO and the Solicitor's Office will work with policy administrators in Cross-Cutting Policy (CCP), who own the prosecution policy and maintain it on a delegated basis, on behalf of the Board of Inland Revenue. CCP has the role of signing Board's Orders to proceed with a criminal prosecution, having regard to investigation reports from SCO and legal advice from the Solicitor's Office. CCP applies a public interest test, as set out in the Code for Crown Prosecutors. Once this test is satisfied, CCP will issue a Board's Order. So each case involves three parts of the Inland Revenue. This tri-partite working has a proven track record, in ensuring a high standard of cases being put before the criminal courts.

3.3 Professional Advisers

The Inland Revenue will seek to prosecute accountants, tax advisers and other professionals who assist their clients, or who act in their own capacity, to evade tax through means of money laundering activities. Professionals are an important stakeholder in the process of ensuring that taxpayers pay the right tax at the right time and the Inland Revenue places great reliance on the integrity of these professionals who act on behalf of their clients.

The Financial Action Task Force on Money Laundering noted in its 2000/01 report that 'Lawyers, notaries, accountants and other professionals offering financial advice have become the common elements to complex money laundering schemes. The trend is mentioned by almost all FATF members'. The report goes onto note that one consequence of the continuing efforts of governments to combat money laundering is an increasing complexity of schemes being operated, increasing the need for the involvement of a professional adviser.

So advisers who enable tax evasion offences are key to the success of these crimes. It is appropriate for the revenue authorities to target them as 'centres of infection'.

The Proceeds of Crime Act 2002 requires certain reports from those in the regulated sector, which will include accountants, tax advisers and other professionals from March 2004. These reports are of their suspicions or knowledge of money laundering of their clients, which may include tax evasion offences. Reports should be sent to the National Criminal Intelligence Service as soon as is practicable after the suspicion or knowledge arises. Making a report is a defence against certain money laundering offences outlined earlier.

When these professionals fail to make a report they commit an offence and may be the subject of a criminal investigation and a subsequent criminal prosecution. The Inland Revenue will take the lead in the investigation and prosecution if the predicate offence of the client is tax evasion and the adviser has failed to report this.

A further offence provided for in the Proceeds of Crime Act 2002 is one of tipping off. A professional adviser is not only obliged to report his or her knowledge or suspicions, but they must not inform the subject of the report that they have done so. Any action which prejudices a related criminal investigation is an offence of tipping off under this part of the Act.

For each of the offences outlined in this part of the strategy and in earlier sections, where the predicate offence is tax evasion, the Inland Revenue will take the lead in countering such offences. It will have regard to this strategy document and to its published prosecution policy in deciding which cases to purse criminally. SCO's dedicated anti-money laundering unit will take the lead within the Inland Revenue in conducting a criminal investigation.

3.4 International dimension

The UK has taken a leading role in promoting the strengthening of links between tax and anti-money laundering authorities. In May 1998, following a UK initiative, G7 Finance Ministers urged OECD to give particular attention to improving the availability of information to tax authorities in order to curb international tax evasion and avoidance. OECD proposed a two prong initiative:

- first, to ensure that financial institutions report all suspicious transactions to the money laundering authorities, including transactions which are (or believed to be) related to tax crimes. Work on this proposal was pursued by the Financial Action Task Force
- second, to increase the flow of information from money laundering authorities to tax authorities, nationally and internationally, without undermining the effectiveness of anti-money laundering systems. Work on this continues to be pursued by OECD's Committee of Fiscal affairs.

The UK, including the Inland Revenue, has actively participated in initiatives to take these two themes forward and will continue to do so. The aims have included sharing experiences, to enable representatives to share information on some of the mechanisms used for both money laundering and tax evasion.

4. STRATEGIC THEMES

4.1 Identification and countering of risks

In line with its broader strategic approach to achieving compliance, the Inland Revenue will identify the risks posed through money laundering. It will identify ways to counter these and it will allocate resources accordingly.

4.2 Maximising effective use of information provided to the Inland Revenue

The revised definition of money laundering to include all acts of tax evasion which generate a financial gain, means that all information gained by the Inland Revenue for the purposes of tackling tax evasion also has usefulness in tackling money laundering offences. So the strategic use of information to tackle tax evasion is effectively mirrored by its use for counter-money laundering purposes. All information powers which are used to tackle tax evasion are relevant here.

A considerable volume of information about tax evasion is expected to be provided by accountants, auditors and tax advisers. This information will be directly relevant to the Revenue in its efforts to tackle tax evasion as it will necessarily concern the professional's knowledge or suspicions or their clients tax evasion.

The offence has been provided for in order for Government bodies to counter money laundering. But the commonality of the money laundering and tax evasion offences means that the Revenue will be able to receive and make use of reports which are purely to do with tax evasion offences.

The reports will be submitted to the National Criminal Intelligence Service (NCIS) in the first instance. NCIS will carry out checks using their other information sources and analytical techniques to identify links to any other wider criminality. NCIS have advised that these reports will carry valuable information about what those suspected of serious crimes are doing with their finances.

If NCIS are satisfied that no wider criminality is evident and that the suspected offences are limited to tax evasion, they will pass the information onto the Inland Revenue and Customs and Excise as appropriate. The revenue departments will work together to share this information and add value to each other's information wherever possible.

Special Compliance Office Intelligence Group will be the receiving point within the Inland Revenue for all information provided by NCIS. SCO will analyse the information and route appropriate cases to other parts of SCO. They will also sanitise the information before passing it onto others, so as not to readily identify the source of the report to NCIS. Failure to do so may result in some awkward circumstances between the Revenue, the adviser and the client. In some cases it may even involve personal safety risks. Similarly, the Service Delivery Support Financial Investigation Unit will receive un-sanitised information form SCO, but will sanitise it before sending it onto staff in the Revenue network.

Only trained and qualified staff will handle this information.

4.3 Effective management of provision of information to other organisations tackling money laundering

Disclosures about money laundering offences to other investigating organisations will be via the gateway in the Anti-Terrorism (Crime and Security) Act 2001. Such disclosures are subject to agreed Memoranda of Understanding with other organisations and the published Code of Practice about how we will manage and operate these. All disclosures will be routed via a single point of contact within SCO.

4.4 Use of expertise

The Revenue has considerable expertise in specialist financial investigations, including the countering of money laundering and tax evasion, especially where complex and contrived structures have been used, including cases involving trusts, often located offshore.

The Revenue has seconded staff to several other organisations involved in countering fraud, including money laundering. We have staff working on these types of duties at the Home Office, Customs and Excise, the National Crime Squad, the National Criminal Intelligence Service, the Assets Recovery Agency and the Serious Fraud Office. It is our policy to make use of secondments, interchange and loans to provide the expertise of our staff to others, to open up lines of communications inter-departmentally and to benefit from the knowledge our staff bring back to the Revenue when they return.

4.5 Working with the private sector – consultation with practitioners

We recognise the value of working with the private sector in tackling money laundering and the value of the contribution this sector can make. There is clear commonality of objectives with the private sector in seeking to eliminate money laundering offences.

We will also consult with the private sector about how we will counter money laundering and seek their views about the impact our actions will have on legitimate trade.

4.6 Ensuring that the Inland Revenue is not being used as a means to launder money

A further dimension to tackling money laundering is to have robust internal controls to ensure that the Inland Revenue itself is not being used a means to launder money. A cheque or bank transfer from the Inland Revenue provides the launderer with a very high level of legitimacy for the funds which generated these.

Some of those laundering criminal money may take the view that the payment of 40% tax is a reasonable price to pay for legitimacy of funds. Revenue staff will need to be aware of this when dealing with sham 'front' companies or when receiving cash or cheques in settlement of tax debts.

Staff awareness at all relevant levels will be vital in countering these types of activity. SCO's anti-money laundering unit will have a leading role to play in developing such awareness.

Index

Locators refer to Paragraph numbers